Critical Aesthetics

Kobayashi Hideo, Modernity, and Wartime Japan

Harvard East Asian Monographs 318

Critical Aesthetics

Kobayashi Hideo, Modernity, and Wartime Japan

James Dorsey

Published by the Harvard University Asia Center
and distributed by Harvard University Press
Cambridge (Massachusetts) and London, 2009

Printed in the United States of America

The Harvard University Asia Center publishes a monograph series and, in coordination with the Fairbank Center for Chinese Studies, the Korea Institute, the Reischauer Institute of Japanese Studies, and other faculties and institutes, administers research projects designed to further scholarly understanding of China, Japan, Vietnam, Korea, and other Asian countries. The Center also sponsors projects addressing multidisciplinary and regional issues in Asia.

Library of Congress Cataloging-in-Publication Data

Dorsey, James, 1961–
Critical aesthetics : Kobayashi Hideo, modernity, and wartime Japan / James Dorsey.
p. cm. -- (Harvard East Asian monographs ; 318)
Includes bibliographical references and index.
ISBN 978-0-674-03284-2 (cloth : alk. paper)
1. Kobayashi, Hideo, 1902–1983--Criticism and interpretation. 2. Aestheticism (Literature) I. Title.
PL832.O28Z63 2009
895.6'09--dc22

2009008233

Index by the author

♾ Printed on acid-free paper

Last figure below indicates year of this printing

19 18 17 16 15 14 13 12 11 10 09

To the memory of

William F. Dorsey, M.D.

Acknowledgments

While working on this book I enjoyed a steady stream of guidance, support, and encouragement from a long list of generous people. I would like to acknowledge and thank at least some of them here. I am grateful to David Fahy, Yōichi Aizawa, John Ross Carter, Jurgis Elisonas, George M. Wilson, Sumie Jones, Alan Tansman, Kenneth Pyle, Matthew Königsberg, and the late Andrew Markus. As my dissertation advisor at the University of Washington, John Whittier Treat engaged my thinking and writing with unfailing attention and great insight; I find that even today almost every critical line I pursue has its roots in something John said or had me read. I am proud to call myself his student and friend. I was also fortunate to work with Jay Rubin during those years. I continue to be inspired by his incredible sensitivity to both the mechanics and potentials of literary expression in Japanese and English; I am also appreciative of his friendship and encouragement. I had wonderful, committed peers as a graduate student, and for their contributions to my thinking I thank: Doug Slaymaker, Jeff Johnson, Rachel DiNitto, Davinder Bhowmik, Christine Marran, Charles Exley, Motoo Kobayashi, and Chiyoko Kawakami. At Dartmouth College I have benefitted from the insight of Dennis Washburn and my other colleagues in the Department of Asian and Middle Eastern Languages and Literatures.

A number of research periods in Japan were made possible by the following organizations: the Japanese Ministry of Education, the Association for Asian Studies Northeast Asia Council, and the Social Science Research Council/Japan Society for the Promotion of Science. In Japan I benefitted greatly from the advice and friendship of

Tanada Teruyoshi, Yoshioka Eiichi, and the late Nakagomi Shigeaki. During the eighteen months that I worked with him, Karatani Kōjin was of immense help in grasping key issues in modern Japanese intellectual history, and his thinking continues to influence me today. I would also like to thank Kuroko Kazuo, whose keen critical sense, encyclopedic knowledge, and social commitment have always been an inspiration.

For my wife, Yukari, no words can suffice to express my appreciation.

This book is dedicated to the memory of my father, William F. Dorsey, M.D. (1921–1985). His understanding of history—especially military history, with its veneer of glory obscuring underlying horrors—informed his lifelong commitment to social justice and world peace.

Contents

Critical Aesthetics

Kobayashi Hideo, Modernity, and Wartime Japan

PROLOGUE
The Anxiety of Interpretation

In the fall of 1996, respected literary critic and academic superstar Frank Lentricchia committed a shocking apostasy: he renounced his belief in literature as a discursive arena for the exploration and exercise of political and ideological influence, and embraced in its place the conviction that "literature is pleasurable and important, as literature, and not as an illustration of something else."[1]

This statement represented a radical departure from the intellectual stance that had made him famous. In 1983, while a professor at Rice University, Lentricchia had secured his reputation in the academy with the publication of *Criticism and Social Change*. In this book he had posed a question that haunts scholars of literature: "Can a literary intellectual . . . do radical work *as* a literary intellectual?"[2] His answer was in the affirmative, of course, and he would later recall that at the time of the book's publication he had been "convinced that a literary critic, *as a literary critic*, could be an agent of social transformation, an activist who would show his students that, in its form and style, literature had a strategic role to play in the world's various arrangements of power; that literature wasn't to be relegated to the Arts and Leisure section of the Sunday paper, as if it were a thing for weekend amusement only."[3] Lentricchia's revolutionary agenda, put forth in powerful prose, earned him a reputation as the "Dirty Harry of contemporary literary criticism."[4] His fierce defense of literary studies as a mode of social activism—as something more than a means for refining aesthetic sensibilities or exploring cultural heritage or revealing the multiplicities of the human experience—

was appealing to many working in the academy. It continues to inspire students and teachers of literature today.

However, in the fall of 1996, Lentricchia, who was by this time a tenured professor at Duke University, made the pronouncement mentioned above: he had, in short, changed his mind about literature's relationship to power and social justice. Whereas he had built his career as a critical theorist and analyst of literary texts, Lentricchia announced that he would thereafter be true to a second, secret side of his literary life:

> The secret me was me-the-reader, in the act of reading: an experience in which the words of someone else filled me up and made it irrelevant to talk about my reading; an experience that I'd had for as long as I can remember being a reader. This secret life implicitly denied that any talk about what I had undergone could ever be authentic. My silent encounters with literature are ravishingly pleasurable, like erotic transport.[5]

His secret self revealed, Lentricchia retreated into the undergraduate classroom to indulge and share these pleasures of reading. Of his life in this safe haven, he writes,

> I become something of a rhapsode. As Plato says in the *Ion*, rhapsodes are enthusiasts. We're out of our minds. Like all rhapsodes, I like to recite from the text. I tell my students that in true recitation, we're possessed, we are the medium for the writer's voice. . . . My listener-students . . . too become possessed. Rhapsode and audience assume a single strange consciousness, not their own: "living," not "knowing," the text. We are simply, and collectively, mad.[6]

In this proclamation, we see his transformation complete. Whereas he had once grappled with literary representations as a means first to understand and later to intervene in the various flows of power in the world, from this point forward in his career Lentricchia would surrender himself to the personal, hedonistic joys available to the connoisseur of literary expression.

Considering his standing in academia and the widespread appeal of his earlier, politically oriented agenda, it is not surprising that this socially conscious critic's apostasy triggered a variety of responses. A consideration of two of them is warranted here for they illuminate a tension in literary circles operant also in the figures examined in this study. One response to Lentricchia's article appeared in the very same journal, *Lingua Franca,* in the form of a reader's letter to the editor, and it offered a cautious embrace of his new vision. The embrace, however, was tenuous, qualified: when "Brother Lentricchia ceases to use the word 'text' when he means 'novel,' we'll know his soul has truly come home."[7] This statement reveals something of the radical nature of Lentricchia's conversion. So different are the positions he has held that they require distinct "languages." If Lentricchia is truly to abandon himself to the act of reading, he must acknowledge that he is reading "novels," not "texts." Furthermore, in the metaphors it employs, this reader's statement also illustrates a widely shared assumption about Lentricchia's new approach. By looking forward to the day "his *soul* [will] truly come *home*" (italics added), this reader is suggesting that Lentricchia's rhapsodic encounters with literature represent some privileged point of origin antecedent to the intellectual analysis that constituted one stage of his career. The implication is that his foray into theory was somehow a betrayal of basic human nature, a contrived attempt, fueled by hubris, to harness the literary imagination to the lesser goals of some secular world.

There is also something undeniably appealing about this apolitical, purely literary (aesthetic) vision. We do experience, at times, a book whose words fill us up, a text that engulfs us. When we give ourselves over to that experience, we do indeed feel as if our "soul" has found its way "home." When we sit down to write or talk about that experience, however, we find that somehow our words are not up to the task. We worry that by the act of interpretation we are somehow doing that original encounter a grave injustice, somehow reducing the private and sacred to the communal and profane. We sometimes succeed in repressing these nagging doubts as we deploy literary texts in an effort to alter the hierarchies of power in the world. They return, however, the next time a bright young student of literature interrupts a lecture to ask, "I loved this novel. It made me laugh, it made me cry. Why do we have to ruin it by analyzing it to death?" Like the converted Lentricchia in 1996 and the cautious reader who applauded his conversion, many would privilege this intoxication of rhapsodic abandonment.

It is easy to imagine other reactions to Lentricchia's apostasy. Whether their claim is rooted in a suspicion of hedonistic pleasures, a Protestant work ethic, or the need to assert political relevance in an age defined by the "war against terror," those who make literary texts a central part of their profession feel compelled to insist, like the younger Lentricchia, that "literature [has] a strategic role to play in the world's various arrangements of power." Not surprisingly, this position was also promoted in the pages of *Lingua Franca* in the form of another reader's reaction to the Lentricchia article. This letter defends the politicization of literary studies, and accuses the Duke professor of a cowardly retreat from the very critical discourse that he himself had helped to propagate. Most germane to the argument here is an unexplored observation in the letter, an observation that indicates that the two literary stances adopted by Lentricchia might not be mutually exclusive after all: the letter-writer observes that, in his denunciation of politicized literary criticism, Lentricchia "certainly hasn't abandoned the terrain of metacritical debate, in which his article intervenes quite conspicuously. . . ."[8] This remark cuts to the quick of Lentricchia's conversion. Issued by a literary theorist in a forum for intellectual debate, even this renunciation of ideological motives has ideological and theoretical ramifications. In fact, Lentricchia's subsequent work suggests that he intended the "conversion" he announced in the *Lingua Franca* article to be precisely that type of metacritical intervention.[9]

At its core, this study explores a similar commitment to literature as a realm complete unto itself. It also examines the paradoxical manner in which that stance, pursued over the course of two decades, itself constituted a "metacritical intervention" of monumental importance in the cultural history of modern Japan.

These tensions as explored in this study can also be productively introduced through reference to Susan Sontag's classic essay of 1964, "Against Interpretation." I discuss it here not only because it substantiates the pervasive nature of these tensions, but also because Sontag's articulation of the issues provides imagery and a vocabulary that proves useful. While Lentricchia's article takes the form of a personal manifesto, Sontag's essay includes a short but carefully formulated history of interpretation's infiltration of literary discourse, as well as a program for liberating the literary from the analytical. Interpretation today, Sontag asserts, is "reactionary, impertinent, cowardly, stifling"; it is

> the revenge of the intellect upon art. Even more. It is the revenge of the intellect upon the world. To interpret is to impoverish, to deplete the world—in order to set up a shadow world of "meanings." It is to turn *the* world into *this* world. . . .
>
> The world, our world, is depleted, impoverished enough. Away with all duplicates of it, until we again experience more immediately what we have.[10]

As Lentricchia would do over thirty years later, Sontag dreams of reversing humankind's relentless parsing of literature and art into its hidden meanings and ideological significations. Where Lentricchia would have us "live" the text rather than "know" it, Sontag would have us "experience more immediately" the works we impoverish through interpretation.

Sontag's program is based on her understanding of the historical and philosophical contexts that have led us to the current state. The penchant for interpretation is rooted in our inheritance of the ancient Greek conception of art as mimesis—as a representation of something else. This paradigm fuels a perpetual need for interpretation, the act whereby that "something" existing antecedent to the work of art, its "true content," can be revealed. Over time the pace of interpretation quickened, and its range grew; the scientific enlightenment pulled even the heretofore immune realms of myth and religion into the fray. Finally, with Marx and Freud the interpreting mind became ubiquitous, and latent content (visible only through interpretation) was now privileged above all else. Understanding had become synonymous with interpreting.[11]

As a cure for this obsession with teasing out latent content through interpretation, Sontag proposes, not surprisingly, a renewed attention to form. It is possible to repel the interpreters, she suggests, by "making works of art whose surface is so unified and clean, whose momentum is so rapid, whose address is so direct that the work can be . . . just what it is."[12] Criticism, too, she argues, must strive for a "transparency" that allows us to experience "the luminousness of the thing in itself, of things being what they are," for this direction alone will prompt the recovery of the senses we need to once again fully experience the world as it is.[13]

Like Lentricchia's manifesto, Sontag's essay is an unequivocal advocacy of an acritical, emotional engagement with art (or literature). It is also—and here again it anticipates Lentricchia's stance—an ironic gesture in that it originates wholly within the realm of intellectual, critical discourse. An artistic/literary appreciation whereby a "work can be . . . just what it is" may be presented as some primal mode of experiencing the world, but for Sontag this is possible only as a "recovered" mode of cognition. It is meaningful and, in fact, recognizable only after the interpretive mode has taken hold. Sontag, like Lentricchia, recognizes the irony inherent in her stance. In an interview held three years after the publication of "Against Interpretation," Sontag claimed "Obviously, if nobody were paying attention to content or meaning or message, then probably I would be talking about that."[14] Sontag's case is another demonstration of how a rejection of critical analysis functions, ultimately, as precisely the sort of "metacritical intervention" it claims on its surface to denounce.

To repeat, this study is an examination of the contours and consequences of a very similar sort of metacritical intervention, one worked in the intellectual world of Japan between approximately 1929 and 1946. It was an intellectual intervention that exercised tremendous influence on a generation of writers and critics, and the literary world of Japan today continues to grapple with its legacy.

Introduction

This study revolves around the career of the Japanese literary and cultural critic Kobayashi Hideo (1902–83), a man whose interpretive angst fueled a lifelong quest to somehow recover a literary experience unmediated by intellectual machinations. To borrow Lentricchia's vocabulary, Kobayashi desired to "live" rather than "know" a literary text. To use Sontag's phrasing, he desired an encounter with art in which the object would not be compromised, in which it could be "just what it is." The phrase that most tellingly captures his spirit, though, might be that coined by the reader cautiously embracing Lentricchia's conversion: few would dispute the claim that more than anything else Kobayashi Hideo longed to find a means whereby "his soul [could] truly come home." Paradoxically, Kobayashi waged his war against interpretation through a genre that is virtually synonymous with it: criticism. In this sense, as Edward Seidensticker has pointed out, "Kobayashi often seems rather close to the great contradiction in the works of the late D. T. Suzuki, who announced his conclusion first, that nothing can be said about Zen, and then wrote volume after volume."[1] Yet somehow Kobayashi made it work. He is indisputably the most influential critic of Japan's Shōwa period (1926–89).

Like Lentricchia, Kobayashi came to treat his experience of literature as intimately personal and ultimately beyond articulation; he explored the sources of that sensibility, its ramifications for modernity, and its potential as a cure for the fractured modern subject. In this sense, throughout his career, his suspicion of interpretive endeavors itself served as a critical intervention in literary and cultural circles. Kobayashi was at times like Sontag, using discursive prose to stem the slide into increasingly invasive abstract interpretations of literature and the world. At other times he wrote more performatively, practicing what he preached, and in the best of these moments he succeeded in restoring what Sontag describes as "works of art whose surface is so unified and clean, whose momentum is so rapid, whose address is so direct that the work can be . . . just what it is." At these times Kobayashi realized Sontag's prescription for healing the pathology of interpretation: "The aim of all commentary on art now should be to make works of art—and, by analogy, our own experience—more, rather than less, real to us. The function of criticism should be to show *how it is what it is,* even *that it is what it is,* rather than to show *what it means.*"[2]

In the best of his performative essays Kobayashi imbues literary classics, historical events, famous personages, and his own temporal moment with the aura of immutable, impenetrable "thus-ness." He clears the interpretive fog surrounding things, and we once again experience their beauty, their power. We viscerally feel the magic, the luminousness, the mystery of them. It is almost, as both Lentricchia and Sontag describe it, an "erotic" experience.[3]

But there is another side to Kobayashi Hideo. During his tour of Japanese colonies on the Asian continent in the late 1930s, Kobayashi marveled at the immediacy of lives so destitute they bridged no thought of the future; on the home front he reveled in the population's silent acquiescence to the demands of the wartime regime while simultaneously calling on it to recognize its patriotism as something as certain as sexual desire; concerning literature, he called for more aggressive assertions of government thought control and censorship. After Japan's surrender in 1945, Kobayashi was, not surprisingly, one of twenty-five literary figures accused of bearing responsibility for the war.[4]

These two aspects of Kobayashi's career, one intimately literary/artistic and the other fully political/ideological, are inextricably intertwined. While the aesthetic vision he embraced holds widespread appeal, the conditions of Kobayashi's formulation and application of it are, of course, specific to this man and his time. It was Kobayashi's personal circumstances, his generation's particular experience of modernity, and his nation's historical trajectory that fused his literary beliefs to an ideology of repression and imperialism. This study attempts to account for these specificities while exploring, too, the more universal question of how renunciations of the interpretive act themselves constitute literary and ideological interventions. Kobayashi's career can serve as a case study of a critical aesthetics, a vision of culture that was both informed by its historical moment and constitutive of it.

The first chapter of this study casts Kobayashi's aversion to interpretation as a reaction to the phase of modernity experienced by his generation. The devastation of the Great Kantō Earthquake of 1923 and the radical changes that took root in the subsequent rebuilding of Tokyo ushered in an era of new, almost animate forms of materiality (technology and commodities), and these demanded a renegotiation of humankind's relationship to them. Recorded in Kobayashi's "Kokyō o ushinatta bungaku" (Literature That Has Lost Its Home, 1933) is his experience of this confusing deluge of modernity's "things"; articulated in "Dentō" (Tradition, 1941) is the method by which Kobayashi would restore the aura of mystery and wonder by rhetorically reconstituting texts and cultural artifacts in ways that rendered them seemingly impenetrable to the analytical mind. This chapter completes the broad characterization, begun in the pages above, of Kobayashi's overriding concerns.

The second chapter narrates Kobayashi's earliest experience of this new phase of modernity through a discussion of his early fiction, written under the influence of the Taishō-era sensibilities largely embodied in the works of novelist Shiga Naoya, with whom Kobayashi shared an affinity. "Tako no jisatsu" (The Octopus's Suicide, 1922), Kobayashi's first published short story, suggests he was on the brink of a Shiga-like career in which art and life, mind and body, spirit and materiality were holistically integrated. Then came the earthquake. Kobayashi's next story, "Hitotsu no nōzui" (One Brain, 1924), reflects a greatly altered consciousness, one in which the borders between materiality and consciousness are blurred in thoroughly modernist style. While he seemed to be on the brink of embracing a style and sensibility akin to that of the Neo-perceptionists (Shinkankaku-ha), Kobayashi subsequently balked at the prospect of plunging into the alienated, fragmented world of modernism. He dedicated himself instead to the Sisyphean task of somehow restoring that original, holistic, Shiga-esque sensibility that he had tasted before the earthquake.

Kobayashi's response to this modernist impulse, something he shared with many of his generation, is explored through two important trajectories in the third and fourth chapters. First is Kobayashi's turn from autobiographical fiction to criticism, the literary genre that best represents the post-earthquake world. The publishing boom of the early Shōwa period had commodified literature and brought it physically and psychologically closer to a broad range of people. This in turn fed the fires of critical interpretation. In order to recover, to recuperate the sensual (as opposed to intellectual) literary experience from within his changed world, Kobayashi had to repel this analytical threat to literary aesthetics. He did just that, redrawing the contours of criticism through a reification of the literary text and an expansion of the role of the intuition of the perceiving subject. In essays such as "Jinsei shakudanka Ranbō" (Rimbaud, Shatterer of Life, 1926) and "Akutagawa Ryūnosuke no bishin to shukumei" (The Muse and Destiny of Akutagawa Ryūnosuke, 1927), Kobayashi began to privilege the intuitive act of "seeing," a cognitive mode contingent at its inception upon a distinction that modernity had obscured: that between perceiving subject and perceived object.[5]

A second, related trajectory is that which brings Kobayashi's literary agenda into the world of politics. This move begins with his award-winning essay "Samazama naru ishō" (The Various Designs, 1929), and the attack on the Marxist worldview that he launches there extends into a debate with philosopher Tosaka Jun (1900–45). Tosaka and Kobayashi represent diametrically opposed stances concerning the "stuff" of modernity: Tosaka, a Marxist, would pull it close, scientifically parsing it to understand its ideological underpinnings, while Kobayashi would distance it, rendering it inaccessible so as to wonder at its beauty. Their interchange, and the evolution of Kobayashi's message from an aesthetic vision to a full-blown worldview, is the subject of the fourth chapter.

The fifth and sixth chapters examine Kobayashi's career from the late 1930s to the early 1940s. During this time Kobayashi wrote increasingly on history as he turned from European literature to the Japanese classics. His interest in ancient ceramics and antiquities also grew, with modes of aesthetic appreciation from this realm increasingly appropriated for his writing on other topics. While these interests parallel those of many reactionary wartime intellectuals, Kobayashi's insistence on the intimately personal and ultimately inexpressible nature of the aesthetic experience precluded his participation in the essentializing discourse on Japanese ethnic identity that rationalized imperialism on the continent. This stance also made possible his hauntingly beautiful paeans to Japan's medieval classics: the six pieces written in 1942 and 1943, and later collected under the title *Mujō to iu koto* (The Fact of Evanescence, 1946). In these essays—perhaps better described as prose poems—Kobayashi rhetorically restores to ancient texts the aura that adheres to an impenetrable, ultimately incomprehensible materiality. In a sense, he approaches these classical works of literature with the same sensibility he brought to the ceramics he so dearly cherished. The manner in which these essays revived a sense of mystery and awe in the realm of literature gave hope to some left-leaning writers, convincing them that art was still possible under the oppressive wartime regime.

The sixth chapter deals with the flip side of this coin: essays from the same period in which Kobayashi focuses his attention not on literature but rather on the subject of Japan's colonies and the war effort. Here we find the disturbing declarations, alluded to above, that prompted some in the postwar years to label Kobayashi a literary figure bearing responsibility for the war. These pieces are not the aberration that some scholars would label them; they are in fact fully in keeping with Kobayashi's earlier works. Nowhere is this more apparent than in "Sensō to heiwa" (War and Peace, 1942), a prose poem inspired by a photograph of U.S. naval vessels aflame after the Japanese attack on Pearl Harbor. The parallels between Kobayashi's artistic vision and these political pronouncements are the reason that Kobayashi's are a critical aesthetics, and in both senses of the phrase: his conception of the beautiful is grounded in a historically and ideologically informed stance, and it engenders subjectivities crucial to the destiny of the nation. More specifically, Kobayashi's compelling aesthetic vision is one prone to perceiving destruction and repression as intimately suited to revealing the sublime beauties of the human condition.

The epilogue treats Kobayashi during the immediate postwar period. The central pillar of the literary revival at the time, writers affiliated with the journal *Shin Nihon bungaku*, included Kobayashi on their list of writers to be purged for complicity during the war. While this movement soon lost its momentum, its initial impact was sufficient to severely damage the careers of a number of writers, Yasuda Yojūrō (1910–81) most prominent among them. Kobayashi, however, soon resumed a position of prominence, and remained an elder statesman of literary studies in Japan until his death in 1983. The literary community (both then and now), it seems, has been willing to pardon Kobayashi for his consistent dedication to literary (or aesthetic) principles. Unlike the many who had deserted Marxist literary stances under the repressive wartime regime, Kobayashi had never betrayed his vision, stubbornly pursuing an intimately literary/aesthetic worldview throughout the war years. Ironically, it was precisely the literary/aesthetic nature of that vision that undergirded his fascist wartime stance.

This study of Kobayashi Hideo, then, participates in a number of discourses. It is an exploration of the roots and consequences of an aversion to interpretation, an aesthetic and ideological stance touted by a wide variety of critics from various cultures and historical moments. In its focus on Kobayashi's obsession with the radically changed materiality of post-earthquake Tokyo, it is also a delineation of this dimension of modernity. The examination of his wartime writings, both the grand achievement of *Mujō to iu koto* and the disturbing proclamations in support of Japan's imperialist regime, addresses the relationship of aesthetics to ideologies of violence. Finally, the study offers a portrait of Kobayashi Hideo, the man whom even such radically different thinkers as Karatani Kōjin and Donald Keene place at the very center of modern Japanese critical discourse: Karatani acknowledges his creation of the paradigm upon which Japanese criticism was built, and Keene credits him with "creating" modern Japanese criticism.[6] Concrete evidence of this influence on the world of Japanese letters was offered by Etō Jun in 1964: all six of the established literary critics writing reviews (*bungei jihyō*) for the major newspapers at that time had careers that were substantially intertwined with Kobayashi's.[7] Kobayashi's broad sphere of influence makes the investigation of his ambiguous legacy all the more important.

To be sure, this story is but one of the many that might be narrated about Kobayashi Hideo. The body of secondary literature on him is enormous and continues to grow daily. It began as a trickle even before Kobayashi was recognized by the literary community, with associates and friends remarking on his work as it first appeared.[8] This trickle became a steady stream after Kobayashi garnered an important literary prize with "Samazama naru ishō" in 1929. Thereafter each new stage in Kobayashi's career triggered a wide range of responses from colleagues, competitors, and observers.

Important attempts to make sense of his broader significance were part of the widespread introspection of Japan's literary world in the days after the close of World War II. Building on the work of earlier thinkers concerned with the ideological ramifications of Kobayashi's literary vision, critics associated with the journal *Kindai bungaku,* the voice of new and renewed left-wing thinkers, had the perspective required to move beyond reactions to particular expressions and to begin an exploration of the wider implications of his overall thought.[9] Certain critics continued work in this vein.[10]

The renowned Kobayashi Hideo researcher Yoshida Hiroo marks the late 1970s and early 1980s as a watershed in Kobayashi studies, but the first true shift in perspective takes place in the late 1950s, with Nakamura Mitsuo's "Kobayashi Hideo ron."[11] Here Nakamura opens a discussion of Kobayashi that foregrounds the literary and artistic dimension of his work by insisting that Kobayashi is not so much a critic as a prose poet.[12] This reorientation calls attention to Kobayashi as the progenitor of a new genre of critical discourse rather than as, say, a particularly insightful explicator of works of fiction and literary trends. This shift in the perception of Kobayashi's role in the literary community helped readers recognize his importance. Unfortunately, it also served to divert attention from the ideological implications of his work. Readers enamored of Kobayashi as a "prose poet" (or in Hosea Hirata's phrase, a "poet manqué"), in surrendering themselves to the beauty of his prose and the allure of his literary sensibility, too often overlook the relationship between the literary sensibility and his wartime stance.[13]

Etō Jun's book, *Kobayashi Hideo* (1961), followed closely on the heels of Nakamura's study, and legitimized this approach to Kobayashi's work. Etō contextualizes Kobayashi by placing him in a lineage of novelists (Natsume Sōseki and Shiga Naoya) struggling to make sense of the self in the context of modern Japan's intersection with the West. In methodology and format this book is indistinguishable from "critical biographies" (*hyōden*) dedicated to poets and writers of fiction: based on Kobayashi's loss of his father at a relatively early age and a tempestuous love affair that almost drove him to suicide, Etō draws a psychological portrait that he then posits as the source of particular modes of thought and imagery that surface repeatedly in Kobayashi's oeuvre of criticism. The result is an interesting portrayal of the personal life and *artistic* temperament behind this literary critic.[14] Subsequent studies of Kobayashi have virtually all drawn to some extent on the approach and biographical detail of this pioneering work.[15]

The next shift in the critical reception of Kobayashi Hideo is the aforementioned late 1970s/early 1980s watershed marked by Yoshida. At this point, Yoshida asserts, the literary community began to consider Kobayashi as neither simply a critic nor a creative writer but rather as "an embodiment of Japanese literary culture" (*Nihon no gengo bunka no hito taigensha*).[16] The impetus for this reappraisal was first the completion of Kobayashi's magnum opus on the Tokugawa intellectual giant for whom the work is named, *Motoori Norinaga*, and then Kobayashi's death in March 1983.[17] Studies from this time period employ a broad spectrum of approaches. Many get at the heart of Kobayashi's significance through a close reading of a particular work.[18] Others explicate Kobayashi's thought by juxtaposing it with the various sources of his inspiration, including the French Symbolist poets, Motoori Norinaga, and Henri Bergson.[19] Still others employ a thematic approach: Kamei Hideo focuses on Kobayashi's struggle with the limits of language, while Aeba Takao contextualizes a number of key essays by revealing how they are in dialogue with both literary and popular culture trends from their time of publication.[20] The interest in Kobayashi continues unabated today; as Yoshida remarks, a study of this writer is very much a rite of passage for all aspiring critics in Japan.[21]

In English there are only a handful of essays on Kobayashi. The earliest are three by the late Edward Seidensticker, who provides a lively introduction to the critic. Seidensticker paints Kobayashi as a writer in conversation with Western thinkers but one who is ultimately heir to an indigenous literary tradition of brief insights and intuitive thinking that, when skillfully exercised, "can be the very music of the race."[22] These essays include a number of extended translations and a consideration of Kobayashi's wartime works and stance. Donald Keene also writes on this critic. His *Dawn to the West* presents the criticism of the Shōwa period in two sections: "Kobayashi Hideo" and "Other Modern Critics"; the former section is ten times the length of the latter. In contrast to Seidensticker's focus on Kobayashi's analysis of domestic literary issues, Keene includes an examination of Kobayashi's work on foreign writers such as Dostoevsky, noting that "it was surely of great importance that a Japanese intellectual should have written with skill and assurance about a European author—neither disqualifying himself because of his nationality nor attempting to impart any specifically Japanese quality to his account."[23]

The first English-language work to fully appreciate Kobayashi as a thinker speaking beyond the confines of his national literature is Paul Anderer's introduction to his book of translations. Though short, his essay convincingly presents Kobayashi as an important thinker addressing such widespread concerns of the twenty-first century as "the culture of cities, the loss and invention of traditions, ideology and aesthetics, narration and the nation-state, the dimensions of the literary self."[24] The translations that Anderer provides, furthermore, support the incorporation of that voice into the ongoing discourse on these crucial issues.[25] Hosea Hirata's writing on Kobayashi Hideo advances the agenda introduced by Anderer, particularly in his "Home and History: Kobayashi Hideo and Other Visionaries of the Past," where he attempts to elucidate some of Kobayashi's sensibilities through references to ideas articulated by Walter Benjamin and Roland Barthes.[26]

Breaking the mold for Kobayashi studies outside Japan, however, is Matthew Königsberg. In addition to his full-length study in German, Königsberg has published an essay on Kobayashi in English, and it is *sui generis*.[27] His intention in this highly critical essay is to right what he sees as a lopsidedness in the approaches to Kobayashi's oeuvre: in a characterization that is true even today, Königsberg laments the fact that so many of the analyses are "panegyrics" where "[r]espect is the dominant tone."[28] His own essay uses Kobayashi's very short 1940 essay "Hitorā no 'Waga tōsō'" (Hitler's *Mein Kampf*) as a touchstone from which to paint a portrait of Kobayashi as a dangerous, egotistical, and irresponsible public intellectual, however gifted he may have been. It is only with this carefully argued and convincingly documented critique that the field of Kobayashi Hideo studies in the English language attains some measure of balance. This current study hopes to follow the lead of Königsberg, and perhaps contribute to the reinvigoration of the often all too respectful discourse on the "god of criticism" (*hihyō no kamisama*), as some have designated Kobayashi.

As even this abbreviated overview of Kobayashi studies suggests, there are myriad approaches to this thinker. This study attempts to account for but a few in order to concentrate on the works of Kobayashi Hideo as an important intersection of aesthetics and ideology. The texts chosen for analysis do not reflect the full range of Kobayashi's oeuvre but rather this particular focus. Furthermore, the labyrinth of intellectual and literary influence, an integral part of Kobayashi studies in Japan, is given only cursory attention; in its place is an attempt to situate Kobayashi in a genuine dialogue with his contemporaries and his age. While this perhaps does a disservice to the cosmopolitan, eclectic roots of Kobayashi's thought, the question of influence seems secondary to a treatment of his formation within, and influence on, a particular historical moment and cultural milieu. It was, after all, these particularities that prompted Kobayashi to seek out the sources he did. The conditions that fostered those choices were part of the modernity Kobayashi experienced. His was an age in which an increasingly porous, mutable materiality prompted a quest to restore the artistic work to a level of concreteness that precluded interpretation and instead inspired awe. These matters are the subject of Chapter 1.

ONE

"An Endless Clutter of Things and Events"

Kobayashi Hideo's literary career spanned virtually the entirety of the Shōwa period (1926–89). Some of the striking vicissitudes of these six decades are explored in this study, beginning in this chapter with the impact of modernity and modernism in Japan during the 1920s and 1930s. While Japan as a nation bounced wildly from the comparatively liberal and democratic Taishō period (1912–26) to the increasingly repressive military regime of the war years, and then on to the occupation period reforms and an eventual economic miracle, Kobayashi's personal and professional life is not marked by such radical fluctuations. It was, in fact, a steady rise to prominence followed by a long, distinguished career at the forefront of Japanese literary culture. A brief overview of this career will provide the larger context for this study's interpretation of certain key points in the evolution of Kobayashi's aesthetic vision and critical agenda.

Born in the heart of Tokyo on 11 April 1902, Kobayashi Hideo's early years were filled with all the privileges of a first-born son in an upper-middle-class family.[1] His father, Toyozō, was an educated man, the holder of multiple patents, and a professor at what is now the Tokyo Institute of Technology. He later served as a technical consultant in industry, and eventually founded his own firm, the Nihon Diamond Corporation. He had studied abroad, and introduced to Japan the latest technologies for cutting and setting precious gems. Though not in opulence, the family lived very comfortably—a large house, recordings of *Faust* and *La Bohème* on the gramophone, tennis, golf, and summers at the seaside.[2]

That early in life Kobayashi interacted with literary-minded peers and schoolmates such as the future poets Tominaga Tarō (1901–25) and Nakahara Chūya (1907–37), as well as the budding critics Kawakami Tetsutarō (1902–80) and Kurahara Korehito (1902–91), suggests something of the privileged environment he enjoyed; it also explains the emergence of his interest in literature. Even in primary school he circulated a magazine among his friends and classmates. Graduating at the top of his class, the thirteen-year-old Kobayashi then entered the prestigious First Middle School. Though he initially balked at the narrow, examination-centered curriculum there, it did enable him to gain entrance into the elite First Higher School (Dai-ichi kōtō gakkō), albeit only after an extra year of cramming to pass the entrance examination.

The first disruption of this comfortable childhood came with the untimely death of his father in 1921 at the age of 46, an event that contributed to a nervous condition that kept the eighteen-year-old Kobayashi out of school for a time. Critic Etō Jun insists that this event marks a psychological turning point for Kobayashi, as it denied him the opportunity to play out the archetypal father-son battle integral to so many literary works of modern Japan, including the work "Wakai," by Kobayashi's own beloved Shiga Naoya. It also thrust upon Kobayashi the role of primary caretaker for his sister and mother, denying him the full extent of his adolescence.[3] This period is also marked by a flirtation with Christianity. Years later his sister would recall how for a time Kobayashi would disappear after supper to attend a neighborhood Bible study group.[4] His mother's subsequent ill health prompted her to move to Kamakura, and Kobayashi commuted to high school from a boarding house in Tokyo.

These disruptions, however, did not prevent him from beginning to write. In November 1922 he published his first short story in a small coterie magazine: "Tako no jisatsu" (The Octopus's Suicide). The story was followed by number of other short works of fiction, including "Hitotsu no nōzui" (One Brain, 1924), "Ame" (Sweets, 1924), and "Ponkin no warai" (Ponkin's Smile, 1924), all completed before he had graduated from high school.[5] Following his matriculation in the French Literature Department of Tokyo Imperial University in April 1925, Kobayashi immersed himself in the worlds of French poets Arthur Rimbaud, Guy de Maupassant, and Charles Baudelaire. High school classmate Hatano Kanji attests to the fact that by his early 20s Kobayashi was reading French with ease, working his way through most of Maupassant's works as well as those of Edgar Allan Poe in French translation. Much of this reading was, apparently, done surreptitiously in the back rows during lectures at school.[6] No passive reader, Kobayashi left his mark on much of what he read: the borrowed volumes he returned to Tokyo Imperial University professor Tatsuno Yutaka had hair, dandruff, and cigarette ashes pressed between the pages, and, not satisfied with merely circling and underlining significant passages, Kobayashi had cut out entire pages to save for future reference.[7]

Of the French writers he encountered at this time, Rimbaud became a lasting obsession. Kobayashi not only wrote his graduation thesis on this poet, but also translated his works extensively into Japanese. His first works of criticism also date to this period, during which Kobayashi wrote essays on writers Satō Haruo, Shiga Naoya, Akutagawa Ryūnosuke, and his friend the poet Tominaga Tarō, who had died tragically in 1925. During the early 1920s Kobayashi was also tormented by his tumultuous romance with Hasegawa Yasuko, an aspiring actress said to resemble Greta Garbo. Their relationship was plagued by Hasegawa's inability to break completely with her former beau, Kobayashi's friend the poet Nakahara Chūya. In fact, so intertwined were the three that Etō Jun refers to the situation as a "bizarre triangular relationship."[8] Furthermore, Hasegawa was infamous for her wildly erratic behavior: she is reputed to have attempted to push Kobayashi in front of a streetcar as well as to have threatened him with a razor.[9]

To these personal crises was added the devastation of the Great Kantō Earthquake in 1923 (discussed in some detail below). Kobayashi and his sister were still living in the family house in Shirokane, Tokyo, when it struck. Though the home was not destroyed, its foundations were seriously damaged, and the house now stood somewhat askew.[10] Kobayashi's main concern, however, was for the safety of his mother, who was convalescing in Kamakura. Having heard rumors that a tidal wave had engulfed that city, Kobayashi set out immediately to see for himself. He borrowed a knapsack, stuffed it with supplies, and caught a navy ship to Kamakura, where he found his mother and uncle sheltering in a shack. Though the tidal wave had never come, their homes had collapsed in the quake.[11]

After his graduation from Tokyo Imperial University in March 1928 Kobayashi established himself in the world of Japanese letters. Recognition came with the critical essay "Samazama naru ishō" (The Various Designs, 1929). Though an essay by Marxist Miyamoto Kenji edged it out for first prize in a literary competition sponsored by the magazine *Kaizō*, "Samazama naru ishō" impressed a wide range of figures in the literary world with its bold and unapologetically subjective critique of a broad spectrum of literary and critical methodologies, not the least of which was the Marxist criticism that dominated the publishing industry of the day. This essay opened doors for Kobayashi, and he soon became a regular contributor to many of the major literary journals. Writing mainly on contemporary fiction and criticism, Kobayashi championed the opposition to Marxist criticism and proletarian literature. He was largely successful in turning the tide against these movements, though it must be said that the government's increasing repression of left-wing writers certainly contributed significantly as well.

Through the 1930s Kobayashi occupied increasingly influential positions, including that of editor of the prestigious journal *Bungakukai*, a post he assumed in 1935. He began lecturing at Meiji University, first on literature and later on cultural history, and married in 1934. He also continued to publish voluminously, everything from reviews of recently published fiction to cultural commentary. He also wrote on foreign cultural icons. His serialized studies of the life and works of Dostoevsky and later of Mozart garnered him an audience beyond the narrow confines of the literary world. So prominent was Kobayashi that few would disagree with Donald Keene's evaluation: "It is hard to imagine what Shōwa criticism would have been like without Kobayashi, though we can be fairly sure that it would not have developed so greatly, nor would it have come to command the attention not only of persons professionally interested in literature but of the general public."[12]

Like the rest of the population, Kobayashi could not but have had his life changed by Japan's aggression on the Asian continent and later its war in the Pacific. Though his activities during this period are examined in Chapters 5 and 6, it bears repeating here that Kobayashi composed some of his most beautiful prose as the war escalated. The six short pieces composed in the wake of Japan's attack on Pearl Harbor, and collected under the title *Mujō to iu koto* (The Fact of Evanescence), are haunting prose poems in which Kobayashi seems almost to be channeling the literary voices of Japan's middle ages. These essays embody the approach to literature that Kobayashi had advocated in more conventional expository prose for much of his career.

Though some of his wartime essays prompted the younger, liberal critics of the postwar years to accuse him of complicity in the country's misguided military endeavors, his unflagging dedication to literary matters seems to have earned him a reprieve, and the postwar years found Kobayashi once again situated at the core of Japan's literary world. Two highlights from his postwar oeuvre are *Kindai kaiga* (Modern Painting) and *Motoori Norinaga.* The former is a collection of essays on painters Monet, Cézanne, Van Gogh, Gauguin, Renoir, Degas, and Picasso. Published as a single volume in 1958, it won him the Noma Literary Award (Noma bungakushō). *Motoori Norinaga,* his magnum opus on the Tokugawa-period philosopher, occupied Kobayashi for more than a decade. He was awarded the Japan Literary Award (Nihon bungaku taishō) in 1978 for this work. Throughout his career Kobayashi was very much a public intellectual, and his reading audience reached beyond the confines of the academic and literary worlds. Something of his overall prestige can be discerned from the fact that he was awarded the Imperial House's Order of Culture (Bunka kunshō) in 1967. Kobayashi continued to write and publish until his death from renal failure in March 1983.

As the above abbreviated biographical sketch suggests, other than the private crises he experienced as a young man, Kobayashi enjoyed a stable home life, and forged a tremendously successful career. What is not readily apparent from this sketch of his personal and professional life are the explosive historical and cultural developments that occurred around him and that he engaged in his thinking. His dialogue with these phenomena is the focus of this study. Of particular importance in the intellectual history of modern Japan are the strategies that Kobayashi developed and propagated when faced with modernity as it manifested itself in Japan.

The sections below introduce a broad range of elements associated with that modernity: a rift in the historical continuum that prompted a problematic and contradiction-ridden relationship with both the past and one's own moment in time; an expanding capitalism with all its concomitant promises and anxieties; a rapid rise of a popular, consumer culture that threatened the conventional role of the intelligentsia; a keen sense of disillusionment that fueled a nostalgia-driven concern with communal and personal memory; and an alienation that left humans groping for a new subjectivity, an authentic mode of being in their rapidly changing world. All of these were matters of concern for the generation as a whole and for Kobayashi in particular.

This study's primary focus, however, is on the effects of the altered materiality ushered in by modernity. Materiality is a point of confluence for many of the trajectories of modernity mentioned above, and as such it is a useful touchstone for tracing the contours of this new era. Materiality registered the rift in history: the landscape of Tokyo, in particular, was virtually unrecognizable after the 1923 earthquake, and the material culture enveloping the population as a whole changed radically in the interwar years. The spread of capitalism and the rise of a consumer-driven popular culture, too, altered materiality: objects were replaced with commodities, which in their plentitude and generic nature functioned in very different ways. Those objects left over from a former time, too, were altered by the arrival of modernity. Humans came to seek in them something stable, something beyond the vicissitudes of time. Things that had once been taken for granted came to be viewed with nostalgia, and this attitude altered the social value of that materiality. In these and many other ways modernity took root through its unique materiality, and subjectivities were formed and preserved in dialectic with this new materiality.

This chapter introduces the new materiality that became particularly prominent in the wake of the Great Kantō Earthquake of 1923, and then proceeds to tie a number of characterizations of modernity to this materiality. Kobayashi's response to these changes is then traced through a number of seminal essays. In one, Kobayashi documents how the too-rapid transformation of the "stuff" of his world alienated him from his place and time; another reveals the outline of the intellectual stance he adopted to reconfigure materiality such that he could engage it in more meaningful and authentic ways. As a whole the chapter portrays, in broad strokes, Kobayashi's aesthetic vision as a reaction to his moment in time.

The Great Kantō Earthquake and the New Materiality

After 1 September 1923, nothing would ever feel quite the same. The Great Kantō Earthquake, with a magnitude of 7.9, ignited a series of dramatic changes in both the cityscape of Tokyo and the mindscape of its inhabitants. First and foremost was the physical destruction and loss of life, the damage caused by the earthquake itself being compounded by the ensuing fires that raged for three days, reducing the city to a burned-out plain. The chaos that erupted rendered accurate statistics on the damage forever unattainable, but most agree that approximately 100,000 lives were lost, up to three quarters of the buildings in the city were either leveled or seriously damaged, and 2,000,000 residents were left homeless.[13] The city would have to be rebuilt and repopulated.

An eyewitness account conveys something of the indescribable sadness of the catastrophe, even for those not directly affected. Matsumoto Masao, 22 years old at the time, witnessed the catastrophe from a part of the city that was largely spared by the ensuing fires, but he movingly captures the scene as the displaced moved out of the ruins of Tokyo:

> People pulling handcarts piled high with all their worldly possessions, individuals shouldering enormous bundles, mothers with a child strapped to their backs and both hands lugging pots and pans—the line of evacuees seemed endless. Some of them asked the residents of the homes they passed if they would buy some of the possessions they had so painstakingly salvaged. Perhaps they were resigned to the fact that they could carry them no further; perhaps they were hoping to muster cash for the road ahead. Many of the residents, for their part, were completely flustered by these appeals: they could not in good conscience snap up the goods at dirt-cheap prices, but neither could they coldly, callously refuse the requests.[14]

This exodus from the heart of the city marked the end of an era. When the evacuees returned, it would be to a city being rebuilt in a far more modern, Western style.

A calamity of this scale alters the consciousness of survivors. The fact that the damage to Tokyo was most extensive in the older downtown area (*shitamachi*) meant that the earthquake opened an enormous rift in the historical continuum. The traditional sensibilities and material culture that had endured in these areas now having been lost, the post-earthquake present seemed immensely distant and irreparably severed from the past. As the city of Tokyo was rebuilt on a landscape wiped clean of tradition and history, its residents felt a new consciousness also taking hold.

Novelist Yokomitsu Riichi (1898–1947), who lived through the catastrophe and witnessed the emergence of the new world that arose in its wake, captured the atmosphere of post-earthquake Tokyo when he wrote:

> In the midst of the great metropolis spread out like an unbelievably vast stretch of burnt ruins, a mutant (*henkabutsu*) of great speed known as the automobile began to loiter about for the first time. Shortly a sound-emitting monster (*kikeibutsu*) called the radio made its appearance, and then a most useful object (*jitsuyōbutsu*) shaped like a bird, the aeroplane, started coursing through the skies. These were the embodiments (*gushōbutsu*) of modern science that came into existence for the first time in our country soon after the earthquake. The sensibilities of the youths witnessing the successive manifestations of these latest contraptions of modern science amid the burnt ruins could not help but be altered in some fashion.[15]

This sensibility-altering landscape is distinguished by the radically altered materiality evoked here by Yokomitsu, who turns to the word "object" (*butsu*) to create four neologisms in what are just two sentences in the original. This materiality is mutating, mobile, and slightly threatening; though inanimate objects, Yokomitsu's neologisms and modifying clauses invest them with a life of their own: mutants loiter, monsters appear, and mechanical birds soar through the skies. This almost animate materiality made possible by the innovations of modernity's technology arrives as a threatening onslaught, and its proliferation is accelerated by the absence of the concrete monuments and established practices of pre-earthquake Tokyo—those restraints had been removed from the physical, conceptual, and literary landscapes by the earthquake. It was a new world in Tokyo, and altered sensibilities were needed to make sense of it.

The events of 1 September 1923 shattered the tenuous confidence of the Taishō period, and marked the advent of a renewed sense of crisis concerning the modernity that was sweeping over Japan. The changes felt so keenly at this point had, of course, started with the appearance of a consumer culture in the Edo period (1600–1868), picked up speed with the opening of the country to foreign intercourse and the nation-building of the Meiji period (1868–1912), and reached maturity during the switch to heavy industries following World War I. Still, the shock of the Great Kantō Earthquake gave everyone pause and, in the appraisal of life that followed, the cumulative effect of those gradual changes suddenly appeared universal, monumental, and irrevocable.

Most striking were the objects (materiality, technology, commodities) that now seemed to occupy a more prominent place in life than ever before; they were produced in abundance, circulated freely, and seemed to exercise a will of their own. Coming to grips with modernity after the earthquake meant renegotiating humankind's relationship with this radically altered materiality. This renegotiation was the challenge faced by writers and intellectuals in Tokyo, Kobayashi Hideo prominent among them. Faced with a cityscape changing so quickly it invalidated his memories, and confronted with a new literary landscape so whimsical it offered no solace, it was incumbent on Kobayashi to somehow reconceptualize materiality and subjectivity in ways that made it possible to engage the world authentically and meaningfully once again.

History, Capitalism, Subjectivity, and Materiality in the Modern Age

The altered materiality that became so conspicuous in the wake of the earthquake was one element in a larger constellation of disorienting developments associated with the modernity that Kobayashi experienced in his youth. Scholars researching modernity and its ramifications in Japan characterize this constellation in a variety of ways, many of which provide conceptual vocabularies useful to this study. An overview of some of them in the following two sections provides an initial context for a discussion of Kobayashi's thought.

Perhaps the broadest definition of modernity in the Japanese context is that offered by Dennis Washburn in *The Dilemma of the Modern in Japanese Fiction*. Rather than tie it to the advent of industrialized societies beginning in the nineteenth century, Washburn treats modernity as a recurring *pattern* of social and cultural reappraisals prompted by what are perceived as ruptures in the historical continuum. As such, Washburn's study examines classical texts such as *Genji monogatari* (Tale of Genji, ca. 1021) and *Hōjōki* (An Account of My Hut, 1212) as well as works from the late nineteenth and twentieth centuries. "To be modern," Washburn writes, "is to possess a heightened sense of the significance of one's present moment: a significance expressed through forms or patterns that seek a still point transcending the human experience of time."[16] This consciousness, he goes on to argue, is intimately tied to subjectivity, for subjectivity "is created out of the struggle to assert one's presentness against the past. Personal and cultural identity are forms of narrative in which an understanding of the modern is the central constitutive element."[17] Washburn points out a troublesome paradox that plagues this quest for a personal or cultural identity: any pursuit of temporal transcendence is inevitably rooted in time—both in its reliance on linguistic expression (which eventually comes to an end) and in its ties to the historical moment—and is hence fated to be superseded.[18]

This study of Kobayashi Hideo draws on two elements of this characterization of modernity: the centrality of a yearning for a temporally transcendent "still point" in which to anchor subjectivity, and the troublesome paradox whereby such resistance to the passage of time is itself ultimately a product of a specific historical moment. Throughout his career Kobayashi consistently denounced anachronistic interpretations of literary texts (such as Marxist readings of classical fiction), and through a circumventing of intellectual analysis, he sought to recover what he believed to be a "still point": the seemingly transhistorical ability to appreciate literary texts (or any form of art) when apprehended holistically through an exercise of intuition. Ironically, this capacity was recognizable only because alternatives had emerged, that is, rigorous analytical methodologies such as the Marxist criticism rampant in the 1920s. Kobayashi's critical vision, therefore, was undeniably rooted in his historical moment. In short, he was caught in the temporal paradox of modernity that Washburn describes.

The modernity that Kobayashi and his generation encountered is also fruitfully interpreted through the economic system constituting it: capitalism. This feature is highlighted in Harry Harootunian's analysis of Japan's encounter with the modern, *Overcome by Modernity: History, Culture, and Community in Interwar Japan*. Examining texts from the end of World War I in 1919 to the infamous "Overcoming the Modern" symposium of 1942 (roughly the same period dealt with in this study), Harootunian traces the rupture in the social fabric to capitalism.[19] Quoting Slavoj Žižek, he states that "capitalism simply 'undermined every fixed social identity' and produced innumerable new subject positions all challenging the fixity of received traditional roles."[20] Most disruptive, Harootunian argues, was the "unevenness" instituted by the inevitably lopsided spread of capitalism. As the face of Japan changed during the shift to heavy industries in the wake of World War I, it became increasingly apparent that, contrary to all expectations, this evolution was allowing for, perhaps even promoting, "unevenness" in the form of ruptures between social classes (blue collar industrial vs. agrarian), geographic areas (urban vs. rural), generations (the *moga* and *mobo*, or "modern girls" and "modern boys" vs. their parents' generation), and historical moments (the modern present vs. "history" or the past). The emerging social disparities were raised to the level of an obsession by the fact that they contrasted so sharply with modern capitalism's implied promise of universal progress and stability.[21]

The attention Harootunian pays to this dimension of the era makes his analysis particularly pertinent to the issues explored here; his topography of the intellectual reactions to capitalism, his analysis of the commodification of culture, and his emphasis on, and characterizations of, the role of memory inform this reading of Kobayashi Hideo's renegotiation of humankind's relationship with materiality. All of these dimensions of modernity are returned to in the discussion below.

A third and final treatment of modernity that has been particularly influential in the conception of this study has been Karatani Kōjin's seminal *Nihon kindai bungaku no kigen* (Origins of Modern Japanese Literature, 1980). This work reconfigured and reinvigorated the readings of post-Meiji literary history, particularly the canonized reading focusing on "the formation of the modern self" (*kindaiteki jiga no seiritsu*).[22] Karatani's greatest contribution was his insistence on revealing and problematizing the discursively fabricated concept of "selfhood" (or, in his terms, interiority [*naimen* or *naibu*]). In this critique he offered a far more nuanced interpretation of the new literary language (*genbun itchi*) that allegedly allowed that "self" to be articulated, suggesting that it is best understood to be a by-product spawned by an inversion (*tentō*) of a new sensibility brought to bear on the depiction of landscape (or, more broadly, exteriority, or *gaibu*).[23] Like much of the work on post-Meiji Japan that has appeared in the twenty-five years since its publication, this study draws on the analysis first worked out by Karatani in *Nihon kindai bungaku no kigen*.

More specifically, Karatani foregrounds a dynamic relationship that opens the door for precisely the type of approach employed in the current study. In the chapter entitled "Naimen no hakken" (Discovery of Interiority), Karatani writes:

> The theme of the exploration of the modern self [*kindaiteki jiga*], however diverse its articulations, dominates discussions of modern Japanese literature. Yet it is laughable to speak of this modern self as if it were purely a mental or psychological phenomenon. For this modern self is rooted in materiality and comes into existence—if I may put it this way—only by being established as a system. What I want to emphasize is the systematicity of the very "inner self" that is usually seen as challenging systems.[24]

Karatani's insistence on accounting for the antithesis against which selfhood (subjectivity) was, and continues to be, postulated is in many ways the inspiration for approaching Kobayashi's thought as rooted in a subjectivity emerging in dialogue with a new form of materiality.

There are, of course, other factors pertinent to this study: the machinations of the state, the momentum of the literary and philosophical tradition (largely anachronistically constructed), and the personal dispositions and conscious choices of individual actors, to name but a few addressed here. Still, the features of modernity highlighted by these scholars—Washburn, Harootunian, and Karatani—are particularly useful in this chapter's introduction to the intellectual stance adopted by Kobayashi in response to modernity. They shaped his generation, including its understanding of history and its deployment of memory in preserving and resurrecting traces of it in the present. It is through an appreciation of this relationship to a rapidly receding past that Kobayashi's texts will be interpreted later in this chapter.

Memory and the Prisonhouse of the Present

In plotting the responses to the "unevenness" generated by modernity's capitalism, Harootunian produces a framework that can easily be adjusted to focus on the materiality of post-earthquake Japan. He outlines two basic strategies. On one side Harootunian situates writers who accepted the grand spectacle of modern life with all its dynamism and incongruities. People like anthropologist Kon Wajirō (1881–1973) and Marxist philosopher Tosaka Jun (1900–45), for example, focused on the "everydayness" of contemporary urban life, and attempted a revolution from within modernity. This revolution was to bring the era to its proper completion in a society bound together by its embrace of science, rationality, and the commodification prompted by capitalism. This response is easily re-articulated in the idiom of this study: these intellectuals enthusiastically embraced the new "objects" (commodities, materiality) that had invaded the landscape. Kon's anthropology of the metropolis's streets and parks chronicled the items and patterns of the new consumer behavior, and Tosaka's Marxism centered on the new material culture as the key to understanding the age. Like Yokomitsu Riichi in the passage quoted above, thinkers in this vein sensed a glorious potential in the new, dynamic materiality.

Harootunian also explicates a diametrically opposed response to this "unevenness" of the modern world, and it is here that memory assumes an important role. Rather than attempt to co-opt or harness the shifts occurring in the landscape and mindsets of Tokyo in the 1920s, some intellectuals sought to ease the anxieties of rapid change by resuscitating, resurrecting, or at the very least preserving premodern modes of existence now on the verge of extinction. Yanagita Kunio (1875–1962) and Watsuji Tetsurō (1889–1960) were two such thinkers who struggled to establish this type of historical continuity.[25] Here too Harootunian's narrative might be understood in terms of the burgeoning ultra-sensitivity to materiality, a primary concern of this study. Though these men were hoping to recover "the traces of a life once whole, coherent, unified, and authentic,"[26] they were in fact doing so by renegotiating their relationship to materiality. This dimension of their work is most evident in the ethnology boom sparked by Yanagita: great energy was invested in the collection and fetishization of the things of everyday rural life.[27]

Harootunian's analysis of the period includes the identification of a significant aptitude exercised by intellectuals in this latter category, an aptitude that plays an important role in Kobayashi's aesthetics as well. With the landscape of Japan, particularly post-earthquake Tokyo, now so radically different, people nostalgic for a mythical past wherein life was more "even" (coherent and authentic) naturally turned to memory for solace. This inclination was so marked, writes Harootunian, that "the construction of memory . . . became one of [modernity's] most principal and enduring forms of cognition. This privileging of memory was a corollary of the valorization of the cultural/aesthetic domain over the political/economic."[28]

The conditions, however, shaped a very distinct form of memory:

> The discourse on the social was concerned with depth, searching for fixed essences beneath the visible skin of contemporary life. It fastened on those traces that would reveal an existence prior to capitalism and modernity. Seeking to repress signs of its own historicity, this discourse pursued the task of constructing a vast synchronic drama that, because it was posited upon forgetting the instituting moment, could not allow into it any diachronic reflection or reference. . . . Instead of attending to the place of production, [these thinkers] resorted to the production of place. The temporal process was incorporated into space. . . . [T]hinkers and writers sought to install in the present a moment of recall or recovered experience, a memory *of* rather than *from* a time before time. . . .[29]

In the crush of change, with the invasion of almost animate objects and the unevenness of the interwar years, the quest for "fixed essences" (or, in Washburn's words, "a still point transcending the human experience of time") was an immensely attractive option.

Though so much had changed, traces of a former existence did remain, though perhaps as nothing more than a sense of longing for something other than the attending present. The response to that longing was, as Harootunian notes, memory, for it seemed the only way out of the prisonhouse of the present. The alternative, history, was undesirable for a number of reasons. As a conscious attempt to explain the present in terms of root causes in the past, history not only privileges the (unsettling) present as the end point to which all previous events had led, but also explicitly renders the past familiar, an act that detracts from the myth of it as an alternative to the here and now. Memory, on the other hand, privileges the past without explicitly establishing a causal relationship with the present. Additionally, seen as an involuntary occurrence, the act of remembering appears immune to the machinations of the recollecting subject, and hence remains untainted by the agendas of the present.

In point of fact, of course, both history and memory are plagued by the same problematic chronological reversal that Nietzsche identified in the cause-and-effect paradigm: the conditions of the present (the effect) determine what among the vast array of past circumstances are highlighted as history or memory (cause).[30] In that the longing for some stable "still point," for "a life once whole, coherent, unified, and authentic," was prompted by a too-rapidly changing present, the resurrection of the past (whether by memory or history) was at best a reactionary denial of the slippery, ever-changing now rather than the pristine premodern mode of existence for which these intellectuals yearned. In this sense both memory and its putative alternative, history, are equally compromised by their nature as "vast synchronic drama[s]," and we are all always "overcome by modernity." Between history and memory, however, there is a difference *of* degree, and it is an important one: in that memory is perceived to resurrect the past in an act "natural" and involuntary, it more effectively erases its own historicity and more convincingly fabricates the type of temporally transcendent experience craved by those disoriented by modernity and its unpredictable new materiality.

Kobayashi was one of these, and many of the features foregrounded by Harootunian are apparent in Kobayashi's deployment of memory as a means of recovering and preserving the type of meaningful existence that modernity was quickly rendering inaccessible. His relationships to the past and to the changed materiality of his present are issues at the core of much of his writing. The sections below interpret a number of seminal works by Kobayashi, demonstrating how his writing engaged the multifarious challenges of modernity in restoring, rhetorically at least, a stable subjectivity able to engage the world authentically and meaningfully.

Memories of the Home One Never Knew

All of the factors discussed above—an anxiety with the materiality of modernity, the longing for (imagined) premodern modes of being, the location of memory at the core of the endeavor to recover what was being lost—are evident in Kobayashi Hideo's 1933 essay "Kokyō o ushinatta bungaku" (Literature That Has Lost Its Home). Here Kobayashi relates a trip he took with poet and novelist Takii Kōsaku (1894–1984). Though less than ten years younger than Takii, Kobayashi is a man of a different world for having been raised in Tokyo during the earthquake and its subsequent kaleidoscopic changes. While Takii speaks so fondly and emotionally of the childhood memories he associates with the rural landscapes rolling past outside the train window, Kobayashi finds himself unable to empathize:

> I was struck by the fact that I do not understand the notion of a "first home," or a "second home"—indeed, what a home of any kind in fact is. Where there are no memories [*omoide*], there is no home. Only a person who possesses layer upon layer of vivid memories built on countless strong impressions from a concrete environment can appreciate the healthy emotions evoked by the word "hometown." Search as I might within myself, these memories simply don't exist. Looking back on my life I can say that since childhood my heart has been tortured by an endless clutter of things and events that have changed too quickly; I did not have the leisure to nurture for later years the substance of powerful memories, substance linked to solid objects and incidents. I do have memories, but they are lacking in concrete substance. I sense something vaguely fictitious about these memories.[31]

The contrast with Takii's guileless and heartfelt sentiments is striking; Kobayashi's sense of alienation is extreme.

The intensity of Kobayashi's anxiety is most evident in his choice of the "lost home" metaphor. The word he uses is *kokyō* (or, alternatively, *furusato*), an emotionally charged word referring to one's birthplace, hometown, or, by extension, any point of origin. This word had grown steadily in sentimental value as so many in the post-Meiji generations had left their country homes for the greater opportunities available in the capital. To these earlier generations the *kokyō* had always served as both a geographical and temporal base against which to evaluate new experiences in the teeming metropolis of Tokyo. Paradoxically, rural origins did not only represent specific local subcultures as distinct from the shared national culture being constructed in the capital (a domestic site of difference). They also stood collectively for a uniform, unchanging, traditional lifestyle (a historical community) antecedent to the modern, cosmopolitan existence in Tokyo. While writers since Meiji had found their rural origins sometimes reassuring, sometimes suffocating, these origins nevertheless always provided a firm point of reference. In the above passage, however, Kobayashi marks the type of "unevenness" that Harootunian situates at the core of the experience of modernity: while Takii still has access, through memories *from* his past, to this stable alternative reality, Kobayashi does not. While the literary world he is writing about may as a whole have "lost its home," Kobayashi states unequivocally that he himself has never known one, yet he yearns for it all the same. Clearly Kobayashi is poised to exercise what Harootunian characterizes as one of modernity's principal forms of cognition, memory; he is on the brink of installing "in the present a moment of recall or recovered experience, a memory *of* rather than *from* a time before time."

The passage cited also narrates the change that has made this recourse to memory a necessity. The cause of his alienation from the "home" is nothing other than the radical change in the nature of materiality. In place of a "concrete environment" (*kakkotaru kankyō*) composed of "solid objects and incidents" (*kakkotaru jibutsu*), Kobayashi finds himself plagued by "an endless clutter of things and events that have changed too quickly" (*monogoto no kagiri nai zatta to hayasugiru henka*). This experience is particularly true for one born and raised, like Kobayashi, in Tokyo, that most modern of locales. "Though I was born in Tokyo," Kobayashi writes, "that fact makes absolutely no sense to me."[32] The reason is that his experience is lacking the "specificity" (*gutaisei*) that would make him a "Tokyoite born in Tokyo" rather than that "abstract being known as a city dweller."[33] The perception of a shift from concrete and solid to amorphous and permeable infects all things. Post-earthquake Tokyo in particular is now a generic urban space; Kobayashi and his generation are no longer Tokyoites but rather ethereal abstractions.

In Kobayashi's mind it is memory that links one to the "home," memory that makes it possible to transcend the "endless clutter of things and events that have changed too quickly" (the modern present) and regain a bygone world where one can react with "healthy emotions" to a fully inanimate materiality ("solid objects and incidents"). The irony of lamenting the loss of a home he has never known does not escape Kobayashi. It haunts him. Sifting through the memories he does have, Kobayashi finds them "vaguely fictitious" (*kakū no ajiwai*), and hence unable to ground him. He is, in fact, struggling to remember a time of which he has no memory, a time or mode of existence that the changes in his sensibilities have rendered inaccessible. Unlike Takii, who has memories *from* a time before, Kobayashi can have memories only *of* a time before.

Kobayashi's awareness and conception of this dilemma is revealed in a second passage from "Kokyō o ushinatta bungaku":

> What I feel when I listen to my mother tell stories of her own childhood is that they are simple, ordinary stories told in a calm manner. But, all the same, they are naturally infused with a powerful emotion. She relates simple memories, but they contain a narrative structure. I envy her that for, try as I might, her stories have something that remains beyond my grasp. The memories I relate do not have a unified narrative structure unless I manufacture some embellishment—or perhaps "crafting for them a subjective dimension in the form of a perspective or critical stance" is a better way to put it. This cannot be the proper path, and I am left brooding over the situation.[34]

Here the powerful memories of a home that Kobayashi had attributed to Takii are replaced by stories told by his mother of her youth. Memory and narrative are interchangeable. Mother's stories are related unselfconsciously, simply, and yet they have all the makings of fine literature in that they are "infused with a powerful emotion," and contain a narrative structure. Radically alienated from the "home" and without memories from it, Kobayashi is unable to reproduce such stories. The clutter of his world demands that he retrospectively order it through "embellishments" (*funshoku*), and the contradiction inherent in having to artificially construct "simple, ordinary stories" (*goku futsū na hanashi*) quite understandably leaves him brooding.

"Kokyō o ushinatta bungaku," particularly the passages quoted above, concisely encapsulates Kobayashi's perception of the crisis of modernity, and a significant portion of his writing is dedicated to compensating for his perceived lack of a stable point of origin, a "hometown of the spirit." This quest is largely one of renegotiating the relationship of humans to an altered materiality, one now almost alive and pressing in from all directions. The proper path seems to lie in the direction of resurrecting premodern modes of existence, or a return to a "home" present before the shift in sensibilities. The "home," however, is one he himself has never experienced, and the memories that he would invoke in its resuscitation are also curiously absent. To appease his nostalgia for that mysterious something that came before, then, he is left with no choice but to deploy the tools and conditions of his modernity. In his own words, he must "manufacture some embellishment," though the phrase is too negatively connoted to do justice to his accomplishment. In this engagement with materiality and memory in an attempt to address a perceived crisis of subjectivity, Kobayashi's agenda is an intimately modern one.

The "endless clutter of things and events" shaped more than Kobayashi's childhood. It persisted into his adulthood, evolving into an overwhelming presence haunting Kobayashi and his generation. The new materiality and the sensibilities it was nurturing were nowhere more apparent than in Kobayashi's professional field of literature. Just as technology had changed the landscape of post-earthquake Tokyo, so too had it altered the world of publishing. The proliferation of the written word changed its place in the cultural constellation of interwar Japan, and Kobayashi Hideo would need to stem its slide into amorphousness, too, in order to recover the sensibilities of the premodern.

World Literature for a Song and the Loss of Aura

In turning to literature as a means of halting the slide into an ever more mutable and abstract present, Kobayashi was following the lead of distinguished predecessors such as Akutagawa Ryūnosuke (1892–1927). Like many writers whose careers blossomed during the Taishō period, Akutagawa defined his world, ordered it, and forged a place for himself in it entirely in literary terms.[35] The literary world that Kobayashi turned to, however, was undergoing a transformation not unlike that of Tokyo itself in the mid-1920s. Here, too, it was the earthquake that marked the turning point.

With virtually all the printing companies in Tokyo burned to the ground in the catastrophe, the publishing industry underwent a major restructuring. A particularly notable literary victim of the earthquake was the journal *Shirakaba*. A hallmark of the harmonious Taishō period, this cosmopolitan, highbrow journal had introduced European art as well as young, idealistic Japanese writers to the educated public. Its first edition, published in 1910, was a printing of 300 copies; its famous issue introducing Rodin reached 1,000 copies.[36] The Shirakaba facilities, however, were destroyed in the earthquake, and the journal was never revived.

The new journal *Bungei shunjū*, on the other hand, was just coming into its own. Although all copies of the September 1923 issue had burned at the printer's during the earthquake, this journal bounced back quickly, and by 1927 was printing runs of 180,000.[37] Its popularity was undoubtedly due to the new concept developed for the magazine by its founder and driving force, Kikuchi Kan (1888–1948). Kikuchi refused to follow the conventional practices of contemporary literary magazines, particularly their penchant for opening with articles so complex that, as Kikuchi put it, only three people would read them—the writer, the editor, and the proofreader. Instead he aimed at a more accessible and eclectic format, something he was fond of describing as *bungaku oden* (a literary hodgepodge or slumgullion).[38] This publication was obviously aimed at a mass market, and its success suggests that the market was ready for it.

This new, consumer-oriented publishing strategy was supported by new printing technology that greatly reduced the time, effort, and expense needed to bring words into print.[39] Taking advantage of this breakthrough and the increasingly broad demand for easily accessible reading material, the publishing house Kōdansha released the magazine *Kingu* (King) in 1925 with an advertising campaign of unprecedented scale. According to Kōno Kensuke, the start of the magazine was heralded by the distribution of 1,700,000 flyers, a mass mailing of letters and postcards, newspaper advertisements, and the mobilization of musical sandwich men.[40] This multimedia advertising spectacle was a grand success: the 500,000 copies of the first edition sold out so quickly that Kōdansha printed an additional 250,000. An issue in 1928 sold 1.5 million copies.[41]

Kingu was the brainchild of Noma Seiji, the founder of the Kōdansha publishing house and a man who did Kikuchi one better in breaking away from the conventions and pressures of the literary community. Whereas Kikuchi had launched *Bungei shunjū* because he wanted a venue in which he, his friends, and young writers could express themselves freely on topics of personal concern, Noma conceived of his magazine purely in terms of the readership it might reach. In his own words, he wanted something that would be

> of interest—of great interest—to the elderly, to children, to women. Something that would be irresistible reading for scholars, businessmen, and housewives—a magazine with an appeal that transcended age, gender, occupation, and [social] standing. . . . On top of that I want it to be instructive, very instructive. . . . [And it had to be] cheap, and not just cheap by ordinary standards—it had to be *really* cheap.[42]

The circulation numbers attest to *Kingu*'s broad appeal, and at 50 *sen* for 352 pages it was certainly cheap. Most important, however, is the fact that right from the very beginning, this publishing venture was conceived of in marketing terms. Publishing was no longer strictly the purview of an elite cadre of literary men; books were now conceived, produced, advertised, and distributed in ways indistinguishable from other commodities.

This commodification and mechanical reproduction of the written word soon spread beyond the confines of mass-produced magazines. A month before the Shōwa era began, publishing house Kaizōsha announced its forthcoming 37-volume collection of contemporary Japanese literature (*Gendai Nihon bungaku zenshū*). These volumes would be made available on a subscription basis only, with each hefty tome of 500 to 600 pages carrying the unbelievably low price of one yen. Taking a cue from the taxis with a flat rate of one yen (*entaku*), these books were referred to as *enpon* (one-yen books), and demand exceeded all expectations. Hoping for sales of 20,000 to 30,000 sets, Kaizōsha soon found itself committed to producing somewhere between 250,000 and 380,000 sets of the collection. With this tremendous reception, Kaizōsha expanded the set from the original 37 volumes to 50 volumes—and later tacked on 12 more. Five years elapsed before the final volume was released in 1931.

Other publishers followed closely behind. Shinchōsha's 38-volume collection of world literature (*Sekai bungaku zenshū*), announced in 1927, eventually sold 580,000 sets. Around the same time Shunyōsha offered a 50-volume set of literature from Meiji and Taishō (*Meiji Taishō bungaku zenshū*), and Heibonsha produced a collection of contemporary popular literature (*Gendai taishū bungaku zenshū*) in 60 volumes. In the early years of Shōwa as many as 200 different *enpon* collections were available, with Heibonsha alone offering over 30 different series. In the advertising copy for their *Gendai taishū bungaku zenshū*, company president Shimonaka Yasaburō acknowledged the degree to which the written word, particularly popular literature, was infiltrating all corners of life:

Though there may be some among the Japanese people who will forget the name [of prime minister] Wakatsuki Reijirō, surely none will forget [literary characters such as] Major Takano, Orinosuke of the Tajima School, Shimizu no Jirōchō, Okinu, and Ogin. The reason? For people who read today, popular literature is, along with rice and salt, a staple of daily life.[43]

Mass-produced versions of literature of all stripes, from these popular pieces to foreign classics in translation, became very much a part of the lives of a broad range of the population.

Needless to say, the effects of this magazine and anthology boom spread beyond the publishing houses and the readership to alter the lives of writers across the spectrum. Kikuchi Kan, founder of *Bungei shunjū*, saw his economic value skyrocket from the 7-yen-per-page rate he was getting from *Chūō kōron* to the 100-yen-per-page fee he was able to negotiate for the story he published in the magazine *Kingu*.[44] Concerning the *enpon* anthologies, Kikuchi called them a "revolution" in publishing for the royalties they provided writers. "That writers have prospered, at least materially," Kikuchi said, "was thanks to the *enpon*."[45]

But these developments were something of a mixed blessing. As literary production expanded to meet the growing demand, the prestige of the man of letters suffered, at least in the eyes of some. Poet, essayist, and fiction writer Satō Haruo (1892–1964) captured the essence of the equivocal outcome of the publishing boom in a lively section of his *Taikutsu tokuhon* (Textbook of Boredom, 1926):

I get the impression that the *bundan* has become just another professional organization, no different from a fraternity of *geta* makers, a gang of rickshaw coolies, a bakers' guild, a gaggle of politicians, or the whole mass of officialdom. It is not my intention to slander the society composed of modern writers as being inferior to other societies; all I am saying is that it is no different from any other profession. That is the simple truth, but I wonder if members of the *bundan* do not think of the lives that they lead as being especially elevated? First of all, is it not true that our work, in relation to the amount of labor involved, is better paid than any other profession? Indeed, literature is now an economically viable occupation for anyone who has the talent to string together a few words; and if he has a modicum of practical wisdom, he can make a fortune as a writer; and, provided he has this practical wisdom, his literary ability is only of secondary importance. All one has to do is to spend ten years or so, like an apprentice serving out his term, close to the atmosphere of the *bundan* and one's manuscripts will somehow or other start to sell. . . . The poverty of members of the *bundan* is now a thing of the past. In this respect ours is a truly wonderful age. Does this mean, then, that literature is now so highly valued by society? And does literature itself enjoy such influence over society? No, that is naturally quite a different kettle of fish. In fact, it would be more accurate to say that the opposite is the case. I would even go so far as to say that literature, as a social phenomenon, has never had less authority than at present.[46]

So, as literature and the written word flooded the market, as royalties and higher commissions filled the wallets of the writers, a concern arose that the integrity of the profession had been compromised.

For better or worse, a fundamental change was indeed taking place. In his prescient 1936 essay "The Work of Art in the Age of Mechanical Reproduction," Walter Benjamin writes: "the mode of human sense perception changes with humanity's entire mode of existence."[47] Though Benjamin in this essay is thinking primarily of the visual arts (painting and film), his observations apply equally to the changes in sense perception that emerged with the new mode of existence ushered in by the mechanical reproduction of the written word as outlined above. As was the case with the invasion of almost animate inanimates (automobiles, radios, airplanes), the flood of literary commodities into the marketplace prompted a new sensibility. Some writers, Kikuchi Kan most prevalent among them, embraced the new literary economy, and spurred on the commodification of literature. Other writers balked at this cheapening (in both senses of the word), sensing in it the imminent demise of an almost sacred aesthetic and intellectual experience. Kobayashi was a major voice among this second group.

Both reactions were based in the new sensibility that, Benjamin explains, is distinguished by the loss of the "aura" that once surrounded the absolutely unique work of art. This loss is prompted by "the desire of contemporary masses to bring things 'closer' spatially and humanly, which is just as ardent as their bent toward overcoming the uniqueness of every reality by accepting its reproduction."[48] The function of distance is particularly important to Benjamin. The conventional attitude toward art is grounded in the image of a painter producing a singular original from a "natural" distance, much like a magician works his sorcery from afar. The age of mechanical reproduction, however, shifts human sense perception toward a paradigm based on the movie cameraman, whose medium is valued precisely because it can be easily reproduced. The cameraman roves freely around and even into his subject, like the surgeon eliminating all distance. Because of these differences in distance, Benjamin maintains, there is "a tremendous difference between the pictures they obtain.

That of the painter is a total one, that of the cameraman consists of multiple fragments which are assembled under a new law."[49] The "total" picture produced respectfully by the painter from a distance generates an aura; the willful rearrangement of fragments carved out of the whole (the method of the cameraman) does not.

The shift from literature as the purview of the economically and educationally privileged to literature as a cheaply produced and aggressively marketed commodity represents the very same collapsing of distance and decline of aura. Literature was pulled close spatially as cheaper prices meant more books lined the shelves in the homes of more people. It was pulled close "humanly" (by which Benjamin means psychologically) by the surgeon-like approach that publishers and editors adopted toward the corpus of world literature. Certain writers were deemed undesirable and were extracted; others were found important and were anthologized. The body of work of any anthologized writer was similarly dissected, and only the most desirable elements were transplanted into the collections. With the launching of each new series, the editors would comb through the multiplicity of fragments, combining them time and time again under new laws that would hopefully yield a bestseller.

Perhaps the most invasive procedure of all, however, was translation. Whereas most foreign literature had long been accessible only to the wealthy and linguistically adept, translation now made it widely available. "World literature," once a near sacred canon preserved in the hallowed halls of the upscale foreign bookstore Maruzen, was now readily available from Shinchōsha—in easy-to-read Japanese translation and for only a yen per volume. Japanese texts, spatially and humanly close from the start, were pulled closer still through a similar act of translation: at least some of the new collections included *rubi*, pronunciation guides to the more difficult *kanji*.[50] In short, through dissection and rearrangement, through editing and translation, literature was made familiar.

The experience of reading would never be the same. To struggle through the French in a novel virtually unknown to one's countrymen, and obtained only after considerable effort and expense, is to surrender oneself to an encounter with a mystical unknown, to lose oneself in the aura of art. To read that same novel as reproduced in Shinchōsha's *Sekai bungaku zenshū* is a different experience entirely: it is plucked off one's very own bookshelf, skimmed leisurely in one's native Japanese, and contemplated with the knowledge that thousands of other readers may be considering the very same work at the very same time. All this, and for the price of a single yen. In this latter scenario there is a sense of confident mastery over the material, an attitude conducive to the deployment of literature in one's own public agenda.

This altered human sensibility contributed to the spread of Marxist criticism, the most influential literary movement of the Shōwa period. Particularly in the early years, Marxism dominated literary discourse: approximately 80 percent of the criticism published in literary and general magazines during the late 1920s and early 1930s was written by Marxists.[51] Explanations for this explosion of Marxist criticism point to its social and historical pertinence, its humanitarian concerns, its promise of parity and simultaneity with Western thinkers, its unchallenged role as comprehensive social theory, and its allure as a mysterious and dangerous doctrine.[52] To these conditions should be added the new "proximity" of texts, a factor that diminished their aura and replaced the aesthetic experience of art with the surgical dissection of texts. Ironically, it was the commodification of literature that made the emergence of Marxist criticism psychologically possible, and this criticism, in turn, became a valuable piece of literary merchandise in the growing market for the written word.[53]

Maruzen Commodities and Literary Artifacts

Though he turned to the literary community for refuge from the strains of a turbulent reality, Kobayashi found there the very same erosion of the concrete and unchanging. Like his birthplace, Tokyo, the literary world was now an "endless clutter of things and events that have changed too quickly." The publishing boom, with its support for new and previously marginal genres, its transformation of centuries of foreign literature into a Japanese language commodity, and its boost to the field of criticism, threatened the literary status quo. Kobayashi's personal distress over the devaluation of literary texts as they flooded the marketplace at increasingly cheaper prices is evident from the very start of his career. In his earliest work of fiction, "Tako no jisatsu" (The Octopus's Suicide, 1922), this anxiety is expressed through the depiction of a visit to Maruzen, the purveyor of foreign books and knowledge to generations of Japanese intellectuals since the Meiji Restoration.

For Kobayashi's literary forebearers, Maruzen, with the foreign literature it offered, played a central role in their identities. The bookstore figures prominently, for example, in "Aru ahō no isshō" (The Life of a Stupid Man, 1927), Akutagawa Ryūnosuke's third-person account of his own descent into suicidal depression and madness. Reaching back to his roots as his life comes to a close, Akutagawa records fragmented memories of his mother and his home, but prior to even these he describes a glorious moment in a bookstore that was most certainly Maruzen. Its place at the very origin of this "life of a stupid man" suggests the primacy of this literary experience in the formation of his entire sense of self. In this famous scene, a 20-year-old Akutagawa is perched on a ladder and skimming the titles of Western literature high on the shelves—Maupassant, Baudelaire, Ibsen, Tolstoy, Nietzsche, Dostoevsky, Flaubert. The failing of the light as night presses in is about to send him down the ladder.

At that very moment, directly overhead, a single bare light bulb came on. Standing on his perch on the top of the ladder, he looked down at the clerks and customers moving among the books. They were strangely small—and shabby.

Life is not worth a single line of Baudelaire.

He stood on the ladder, watching them below.[54]

Foreign literature raised the young Akutagawa above the crowds; it provided him with an almost omniscient perspective. As Seiji Lippit notes, this scene shows that "space is thus organized according to an opposition between the world of the imagination and intellectual activity, on the one hand, and the economic realm of labor and consumption ('clerks and customers'), on the other."[55] The title of this episode is "The Era" (*Jidai*), a fact that reflects the degree to which Akutagawa felt his experience was shared by his peers.[56]

Kobayashi's pilgrimage to Maruzen, however, came some ten years later, and his experience illustrates his dismay at the increasing commodification of literature. "Tako no jisatsu" is an autobiographical story, written in the style of Kobayashi hero Shiga Naoya (1883–1971). It recounts the day-to-day doings of Kenkichi, Kobayashi's alter ego. On a walk along the beach in Kamakura one night, the introverted Kenkichi comes upon a crowd listening to speeches delivered by members of a new religious group. Kenkichi stops to listen, but soon finds himself fidgeting. When a young woman sitting next to him directs a disapproving glance his way, he suddenly stands up to leave.

He found himself walking along the beach, and it struck him how far removed he was from what those people called their religious life. He could

> understand their feelings because as a middle-school student a sentimental longing had inspired him to seek religion as well. Now, though, he could not imagine naively losing himself in any religion no matter what hand life dealt him. . . . He suddenly remembered having once briskly walked along this coast on a chilly day in early spring and being overwhelmed by a burning desire for knowledge. He had been confused as to where to begin this quest. He had entered Maruzen, a five-yen bill clutched in his hand, but had lost all sense of which books to buy. He had grown furious at the other customers, thinking "How can they possibly buy their books so nonchalantly?" On the verge of tears, he had fled the bookstore. As he stared now at the golden froth of the waves, he felt them form eddies in his own mind, and these memories of himself were pulled under and disappeared.[57]

Like Akutagawa, Kobayashi had turned to Maruzen and the foreign literature it sold in hopes that it might fill some spiritual void and distinguish him from the unthinking crowds. The aura of the establishment, however, has dissolved, and a disappointed Kobayashi runs into the street with tears in his eyes.

Interestingly, it is an encounter with religion that sparks this memory of Maruzen. Many late-Meiji and Taishō literary figures had flirted with Christianity in their youths, only later to funnel their spiritual energies into literary channels.[58] While this trajectory is perhaps most readily apparent in the Shirakaba writers, the group with whom the young Kobayashi felt the closest affinity, even Akutagawa seemed to find Christianity and literature surrogates. In an inversion of the conventional trajectory, the disintegration of his literary vision was accompanied by a re-evaluation of Christianity, something he sincerely investigated in the tortured final year of his life.[59] In the passage quoted above, Kobayashi alludes to his own fleeting infatuation with Christianity during his late teens. That his declaration of his disillusionment with religion should lead to a memory of Maruzen suggests something of the degree to which literature filled a void as spiritual as it was intellectual or aesthetic. As for so many others, it was a desire for an experience of transcendence through the aura of art that prompted Kobayashi to step into Maruzen's world of foreign literature.

The sought-for experience is nowhere to be found. Perhaps because they are now too plentiful, Kenkichi (Kobayashi) cannot identify the books that will satisfy him. Worse, while his interests and abilities resemble those of Akutagawa before him, they are no longer sufficient to lift him above the milling crowds. To the story's protagonist the books represent almost sacred scriptures; to the customers they are but commodities to be purchased "nonchalantly" (*nonki ni*). In short, the entire literary enterprise has been compromised, and there is nothing to do but flee. The despair would escalate exponentially in the *enpon* boom that was but a few years away.[60]

With the world around him, and particularly the city of Tokyo, changing too quickly, and with the conventional refuge of literature equally confused and commodified, Kobayashi is left with no choice but somehow to artificially reconstitute the materiality of literature just as he must conjure up a "home" through unreliable memories. This project would require some years to complete, and in the interim Kobayashi would flirt with various accommodations of the new commodified literature. His 1924 story "Hitotsu no nōzui" (One Brain) approaches the narrative style of modernist Yokomitsu Riichi, and the theory of language Kobayashi expresses in his award-winning "Samazama naru ishō" (The Various Designs) shares certain perspectives with understandings put forth by Yokomitsu as well as by Kataoka Teppei (1894–1944), both theorists of the Neo-Perceptionist group (Shinkankaku-ha).[61]

However, in some of his most successful performative essays, Kobayashi manages to resurrect, for a moment, the experience of literature before it was cheapened, commodified.[62] He reestablishes psychological distance, renders the text whole and impermeable, and thereby restores its aura. This modus operandi is nowhere stated more clearly than in the 1941 essay, "Dentō" (Tradition), in which Kobayashi reflects on his experience of researching and writing on Dostoevsky. The following extended quotation concisely captures the essence of how Kobayashi would return a stable impermeability to literary texts that were increasingly losing their aura in the whirl of interpretations, translations, and reproductions.

> There was a time when I very carefully read the literature of Dostoevsky. When I first began to fish around in the documents concerning his life and times, I turned up evidence of many historical conditions that seemed to explain how his literature came to be, or even how it was inevitable that it should arise. However, as the range of documents that I read expanded, and I doggedly pursued my research, things started to fall apart. One after another, strange, paradoxical facts appeared, leaving me at a loss as to how to choose between them and what they might mean. It seems that we have to take things this far. It is when we stop in the middle of this process that we experience relief at having solved the mysteries while in fact we have done nothing but scrape together from the historical facts those elements that are easiest for us to understand. And that is not all; there is an even

graver misunderstanding that arises from this misplaced sense of relief. When we have uncovered the historical conditions that gave rise to the work, we become utterly convinced that its power is reducible to the sum of those various elements we identified through our analysis. We claim that having started from the vague, unstable wonder we felt when we first encountered the work, we have arrived at a more certain, exquisite understanding of it. Something has been gained, to be sure. But who can say what has been lost in the process?

The work must be pursued to its conclusions. Suffering in the confusion caused by too many documents, being overwhelmed by the disorderly jumble of historical facts—it is good to have a keen taste of these experiences. There are things that cannot be truly understood without them. On one side we find the startling disorder of history, and on the other we discern the astounding harmony and order of the work of art. How did the integrity of the work of art emerge from such a disorderly reality? We lose sight of the thread linking these two worlds, and are left mystified. Having been pushed to our wit's end, however, is not all for naught as we suddenly realize that there is nothing to do but once again turn to the text, to go back to where we started. We may feel that we have toiled in vain but this feeling, too, serves its purpose. Returning empty-handed to the place where we started, we truly appreciate the work of art for the first time. The conditions behind its emergence—those we deemed necessary, those we could only think of as coincidental, and that jumble we left behind as incomprehensible—we understand that all of these are absorbed and manifest in the immutable harmony of the mysterious living thing that is the work of art. We leave the realm of the mystery and circle around it only to find it remains unsolved. But the light shining forth is now brighter, and the mystery is now more beautiful than before.[63]

Here Kobayashi begins his examination with an approach that Benjamin would have likened to a surgeon's. He pulls the text close, begins to dissect it, and rearranges the fragments under some new law. He employs the historically sensitive, interpretive approach employed by the contemporary critical community and made physically and psychologically possible by the publishing boom of the late 1920s. (Unable to read Russian, Kobayashi had access to Dostoevsky only in translation.) Kobayashi stops short, however, when he realizes that to approach the text in this manner is to accept it as part of that new, dynamic, porous materiality (the commodity) that lends itself to infinite mutations and reproductions; to proffer yet another interpretation is to further commodify the text, to contribute to the already overwhelming clutter of the literary world. Worst of all, to pursue this approach is to diminish the aesthetic experience, that feeling of "vague, unstable wonder."

For these reasons Kobayashi reverts to a position within Benjamin's other paradigm, that of the magician. Like the magician (or painter), Kobayashi reestablishes a "natural" distance between himself and the object. He does this by insisting on our ultimate inability to exhaustively explain the text, an assertion that serves also to reestablish the aura, or "mystery," of the work of art. It is "a living thing" (*ikimono*) only in the sense that it must be appreciated as a whole; in all other respects Kobayashi has rendered the literary text a solid, impermeable, and static object of aesthetic appreciation. "We leave the realm of the mystery and circle around it only to find it remains unsolved. But the light shining forth is now brighter, and the mystery is now more beautiful than before." This untouchable text is uninterpretable; it is immune to reproduction or mutation; it is a specimen of "premodern materiality." Perhaps most importantly, it is beautiful—and beautiful because of how Kobayashi has situated himself (and by extension other readers) in relationship to it. Not surprisingly, Kobayashi's stance vis-à-vis the text is not unlike that found sometimes in the work of Susan Sontag, whose essay "Against Interpretation" was discussed in the preface to this study. Cary Nelson captures that stance in his description of Sontag's writing: "Sontag never finally assumes an easy familiarity with her subject but rather draws its difficult negating otherness ever closer to herself. Her work may be understood, in a way, as a search for a text that is utterly unknowable, a text that will always elude and contradict what we may say about it, a text, in short, that cannot be contaminated by critical rhetoric."[64] This description captures the essence of Kobayashi's attitude toward Dostoevsky as expressed in the passage quoted above.

Also evident there are the complex workings of memory, what Harootunian identified as "one of [modernity's] most principal and enduring forms of cognition." Like other thinkers battling the diminution of sensual experience accompanying this latest phase of modernity, Kobayashi attempts to somehow resuscitate something of a nearly extinct past by "recollecting" alternatives to the present based on some vestigial presence. Kobayashi generated a vision of a "home" he had never known based on yearnings rooted in a distrust of the present. In the passage quoted above, he again acts on this nostalgia, narrating his experience as a memory of an authentic textual encounter ("there was a time when . . ."). He does so, however, from a radically different vantage point—that of a very different present. The aesthetic power of the original encounter with the holistic text is anachronistically posited from a point at which it has been sullied by conscious thought. Kobayashi's use of memory is, as Harootunian phrases it, a process whereby the writers "install in the present a moment of recall or recovered experience, a memory *of* rather than *from* a time before. . . ."

Kobayashi was not the only one to attempt the resurrection of a more coherent and authentic past through a renegotiation of humankind's relationship with materiality. In fact his vision overlaps in many places with that of contemporary ethnographers, many of whom experimented with "things" in a much more literal sense. People like Yanagi Sōetsu (1889–1961) and Shibusawa Keizō (1896–1963), in particular, dedicated themselves to collecting, cataloging, and preserving actual artifacts: Yanagi was first the driving force behind the museum of Korean art that opened in Seoul in 1924, and later championed indigenous folkcrafts (*mingei*); Shibusawa played a central role in founding, running, and bankrolling the Attic Museum, with its enormous collection of folk implements (*mingu*). Through these objects the ethnographers hoped to preserve access to an alternate, premodern world by making possible a concrete encounter with a part of it. The objects could provide an authentic experience antecedent to the written representations that had come to serve as poor substitutes for such in the modern world. The source of these objects was, of course, the rural villages of Japan, a space the ethnographers looked to for "that sense of a totality that is anterior to practicing subjects."[65]

Like these men, Kobayashi collected literary "artifacts," which he anachronistically inscribed with qualities diametrically opposed to the new mass-produced commodities. Commodities were abundant, for convenient use and disposal, composed of interchangeable parts and hence prone to infinite rearrangement; artifacts, on the other hand, were increasingly rare and therefore precious, suitable for preservation and appreciation; they were seamlessly integrated wholes and somehow sacred. Kobayashi's penchant for turning literary texts and even authors into "artifacts" was paralleled and informed by an enduring interest in ancient ceramics and antiques, an interest that can be traced back to his childhood friendship with collector and legendary appraiser Aoyama Jirō.[66] The concrete, enduring beauty of these things, a beauty he found impervious to linguistic explanation, became a model for Kobayashi's appreciation first of literary texts (as suggested by the passage on Dostoevsky quoted above) and later of the world at large (as evidenced in his essays on the war).[67] This feature of Kobayashi's method grew so prominent, in fact, that his contemporary Sakaguchi Ango argued quite convincingly in 1947 that Kobayashi's essays exhibit the sensitivities not of a literary figure but rather those of an "appraiser of antiques" (*kottō no kanteinin*).[68]

Kobayashi's resurrection of the "lost home" through the deployment of a recovered memory was rooted in his generation's sense that a radically altered materiality had invaded the landscape in the years after the earthquake of 1923. In erasing history from the cityscape, this catastrophe inaugurated an influx of new technologies and lifestyles, both of which contributed to the flood of commodities on the market. Even a short ten years after the earthquake, so much had changed that Kobayashi's childhood memories struck him as "fictitious," and in place of experiences of solid objects and incidents, he recalls only an "endless clutter of things and events that have changed too quickly." He found the same to be true in the world of literature, the traditional refuge for those with a literary bent. The publishing boom of the early years of the Shōwa period had so diminished the once elite and exquisite experience of literature that it no longer served to soothe the soul.

Without recourse to literature as it existed at the time, Kobayashi was forced to undertake a more radical restructuring of the world. At the core of this project was a renegotiation of humankind's relationship to materiality, an arbitration that required first and foremost rendering "things" inert, immutable, and ultimately immune to the machinations of the human mind. This vision was not limited to literature but was extended to all fields of culture, to politics, and to warfare; without restructuring the world, the experience of the aura of the aesthetic object was unrecoverable. The shift in materiality that shaped Kobayashi's career became apparent in the days after the earthquake, and the manner in which it affected him is the subject of Chapter 2.

TWO

Making Shiga Simple

The previous chapter introduced critic Karatani Kōjin's observation that modern subjectivity is "not purely a mental or psychological phenomenon," but is rather "rooted in materiality and comes into existence . . . as a system."[1] This system, a dialectically evolving relationship giving shape to both subjectivity and materiality, changed radically between the closing years of the Taishō period and the early years of the Shōwa era (1926–89). This chapter examines the subjectivity-materiality systems on both sides of this divide, marked by the earthquake that both spurred on the shift and called attention to it. The Taishō sensibilities are represented in the Shirakaba writers, particularly Shiga Naoya, whose literary alter egos exhibited the same confident, cosmopolitan perspective and aura of self-realization as the writer himself. While critic Hirotsu Kazuo (1891–1968), writing before the earthquake, could read this Shiga persona as a mask deployed to ease the anxieties of modernity, the system that fell into place after 1923 prompted a very different reading by Kobayashi Hideo. Though he understood the Taishō literary giant in much the same way as did Hirotsu, his inflection of Shiga's accomplishment bore the mark of the very different, post-earthquake Shōwa sensibility. In short, Kobayashi took the Shiga persona at face value. He saw in that confident, composed persona a timeless subjectivity in which mind and body, the abstract and the concrete, were in a balance that allowed for an intuitive apprehension of the world that was hardly possible any longer.

Why did Kobayashi apotheosize Shiga in this manner and to this extent? Simply put, Kobayashi himself experienced traces of that Taishō/Shirakaba sensibility as a young man, and its dissipation in the chaotic modernity of Shōwa prompted him to seek to revive it. In this quest he turned to novelist Shiga Naoya, the most representative member of the Taishō literati and a writer for whom he had shown an early interest and an enduring admiration. In emulation of Shiga, Kobayashi wrote his first works of fiction; to Shiga he fled for consolation during a personal crisis; with Shiga as a touchstone, he composed the criticism that ordered his literary world. In all things, Shiga embodied the spiritual "home," the self-realized subjectivity of the Taishō intellectual that had been lost in the crush of modernity. Through his reading of Shiga, Kobayashi attempted to reinstate a subjectivity able to forego the cerebral machinations of the modern world, able to resist the alluring labyrinth of political, ideological, and psychological interpretations. Through Shiga, Kobayashi hoped to resurrect a subjectivity sufficiently confident to trust its intuition and bold enough to surrender itself to an uncompromised encounter with the beautiful.

Ironically, this subjectivity, which Kobayashi posits as timeless and somehow natural, was a largely imagined entity, one fabricated in response to the very different subjectivity that had taken hold as modernity progressed. It was retrospectively constructed, one product of the widespread attempts by disillusioned Shōwa thinkers "to install in the present a moment of recall or recovered experience, a memory *of* rather than *from* a time before time," as Harootunian characterizes the gesture.[2] In that a new system of materiality and subjectivity was in place, Kobayashi could not recover that former sensibility; in fact, he could not even envision it save through the lens of that which had replaced it. The venue that was open to him was to fabricate an imagined approximation of it, and this task required from him an intervention. Kobayashi did precisely this, portraying Shiga's genius as resting in the writer's "unassailable simplicity" (*dō shiyō mo nai tanjunsa*). This characterization buttressed the corpus of Shiga's work against the analytical parsing and intrusive interpreting that had compromised an intuitive appreciation of his writing; in a sense it restored to Shiga's fiction the nature of impenetrable materiality. The Shiga persona, whether exhibited in the writer or in his protagonists, simply was what it appeared to be. This approach to Shiga was not the natural, ingenuous reading that Kobayashi suggested it was. Rather it was a cognitive method, and one that required considerable rhetorical finesse on Kobayashi's part. In other words, Shiga's "simplicity" was anything but. It had to be constructed.

This chapter in Kobayashi's intellectual development is rooted in the Taishō period, as it was in the short course of these fourteen years that Shiga Naoya and the Shirakaba sensibility reached full maturity. Comparing the critiques of Shiga offered by Hirotsu Kazuo and Kobayashi, coming as they did from two different "systems," we see both sides of Taishō culture revealed: its self-absorbed, political complacency and its spiritually attuned and exquisitely cultured subjectivity. An explanation of the roots of the Shōwa nostalgia for the latter of these two dimensions can then be teased out of a reading of two short stories by Kobayashi, the first composed in the years immediately preceding the 1923 earthquake, and the second written shortly after. In the earlier story, "Tako no jisatsu" (The Octopus's Suicide, 1922), Kobayashi demonstrates a subjectivity rather close to Shiga's. The latter story, "Hitotsu no nōzui" (One Brain, 1924), however, demonstrates the manner in which the world has changed and the degree to which the borders between materiality and subjectivity have been blurred. This blurring, in fact, is actually the theme of that second story, Kobayashi's first after the earthquake. The threat of materiality and the concomitant fracturing of subjectivity in this story explain why Kobayashi was later to seek so desperately the certainty and calm of Shiga's world. They also indicate why Kobayashi would abandon fiction in favor of criticism. With the self overwhelmed by the new materiality of the modern world, Kobayashi could no longer reproduce the sort of intuitive insights that had marked Shiga's sensibility. However, by buttressing the traces of that fading sensibility, he could begin to reconstitute something of that world. Criticism was the genre most conducive to this enterprise. It was only in this genre that he would be able to realize the dream of Taishō in the confusing modernity of the Shōwa world.

The Politics of the Literary Imagination in Taishō

Paradoxically, the Taishō period represents both a blossoming of internationally minded liberal culture and a moment when the seeds of later imperialism were planted. These two realms operated in isolation from each other, with only the most fleeting of points of conflict. While historical and cultural contingencies made this possible for a time, as the Shōwa era progressed, the two realms collided. Kobayashi Hideo forged and propagated his critical and aesthetic vision as these domains suffered increasing discord. His yearning for the disappearing Taishō sensibility, however, led him to continue to work for its revival, and it prompted in him the attitude toward Japan's imperialism that is explicated in Chapters 5 and 6. His refusal to engage the political realities of Japan's war on the continent and in the Pacific, choosing instead to reify those pursuits as immutable realities, can be traced back to the formation of his sensibilities under the influence of the Taishō system of materiality-subjectivity. For this reason, the dual, conflicting dimensions of Taishō culture are important for an understanding of his work.

Indeed, at one level, the Taishō period represents a golden moment, a time when politically, economically, and socially the frantic labors of the Meiji period came to fruition.[3] That Japan had indeed fulfilled the Meiji dream of successful modernization had been proven by its successes in first the Sino-Japanese War (1894–95) and then the Russo-Japanese War (1904–05); in the Taishō period Japan took the next, more civilized, step toward membership in the world community by joining the League of Nations (1920). The frenzied industrialization, too, now paid off, and Japan was able to take full advantage of the economic opportunities offered by World War I, a war fought elsewhere.[4] The resulting material prosperity eased various domestic tensions, smoothing the way for an increasingly inclusive, democratic system of government.[5] Political parties wielded increasing influence, the prime ministership being awarded to a party leader almost as a matter of course after 1918. Though ultimately unfulfilled, there was optimism concerning the future of a broad-based democracy. This sense of inclusivity is also apparent in the emergence of women's voices such as those heard within the forum of Hiratsuka Raichō's (1886–1971) magazine *Seitō* (Bluestockings), first published in 1913. Though reactionary elements worked to suppress this discourse, the liberal tone of Taishō was such that an open, lively debate on the proper "new woman" (*atarashii onna*) continued for over a decade.[6]

Emerging at the same time as these developments were intellectual movements that availed themselves of Japan's increased commerce with the rest of the world, its perception of itself as now economically and culturally on a par with the West, and the freedom of expression that the liberal atmosphere promoted. Representative is the work of Yoshino Sakuzō (1878–1933), professor of political history at Tokyo Imperial University, and philosopher Nishida Kitarō (1870–1945), an enormously influential teacher and writer based at Kyoto Imperial University. Yoshino re-examined the concept of Western democracy in light of Japan's emperor system and its other political traditions; Nishida adopted the Western discourse of philosophy, but articulated his ideas with sensitivity to the possible contributions of the Buddhist tradition. In their incorporation of indigenous institutions and traditions into their confident contributions to once-foreign academic discourses, these intellectuals were typically Taishō.

However, as mentioned above, the Taishō period had a second face as well. Harootunian, for example, locates in those years a shift, ultimately calamitous, in the relationship of the individual to the state. The operative terms in the Meiji era had been the advancement of "civilization" (*bunmei*) through "education" (*shūgyō*), while in Taishō the concern was with "culture" (*bunka*) as a product of "cultivation" (*kyōyō*). Harootunian writes:

> The former meant a commitment to discipline, practical education and self-sacrificing service; the latter . . . stressed personal self-cultivation and refinement. The idea of *shūgyō* enjoined men to act publicly and to serve goals larger than themselves; *kyōyō* required men to operate in the private sphere and to serve only themselves; the former subordinated private choice to public expectation, the latter subordinated public to private considerations.[7]

While this shift led to the "triumph of that conception of private interest and atomized individuality which is at the heart of the liberal political and social creed,"[8] it did so at the expense of a politically and ideologically engaged subjectivity. Ultimately, Harootunian asserts, the privileged discourse of culture led "not simply to indifference, but to the deployment of culture as a surrogate for politics."[9] In short, the implication is that while the individual once conflated personal aspirations with those of the nation, in Taishō he or she began to conceive of them as entirely unrelated concerns, thereby inculcating a politically naive subjectivity.

Karatani Kōjin paints a similarly cynical portrait of Taishō. The period, Karatani writes, is marked by a "consciousness of autonomy, as tension between Japan and the West began to ease following the Russo-Japanese War, and Japan proclaimed its separation from Asia."[10] This easing of the East-West tension that since Meiji had shaped most discourses engendered what Karatani sees as the defining characteristic of the period:

> a self-complacency that can introduce anything from the outside without actually maintaining a conception of the exterior; or conversely, a delusionary, insular mentality that thinks of itself as worldwide, even though it is entirely

local; or further, the self-deception of being unaware of "invasion," even while Japan is in fact advancing mercilessly throughout the world.[11]

Like Harootunian, Karatani sees the age as one in which eyes were naively turned inward.

Both critics imply it was this introverted mentality of Taishō that made the beginnings of the imperial state possible. The argument paints the Japanese intelligentsia as too concerned with personal cultivation or too insular in their thinking to fully realize that certain contemporary events augured the repression that was soon to come. To be sure, in retrospect at least, it seems obvious that Taishō intellectuals would have been better served by adopting a more strident response to the acts and edicts promulgated by the Meiji government in its final years. Particularly ominous was the issuance of the Imperial Rescript of 1908 (Boshin shōsho), which, through the various government crusades inspired by it, initiated a campaign of national mobilization intended to stem the rising tide of "selfish" pursuits and to reestablish citizens' affinity with national interests.[12] Other disturbing developments were more readily apparent. While the establishment of a protectorate over Korea in 1905 may have first appeared as an act of benevolent guardianship, the outright annexation of the territory in 1910 sent a clear message of imperialist intent. That Japan intended to further pursue this track was made clear in the Twenty-One Demands of 1915 and the Siberian Intervention (1918–22), both of which revealed Japanese designs on China as well.

Furthermore, the draconian repression of free speech and the shrewd system of censorship that would fully emerge some two decades later were also presaged at this time by the High Treason Case (Taigyaku jiken). An ill-conceived and easily foiled attempt on the emperor's life prompted first a massive round-up of left-wing thinkers and then a secret trial in 1911. Though only four of the accused could be convincingly tied to the plot, this trial resulted in, on the grounds of lèse majesté, 24 death sentences (half of which were promptly commuted to life imprisonment). In the wake of the incident, some 90 volumes of "suspect" writing were banned, and the Minister of Education established a committee to reform literature, a perceived source of the subversive thought at the root of the plot. As inauspicious as these developments were, none provoked a sustained objection from writers.[13] These facts prompt Harootunian, Karatani, and others to characterize Taishō-era thinkers and writers as politically naive and self-complacent.

It is exceedingly difficult to reconcile these two faces of Taishō, one progressive and cosmopolitan and the other politically apathetic and insular. Viewing the age as liberal, and speaking of a "Taishō democracy," has prompted a reductionist reading of the militarism and imperialism of Shōwa as a mere "aberration" in an otherwise smooth progression to a liberal, democratic state. On the other hand, condemning the period as overly credulous and politically complacent belittles what were genuine victories for a progressive agenda. The most productive approach, then, is to acknowledge the influence of both dimensions by conceiving of the individual's relationship to the state from a different perspective. If, as Harootunian would have it, the Meiji period is viewed in terms of the pursuit of civilization through education (though perhaps "training" is a better translation of *shūgyō*) wherein individual interests were conflated with those of the nation-state, then the Taishō period's concern with culture through cultivation (*kyōyō*) in a realm largely indifferent to political ideologies is not necessarily a case of the ostrich sticking its head in the sand. It may very well be taken as the beginnings of a subjectivity capable of resistance precisely *because* it was indifferent to the national agenda. As Harootunian himself writes, the assertion of private interests (anathema to the Meiji state) lies at "the heart of the liberal political and social creed."

This being said, it should be noted that, with a few significant exceptions, writers during these years did not see their work in explicitly oppositional political terms.[14] Indeed, as demonstrated by Jay Rubin in his analysis of speeches, stories, and plays inspired by the High Treason Case, even those writers who had privileged information about the injustices being committed viewed the role of the writer within a paradigm that precluded the distinctly adversarial role of the social activist. To them, fiction (including autobiographical fiction) was a realm for exploring the ideas and ideals of each individual, independent of developments in the public realm.

Now, while writers may not have consciously imagined themselves as oppositional voices, their stances often had political implications. Speaking of the late-Meiji naturalists, but expressing an observation that applies equally to all creative writers under a repressive state, Rubin claims: "Instead of accepting the values of their elders, they were looking inside themselves. These writers . . . were the silently read conspirators of the young. They were subversive agents threatening communal solidarity not with obscenity but with something far more insidious: privacy."[15] Though Rubin does not offer an extended, theoretical conclusion based on his research, the implications are clear and convincing: the literary imagination is innately liberal; it is subversive of organizing, controlling, and totalizing mechanisms such as those instituted by the Meiji state.

While Kobayashi's career suggests that the literary imagination can at times inspire support for imperialism and totalitarianism (again, see Chapters 5 and 6), literature's threat to national solidarity in these years was very real. However the writers may have conceived of their position vis-à-vis the state, quite clearly the state considered many of them to be threats to public morals and the national agenda, as the expanded system of censorship attests. One might also point to the pending rise of proletarian literature and Marxist criticism in the early Shōwa period, both movements that posited the writer as critic of the state, enabled by the Taishō cultivation of a sense of the autonomous individual. The point is that the script for Japan's literary and cultural evolution during the 1930s was *not* written during the Taishō period. Rather, the particular configuration of liberal forces reveling in their relative autonomy from state mechanisms of control set a model of literary sensibilities that Kobayashi Hideo, for one, used as a touchstone throughout his career. These literary sensibilities and their relationship to the state are best traced through the work of the Shirakaba group.

The Shirakaba Writers

The literary side of the Taishō era is virtually synonymous with the writers of the Shirakaba group: Mushanokōji Saneatsu (1885–1976), Shiga Naoya, Satomi Ton (1888–1983), Yanagi Muneyoshi (also known as Sōetsu, 1889–1961), Arishima Takeo (1878–1923), and Nagayo Yoshirō (1888–1961).[16] These men were all born to wealthy families within ten years of one another, and they were all graduates of the exclusive Gakushūin, or "Peer's School." The education they received there included a healthy dose of foreign languages and literatures, and the elite student body inculcated a consciousness of themselves as possessors of impeccably cultured tastes and sensitivities. In short, at the level of the individual, they embodied the ethos of the Taishō era: financially prosperous, socially secure, and both assured and cosmopolitan in their worldviews. Their literary subjectivity, especially as expressed in the works of Shiga Naoya, exercised a powerful influence on a broad range of writers, Kobayashi Hideo included.

Brimming with confidence, the Shirakaba authors during the early Taishō era exulted in their polished, cultured selves. Mushanokōji Saneatsu summarized their shared aspiration in the phrase "exercise the abilities of the self" (*jiko o ikasu*). This objective was based on the premise that lying deep within an individual, below the level of conscious thought and intellectual machination, rests an innate ability to instinctively appreciate and create beauty. Mushanokōji elaborated on this idea in the group magazine, *Shirakaba*, in 1911:

> I believe that seeing the beauty or unsightliness of an object, rejoicing in it or lamenting over it, is not something done through my own efforts. I believe it is the way I am made that causes me to be thus affected. And so I think that, in my case, reacting in a particular way is the result of having been made such that I respond to a particular object in that manner. To honestly express what I feel when I am thus affected is, essentially, to hint at the spirit [*ishi*] of that particular object.[17]

This statement is significant in two respects. First, it reflects the concept of the atomized individual that emerged in the Taishō period. The "I" is an unexamined, autonomous being, existing in a realm untouched by external factors. Second, in Mushanokōji's statement, materiality is represented as "objects" beyond intellectual analysis and understanding; they are entirely a matter of a physiologically triggered, intuitive *appreciation*. Approached in this manner, the materiality of these objects is not dissected and therefore not compromised. Materiality remains "hard and fast," ultimately incomprehensible to the intellect but susceptible to intuitive apprehensions of its aura or "spirit." The dual poles of subjectivity and materiality, then, are mutually dependent, existing as a "system," as Karatani would call it. It was this system that was to be irrevocably altered by the invasion of the new materiality in the wake of the 1923 earthquake.

The literature of the Shirakaba group can be read in much the same manner as the Taishō period as a whole. On the one side, the confidence and sincerity exuding from their work struck many as a welcome change from the sometimes suffocating narrowness and pessimism of naturalism's "I-novels" (*watakushi shōsetsu*). For example, Akutagawa Ryūnosuke (1892–1929), a writer whose temperament could not have been further from that of the Shirakaba writers, wrote: "Most of us were happy that Mushanokōji had thrown open wide the skylight of literary society and let in some fresh air."[18] This "fresh air" seems to have been one of the few things to give the tortured Akutagawa solace. In his autobiographical "Haguruma" (Spinning

Gears, 1927), the story of his cynicism and doubts slowly driving him insane, Akutagawa writes of his reaction to Shiga's *An'ya kōro* (A Dark Night's Passing, 1921–37): "I sprawled on the bed reading *A Dark Night's Passing*. Everything about the protagonist's spiritual struggle was painfully familiar to me. Compared with him, I felt like such an idiot that it brought tears to my eyes—which, in turn, lent me a degree of peace."[19] The "I" of Akutagawa's autobiographical story is enveloped in such a nightmarish battle for his own sanity that Donald Keene has gone so far as to say that after reading the story "we can only marvel that Akutagawa did not kill himself sooner."[20] The fact that even at this psychological extremity Akutagawa was moved by the "spiritual struggle" of Shiga's hero speaks volumes about the appeal of the Shirakaba subjectivity.

However, just as the progressive advances of the Taishō era are often dismissed in favor of a focus on the insular nature of the overriding *kyōyō* mentality, the subjectivity of Shirakaba members has time and again come under attack for being excessively self-absorbed and grossly naive. As critic Honda Shūgo asserts, this dimension of the group is evident in their various slogans:

> The people in the Shirakaba school shared, to some extent, a tacit self-affirmation [*jiko kōtei*] that deemed what they were unaware of, useless, and what they could not comprehend, meaningless. The phrase "hurrah for ignorance" [*muchi banzai*] was a divine revelation unique to Mushanokōji, but such heaven-sent self-affirmations that proudly displayed an "obliviousness to the world" [*seken shirazu*], a "happy-go-lucky" nature [*omedetaki hito*], or a "child-like temperament" [*kodomorashisa*] were not monopolized by him.[21]

While such subjectivities allowed for the aura of sincerity and authenticity that appealed to so many readers, it is not surprising that they also struck others as ludicrously simplistic. Poet and critic Ikuta Chōkō (1892–1930), for example, took them to task on this count, suggesting in a 1916 essay that they represented a retreat from the level attained by the Naturalists of the previous generation.[22] Others took the critique one step further to reverse the syllables of the group's name and refer to them as *bakarashi(i)*, "idiotic."[23]

Textual evidence supporting such accusations is readily available. Honda, for example, points out that Mushanokōji's play "Momoiro no heya" (The Peach-Colored Room, 1911) is representative of the general Shirakaba rejection of social concerns: the "peach-colored woman" dismisses the pleas of the repressed people outside her door on the grounds that each individual's greatest responsibility is to him or herself.[24] Shiga's "Horibata no sumai" (My House by the Moat, 1925) is another example: the protagonist agonizes over whether to intervene in the imminent drowning of a cat, trapped and doomed for having killed chickens. He eventually decides not to lift a finger, and justifies his decision by likening it to the merciless attitude adopted by God toward the suffering in the world.[25] Literary representations of such subjectivity would seem to underscore the criticism of the group as hopelessly disengaged from the pressing social issues right outside the doors of their "peach-colored" rooms.

Yet, as argued above, such subjectivities are not necessarily antithetical to a liberal, progressive society. Rather, in their stubborn insistence on the sanctity of the individual and their privileging of the inner life, these writers fuel the idealism necessary for any progresssive social agenda. In fact, some of the Shirakaba writers themselves experimented with a social activism based on their ideals. Though ultimately a failure, in 1918 Mushanokōji instituted his "New Villages" (*atarashiki mura*) movement, a series of agriculture communes dedicated to realizing the humanitarianism of Tolstoy, and in 1922 Arishima Takeo turned over his family land in Hokkaidō to the tenant farmers who worked it.[26] Though perhaps based more on utopian visions than on a political agenda, the fact remains that the subjectivities nurtured by these Shirakaba writers included concerns that spilled over into the social realm.

Perhaps more important than these isolated acts, however, is the example set by these men in their literary works.[27] Their ability to pursue their personal literary agendas regardless of increasingly disruptive state intrusions and their single-hearted concern with being true to themselves at all costs served as a model of what *could* be possible for all writers. As such their example inspired the more socially engaged writing of the early Shōwa period: proletarian literature and Marxist criticism. The attraction exercised by the Shirakaba worldview on succeeding generations of writers is attested to by the enduring respect shown Shiga Naoya, perhaps the most well-known of the group. Even such socially engaged intellectuals as radical proletarian writer Kobayashi Takiji (1903–33) and one-time Communist Party member Shimaki Kensaku (1903–45) held Shiga in awe. Kobayashi Takiji, who died at the hands of the police in 1933, praised Shiga for his prose; Shimaki was so taken with Shiga's *An'ya kōro* that he took part of his pen name from its protagonist, Tokitō Kensaku.[28] Something in the Shirakaba subjectivity was deemed inspiring by writers with a clear social and political agenda; something in the literary imagination, even taken to its apolitical extreme, was empowering to thinkers more explicitly engaged with political ideologies from a point of resistance.

Like so many others raised in the ethos of Taishō and coming of age as readers of the Shirakaba school, Kobayashi Hideo was enamored of this subjectivity. He found an ideal artistic subjectivity particularly in the figure of Shiga Naoya, a man Kobayashi saw as perfectly synthesizing the dualities that torment all moderns. Kobayashi had inherited certain traits of this subjectivity himself, as his earliest work of fiction attests. The new materiality of post-earthquake Japan, however, had rendered that subjectivity increasingly distant, and it was only through the genre of a much altered criticism that he would later be able to revive it. Nevertheless, Kobayashi inherited the Shirakaba group's unshakable faith in the intuitive insights of the self, and this subjectivity is at the root of his most memorable criticism. Moreover, his stubborn refusal to respond to the vicissitudes of ideology and politics inculcated by this literary stance allowed Kobayashi to remain true to his personal literary vision during the tumultuous war years, a time when so many others compromised their beliefs.

But there is another side to the workings of this literary subjectivity. Or, stated more precisely, when resurrected within a different system of subjectivity-materiality, this literary stance inculcates previously absent inclinations. The exercise of the Shirakaba-esque intuitive appreciation is predicated upon a sharp distinction and significant distance between subject and object. As the invasion of the new, infinitely interpretable materiality progressed, this distance was closed, and the aura of the work of art was diminished. In order to buttress that fading aura and preserve the exquisitely aesthetic dimension of an experience of art or literature, Kobayashi was forced to rhetorically reconstruct an intellectually impenetrable materiality that was hermeneutically resistant and economically remote to the same degree as literature in pre-earthquake Japan. This effort required mounting an extreme resistance to the interpretive trends of the time and a reification of materiality so absolute that, in exchange for the recovery of an ability to intuitively appreciate beauty, the ability to critically and analytically engage the world was suppressed. Furthermore, the revival of the Taishō sensibility in the very different atmosphere of Shōwa ultimately resulted in a glorification of that very political indifference in the name of the aesthetic experience.

Hence, while the infinitely literary nature of Kobayashi's vision kept him aloof from the jingoistic propaganda of the war years, it also prompted him to affirm the realities of war as well as to celebrate them as a circumstance beyond interpretation, and hence conducive to the mode of intuitive appreciation upon which the fully aesthetic experience rested.

The precise nature of the Shirakaba subjectivity that Kobayashi retrospectively constructed is evident in his essays on Shiga Naoya. Not only does Kobayashi's reading of this Shirakaba giant reveal the contours of the literary vision Kobayashi himself embraced, but in these essays can be found the very techniques whereby Kobayashi resuscitated a world wherein that literary vision would still be viable. The subject is best treated by comparing Kobayashi's interpretation of Shiga with that of critic Hirotsu Kazuo, from whom Kobayashi takes his cue.

Reading Shiga Before and After the Earthquake

As Usui Yoshimi notes, Hirotsu Kazuo's "Shiga Naoya ron" (A Study of Shiga Naoya) defined the contours of virtually all subsequent readings of this author, and at the early date of 1919.[29] It is a surprisingly prescient essay, seeming to predict the entire trajectory of Shiga's career. In its balanced perspective and guarded praise for this author, it reflects the stable confidence of the Taishō era. This piece by Hirotsu informs every corner of Kobayashi's reading of Shiga, and it is in Kobayashi's transformation of the nuances that his particular dilemma and his proposed solution are apparent.

One of Hirotsu's central points is that Shiga's artistry is rooted in his artistic manipulation of the specific and concrete. At a time when the literary community was divided into the naturalists and those pursuing more imaginative themes, Hirotsu saw in Shiga a successful blending of the two extremes.[30] Although "Shiga is a precious artist, unsurpassed in his creativity," Hirotsu asserts, it is impossible to place him entirely in either the "artistic" (*geijutsu-ha*) or "real life" (*jinsei-ha*) camps.[31] This balanced perspective is a product of Shiga's ability to artfully craft his stories without recourse to excessive abstraction. Shiga draws on things he has personally seen, heard, touched, and felt, Hirotsu writes, and "one gets the impression that he does all he can to avoid rendering a hasty interpretation of it. The concrete over the abstract, the particular rather than the general—

Shiga's bright, piercing vision always examines the world from this perspective. In this sense he is a thoroughgoing realist."[32]

Because of his unflagging attention to concrete detail and his aversion to abstract expression, Shiga's philosophy and view of life are never explicitly revealed in his works. Hirotsu characterizes this element of the writer's craft with images reminiscent of Susan Sontag's call for artists to fashion "works of art whose surface is so unified and clean, whose momentum is so rapid, whose address is so direct that the work can be . . . just what it is."[33] Hirotsu appreciates Shiga's works in this manner, though he deviates from Sontag's unequivocal approval of such resistance to interpretive endeavors. Shiga's works, Hirotsu writes, have a surface "far too smooth" (*amari ni mo nameraka sugite*) for critics to easily interpret, but regardless of that fact, beneath that slick surface, somewhere in the depths, rest hidden clues to the author's philosophy of life. Hirotsu warns us that, without constant vigilance, those indicators will pass unnoticed.[34]

Hirotsu himself remains vigilant, and he succeeds in parsing the psychology behind Shiga's works. While the harmonious, balanced self, grounded in the immediacy of concrete realities, produces the "smooth" surface of Shiga's works, Hirotsu points out that underneath lies "an acute, complex, and pathological sensitivity born from modern civilization."[35] It is in order to soothe that "pathological sensitivity" that Shiga exercises his artistry on the world, painstakingly eliminating through his fiction any "discord, contrivance, injustice, and unsightliness." In his unwillingness to compromise with any such unpleasantness, Hirotsu claims, Shiga is a "horrifyingly selfish individual."[36]

In short, Hirotsu sees in Shiga both sides of the subjectivity that distinguishes the Taishō era. He expresses great respect for Shiga's "sharp mind, pure heart, and powerful personality," but he laments the fact that the writer has become increasingly introverted in his attempts to mollify that pathological sensitivity and defuse its explosive nature. "The time must come," Hirotsu declares, "when Shiga will open his eyes once more to what lies outside the harmonious world he has constructed in his own life."[37]

Hirotsu's reading, then, acknowledges and revels in the artistry of Shiga, but without surrendering his critical perspective. He plunges beneath the smooth surface of Shiga's work to reveal it as a salve fashioned by the irritated, confused soul of a modern man, and he expresses hope that Shiga will turn his attentions to the outside world once again. While Hirotsu read Shiga from within the comforting confines of the Taishō period, Kobayashi looked to him from a very different moment in the Shōwa era. In the ten-year interim between Hirotsu's essay and the first from Kobayashi, the invasion of the new materiality, the commodification of literature, and the new critical approaches spurred on by these developments had diluted the aesthetic experience. Because of his very different present, Kobayashi's reading of Shiga focused on traces of the worldview in which that pure, intuitive aesthetic experience was still possible. Furthermore, through his reconfiguration of Hirotsu's reading of Shiga, Kobayashi resurrects it. In contrast to Hirotsu's critical analysis, Kobayashi posits Shiga entirely as an object of intuitive appreciation, a distant literary artifact immune to explicitly intellectual interpretation and therefore amenable to an aesthetic experience the likes of which was increasingly rare in the critical, cerebral world of post-earthquake Shōwa.

Kobayashi's perception of this writer is shaped by excesses he perceived in both the literary trend that preceded Shiga (the Naturalist writers of the late Meiji period) and those that followed him (the Marxist critics and proletarian writers of early Shōwa). This context for his reading can be found in Kobayashi's "Watakushi shōsetsu ron" (A Theory of the I-Novel, 1935).[38] This essay ranks among the most well known of his works, as famous for its informed, confident, and original interpretation of foreign literary traditions (particularly French) as it is for its convincing reading of the domestic literary community in the late Meiji period.[39]

Concerning the Japanese Naturalist writers who had dominated the *bundan,* Kobayashi's complaint was that they had neglected to address the broader philosophical and social issues that framed the works of their European inspirations:

> Writers in our country certainly did absorb a series of decontextualized philosophies, at least to the extent that these appeared in the techniques of Western authors. These philosophies, however, did nothing but feed their dreams. Such foreign thought was incorporated by them only at the level of technique, and it was at this level alone that such thought lived on. What was adopted was not so much philosophies as it was mere impressions.[40]

More concretely, Kobayashi criticizes famed Naturalist Tayama Katai (1872–1930) for forgoing the tortuous process whereby his idol Maupassant forged his literary vision and instead simply adopting the end product, the technique (*gihō*) fashioned to accommodate that vision. This technique was one whereby the writer turned his or her eyes from the stars (abstractions and ideals) to the ground beneath their feet (sordid realities).[41] In short, Katai (and the Naturalists who followed) developed a "tunnel vision" focused on the realities of everyday life without engaging the larger intellectual context (the philosophy of positivism) that had prompted that approach. For this reason Japan's Naturalist writers, Kobayashi argues, had been unable to forge the type of "socialized self" (*shakai-ka shita watashi*) that made European writing so vibrant.[42]

In contrast to the Naturalists' suffocating concern for the minutiae of everyday life, the Marxist critics and proletarian writers who succeeded Shiga in the years after the earthquake exhibited, in Kobayashi's eyes, an excessive interest in the opposite pole: theory and philosophical abstractions. Kobayashi's antagonistic relationship with these literary trends is the primary focus of a later chapter; suffice it to say at this point that in "Watakushi shōsetsu ron" Kobayashi does express an appreciation for Marxism-inspired literature's concern for both the theretofore absent "philosophy" and a society larger than the *bundan*. To balance this praise, however, he chastises theory-based literature for ignoring concrete realities:

> Never before had writers relied so heavily on thought, never before had they struggled to compose based on a theory. Furthermore, this was also a time of unprecedented authorial disregard for their own corporeality [*nikutai*]. It was not that authors had forgotten to internalize or embody their philosophies; it was that they were intoxicated by philosophies too cold-blooded to permit either internatlization or embodiment. The significance of these literary movements lies entirely in their ability to intoxicate..[43]

Marxism-influenced literary trends had, in effect, overcorrected for the shortcomings of the Naturalists. The scales had been tipped too far in the direction of "cold-blooded" conceptual understandings and abstractions.

Kobayashi Hideo appreciated Shiga Naoya for his ability to avoid both excesses, synthesizing an abstract understanding of art with an attention to the concrete and personal. Kobayashi expresses this in "Watakushi shōsetsu ron" by insisting that since the advent of the I-novel, "no writer has succeeded as well as Shiga has in boldly, even violently, wresting from his own life a work of art; no one has adhered so scrupulously as he to the approach of the personal novel [*shishōsetsu*], in which the logic of everyday life becomes the logic of literary creation."[44] In other words, abstract aesthetics and the everyday realities were seamlessly integrated in Shiga, whose art and life, worldview and plebeian tasks, intellect and emotions are in perfect accord.

Kobayashi's appreciation of this writer had begun long before this 1935 essay, and it continued throughout his long career. Early evidence of this admiration includes a now-lost critical essay titled "Shiga Naoya no dokusōsei" (The Originality of Shiga Naoya), which Kobayashi probably wrote in 1926 and sent to Mushanokōji Saneatsu sometime before January 1927. Mushanokōji praised it and promised to publish it if Kobayashi was unable to find a more lucrative venue. The essay was never published, but indications are that it served as the cornerstone of a later essay, "Shiga Naoya" (1929).[45] This was followed by references to Shiga in many critical essays and, in 1938, a second essay dedicated entirely to this writer: "A Study of Shiga Naoya" (Shiga Naoya ron).[46] As the brief comments on Shiga in "Watakushi shōsetsu ron" suggest, Kobayashi's reverence for Shiga is rooted in the manner in which the writer could avoid intoxication with abstractions and instead focus on concrete specifics. This point was first made by Hirotsu, and Kobayashi returns to it in a variety of guises in his longer essays on Shiga: "Shiga is aware of no gap between thought and action. . . . Truly, for Shiga, to think is to act, and to act is to think."[47]

Kobayashi finds Shiga's full integration of art into life reflected most clearly in the story "Wakai" (Reconciliation, 1917), certainly Kobayashi's favorite. "Wakai" is the story of a young writer's attempts to narrate and thereby heal (or perhaps heal and thereafter narrate) his strained relationship with his father. He is plagued throughout by a stubborn refusal to compromise either his artistic policies or his true feelings. Kobayashi quotes a passage wherein the narrator, a Shiga alter ego named Junkichi, attempts to deploy fiction in the shaping of his real life: he plots a story with a horrifying escalation of father-son hostilities in the belief that writing it will somehow preclude an actual occurrence. His musings on this plot then take a sudden turn in which the imagined hostilities prompt the vision of a tearful reconciliation.

It is then time for the real world to intrude on Junkichi's imaginative manipulation of it: a further deterioration of his real-world relationship with his father raises the possibility that the imagined catastrophic scene might actually occur, and without the happy resolution. Shiga/Junkichi is therefore forced to abandon the story, at least until real-world events had progressed further.[48] All of this is included within the pages of "Wakai," which is ultimately Shiga writing about himself being unable to write the story.[49] Kobayashi, for his part, sees in this story evidence of Shiga's creative process being fully intertwined with his real life (*jisseikatsu*); for Shiga, writing is an act as natural as moving one's arms and legs.[50] This sincere engagement with an existence in which life and art are inseparable is what Kobayashi admires in Shiga.

Kobayashi sees this incorporation of the abstract into the concrete at the level of style as well. While the confusion of the modern world drives authors into emotional and conceptual flights of fancy with little or no connection to the concrete world, Shiga avoids this: "Shiga's delicate sensibilities (*shinkei*), too, struggle to break free from corporeality (*nikutai*), but his corporeality grasps it, refusing to let go. When his delicate sensibility does separate from the physical, his intellect will not supply it with abstract images and it painfully touches down again in real life, where Shiga then seeks the images he needs."[51] Kobayashi illustrates this point with an example from "Ko o nusumu hanashi" (The Kidnapping, 1914). Here a psychologically unbalanced protagonist first speculates on the future education of a charming child he hopes to kidnap, only later to find these abstract musings brought up short by a very different corporeal reality: a "small girl with her smelly hair . . . snoring lightly in her sleep."[52]

Though Kobayashi offers no further examples, emotional flights of fancy are reigned in by corporeality in many of Shiga's works. The story "Wakai" provides a clear example. At the moment of the sudden dissipation of the enmity between father and son, while all are weeping for joy, the narrator's grateful mother bows vigorously to him. When he returns the bow, "delicate sensibilities" are reigned in by the physical: "I had no choice but to bow over her head and, since she was just on her way up at that moment, my mouth hit against her hairdo."[53] The shock of Junkichi, emotionally overwhelmed by the sudden reconciliation, suddenly finding his mouth filled with his mother's oiled hair quickly brings a transcendent moment back to earth. One might also consider the close of *An'ya kōro*, in which Kensaku has his revelation on the mountaintop only to succumb immediately to a severe case of diarrhea.[54] Thought and action, art and everyday life, sensibilities and corporeality—like Hirotsu, Kobayashi reads in Shiga a balanced grounding of abstractions in a concrete reality.

While Kobayashi follows Hirotsu Kazuo's lead in identifying this distinguishing mark of Shiga's work, he proceeds to draw very different conclusions. While Hirotsu interprets the calm exterior and seamless surface of Shiga's works as a balm covering "an acute, complex, and pathological sensitivity born from modern civilization," Kobayashi insists it is evidence of Shiga's having transcended precisely that. In an obvious allusion to Hirotsu's essay, Kobayashi writes:

> People say that modern man's sensitivities are pathological and acute. While they may indeed be in an unhealthy state, they are most certainly not acute. The eyes and ears of the ancients were incomparably sharper than ours today. All that we have today are sensitivities fragmented and convoluted from having been subject to complex stimuli unimaginable to the ancients. . . . Perhaps what has crushed our system of sensitivities is not an unhealthy physiology but rather a surplus of abstract concepts. . . . In other words, our sensitivities have shifted from the physiological acuity of the ancients to a conceptual complexity.[55]

Shiga, Kobayashi suggests, has inherited that "physiological acuity" (*seiriteki eibin*) of the ancients. He is not tortured by a "surplus of abstract concepts" (an affliction Kobayashi himself confesses to in "Kokyō no ushinatta bungaku") but rather is capable of letting "his sensations decide his preferences, and these, in turn, unerringly set his conscience."[56]

This subjectivity arises in conjunction with a very specific sort of materiality. A "physiological acuity" reaches not toward a conceptual or abstract understanding, but rather an intuitive apperception. To represent this mode of existence Shiga always returns to corporeality, the concrete specifics of his world. Rather than seek to penetrate beneath the surface and risk losing oneself in the labyrinth of interpretations and permutations, Shiga employs the "mode of the ancients," remaining on the surface. "In short, just as the men of old equated one's personality with one's face and actions, so too does Shiga believe that the nature of the self is expressed in countenance and behavior," writes Kobayashi.[57] This reading is an unequivocal affirmation of the Shirakaba subjectivity, a subjectivity that places total trust in the intuitive apprehension of the concrete specific. While Hirotsu recognized it and couched his appreciation of it cautiously, the shifting world that Kobayashi was experiencing prompted him to laud it acritically as a true method of cognition that had been in place since time immemorial.

In keeping with this rewriting of Hirotsu's critique along unequivocally positive lines, Kobayashi replaces Hirotsu's characterization of Shiga as a "horrifyingly selfish individual" with a more affirmative euphemism: "ultra-egoist."[58] Not only is the negative connotation muted by the rephrasing, but what had begun as something of a prosaic rebuke is transformed into a philosophical concept by the use of the English word (rendered in *katakana* as *urutora egoisuto*). Taken as evidence of Shiga's uncompromising personal vision, this interpretation of Shiga's subjectivity also renders moot Hirotsu's critique of Shiga's increasingly introverted stance.

Kobayashi's reading of Shiga presents a puzzling question. If, as Kobayashi argues in "Watakushi shōsetsu ron," it is the "socialized self" that serves as the indispensable core of literary creation, in what manner is Shiga's subjectivity "socialized"? Kobayashi does not explicitly address the question, but the implication is that Shiga's stubborn insistence on the conflation of his personal life and his literary agenda constitutes a viable societal stance. This subjectivity is certainly not a "socialized self" in the sense that pressing issues of social justice and political ideology are explicitly addressed in his works. Still, Shiga's insistence on a life centered on "exercising the abilities of the self" (*jiko o ikasu*)—Mushanokōji's motto for the Shirakaba school—through the pursuit of literature does imply a certain relationship to society. In remaining willfully outside the organizing and totalizing machinations of the state, in stubbornly refusing to define itself in opposition to political ideologies, and in wholeheartedly dedicating itself to realizing aesthetic beliefs in the concrete specifics of everyday life, this subjectivity is in its own way "socialized." While Marxist critics and proletarian writers link the self to society through political ideology, Shiga (and Kobayashi himself) forge the link through aesthetic principles. In a Shōwa environment where the intimately human experience of fine art or literature *as fine art or literature* was slowly being eroded by commodification and a concomitant hyperactive intellect, this Shiga-esque subjectivity surely seemed not only viable but absolutely indispensable.

Kobayashi is writing for a Shōwa audience that is reading literature in a manner increasingly like Hirotsu Kazuo's, that is to say critically and with an eye to psychological motivations and abstract worldviews. This cerebral approach must be subverted, for not only is it antithetical to the lessons Kobayashi would have us learn from Shiga, it is also the very approach that impoverishes the aesthetic experience that Kobayashi hopes to revive. The era being what it is, however, Kobayashi has no choice but to accept the paradoxical task of employing critical interpretation to dismantle the analytical approach to Shiga and, by extension, all art and literature. This act alone will leave Shiga's stories intact, allowing the reader to bask in the aura of art, rather than parse the works in order to intellectually understand something as ethereal as Shiga's "acute, complex, and pathological sensitivity born from modern civilization."

Kobayashi accomplishes this by re-establishing the distance Benjamin identified as so crucial to the aesthetic experience. This move is most readily apparent in the temporal distance Kobayashi insists upon in considering Shiga. In spite of the fact that Shiga was less than twenty years his senior, and in spite of the fact that Shiga wrote "Wakai" only twelve years earlier, in his 1929 essay Kobayashi links Shiga's sensibilities to those of the "ancients" (*kodainin*), and refers to them as "classical" (*kotenteki*) and even as evincing a "primeval nature" (*genshisei*).[59] These characterizations stand in sharp contrast to Hirotsu's insistence that Shiga's pathological sensitivity is a product of the modern age, an insistence that draws his subject close and enables Hirotsu to work a critique.

In addition to this temporal distancing, Kobayashi also reconfigures the reader-text (or reader-author) relationship by effacing the interpretation-inducing literary text and replacing it with an object more easily perceived as immutable materiality: a painting. Writing again on "Wakai" in his 1938 essay on Shiga, Kobayashi finds there

> a certain unassailable . . . calm simplicity. The author does not need many words to express it and the reader who explores it is all but fully deprived of a critical language to describe it. . . . Looking at Shiga's work is like gazing at a splendid work of art; in a word, one's heart grows quiet, and none of the conventional approaches are applicable. Since such quietude is hard to bear, readers quite naturally start to speak of Shiga's works in the manner of a connoisseur of art. They take pleasure in making such ridiculous pronouncements as "Of his short stories, I like 'Kinosaki nite' [At Kinosaki] best," or "'Takibi' [The Bonfire] is superior" . . . [But] I believe that a wide assortment of fascinating issues rise to the surface when we place the unassailable simplicity of Shiga's works in the literary world of today with all its complexities and confusion.[60]

While the critical age and genre in which he works forces Kobayashi to justify his approach in terms of its implications for contemporary conceptions of literature, the movement in this passage is undeniably toward a reification of the literary text as impenetrable materiality, as concrete as a "splendid work of art" on the wall. The visual arts, too, are subject to interpretation, of course, but it is clear here that Kobayashi is positing them as a paradigm for pure aesthetic appreciation, the trigger for an almost religious epiphany inexpressible in words. Just as Shiga's artistry lies in his presentation of a concrete world uncompromised by intrusive interpretations, Kobayashi's rhetoric renders Shiga and his texts a solid materiality immune to "critical language" (*hihyōteki gengo*) and conventional approaches (*hō*). Hirotsu had identified the interpretive resistance of Shiga's work only to interpret *that*; Kobayashi reifies and apotheosizes that interpretive impenetrability, prompting readers once again to experience art at a level antecedent to analysis and intellect.

In passages like that quoted above we see the manner in which support of a thoroughly literary imagination—indeed one literary to the extent that it is all but exhaustively defined by its apoliticality—can brush up against the most political of ideologies: fascism. In undermining skeptical interpretive tendencies so that readers may once again indulge that most human experience of awe in the face of an aesthetic artifact, Kobayashi Hideo promotes the type of self-obliterating aesthetic moment associated with fascism. Alan Tansman has explored this literary fascism in the Japanese context, finding in various works of the 1930s and 1940s a penchant for moments of "repose" (*ansoku jōtai*) underpinned by acts of horrible violence:

> As a balm for the wounds of modernity, literary works evoked moments of repose in scenes where the agitated movement of modern, linear time temporarily ceased, and senses fractured by modern stimuli could rest in a moment of simultaneity. In such moments of repose, fragmented perception is rendered whole, as senses merge or are confounded in a glare that completely absorbs (or completely effaces) the perceiver of the scene. Such scenes, which present moments of perceptual blending or simultaneity such that linear time gives way to space, suggest doubts about the universality of Western notions of teleology. They are aesthetic moments of Japanese authenticity that unite in one moment the deepest past with the immediate present and the distant future.[61]

It is not difficult to imagine the manner in which the demands for selfless sacrifice in wartime propaganda exploited this aesthetic. As Tansman notes, the apotheosis of such totalizing moments in literary works "fueled a fascistic ideology in the real world—an ideology that promised a cure to modern alienation through submerging the self in the state and war. . . . [Such writing] occupied an aesthetic sphere uncomfortably close to the political world where self-immolation was a real possibility."[62]

A full exploration of this aesthetic's links to the military aggression and imperialist mission of Japan's 1930s and 1940s will be made in a later chapter. Here it will suffice to note the contours and nature of Kobayashi Hideo's invocation of this artistically triggered moment of quiet rapture, and the manner in which it prepares subjectivities for the more overt calls for apocalyptic self-effacement that would come in the propaganda of wartime Japan. Walter Benjamin is again useful for characterizing the way in which the mysterious realm of aesthetics can inform political machinations; he himself was, after all, one who keenly felt the pull of both, as Mark Lilla convincingly argues.[63] Faced with an increasingly commodified, mechanically reproducible world much like Kobayashi's, Benjamin noted how it sweeps away "outmoded concepts, such as creativity and genius, eternal value and mystery—concepts whose uncontrolled (and at present almost uncontrollable) application would lead to a processing of data in the Fascist sense."[64] It was precisely these "outmoded concepts" ("creativity and genius") that Kobayashi revives in his reading of Shiga as he portrays the unmatched brilliance of this writer who taps into the sensitivities of the ancients ("eternal value") to produce art that defies anything but an awed silence ("mystery"). Interestingly, Benjamin himself represents his idea of "the processing of data in the Fascist sense" with the example of one standing in awe before a masterpiece of painting: "A man who concentrates before a work of art is absorbed by it. He enters into this work of art the way legend tells of the Chinese painter when he viewed his finished painting."[65] This absorption is precisely the experience that Kobayashi would have us undergo with the works of Shiga Naoya before us, and he turns to the same metaphor to represent it. Overwhelmed, or "absorbed," by it as we are by a "splendid work of art" (*migoto na bijutsuhin*), our most basic tool of personal assertion, language, and the critical consciousness it produces are both swept away.

In his relentless quest to reinstate such aesthetic epiphanies, Kobayashi exhibited an increasing obsession with arts less susceptible to the intrusion of linguistic interpretation. His growing interest in antique artifacts was mentioned in the previous chapter. The visual arts he turns to here in shaping our perception of Shiga also grew in importance to Kobayashi: *Kindai kaiga* (Modern Painting), Kobayashi's award-winning study of such artists as Paul Cézanne, Pablo Picasso, Vincent van Gogh, Auguste Renoir, and Edgar Degas, was serialized between 1954 and 1958, and was, significantly, inspired by a trip, Kobayashi's first to the West, to see the actual paintings (as opposed to reproductions) with his own eyes.[66] Music was equally amenable to this mode of appreciation, and Kobayashi's work on the composer Mozart is one of his most well known.[67]

In this reading of Shiga Naoya, the one writer for whom Kobayashi expressed nothing but admiration, we see the resuscitation of the Taishō subjectivity in a very different Shōwa world. Whereas the Shirakaba group's confidently intuitive and infinitely literary self had been forged in dialectic with the rarefied arts and stable materiality of the Taishō era, the years following the earthquake had altered the mindscape of Shōwa intellectuals. With commodities, including literary texts, rampant in the marketplace, the arts and the world were drawn close for inspection and dissection. While this facilitated interpretation and intellectual understanding, it also compromised the integrity of the intuitive aesthetic encounter, and rendered literary texts hardly more than a subcategory of political discourse. The revival of the intimately human experience of aesthetic appreciation required not only a reorientation of subjectivity but also a reversal of humankind's increasingly intimate relationship with "things." Kobayashi found traces in Shiga of this now obsolete relationship, and deployed this writer in his attempt to resurrect it. He did so by positing a reader-text (or reader-author) relationship based on the textual vestiges of the Taishō worldview he excavated from Shiga's work.

Like so many aspects of the Taishō era, the subjectivity that Kobayashi resuscitated through his reading of Shiga Naoya was a double-edged sword. On the one side it represented a reaffirmation of a self beyond the clutches of the increasing politicization of daily life that had begun in the Taishō period and reached new heights in Shōwa. The subjectivity Kobayashi was resuscitating was somehow more human for its ability to be moved by beauty. This movement seemed to be in constant dialectic with the fascist aesthetic. As Tansman rightfully notes, in the writers in whom he locates a fascist tendency, an equally powerful voice of resistance was also present. These writers, he claims, "could not help but resist the fascist moments they evoked. They could do this—they could not *but* do this—precisely because their writing was literary. Literary writing has the power to resist the clichés of instrumental knowledge."[68] Such was also true of Kobayashi Hideo; as the discussions in Chapters 5 and 6 will reveal, he opposed the simplistic nationalism that ran rampant from the late 1930s (while simultaneously reveling in the opportunities it provided for aesthetic reverie).

Having stood on the perimeter of that Taishō ethos, Kobayashi inherited both sides of the Shirakaba subjectivity, both its celebration of the human capacity for an intuitive apprehension of beauty *and* its stubborn refusal to directly engage political realities. Before this subjectivity was fully internalized, however, the materiality that dialectically informed it was dramatically swept away in the fiery destruction of the Great Kantō Earthquake. His attempt to resurrect that fading ethos required summoning once again an exteriority or materiality that was resistant to intellectual parsing and cerebral analysis. His transcription of the complexities of Shiga Naoya and his literary world into the "unassailable simplicity" (*dō shiyō mo nai tanjunsa*) of a reverence-invoking painting is one example of how he accomplished this feat. Such transcription was made necessary by the greatly changed world of post-earthquake Tokyo.

The remaining two sections of this chapter explore the divide between those two worlds through an examination of two of Kobayashi's earliest works of fiction. In "Tako no jisatsu" (The Octopus's Suicide), Kobayashi reveals just how close he was to that integrated, innately artistic subjectivity of Shiga and the Shirakaba writers; "Hitotsu no nōzui" (One Brain), written after the earthquake, is a record of Kobayashi's encounter with the unsettling materiality of the new world, something he would have to reconstruct along different lines in order once again to approach the artistic epiphanies that had once been possible.

Approaching Shiga: "The Octopus's Suicide"

That the affluent, cosmopolitan, and cultured upbringing so typical of Taishō writers instilled in him a subjectivity close to that of the Shirakaba writers is evident in Kobayashi's earliest work, which bears a striking resemblance to that of Shiga Naoya. This piece of fiction, "Tako no jisatsu," was published in the coterie magazine *Kyōon* in November 1922, when Kobayashi was 20 years old. It was long referred to as the "phantom story" because, though its existence was never in doubt, no copy of it could be found, and for years Kobayashi scholars were limited to speculation as to its nature.[69] When a copy was later unearthed, over 50 years after its original publication, Kobayashi himself dismissed it as nothing but a study and thus not worthy of inclusion in his *Collected Works*.[70]

Traces of Shiga can be detected throughout "Tako no jisatsu." One clear indication that this writer figured prominently in Kobayashi's mind as he wrote the story is the name of the protagonist, Kenkichi. As Aeba Takao points out, this name is almost certainly an allusion to Shiga's hero in *An'ya kōro*, Tokitō Kensaku.[71] Also suggestive is the fact that Kobayashi is known to have sent a copy of the story to Shiga, receiving a letter of praise in return.[72] Again like Shiga, Kobayashi adopts a third-person narrative voice for an overwhelmingly autobiographical account. In this story, Kenkichi is living with his younger sister and his mother, who is suffering from tuberculosis. The location is Kamakura, where the family has moved in hopes that the fresh air of this seaside town will improve the mother's health. Flashbacks to the previous year relate the untimely death of Kenkichi's father. All of these elements of the narrative, including some of the characters, match precisely Kobayashi's own situation in 1921 and 1922.[73]

"Tako no jisatsu" progresses along a subdued plot line, and is without an overwhelmingly dramatic climax, both features of much of Shiga's work. The first half of the story focuses on Kenkichi's interaction with friends Yaeko and Shibutani and an evening walk along the beach; the second half situates Kenkichi with his mother and sister at home, where concern for the mother's illness dominates the conversation and life in general. On the morning after a late-night medical emergency in which his mother coughs up blood, Kenkichi reluctantly leaves her in the care of his younger sister as he travels to Tokyo for the service commemorating the one-year anniversary of his father's death. The story closes with Kenkichi finding some contentment in his weariness as the train approaches his destination.

Far more convincing evidence of Kobayashi's affinity with Shiga's sensibility, however, is the extent to which his protagonist, much like Shiga's, evaluates all elements in his world based on an initial intuitive reaction. With unshakable confidence, Kenkichi labels each and every thing encountered as, essentially, good or bad.[74] True to the general Shirakaba tendency to privilege such intuitive appreciation over intellectual analysis, in Shiga's diary entries and the stories fashioned around them, the expressions "pleasing" (*yukai*) or "displeasing" (*fuyukai*) appear with inordinate frequency.[75] Though the vocabulary used is slightly more varied, the same is true of Kobayashi's "Tako no jisatsu": the marks Kenkichi's *geta* leave on the sand "annoyed him" (*iya na kimochi ni shita*); the performers on the beach "filled him with hate" (*ken'o no nasake ga waita*); carefree customers in a bookstore "anger him to the point of tears" (*hara o tatete nakitaku naru*); his sister's naiveté "irritates" him (*ira ira shite*); the religious neighbors who preach to his weakened mother "infuriated" him (*hara o tateta*).[76] Like Shiga, Kobayashi was keenly attuned to his intuitive reactions, mostly negative, to people and things. The painstaking recording of them points to Kobayashi's Shirakaba-esque faith in the validity of such instinctual reactions.

"Tako no jisatsu" also reflects Kobayashi's acute consciousness of Shiga in the protagonist's struggle to maintain that balance between mind and body—or between nerves (*shinkei*) and corporeality (*nikutai*)—that the later Kobayashi would find so appealing in Shiga. Throughout "Wakai," for example, Shiga's alter ego (Junkichi) refuses to force out an apology at odds with his true thoughts and emotions, stubbornly waiting instead for the moment when a sincere gesture of appeasement can arise spontaneously and naturally from his mental state and the situation at hand. The eventual glorious reconciliation with his father represents precisely such a confluence of mental state and concrete circumstances, and the authenticity of the moment is what guarantees that the healing of the rift will be permanent.

Kobayashi's protagonist, Kenkichi, longs for a similar coincidence of thought and action. He is plagued by an overactive intellect, and this propensity contributes to his annoyance at virtually everything around him. This quirk of his personality is introduced very early in the story:

> He felt annoyed on remembering how he had been up late the night before, talking to a friend. The two of them had debated excitedly. "Just like two gramophones blaring," he thought.
>
> "A little beer is all it takes to get the records spinning. And not to be outdone, he spins his own. What a pair of idiots!"
>
> Suppressing the bitter grin spreading across his face, he consoles himself with the thought that at least he's no gramophone now. He then instantly corrects himself: the only reason is that the records aren't spinning at the moment. Kenkichi felt the anger welling up in him as he realized his same old habit was once again rearing its ugly head—in spite of the fact that he would always end up mentally piecing together some sort of half-baked conclusion, he would still first insist, for some odd reason, on skeptically picking everything apart and spinning it all round and round in his head before being satisfied.
>
> "Who the hell cares! I'm taking a swim!"
>
> With that he plunged into the cold waters.[77]

Unable to attain balance, Kenkichi lunges from one pole (the mind) to another (the body).

Kenkichi's hypertrophied mind also prevents him from an engagement with events in the material world. To keep his bedridden mother company, Kenkichi pulls a chair out onto the porch and sits reading *Anna Karenina*. His mother points to something out in the garden:

> "My, my, sparrows are such light little things, aren't they? Look, there's one perched on a pine needle!"
>
> "Huh?" said Kenkichi. By the time he had raised his eyes from the book, the sparrow was no longer there.[78]

What the life of the mind prevents is not merely the appreciation of little things: Kenkichi misses his dying father's final hours in order to sit for his entrance examinations for higher school. Kenkichi's head is full, and he struggles to empty it so that he can act. This condition is represented metaphorically by Kenkichi banging his palm against the side of his head in an attempt to clear the water from his ears after a swim. Yaeko, the young woman he is enamored with, says, "You should build a tiny little pump and suction it out."[79] No such thing, of course, can relieve Kenkichi.

Kenkichi's plight in "Tako no jisatsu" is juxtaposed with an alternative. His friend Shibutani, the polar opposite of Kenkichi, is unconcerned with the world of books and abstract thought, and instead revels in the physical: he is a strong swimmer and, fittingly, a student at a military academy. The following exchange between the two friends, however, makes it clear that Kenkichi finds existence entirely in the realm of the physical equally undesirable. When Kenkichi refuses to swim because he's sleepy after his late night debate with friend Osamu, Shibutani chides him:

> "Him, eh? Another guy who wants to carry around a copy of *The Origins of Love and Understanding* and be a slacker like you! Boy, there are just too many depressing guys at your school, Kenkichi," said Shibutani.
>
> "Who are you to talk? Are you trying to tell me that there are nothing but great guys at a school like yours, where you have to get whacked with a stick three thousand times just to graduate?"
>
> "Go to hell!" said Shibutani, and he shuffled down toward the water.[80]

As this exchange makes clear, as dissatisfied with his overactive mind as he is, Kenkichi is not willing to denounce it in favor of the unexamined physical life of one like Shibutani.

Just as many of Shiga's stories build toward a moment in which the protagonist is able to act authentically, so too does "Tako no jisatsu" climb toward an incident in which Kenkichi is able to act spontaneously and with perfect certainty. This occurs on the train ride to Tokyo to attend the service commemorating the one-year anniversary of his father's death. Kenkichi is restless, unable to concentrate on the book he is reading. He amuses himself by watching the comfortable and archetypal interaction between two fellow passengers, a mother and her adult son. When the son steps off the train for a moment at Yokohama, a stranger takes his seat, thereby preventing the pair from sitting together upon the son's return. Though the mother and son exchange glances and seem resigned to the new seating arrangement, Kenkichi is not:

> To Kenkichi the expression on the faces of these two people was unbearably sad.
>
> "Excuse me, sir, but would you be kind enough to trade seats with the person sitting next to you?"
>
> It had definitely been Kenkichi himself debating whether or not to say this. But what made him say it was something other than himself. This sort of experience was very familiar to Kenkichi. During his second or third year of middle school, when he would wonder whether or not to do something reckless and for which he would later be scolded, there would be something giving him a shove from behind, and before he knew it the act would be over and done with. At the exact same moment that Kenkichi had spoken, the son had stood up and said, "Would you mind?," thereby making the seating change seem as if it had been done at his request. Kenkichi realized that had this not been the case he would not have been able to hide his look of triumph over this somehow happy experience of having unexpectedly acted brashly.[81]

Though without the wider ramifications or narrative impact of Shiga's moments of authenticity, this moment represents a similar breakthrough for Kobayashi's protagonist.[82] For an instant he attains that state wherein thought and action arise simultaneously and are perfectly synthesized. And again like Shiga, after this moment of elevated existence, Kobayashi pulls the narrative back into the realm of the concrete: Kenkichi immediately feels awkward every time his eyes meet those of the other men.

Following this experience, "Tako no jisatsu" quickly comes to a close. Kenkichi recalls Yaeko's anecdote, from which the story takes its name. She had told him that she once saw an octopus commit suicide, eating its own legs to stave off starvation. Kenkichi remembers the optimistic interpretation she had appended to the story:

> "But, after a week or so goes by, maybe the octopus grows its legs back, one by one, and comes back to life."
>
> For an instant he saw Yaeko's beautiful eyes before him. The octopus that grew back its legs one at a time would soon commit suicide again. Disillusionment and strained smiles—it struck him that these were the links that held his life together.[83]

The octopus eating its own legs time and again is a metaphor for Kenkichi's mind feeding on itself in an endless cycle of self-analysis and self-doubt. Although there is no escaping this cycle, through this incident on the train Kenkichi has realized that there are fleeting moments of reprieve ("strained smiles").

In so many ways, then, "Tako no jisatsu" is the work of a quintessential Taishō literary youth. Sharing a personal background similar to that of the Shirakaba writers, and experiencing an emotional affinity with them, Kobayashi demonstrates in this story a strikingly similar obsession with the integration of mind and body that marked their subjectivity. The "system" of materiality and subjectivity that made such expression possible, however, was to collapse in the year that followed as Kobayashi's personal circumstances changed, and, more importantly, the Great Kantō Earthquake so radically altered the world around him.

The Invasion of Materiality: "One Brain"

If there is something that distinguishes the mood of Kobayashi's "Tako no jisatsu" from Shiga's stories, it is the author/protagonist's obsession with the authentic moment as an end in itself rather than as simply a catalyst for the changed circumstances it will bring. In Shiga's "Wakai," Junkichi's sincere reconciliation with his father not only brings a lasting harmony but also a mental state conducive to writing the story of the stormy relationship. Kobayashi's Kenkichi, on the other hand, though not without personal concerns, longs for such a breakthrough simply for the personal spiritual satisfaction that it will provide, and his circumstances are not substantially altered by that "happy experience" on the train. What had been a means to an end for Shiga has been transformed in Kobayashi's story into an end in itself. This fact suggests that the balanced synthesis of sensibilities and corporeality possible in Shiga's Taishō was slowly slipping from Kobayashi's grasp.

This increasing alienation from the Taishō sensibility can be attributed to the change in Kobayashi's personal circumstances and the disquieting emergence of the new system of materiality-subjectivity in the days following the Great Kantō Earthquake. While a number of critics have remarked on the extent to which this story is reminiscent of the literature of Shiga Naoya,[84] the similarities pale in comparison to those present in the earlier, pre-earthquake "Tako no jisatsu." "Hitotsu no nōzui" is in fact a radical departure from the style of Shiga; in tone and imagery it is much closer to the works of modernists like Yokomitsu Riichi or the young Kawabata Yasunari.

This story is a mixture of travelogue (*kikōbun*) and fiction that relates an irritable young man's winter trip to the Yugawara hot springs, about 60 miles from Tokyo, on the border between Kanagawa and Shizuoka prefectures. It describes the ferries he used, the landscape, and the people he encountered, but most of the prose is dedicated to conveying the anxiety the protagonist feels in a world that simply no longer makes sense. His confusion and irritation arise from his inability to maintain the sharp distinctions between subject and object, self and materiality, animate and inanimate. These categories having been corrupted, the sort of intuitive insight that Shiga had exercised (and that, in fact, to a lesser extent Kobayashi himself had exercised in the earlier story) is impossible, and the protagonist slips deeper and deeper into a surrealistic world.

Significantly, the specter of the earthquake looms over the story's setting.[85] While the destruction had been worse in Tokyo, of course, even outlying rural areas had been affected. In the protagonist's mind the changes in the landscape merge with the physical existence of the inhabitants:

> Making use of the waves, the pilot pushed the boat out to sea and hopped in. Soaked through with the seawater, the bottom half of his pant-leg had changed in color. From it cold drops of water dripped onto the dry white planks of the boat. When I glanced at his leg, I noticed on his shin a horrible purple scar that was a full foot long. It evoked feelings of pity and revulsion in me. . . . There had been a landslide during last September's earthquake, and it had left the red, raw surface of the mountain exposed. The yellow strata looked like clumps of fat. Woven into the mountain at one spot was a purple streak reminiscent of that scar on the boat pilot's leg.[86]

The same feature is evident in the "sooty" youth standing in the burnt-out scenery of Manazuru.[87] The earthquake has changed the world, scarring the landscape and, by association, everything in it.

The "I" of "Hitotsu no nōzui" is similarly swallowed by and at the mercy of his environment. He boards a ferry and stands on the deck waiting for it to depart: "When the rattling of the machinery below began, two or three rings of smoke shot out of the smokestacks and disappeared into the gray sky."[88] As the weather turns colder on deck, he retreats into the shared quarters below, a dark and grimy space lined with enamel sinks to accommodate those who succumb to seasickness. These sinks fill the cabin with a din as vibrations from the ferry's engines set them rattling. The occupants are equally distasteful, and yet the protagonist cannot distance himself from the scene. Like theirs, his existence is entirely shaped by the environment:

> Like ugly, odd knickknacks [*okimono*], these people all silently shook from the engine's vibrations. My own body too, of course, was forced to tremble to the same rhythm. I found this fact unbearable, but I was unable to discover some means by which I alone could be immune. I felt as if the pistons had been set up directly below where I sat. I clumsily removed a cigarette from the sleeve of my kimono, but when I lit it [with some charcoal from the brazier] the tip pushed through into the ashes because my hands were vibrating. I grimaced and pursed my lips to exhale. Quite unexpectedly the smoke shot out in little rings, one right after the other. No matter how softly I tried to exhale the smoke, it formed smoke rings. This cheered me up a bit and, recalling the smokestack on the roof of the cabin on deck, I repeated my little smoking game.[89]

Subject like all the rest to the ferry's vibrations (an allusion to the trembling of the earthquake?), the protagonist is unable to maintain his aloofness. So invasive is this physical environment that he becomes part of the ferry itself, a smokestack blowing smoke rings.

Balancing the intrusion of external materiality into subjectivity (the ferry replicated in the protagonist) is the pushing of subjectivity into the outside world in the form of materiality. This motif takes the form of the protagonist's obsession with his head and brain, the aspect for which the story is named. As the narrative progresses, the brain is objectified to an ever greater extent, further and further alienated from its natural seat and role. The first reference comes early in the story:

> While looking absentmindedly at the movement of the waves, I began to feel an odd pressure. I took off my hat, stuck my fingers into my hair, and tried wildly scratching my head. Somehow the inside of my skull felt itchy to me. I'd heard of diseases in which a tumor forms on the brain. Could one of those things be taking shape somewhere in my own head? I could live with pain but I thought that an itchiness in the head was more than I could bear.[90]

The seat of consciousness is depicted here in its most concrete form, the brain, and its corporeal nature is highlighted in its susceptibility to a plebeian itchiness.

This image is repeated in the representation of the brain of the maid working at the protagonist's inn. He is annoyed at her chatter while she serves his meal, finding her talk meaningless. "I imagined her yellow brain, disgustingly smooth like an ostrich's egg, there behind the wide expanse of her forehead."[91] When she spreads out his bedding and says goodnight, he again thinks of her, and subsequently himself, in terms of the brain: "So the ostrich egg is going to sleep. I no longer found it amusing. I listened to the sound of her sandals as she went down the corridor. If I took my own brain out, I wonder what kind of ugly shape it would have?"[92] Increasingly the brain is portrayed not as the seat of consciousness or subjectivity, but rather as just another element of the concrete world.

The loss of a subjectivity opposed to and independent of the material world reaches an extreme as the story comes to a close. While the physical nature of the brain has been highlighted throughout the story, it had at least remained separated from the world by the walls of the cranium. In the closing passages, however, even this barrier disappears: "I felt like I was carrying my own brain in an ornamental glass case, wondering all the while whether or not it would break. However, at some point, it was already broken. In its place was a lump of rock."[93] This scene completes the transformation from a world wherein subjectivity is distinct from the material world to a world where the two are completely indistinguishable. Just as the world in the form of the vibrating ship had engulfed the would-be aloof observer of that world, so too has the essence of that observer been thrust into that material world and become fully a part of it.

This confusion of subjectivity and materiality renders a Shiga-esque revelation unattainable. Moments such as Kenkichi's experience on the train, that moment in which his mind and body converged in a spontaneous action, are no longer conceivable because the boundaries to be crossed are blurred from the very start. All is part of a confused realm in which animate and inanimate are inseparable. The subjectivity in this story is all but completely alien to the sensitivities that Kobayashi would later locate in Shiga. In "Shiga Naoya ron" Kobayashi writes: "Though it may seem always visible to us, the fact is that nature is always behind a curtain. What we see when we whisk that curtain aside—a mountain, a bird, a pocket watch—when we clearly see what lies there and grasp it, that is true poetry. . . . Shiga's realism is in this sense truly poetic."[94] In "Hitotsu no nōzui," however, the protagonist never manages to whisk the curtain aside for that revelatory moment of poetic insight. In an attempt to write late one night in the inn, the protagonist finds that he is "not able to see things clearly" and that he is merely "fumbling with [his] melancholy *behind a curtain* separating [him] from the outside world."[95] He succeeds only in doodling over and over again on the manuscript paper a smooth yellow rock that, not surprisingly, he associates with his own psychological state.[96]

The only aspect of materiality that the protagonist can fix his sight on is that infused with his own subjectivity. Later, in a scene reminiscent of the protagonist being vibrated by the ferry's engines, again the physical environment engulfs him and prevents an objective observation:

> I was sprawled out in the bathtub. On the far side of the bathing room's glass windows, the snow-covered electrical lines sagged heavily. A sparrow alit on the line. The snow fell with a thud, revealing the insulated black lines. The sparrow was as plump as a rubber ball. From time to time the white steam from the hot spring obscured the electric line and the sparrow.[97]

Here, too, the boundaries between perceiving subject and perceived object are blurred, making that intuitive leap of understanding impossible.

The integration of the human faculties that Kobayashi had praised in Shiga is also strikingly absent. Kobayashi expressed this harmonious synthesis as follows: "People speak of the beauty of Shiga's depictions of nature. Such beauty can only be expressed by writers in whom 'observation' and 'emotional response' indicate the same act."[98] And yet in Kobayashi's work in the wake of the earthquake this holistic appreciation of nature is painfully lacking: "The sound of equipment cutting down trees reverberated in the clear air. There was the scent of fresh wood in the air. I felt that its rare freshness did not at all suit me. And yet, in spite of that, it did strike me as fresh."[99] Here the "emotional response" (*kandō*) does not coincide with the "observation" but rather is itself observed. The intuitive certainty that Kobayashi would later champion in Shiga's work is nowhere to be seen.

For all of these reasons the story is distinctly different from the works of Shiga, and different even from Kobayashi's own approximation of them in "Tako no jisatsu." What emerges in "Hitotsu no nōzui" instead is a fragmented subjectivity moving through an alien landscape. At times the story seems close to the writing of Yokomitsu Riichi, known for employing a high-speed, almost cinematic visuality in his prose.[100] In "Hitotsu no nōzui," one such scene comes when the protagonist leaves Manazuru for the hot spring:

I took the bus to Yugawara. Electricity poles left standing after the fires and the sooty boy seeing us off shot past in the plastic window. Once over the ridge, the road wound gently along the coastline. Grimy fishermen's houses that seemed about to succumb to the oppressive, snow-filled clouds lined the road on the right. On reed mats spread out before their entrances were shells, presumably oyster shells. Each one of these dully reflected the dismal colors of the sky. We passed handcarts, dogs, pedestrians and all sorts of other things . . . one right after the other they caught my eye. The more my weary head tried to ignore them, the more my eyes sought them out. My vision fastened on a piece of hay spinning around on the wheel of a cart, and on everything from the face of the man pulling it to the strip of cloth tied around his brow. I read the graffiti and posters on the electric poles. It annoyed me and with great effort I tore my eyes away from the plastic window.[101]

The rapid sequence of disconnected images reflects the racing of the protagonist's overactive mind. The representation suggests cinema, complete with the containment of the images within a screen-like frame, the window.[102]

Yokomitsu embraced an eclectic mix of modernist literary techniques, and Kobayashi does the same in this story.[103] The kaleidoscopic series of images sometimes gives way to a surrealism close to that experienced by Alice in Wonderland. Out for a walk, the protagonist is confronted by the conductor of the bus he had arrived on the day before. He objects when the conductor tells him to get on board:

"Isn't it too early?"

"It certainly is not." With numbed hands, the ticket-taker tucked up his green sleeve and looked at his big wristwatch. The man on crutches peered over and noisily flipped open the lid of his own watch, every bit as cheap as the ticket-taker's.

"You're 40 minutes fast," he said.

"This is the harbor's watch, so it's got the right time. After all, even if it *is* 40 minutes fast, the boat leaves according to harbor time."[104]

The ticket-taker's absurd assertion, the mysterious man on the crutches—no matter where the protagonist turns, the world is either obscured from view or patently incomprehensible.

In the final section of the story is another surrealistic scene in which once again the brain, seat of subjectivity, is projected onto the landscape:

> I walked along the water's edge, red like rust. Each time the teeth of my *geta* bit into the soft sand, ocean water would quietly ooze up into the holes. As I walked along, staring down at my feet, this seemed to me like water oozing out of my brain. Step after step I sank the teeth of my *geta* into the soft surface of my head as I mumbled "The water oozes in, the water oozes in." Eventually I came to the end of the narrow beach at the water's edge. I turned, thinking to go back the way I had come, and was faced with the tracks of my *geta* continuing in a line in the sand. I was shocked, feeling I had been confronted with something I had never anticipated. Irritated, I hastily tried to make each and every one of those tracks coincide with the *geta* tracks left on my brain. I was unable to take a single step forward. I collapsed on a rock that happened to be at my side.[105]

This scene is fully modernist in tone. The fragmented subjectivity represented in the protagonist's brain merging with the landscape, the geometric pattern of the *geta* tracks on the sand, the visceral feel of oozing fluids in the brain and on the beach—all of these things suggest that the Kobayashi of 1924 was much closer in spirit to the emerging modernist movement than he was to the Shirakaba connoisseurs whom he had admired and emulated before the world was altered by the earthquake.

Kobayashi was by no means the only writer to exhibit in the earthquake's wake a concern with materiality that bordered on obsession.[106] As noted above, Neo-Perceptionists such as Yokomitsu Riichi also found in it an inspiration for a new literary style.[107] This natural disaster so powerfully influenced their work, in fact, that some critics even labeled it "earthquake literature."[108] Yokomitsu, for his part, himself emphasized the psychological effects of the earthquake on those who lived through it, going so far as to equate it with the European experience of World War I.[109]

The other literary movement to emerge in the wake of the earthquake—proletarian literature and Marxist criticism—exhibited a similar hypersensitivity to materiality, and not simply in their interest in the commodity. "Semento-daru no naka no tegami" (Letter Found in a Cement Barrel, 1926) by Hayama Yoshiki (1894–1945) is a perfect example. A young man has fallen into a crusher and his body has been mixed into powdered cement. The letter his girlfriend slipped into the cement sack projects his human qualities onto the structure to be built, and asks to be informed where and how the cement is used.[110] As in Yokomitsu's work and Kobayashi's story, the boundaries between the human and the material are hopelessly blurred.[111]

The confusion and intense angst evident in Kobayashi's "Hitotsu no nōzui" are products of the changed materiality of the post-earthquake world. Gone are the traces of the Shiga-esque sensibility that Kobayashi himself had seemed on the brink of inheriting. Or perhaps it might be more accurate to say that with the rupture of the earthquake, these Shiga-esque sensibilities came into existence for the first time, for it was only after Kobayashi was fully alienated from that Taishō ethos that it became possible to retrospectively construct it in the manner in which he did. The "unassailable simplicity" of Shiga, heir to the wisdom of the ancients, became not only visible but also an absolute value only after an already complex world had been rendered all but completely incomprehensible by the earthquake and the changes that occurred in its wake. Until that time this "god of the novel" (*shōsetsu no kamisama*) had been, as Hirotsu Kazuo put it before the earthquake, the possessor of "an acute, complex, and pathological sensitivity born from modern civilization."

Such is the operation of memory. It resurrects what has come before in response to the present. It does so by excavating and explicating traces of that which came before, traces that appear only because they console those who come after. These features of the phenomenon are responsible for the somewhat convoluted timeline of this chapter: to understand the fabricated nature of Kobayashi's portrayal of the "timeless" simplicity of Shiga, a touchstone for much of his criticism, it is necessary to reach back in an attempt to historicize it. In Kobayashi's earliest piece of fiction, "Tako no jisatsu," he exhibited sensibilities not unlike those of the writer Shiga. As the world represented in "Hitotsu no nōzui," a world wherein materiality threatened autonomous subjectivities, took hold, Kobayashi would glorify with increasing intensity those sensibilities. Such intuitive appreciations of a hard and fast world were no longer feasible, however, and Kobayashi's only recourse was to rhetorically reconfigure both materiality and subjectivity in such a way as to reproduce the aesthetic experience he believed had once been possible. This reconfiguration was no simple task as it went against the grain of the modernist ethos of so much of Kobayashi's generation. Making

Shiga simple required the deployment of powerful argumentation, as his essays on this writer show.

This resuscitation of the ideals of the Taishō literary youth inculcated in Kobayashi that same stubborn independence that marked the subjectivities of the Shirakaba writers, and this independence prevented Kobayashi from later wielding his pen for any explicit justification of Japan's war effort. However, as will be further argued below, the reification of materiality so integral to Kobayashi's aesthetics also prompted him to support the war for the manner in which it produced subjectivities amenable to the intuitive apprehension of the world, the mode of existence wherein beauty could again be felt rather than intellectually explained. Ironically, Kobayashi saw the war in much the same terms as he saw art and literature: phenomena that, if only we surrender ourselves to them, may ultimately heal the rift between mind and body and make us whole once again.

THREE
Seeing Past Akutagawa

As his story "Hitotsu no nōzui" suggests, by 1924 Kobayashi Hideo had fallen into the vortex of a fragmented modernity in which the conventional boundaries of self/other (or animate/inanimate) had been compromised to a point that it was no longer possible to experience a Shiga-esque epiphany, that revelatory moment in which once disparate poles suddenly come into perfect accord. Therefore, in his quest to resurrect the Taishō sensibility within the very different system of subjectivity-materiality in the Shōwa era, Kobayashi had to do more than simply voice an appreciation of traces of it in the works of Shiga Naoya. Such would have been nothing more than a eulogy. To resurrect it Kobayashi would have to reconfigure the relationship of subjectivity to materiality in ways that would make that experience possible once again. In his writings on Shiga, therefore, Kobayashi faced a double challenge. He had to portray Shiga as a sage-like visionary without resorting to an interpretive, analytical language that would have depleted the very sort of aura that Kobayashi was trying to build around Shiga. His stance vis-à-vis Shiga is clearest where he writes: "Looking at Shiga's work is like gazing at a splendid work of art; in a word, one's heart grows quiet and none of the conventional approaches are applicable."[1] Rhetorically rendering Shiga's work as art immune to intellectual interpretation, Kobayashi was striving to make it possible for readers to appreciate it intuitively in much the same way as Shiga himself had apprehended the world.

The current chapter explores this same stage in the development of Kobayashi's thinking from another angle. Although the receding sensibilities of the past were located in the work of Shiga, Kobayashi turned to the novelist Akutagawa Ryūnosuke to expose the noxious influences of the hyper-intellectual modern present. If Shiga inspired his ontology, the critique of Akutagawa helped Kobayashi forge his epistemology. This endeavor would prove to be very difficult as Kobayashi was in essence attempting to short-circuit the analytical thinking that was infiltrating aesthetic and literary realms, and he was deploying, ironically, the genre of criticism to do it. In the process Kobayashi evolved from a writer of fiction to a literary critic, a conversion that took place much more gradually than is commonly recognized.[2] The first important step in this conversion was the essay Kobayashi himself would later call his first critical work: "Akutagawa Ryūnosuke no bishin to shukumei" (The Muse and Destiny of Akutagawa Ryūnosuke, 1927).[3]

This essay was Kobayashi's contribution to the epidemic of literary soul-searching that this writer's suicide had triggered in 1927. With the avalanche of essays attempting to explain the significance of the tragic demise of this quintessentially modern intellect, Japan's literary community was in fact grappling with the entirety of the subjectivity-materiality system established with modernity. As Seiji Lippit convincingly argues, Akutagawa's later writings embody the "disintegration of [the] ideology of literature, together with its capacity to organize a consciousness of modernity. . . . This dissolution is manifested in practice as the fragmentation of literary form in Akutagawa's last works, and in theory as Akutagawa's notion of the 'plotless novel'."[4] This "disintegration" is precisely what Kobayashi experienced, as evidenced in the changes between his own two early stories. There was a sense of urgency in Kobayashi's writings on Akutagawa arising from the fact that he undoubtedly recognized many parallels between that writer and himself, as Aeba Takao points out.[5] Critic Kamei Hideo amplifies this claim, stating that Kobayashi was, in fact, closer in temperament to Akutagawa than to this hero Shiga.[6]

Kobayashi's harsh portrait of Akutagawa reveals the basic contours of his strategy for dealing with the fragmented, disorienting modern world, the "endless clutter of things and events that have changed too quickly," as he phrased it in "Kokyō o ushinatta bungaku." To this end Kobayashi focused on the paradoxes in Akutagawa's works, themselves a reflection of the struggle to make sense of the fragmented modern world. Kobayashi condemned Akutagawa's attempt to make sense of the world by parsing it, in a Cartesian manner, into its component parts. Rather, Kobayashi would argue, the artist's proper mode is a more holistic, acritical, and intuitive application of "seeing" (*miru koto*). This metaphor for his epistemological approach was to become a mainstay of Kobayashi's criticism, and in his reconfiguration of this dominant epistemological metaphor of the age of Enlightenment, Kobayashi joins in a larger philosophical discourse that includes European philosophers such as Henri Bergson (1859–1941) as well as Japanese thinkers such as Nishida Kitarō. This chapter introduces the "ocularcentrism" of modernity in order to use its vocabulary later in tracing the philosophical revolution fought in various circles in an attempt to overcome modernity's challenges. In France, Bergson confronted the legacy of this vision-based epistemology; in Japan, Nishida worked along parallel lines. A discussion of their work sets the stage for Kobayashi's engagement with the modernity represented in the works of Akutagawa Ryūnosuke, an engagement that takes place within this larger discourse. The chapter closes with an exploration of how Kobayashi's "seeing" reshapes critical discourse and a discussion of its relationship with the similar critical agenda pursued by the Japan Romantics (Nihon rōman-ha).

Vision as an Epistemological Metaphor

It is not surprising that Kobayashi Hideo would co-opt the idea of "seeing," or vision, in articulating his epistemological alternative for modern man. As Martin Jay so convincingly demonstrates, since the Enlightenment, vision has served as the most pervasive metaphor for knowledge of all stripes, and its specter permeates language and thought to a degree unmatched by any other sense. As Jay notes, eyes, the instrument of vision, serve as both our "window on the world" and the "mirror of the soul."[7] As such, vision is the metaphor through which we conceive not only of what is "out there" (knowledge of the material world), but also of who we are "inside" (self-knowledge). Walter Benjamin, a thinker whose ideas are central to this study, is a case in point. In exploring how technological advances alter human sense consciousness, Benjamin offers the painter and the cameraman, both manipulators of *visual* images, as representatives of evolving human sensibilities.[8] The education of Taishō-era intellectuals such as Kobayashi was centered on the Western tradition, and it instilled in them a similar epistemological framework.

Therefore, considering the ubiquity, flexibility, and potency of the visual metaphor, it is in some ways natural that Kobayashi Hideo, similarly engaged with the nature of knowledge in a time of mutating materiality, also turned to "seeing" as a metaphor for his brand of knowledge-seeking. It was only in his construction of an alternative mode of "seeing" that he would turn to the indigenous Japanese tradition for inspiration and vocabulary.

As Jay reminds us, the dominance of the visual metaphor dates back to the very inventors of philosophy, the Greeks. Their visual culture inculcated three traits that shaped epistemological exploration, but these very characteristics seemed no longer valid to the thinkers dealt with in this chapter. First, an obsession with visuality tends to efface temporal concerns, privileging "static Being over dynamic Becoming, fixed essences over ephemeral appearances."[9] Second, the ocularcentrism of Greek culture inspired the distinction between subject and object, the viewer and the viewed. Born from this distinction was the idea that the viewing subject is disengaged from the object of the gaze. A third characteristic of Greek philosophy that can be attributed to the ocularcentric perspective concerns distance. Sight being the most efficient tool for predicting what is, literally, looming on the horizon, the philosophical systems germinated under its sway naturally prioritized knowledge that could predict the future. That is to say, priority was given to knowledge that lent itself to the harnessing of the world to man's needs.[10] In Jay's summary, "Once the battle against Sophism, which defended rhetoric and the ear, was won, Greek philosophy could elevate a visually defined notion of disinterested, monologic, epistemic truth over mere opinion or *doxa*."[11] So pervasive was the visual metaphor that even dissent such as Plato's myth of the cave was expressed within it.[12]

Descartes was a seminal figure in the development of this ocularcentric epistemology; he instituted a new dichotomy in the understanding of understanding. Descartes's positing of his famous insight *cogito ergo sum* at the base of all knowledge, once anchored by the assurance of the mind's correspondence to the natural world through the existence of God, provided an autonomous, stable subjectivity from which to observe and chart an objectified world. This strain of Descartes's thought launched the "dominant scopic regime of the modern era": Cartesian perspectivalism.[13] Curiously, Descartes's "I think therefore I am" also provided the grounds upon which a contemplative tradition was to emerge. With the self being the only unassailable object of knowledge, followers of Descartes had the option of pursuing their skepticism by withdrawing into reflection. Jay describes this tradition as "identitarian reflexivity, in which the subject is certain only of its mirror image."[14] This chapter in the story of philosophy demonstrates again the dominance of the metaphor of vision: whether Descartes's insights prompted a turning of the eyes outward or inward, the primacy of the visual metaphor for pursuing knowledge remained unchallenged.

It was, of course, the former of these two strains, Cartesian perspectivalism, that occupied the mainstream of thought, its authority buttressed by the technological advances that it had made possible through the positivism and empiricism derived from it. This brand of ocularcentrism was transcribed in the literary realm in a variety of modes, the most extreme example being Naturalism. Here the model of the "scientific method," as applied by Émile Zola in such works as *Thérèse Raquin*, inspired writers to adopt largely omniscient narrative voices in their "objective" observation of the characters they created.[15] But Cartesian perspectivalism reverberated beyond simply this movement; it was evident wherever literary texts sprung from a unified, hegemonic authorial or narrative voice. In the context of the Japanese literary tradition, it is possible to conceive of the *genbun itchi* movement as a manifestation of the quest for what Jay terms a "disinterested, monologic, epistemic truth."[16] This language-reform movement reduced the polyglossia of the Japanese language, making possible—perhaps inevitable—the unified subject position that came to dominate the Japanese novel: the I-novel (*watakushi shōsetsu*) of the late Meiji and Taishō periods.[17]

This subjectivity was to face a crisis in the late nineteenth and early twentieth centuries in both the West and Japan. Jay writes: by "the nineteenth century what many have called the hegemonic scopic regime of the modern era, Cartesian perspectivalism, was beginning to waver as never before."[18] Ironically, this crisis was prompted in some places by the increasing refinement of the visual mode of cognitive organization; in short, the realization of the paradigm made clear its limitations.[19] In Japan the threat to ocularcentrism arrived in the form of the new materiality invading post-earthquake Japan. The accelerating pace of change and the blurring of animate/inanimate boundaries discussed in Chapter 1 inverted the hierarchy of Being over Becoming as well as invalidated the conventional subject/object distinction, both central concepts of Cartesian perspectivalism.

In Japan's literary arena, this turning point was most conspicuously revealed in the career of Akutagawa Ryūnosuke, a central figure in this chapter. In a literary community dominated by the I-novel and its "centered" subjectivity, Akutagawa was an anomaly. As Dennis Washburn notes, his stories are distinguished by

> the lack of an absolute point of reference. They are often based on classic tales that Akutagawa made new simply by fragmenting the perspective. The characters' viewpoints are purposely decentered to reveal the fact that viewpoint is not absolute; the irony resulting from the gap between what the characters know and what the reader knows reduces the credibility of the account and renders the truth of the story relative, dependent on individual interpretation. The compensation for this ironic denial of absolute truth is that the narrative as a whole seeks credibility by asserting that the contingency of life and art is an inevitable condition of human experience. The literary self is moved to the margins in an effort to regain narrative credibility.[20]

Akutagawa, it might be said, was caught in the middle. On the one hand, he was pushing Cartesian perspectivalism to its extremes by positing multiple, incongruous points of view; on the other hand, he was (at least early in his career) juxtaposing these viewpoints in such a way as to create an aesthetic whole. Washburn calls this "narrative credibility"; Japanese critic Usui Yoshimi, borrowing from Akutagawa's own "Geijutsu sono ta" (Art and Other Topics, 1919), refers to it in terms of the "completion of the piece" (*sakuhin no kansei*).[21] Seiji Lippit, for his part, characterizes it as a mediation: for Akutagawa, he writes, "'literature' mediated between the particular world of the individual and the universal world of modernity, serving as the conceptual basis for his self-consciousness."[22]

This delicate balance between the confusion of multiplying perspectives and "credibility" is precisely what crumbled in this writer's later works. In the kaleidoscopic rush of such works as "Haguruma" (Spinning Gears, 1927), narrative credibility, in the conventional sense, dissolves before the reader's eyes. In these works, as Washburn succinctly puts it, Akutagawa's "unwillingness to abandon a detached, relativistic perspective in order to create the fiction of a transcendent self results in a hyper-rational, schizophrenic narrative voice. The late autobiographical stories reveal a desperate desire to break through the endless regressions of a relativistic outlook."[23] Akutagawa dramatically and tragically played out the epistemological implosion of Cartesian perspectivalism.

The dead end confronted by the pursuit of knowledge rooted in a visual metaphor prompted reconsiderations in both literature and philosophy throughout the world. Jay points out three changes by which philosophies rooted in Cartesian perspectivalism responded to this moment: the "first concerns what can be termed the detranscendentalization of perspective; the second, the recorporealization of the cognitive subject; and the third, the revalorization of time over space."[24] All three of these shifts are presaged in the works of Henri Bergson, whose ideas resonated in Japan through the work of Nishida Kitarō and Kobayashi Hideo. Though characterized in a variety of ways, Bergson's significance in initiating this shift in the European context is being increasingly recognized. Jay makes him a central figure in his study, claiming Bergson's "explicit devaluation of vision was to have a profound, if not always explicitly acknowledged, effect on twentieth-century thought."[25] In his survey of French philosophy in the last century, Eric Matthews credits him with breaking from the epistemological tradition of the natural sciences (which Jay places squarely in the lineage of ocularcentrism) so convincingly that "most of twentieth-century French philosophy can be seen as a series of footnotes to Bergson."[26]

The Revolution of Henri Bergson

The three deviations from Cartesian perspectivalism that Jay highlights in his study—the destranscendentalization of perspective, the recorporealization of the cognitive subject and the revalorization of time over space—all find expression in Japan, and all are integral to the thought of Kobayashi Hideo. These innovations can be traced in Europe to Bergson and, through him, in Japan to thinkers like Nishida Kitarō and Kobayashi Hideo. Though a pursuit of the precise lines of influence is beyond the purview of this study, an introduction of a few points from Bergson situates Kobayashi in the context of a broad epistemological revolution as well as brings into focus some of the particulars of his reading of Akutagawa.

Bergson posited at the core of his philosophy a concept that corresponds closely to what Jay labeled the revalorization of time over space. This linchpin is Bergson's concept of duration, the unfolding of phenomena over their full trajectory through time.[27] Although a holistic understanding is contingent on an appreciation of this sort, it is often derailed by a focus on one frozen moment from the full duration. This blind spot is a product of epistemologies driven by the visual metaphor; Bergson characterizes it as "cinematographical."[28] The cinematographical mode of understanding is, as the name suggests, based on an intellectual analysis of a dynamic whole by parsing it into static, homogeneous images and ideas, much like cinema is composed of a string of separate, static photographic exposures. While such disarticulation has made possible important scientific and technological advancements, this mode of "vision" blinds us to the essence of life as it is revealed over the course of a particular duration.

The most famous examples Bergson offers for our understanding of the unique qualities of duration are drawn from Zeno's paradoxes, one of which presents Achilles allowing a tortoise a head start in a footrace. In order to overtake his opponent, Achilles must first reach the point from which the tortoise started. By the time he has accomplished this, the tortoise has, of course, moved forward, even if only ever so slightly. Achilles now sets out to reach the tortoise's new position, but by the time he reaches it, the tortoise has moved still farther forward. Straight "cinematographical" logic suggests that this series of "snapshots" will continue endlessly, with Achilles having no chance of ever overtaking the tortoise. The problem stems from our contention that "we may disarticulate as we will the movement of Achilles and, as we will also, the movement of the tortoise: thus reconstructing both in an arbitrary way, according to a law of our own which may be incompatible with the real conditions of mobility."[29] Bergson's solution is to view the paradox in terms of "movement" through the duration of the action. If we examine the movement of Achilles and the tortoise from start to finish, it is clear that Achilles will emerge victorious.

Duration is distinguished by its unity and multiplicity; the footrace is simultaneously both a single dash from start to finish and a series of individual footsteps. Comprehension of duration as such, according to Bergson, can be satisfactorily achieved in only one manner: through intuition:

> However much I manipulate the two concepts [unity and multiplicity], portion them out, combine them differently, practice on them the most subtle operations of mental chemistry, I never obtain anything which resembles the simple intuition that I have of duration; while, on the contrary, when I replace myself in duration by an effort of intuition, I immediately perceive how it is unity, multiplicity, and many other things besides.[30]

This conclusion—that intuition is the key to a holistic understanding of duration—is perhaps the most important consequence of Bergson's prioritizing of time over space.

The intuition that Bergson inserted at the core of his philosophy represents his most radical break with Cartesian perspectivalism. It also allows for a qualitatively different manner of knowing, one that ultimately exhibits the "detranscendalization of perspective" that Jay identifies as integral to the overall epistemological shift away from ocularcentrism. Intuition, unlike rational analysis, is not a utilitarian mode of knowing. However, this deficiency is more than compensated for by its absoluteness. In his "An Introduction to Metaphysics" (1903), Bergson writes:

> Philosophers agree in making a distinction between two ways of knowing a thing. The first implies that we move round the object; the second that we enter into it. The first depends on the point of view at which we are placed and on the symbols by which we express ourselves. The second neither depends on a point of view nor relies on any symbol. The first kind of knowledge may be said to stop at the *relative*; the second, in those cases where it is possible, to attain the *absolute*.[31]

Albeit with reservations as to the persuasiveness of the argument, Jay quite rightly characterizes this recourse to intuition as Bergson's way of overcoming the obstacles posed by "intellectual analysis, linguistic symbolization, and visual representation."[32]

Bergson's expression of this mode of knowing as "absolute" at first glance seems to be moving toward a transcendentalizing of perspective rather than away from it. This impression is a product of his critique of Cartesian perspectivalism: by deflating the objectivity of the scientific method, by highlighting its limited and ultimately over-determined perspective, Bergson inadvertently implies that the intuitive alternative transcends the liabilities of perspective. When considered in context, however, Bergson's intuitive knowledge is revealed as "absolute" only in the most limited of realms, oxymoronic as that may seem.

The extreme relativity and limitations of the "absoluteness" of intuitive understanding is hinted at in the above passage, where Bergson insists that it is not dependent on the "symbols by which we express ourselves." This is to say that intuitive cognition, as an infinitely personal experience, is ultimately incommunicable; it cannot be reduced to linguistic articulation or conceptual formulation. To quote again from Bergson's "An Introduction to Metaphysics":

> Abstract ideas . . . [are] incapable of replacing intuition . . . For on the one hand these concepts, laid side by side, never actually give us more than an artificial reconstruction of the object, of which they can only symbolize

certain general, and, in a way, impersonal aspects; it is therefore useless to believe that with them we can seize a reality of which they present to us the shadow alone.[33]

The point is that the symbolic gesture, whether linguistic or conceptual, relies on a universalizing gesture that reduces the phenomenon to its most generic components. In doing so, it erases the glorious specificity, or particularity, of it. Phrased in terms of Bergson's concept of duration, abstract ideas harvest the unity while discarding the multiplicity contained therein.

Not surprisingly, being a philosopher, Bergson rehabilitates conceptual thinking on the very next page of this text. He does so, however, by reconstituting it along lines that emphasize multiplicity over unity and a dynamic Becoming over a static Being:

[Metaphysics] is only truly itself when it goes beyond the concept, or at least when it frees itself from rigid and ready-made concepts in order to create a kind very different from those which we habitually use; I mean supple, mobile, and almost fluid representations, always ready to mould themselves on the fleeting forms of intuition.[34]

In this manner Bergson frees metaphysics from Cartesian ocularcentrism and its obsession with instrumental scientific knowledge. His philosophy emphasizes the sort of intuitive insight more conventionally associated with the creative arts, particularly the moments of almost mystical insight so often inscribed at their core. The "absolute" nature of the brand of knowledge Bergson champions, then, is clearly very different from that pursued by the ocularcentric scientific method. Intuitive knowledge is "absolute" not in the sense that it transcends the limitations of any perspective, but rather in the sense that the particular, extracted from the world of universals, attains a sort of absoluteness, an aura of perfection generated from the fact that it has been rendered immune to generalizations and disarticulations. It is the unassailable absoluteness seen in the intuitive insight of the artist (or the mystical visionary), rooted in a deeply personal, virtually inexpressible, and unshakably assured belief.

As these points suggest, Bergson's philosophy represents a fundamental break with the epistemology that had dominated virtually the entire post-Enlightenment world. All three of the premises central to Cartesian perspectivalism are shattered. Through Bergson's prioritizing of duration (a temporal rather than spatial concept), the disarticulation of reality into static component parts is discredited, and Being gives way to a sense of all things in a fluid state of Becoming.

Second, the intuitive mode of knowledge through which we "enter into" a thing rather than examine it from various external vantage points erases the conventional subject/object distinction. Third, with Bergson's emphasis on the infinitely personal and ultimately inexpressible nature of the intuitive insight, a concern for the *experience* of knowing rather than for what is known replaces Cartesian perspectivalism's obsession with deployable knowledge .

All of these qualities are evident in the parallel epistemological revolution taking place in Japan. Its seeds were planted during the Taishō period, and its maturation occurred in the Shōwa era. While Kobayashi's version of this revolution is outlined later in this chapter, the results of it have in fact already been introduced. Chapter 1 offers an extended quotation from Kobayashi's essay 1941 essay "Dentō" (Tradition). There, in his discussion of his study of Dostoevsky, Kobayashi had chronicled his original disarticulation of this writer's work in hopes of discovering the historical conditions that gave rise to it. He relates how for a time he entertained the idea that he was arriving at some more exquisite knowledge, only to conclude eventually that this was but an illusion that ultimately detracts from our experience of this Russian writer. Instead, the work must be appreciated holistically, recognizing that the individual pieces are in fact "absorbed and manifest in the immutable harmony of the mysterious living thing that is the work of art."[35] Kobayashi's revolt against Cartesian perspectivalism can be read in his description of this experience. He arrived at the intuitive mode of knowing recorded in that passage through his treatment of Akutagawa, a treatment configured by his understanding of Bergson and of philosopher Nishida Kitarō.

Nishida Kitarō: A Bergsonian Shift in Taishō Japan

The influence of Marxist thought on Taishō and early Shōwa Japan has been thoroughly explored in a myriad of ways by a wide variety of scholars. Bergson's influence, however, has not received as much attention. Writing about the late Taishō period, Aeba Takao has stated "there can be no denying the fact that Marx and Bergson both brought 'materiality' [*busshitsu*] to Japan, and together they presented a new perspective from which to view the internal and external dimensions of existence."[36] In addition to Kobayashi, Aeba points to three thinkers who were working along the lines laid out by Bergson: Nishida Kitarō, Miki Kiyoshi (1897–1945), and Mori Arimasa (1911–76).[37] Of these men, Nishida Kitarō exercised the widest influence. Ōoka Shōhei, for example, insists that an understanding of Kobayashi Hideo and his generation is predicated on a familiarity with Nishida's *Zen no kenkyū* (An Inquiry into the Good, 1911).[38] Kamei Hideo alludes to this claim in his study of Kobayashi, adding, "behind Kobayashi's distaste for reality and his sense of an oppressive materiality is hidden a powerful longing for the subject/object conflation of [Nishida's] pure experience [*junsui keiken*]."[39]

The parallels between Nishida's thought and Bergson's philosophy are indeed striking. The degree to which the similarities can be attributed to direct influence is a matter outside the scope of this study, and perhaps ultimately of only marginal importance in any case. Suffice it to note that although Nishida's strengths were in the German and English thinkers, and most of his references in *Zen no kenkyū* are to Hegel, Schopenhauer, Schiller, and Schelling on the German side, and Dewey, William James, and Locke on the English, it is clear that Nishida was aware of Bergson's ideas, and that he took them very seriously.[40] Nishida not only wrote a number of essays on Bergson, but also, in 1941, he went so far as to say that "it was only after I familiarized myself with Bergson's thought that I was able to formulate my idea of 'pure experience' and publish my *Zen no kenkyū*."[41]

Though Aeba points specifically to Nishida's "Jikaku ni okeru chokkaku to hansei" (Intuition and Reflection in Self-Consciousness, 1917), an affinity with Bergson can, as Nishida's statement suggests, indeed be seen in the book that launched Nishida's career. *Zen no kenkyū* outlines Nishida's concept of pure experience, an epistemological approach that shares much with Bergson's (and Kobayashi's, too, as we shall see). Nishida's intellectual agenda reflects the degree to which, through the Taishō period and into the early years of Shōwa, the desire to slip the binds of an ocularcentric, scientific epistemology fueled the thinking of a broad range of thinkers.

In general terms, Nishida's work parallels that of Bergson in its pursuit of a conception of truth very different from that propagated by positivism and empiricism. As outlined above, Bergson sought to redirect our attention to the unique aspects of experience, as these are too often lost in the emphasis on the universalities and abstractions so crucial to scientific thinking. Nishida, too, points us toward the unique and specific:

> There are various arguments about what truth is, but I think truth is that which comes closest to the most concrete facts of experience. Truth is some-

times said to be universal, but if by this one means abstract commonality, then what one is designating is actually far removed from truth. The culmination of truth is the most concrete, direct facts that synthesize various facets of experience. . . . Perfect truth pertains to the individual person and is actual. Perfect truth therefore cannot be expressed in words, and such things as scientific truth cannot be considered perfect truth.[42]

This emphasis on the concrete (the individual, the particular) indicates that Nishida stands with Bergson in opposition to the philosophical lineage seeking universals. Nishida also parallels Bergson in positing truth as something so singular that it cannot be expressed in words.

Second, Nishida's concept of pure experience shares many qualities with the intuitive insight championed by Bergson.[43] Nishida's most concise definition of pure experience is found in the opening lines of *Zen no kenkyū*:

To experience means to know facts just as they are, to know in accordance with facts by completely relinquishing one's own fabrications. What we usually refer to as experience is adulterated with some sort of thought, so by *pure* I am referring to the state of experience just as it is without the least addition of deliberative discrimination. The moment of seeing a color or hearing a sound, for example, is prior not only to the thought that the color or sound is the activity of an external object or that one is sensing it, but also to the judgment of what the color or sound might be. In this regard, pure experience is identical with direct experience. When one directly experiences one's own state of consciousness, there is not yet a subject or object, and knowing and its object are completely unified. This is the most refined type of experience.[44]

In addition to the erasure of the subject/object distinction, Nishida's pure (or direct) experience also shares with Bergson's intuition a conviction that this mode of knowing provides for an absolute form of knowledge, an unquestionable certainty: "It is in the state of direct experience—when subject and object merge with each other and we are unable, even if we try, to doubt the utter singularity of the realities of the universe—that we have conviction about truth."[45] The experience resembles the sudden flash of insight of the mystic, yet another attribute of Nishida's thought that has analogues in Bergson's system.

A third and final dimension of Nishida's philosophy that reveals the extent to which Taishō Japan was experimenting with ideas similar to Bergson's is the attention paid to the internal quality of the experience itself rather than a concern for the deployable knowledge to be gleaned from it: "The meanings of, or judgments about, an experience are simply expressions of its relation to other experiences; they do not enrich the content of the experience. Meanings or judgments are an abstracted part of the original experience, and compared with the original experience they are meager in content."[46] This is reminiscent of Bergson's emphasis on the need to be free from ready-made concepts and instead revel in "supple, mobile, and almost fluid representations." The emphasis in both thinkers is on the act rather than the result.

This attribute of Nishida's thought was so much at odds with the overall trajectory of contemporary philosophy and analytical thought that it attracted immediate criticism. At a time when the only knowledge that seemed worth having was deployable knowledge, Takahashi Satomi quite predictably asked, in his largely favorable 1912 critique of Nishida's *Zen no kenkyū*, the question on everybody's mind: what is one to do with the fact of the experience, where does one go from there?[47] James Heisig raises much the same objection: "The difficulty with his idea of active intuition was that once spoken, there was nothing else to be said about it. As a standpoint, it served to criticize other standpoints, but did not lead him much further."[48] As we will see, much the same sort of criticism would be directed against Kobayashi's work, based as it was on an epistemology that arose from the same wellspring as Nishida's.

Making Sense of Akutagawa

Like Henri Bergson in France, Nishida Kitarō was responding to problems perceived to be innate to Cartesian perspectivalism. In the Japanese literary community, these problems were addressed in the form of responses to the career of Akutagawa Ryūnosuke, whose suicide in 1927 had an impact on the world of letters that is hard to overstate. The suicide of a literary figure was certainly not unprecedented: Kitamura Tōkoku had killed himself in 1894, and Arishima Takeo as recently as 1923. These suicides, however, did not reverberate in the literary world to the same extent that Akutagawa's did. "Akutagawa's expression of 'vague anxiety' as the cause of his suicide, coupled with the turbulent and transitional character of the 1920s, transformed his death from a personal, private catastrophe into a general historical allegory, an empty vessel into which a variety of narrative interpretations could be projected," as Seiji Lippit phrases it.[49]

The intensity of the shock is attested to by the veritable avalanche of essays and magazine articles that appeared shortly after the suicide, each trying to make sense of it. Akutagawa took his life on July 24, 1927. In September of that same year alone seven magazines—*Kaizō, Chūō kōron, Bungei shunjū, Bunshō kurabu, Mita bungaku, Jōsei,* and *Fujin kōron*—all ran special issues dedicated to him. These magazines printed a total of 65 essays with contributions by a total of 52 literary figures.[50] These numbers are astounding, especially in light of the fact that they include neither the essays scattered in magazines *not* dedicated entirely to Akutagawa, nor those that emerged after September of that year. The extent of the reaction is attested to by more than the numbers alone. The list of writers who contributed essays on Akutagawa resembles a "who's who" of the contemporary literary world, including everyone from Tanizaki Jun'ichirō (1886–1965), Hirotsu Kazuo, and Shiga Naoya, to Chūjō (Miyamoto) Yuriko (1899–1951), Uno Chiyo (1897–1994), and Okamoto Kanako (1889–1939). The shock was not only intense, but was felt across a broad swath of the literary world.

The tremendous impact of this event owed much to the fact that Akutagawa's suicide was indeed taken as a "general historical allegory." An active, highly esteemed member of the literary community, Akutagawa mysteriously attributed his decision to take his own life to "simply some vague anxiety concerning my future" (*nanika boku no shōrai ni taisuru tada bon'yari shita fuan*), and it was this enigmatic statement that opened the door to infinite speculation.[51] Further fueling the debate was the perception that Akutagawa represented the modern intellectual, and that he should choose to take his own life raised doubts concerning the fate of all modern intellectuals.

Critic Inoue Yoshio summed up these shared reactions when, in 1932, he wrote:

> Even today we cannot forget the violent shock we felt when, five years ago, the death of Akutagawa Ryūnosuke was announced. . . . It was at this time that we clearly realized just how persistently death had been bearing down on all of us. The problem was no longer "someone else's business," as had been the case with Arishima Takeo's death. This was a question of our very own demise. Naturally, Akutagawa's death was the occasion of a fundamental wavering among the young writers. . . . At the very least, Akutagawa's death was thrown, in the form of a question that absolutely required some sort of answer, at writers who tried to live the day in good faith. Only those who could somehow transcend Akutagawa's death would be able to live from that day forth without the temptation of suicide. For example, today we can no longer relate indifferently to things such as intellectualism [*shuchishugi*]. What Akutagawa has already proven with his death is nothing other than the impotence of our intellect [*chisei*].[52]

This passage suggests the extent to which the younger generation in particular felt an affinity with Akutagawa. It also emphasizes how closely Akutagawa's reputation was tied to issues of the intellect (as opposed to purely literary or aesthetic concerns), and the extent to which many shared his skepticism concerning its efficacy. As Inoue, speaking for his generation, states, Akutagawa's suicide was seen by many as proof of the "impotence" of the intellect. This intellect was quite firmly planted in the Cartesian perspectivalism that informed virtually all corners of modern intellectual life.

Kobayashi Hideo, 25 years old at the time of Akutagawa's death, was but one of many to contribute to this discourse. Through a comparison of other contemporary readings of the incident, the radical nature of Kobayashi's interpretation becomes clear. Whereas the leading critics of various contemporary schools analyzed Akutagawa's works and suicide in terms of what aspects of the intellect rightly infused literature, Kobayashi alone addressed the question of what constitutes the intellect itself; Kobayashi alone advanced an intimately literary alternative to the conventional modes of knowing. The parameters he established in this epistemological inquiry shaped much of his later criticism.

As such Kobayashi's treatise is significantly different from the essay by the established *bundan* figure Masamune Hakuchō (1879–1962) that appeared in the magazine *Kaizō* in October 1927. Hakuchō accepted the conventional understanding of Akutagawa as the quintessential intellectual, but, true to his Naturalist school roots, lamented the writer's inability to balance his cerebral machinations with a grounding in lived experience. This critique is very much informed by the suspicion of fiction shared by many in his generation and so tellingly captured in a famous passage by critic Kume Masao:

> To be sure, a Balzac can write a voluminous narrative like *The Human Comedy* and portray his usurers and aristocratic ladies so vividly that they seem to come alive. Yet I cannot but regard such narrative as a fabrication, nor can I place in it the trust I do in even the most off-handed remark the author might make about, say, the difficulties he encountered writing his stories. . . . Tolstoy's *War and Peace*, Dostoevsky's *Crime and Punishment*, and Flaubert's *Madame Bovary* [are] really no more than popular novels. . . . In the final analysis, they are mere fabrications—just so much entertainment.[53]

Hakuchō's reading of Akutagawa is rooted in a similar perspective. He writes of how he enjoyed Akutagawa's "Kumo no ito" (The Spider's Thread, 1918), but adds that it struck him "as but a dream had while dozing in a cozy study warmed by a heater."[54] In other words, the story comes from a standpoint too comfortable, too removed from the complexities and challenges of life lived in the real world. Hakuchō, in fact, labels the story "trite."[55]

Hakuchō does have high praise, however, for one of Akutagawa's stories, "Jigokuhen" (Hell Screen).[56] This tale of ancient Japan features a painter whose lord punishes him by forcing him to witness his own precious daughter's death in a burning carriage, all for the sake of verisimilitude in his art. In that the tale deals with the suffering of an artist, Hakuchō finds in it an allegory for Akutagawa's own struggles. Akutagawa's personal investment, therefore, allows him to attain new heights in this work of fiction: "Akutagawa, who had dealt only with the exposure of common human emotions and paradoxical psychologies, here has seen the shape of human existence stripped of its mask."[57] For literature to reach its full potential it must be an internalized, personal quest, and include the conviction and investment of sincere soul-searching.

This reading of Akutagawa's work, particularly the story "Jigokuhen," suggests that Hakuchō would leave Akutagawa's brand of intellect intact but have it incorporated into an existence in which life and art, analytical capabilities and lived experiences, are in equilibrium. The two poles themselves, however, are accepted by Hakuchō as distinct. As such his critique does not extend to the nature of Akutagawa's analytical approach to the world; it does not question the writer's penchant for the disarticulation of phenomena and the juxtaposition of perspectives in the pursuit of the elusive truth. The intellect born of modernity remains intact in this Naturalist's reading of Akutagawa Ryūnosuke.

A second rejoinder to the question posed by Akutagawa's death came from the newly-arisen Neo-Perceptionist (Shinkankaku-ha) literary movement. As mentioned above, this movement, modernist in nature, appeared in response to the rapid advances in technology and the sweeping changes in landscape and society during the latter half of the 1920s. The swift and incessant pace of transformation altered this group's conception of truth. Member Kataoka Teppei (1894–1944), for example, wrote:

> Of course even the Neo-Perceptionist School recognizes objective truth. However, that objective truth is a truth for but an instant. Therefore the Neo-Perceptionists do not simply use that truth as a starting point. They do not simply start from that truth and return to it. This is because the objective

truth of the moment of departure and the objective truth of the moment of return differ in content.[58]

It was this perspective that the group, represented by Kataoka's "Sakka to shite no Akutagawa-shi" (Akutagawa as an Author, 1927), brought to their understanding of Akutagawa's death.

Like Hakuchō, Kataoka acknowledges the considerable intellectual powers that Akutagawa had brought to bear on his writing. His objection, however, was to Akutagawa's failure to fully pursue his various observations to their conclusions. Instead, Kataoka argues, Akutagawa developed his wit (*kichi*) to serve as "a damper holding in check the explosive nature of the passions. And so, the sharper this wit becomes, the less explosive things are."[59] In Akutagawa's longing for a "balanced, moderate expression,"[60] he reveals his inheritance of the "spirit of the oriental literati" (*tōyōteki bunjin katagi*).[61]

While Hakuchō's objection was to the manner in which Akutagawa's intellect failed to incorporate lived experience, Kataoka's critique is one of degree: a prisoner to aesthetic values of a bygone era, Akutagawa was unwilling or unable to surrender himself fully to the volatile machinations of a mind in the modern world and inevitably pulled himself up short in order to reaffirm a balanced worldview. As was the case with Hakuchō's critique, Kataoka's essay is ultimately rooted in aesthetic concerns. Akutagawa's ultimate assertion of authority over his potentially explosive fictional world, a move Kataoka characterizes as the author suddenly "grinning broadly" or "sneering," is disappointing because it is "crass."[62]

The third and final essay discussed here to contextualize Kobayashi's contribution was generated not on aesthetic grounds but rather from an explicitly ideological standpoint. This essay, perhaps the most famous contemporary critique of Akutagawa, is Marxist critic Miyamoto Kenji's (1908–2007) "Haiboku no bungaku" (The Literature of Defeat, 1927).[63] Proceeding along the conventional lines of Marxist criticism, this essay affirms the supremacy of the modern intellect while simultaneously rejecting its manifestation in Akutagawa, where it has been distorted by social and class factors. To Akutagawa, Miyamoto writes, "knowledge was, first and foremost, his weapon in life. . . . I must emphatically point out the blatant bourgeois narrowness in his 'vast store of knowledge.'"[64] Thus, while Miyamoto does begrudgingly acknowledge Akutagawa's fine intellect, he casts it as one limited by its bourgeois base and distorted by its use as a compensatory "weapon."

Interestingly, in making his point, Miyamoto turns to "Jigokuhen," the same Akutagawa story that Hakuchō had so enthusiastically praised. Whereas Hakuchō had found it powerful for its depiction of the struggles of the artist, Miyamoto believed the story revealed the ultimately untenable stance assumed by this bourgeois writer: Akutagawa could not, even in the fictional world of this story, sustain a commitment to art at all costs, and the story closes with the painter taking his own life. Miyamoto is suggesting that the same was true for Akutagawa the man, and the lesson to be learned is that art must ultimately be sublimated to moral and political agendas.[65]

True to Marxist ideology, Miyamoto expresses a belief in teleological development through the dialectical process. To this end the contradictions in Akutagawa's life—the intellect versus passion, art versus morality/society—had to be resolved:

> Paradoxes are things that can never be resolved unless they are reclaimed through a resolution at a higher plane. The temperamental romantic was in conflict with the realist in terms of a view of life. Like grinding cogwheels, the philosophical skeptic was, of course, eternally working against the political communist. And that is not all. The combination of these various units could not but bestow anxiety and suffering on the position held by Akutagawa, a position in which a balance between the two poles was artificially maintained through the buttressing of the intellect.[66]

Miyamoto sees, then, Akutagawa's brand of intellect, the intellect he developed as a "weapon" with which to overcome his feelings of social inferiority, as a hindrance to the proper dialectical progression of thought. It "artificially" buttresses the contrasting poles of his thought, preventing a true understanding of the world.[67] Here too, as with the other critiques, the nature of Akutagawa's intellect is never questioned. Rather, it is the uses to which it is put that are questioned.

These three critiques, typical of the general discourse treating Akutagawa's suicide as representative of the crisis of the modern intellect, provide a context for appreciating Kobayashi's essay on this author. Like the others, Kobayashi focuses his examination on the nature and application of Akutagawa's intellectual capacities, particularly their relationship to the challenges posed by paradox and contradiction. Unlike these other critiques, however, Kobayashi's concern is *not* ultimately with the aesthetic effect or ideological ramifications of Akutagawa's brand of thought. Instead, it is the nature of the modern intellect itself—thought bound by the demands of Cartesian perspectivalism—that Kobayashi calls into question. As Kubota

Michitarō rightly points out, Kobayashi's critique of Akutagawa is an epistemological one; he questions the very manner in which Akutagawa, and by extension his generation of thinkers, seeks knowledge.[68] The aspects of Akutagawa's intellect that Kobayashi calls into question are, ultimately, all products of the Cartesian perspectivalism that ruled the day. Consequently, the alternative mode of knowing that Kobayashi began to articulate in this 1927 essay on Akutagawa, not surprisingly, evidences many of the traits that distinguish the philosophical systems of Bergson and Nishida from that paradigm as it faltered under the full weight of modernity.

Kobayashi Hideo on Akutagawa and the Paradox

Kobayashi's turn to criticism with his essay on Akutagawa coincides with an intensely tumultuous period in his personal life: the time of his father's untimely death, his mother's illness, and his torturous relationship with Hasegawa Yasuko. He took solace, though, in his study of the French Symbolist poet Jean Arthur Rimbaud (1854–91), whom he discovered when he was a student in the Department of French Literature at Tokyo Imperial University. In Rimbaud, Kobayashi found a compelling articulation of life lived in literary rebellion and at the borders of sanity, things that resonated with Kobayashi's own experiences and literary aspirations. Rimbaud's renown validated an experience of youth that Kobayashi shared. The affinity is perhaps best summed up in a line from Rimbaud's *Alchimie du Verbe*, which Kobayashi quotes in his first essay on the poet: "Then I explained my magical sophisms by the hallucination of words! I ended by finding something sacred in the disorder of my mind."[69]

It was precisely his own personal experience of such a "disorder of [the] mind" that Kobayashi had begun to explore in his fiction, first in "Hitotsu no nōzui" and later in "Onna to Ponkin" (The Woman and Ponkin, 1925), a story that Awazu Norio describes as "the story of a meeting, consisting of communication by language without understanding."[70] In many ways it was Kobayashi's understanding of Rimbaud, an understanding heavily influenced by Symons's *The Symbolist Movement in Literature*, that underpinned his reading of Akutagawa and set his critical agenda.[71] In their differing approaches to the disorientation of the modern mind, Kobayashi found the clues he needed to forge his own literary vision. The general contours of that vision are all present in his essay on Akutagawa.

Kobayashi's "Akutagawa Ryūnosuke no bishin to shukumei" was published in Mushanokōji Saneatsu's journal, *Daichōwa* (Great Harmony), in 1927. This choice of publication venue reflects the manner in which Kobayashi was to respond to the tortured psychology of the "disordered" mind he shared with both Akutagawa and Rimbaud: by reaffirming and resurrecting his initial affinity with the intuitive, harmonious aesthetics of the Shirakaba school. The journal *Daichōwa* was, in fact, Mushanokōji's attempt to revive the spirit of the group's earlier journal, *Shirakaba*, which had closed with the Great Kantō Earthquake. The title of the journal was intended to suggest something of the contributors' longing for the more balanced world that the Shirakaba writers had once offered; as the editors wrote in the first issue: "We will turn from small harmonies (*chiisai chōwa*) to ever greater harmonies (*daichōwa*). . . . By recording as honestly as possible the things we have thought and felt, we hope to touch the hearts of others."[72] Kobayashi's essay on Akutagawa was in keeping with the journal's overall goal. Though he borrows from the romantic vocabulary of his French Symbolist poets, Kobayashi sought to restore harmony to the world through his reading of the tortured Akutagawa.

This literary turn back toward his Taishō/Shirakaba roots was soon to be physically reenacted by Kobayashi. After he abruptly left Hasegawa Yasuko in May 1928, Kobayashi proceeded directly to the Kansai area, where he frequently called on Shiga Naoya at his residence in the city of Nara.[73] It is not surprising that Kobayashi should turn toward Shiga and the Shirakaba ethos at this point in time. As mentioned in the previous chapter, Akutagawa himself had written in "Haguruma" of the comfort he took in reading Shiga's *An'ya kōro*. As his first story, "Tako no jisatsu," suggests, Kobayashi had once been very close to Shiga in terms of literary sensibilities. His second story, the post-earthquake "Hitotsu no nōzui," and the infatuation with Rimbaud, however, attest to how foreign to him those sensibilities had become. This return to Shiga and the Shirakaba-esque, therefore, was to be a very conscious, hard-fought battle to regain a mode of viewing the world that had once been almost natural to him. In other words, Kobayashi would now need a theory of sorts, or a method, and his essay on Akutagawa represents the beginnings of his endeavor to construct just that. It is only by thinking through Cartesian perspectivalism and its collapse in Akutagawa's works that Kobayashi would be able to painstakingly recognize and reconstruct the harmonious simplicity of Shiga.

In that Kobayashi's agenda in his writings on Akutagawa is so much more ambitious than that of Masamune Hakuchō, Kataoka Teppei, and Miyamoto Kenji, his "Akutagawa Ryūnosuke no bishin to shukumei" is far harsher in tone. In order to clear the discursive space for his radical substitution of sensibilities, it is incumbent on Kobayashi to call into question both the significance of Akutagawa's suicide and this writer's status as intellectual par excellence. Concerning the former, Kobayashi writes:

> Suicide—this was one dramatic scene in the life of Akutagawa; it was truly a horrible act. However, it was simply this and nothing more. There is no logical connection between his works and his suicide, and if there was to be something important here, it would be not the suicide itself, but rather the theory behind it. . . . I should like to ignore all the various, neat labels that have been attached to Akutagawa by so many people.[74]

Kobayashi reiterates this sentiment years later in the short postscript he adds to the essay: "I was unable to feel the slightest sympathy or empathy on the occasion of Akutagawa's suicide."[75] Considering Akutagawa's prominence in the literary world of the time and the seriousness with which that community considered his suicide, Kobayashi's rejection of the larger significance of the death is bombastic, iconoclastic. It was probably possible for him to articulate it only because he was still a student beyond even the peripheries of the literary world.

Equally shocking is Kobayashi's repudiation of the writer's status as an intellectual. While figures such as Hakuchō, Kataoka, and Miyamoto had lamented variously the sterility, reservedness, or misdirected nature of Akutagawa's mind, none had gone so far as to unequivocally reject it in its entirety. Kobayashi does just that:

> He is not at all the intellectual writer that people believe him to be. He was a writer who possessed nothing but nerves [*shinkei*]. All of his works, from "Hana" to "Kappa," are primarily the fixing of a paradoxical psychology, yet I have never once felt in his works the passion of the intellect. The excessively nervous and feeble angle from which he looked at life is a fact I believe all too many people have overlooked.[76]

In both his denigration of the suicide and this reduction of Akutagawa's intellect to a jittery conglomeration of nerves, Kobayashi emerges as the harshest critic of Akutagawa in the months immediately following his death. The criticism is perhaps sharpened by the fact that in reducing him to "nerves," Kobayashi is in fact taking Akutagawa at his (fictional) word.[77]

Kobayashi's disparagement of Akutagawa's intellect is based largely on how the writer dealt with the matter of paradox, the true test for the intellect in Kobayashi's mind. In his concern for the paradox—those statements that seem to run contrary to logic and yet be true all the same—Kobayashi is taking a path trod by Bergson. As discussed above, Bergson's important conception of duration was rooted in his examination of Zeno's paradox of Achilles pursuing the tortoise. For his part, Kobayashi turns to a mathematical metaphor, explaining that the true paradox appears as a "remainder" after we have worked our "computations" on life. If, after we have genuinely struggled to fully account for everything, that remainder lingers, the paradox is a genuine one. The example Kobayashi gives is from scripture: "Blessed are the poor in spirit" (*kokoro no mazushiki mono wa saiwai nari*). Wrestling with these true paradoxes can, Kobayashi warns, drive one to the brink of suicide.[78]

Although he shows great respect for the challenges presented by such genuine paradoxes, Kobayashi insists that most often these challenges to the mind are nothing more than chimeras born of a disingenuous disarticulation of phenomena. In this objection we find echoes of Bergson, who resolved the paradox of Achilles chasing the tortoise by insisting that it was simply the parsing of the race into disparate moments that generated the paradox. Considered over the course of its duration, it becomes clear that Achilles will soon move to the forefront. Kobayashi locates in Akutagawa a similarly fallacious disarticulation. Rather than encounter the paradox as an irrefutable "remainder," Kobayashi writes, Akutagawa goes actively in search of such incongruities, approaching life with

> paradoxical antennae. . . . He attempts to view the flow of a continuously changing reality from each and every angle; he tries to analytically break down reality into a stage and what goes on behind that stage. As the collection of the various paradoxical landscapes he has discovered grows richer, as it grows increasingly exquisite, he has the illusion that he is approaching reality. Reality, however, without fail, eludes him.[79]

This representation of the technique Akutagawa employs in his fiction is accurate, and it reflects the manner in which he was exploring the very limits of Cartesian perspectivalism. Kobayashi does not mention a particular Akutagawa work here, perhaps because so many seem to fit the description. "Yabu no naka" (In a Bamboo Grove, 1921) is a fine example. This story, made famous in the West through director Kurosawa Akira's adaptation in the film *Rashōmon*, explores a murder through a juxtaposition of four "testimonies" (by a woodcutter, an itinerant Buddhist monk, a constable, and an old woman) and two confessions (one by the murderer and one by the wife of the victim). Even the perspective of the murdered man is included, related through the mouth of a spiritual medium.[80] The result is a disturbing indeterminacy in which the truth does indeed elude us.

Kobayashi's objection to the Cartesian disarticulation of phenomena evident in Akutagawa's works is echoed in various parts of the essay. In his mistaken efforts, Kobayashi writes, Akutagawa "attempts to solidify reality in all its component parts; he attempts to freeze life at each and every point in its progression."[81] Elsewhere in the same essay he writes, "With his nerves Akutagawa broke life down into minuscule parts."[82] Five years later, in his "Gyakusetsu to iu mono ni tsuite" (On the Paradox, 1932), Kobayashi returned to the issue. In contrast to Akutagawa's somehow smug, analytical use of the concept in a teleological framework, Kobayashi insists that "at the root of the true paradox there must always be brutally frank observation; there must be a piercing wisdom that intuits an indivisible reality. A paradox is not something to be toyed with; it arises naturally. It is the straightforward expression of an analyst who has sincerely explored a changing reality, taking into account all of its changes."[83]

Kobayashi here reiterates both his rejection of a Cartesian dismantling of the whole (his evocation of an "indivisible reality" [*warikirenai genjitsu*]) and his objection to the reduction of a dynamic reality to a static form. In both of these objections to the Cartesian perspectivalism ruling modernity's intellect, Kobayashi reveals his affinity with the alternatives explored by both Bergson and Nishida.

Kobayashi also shares with these thinkers dissatisfaction with the incessant pursuit of deployable knowledge at the sacrifice of all else. The prioritizing of such knowledge is all part of the ocularcentric worldview; sight, in a most literal sense, allows us to see what the future will bring, and the epistemologies rooted in the metaphor of sight are therefore intimately linked with knowledge that will allow us to deal with that future, that is, deployable knowledge. Though Akutagawa stretches the boundaries of this paradigm to its breaking point by introducing mutually exclusive yet equally trustworthy perspectives, at a deeper level he is still beholden to it. "Yabu no naka," for example, is engaging precisely because the reader wants to "solve the case," to reach a conclusion. Though ultimately frustrated, the reader wants to resolve the paradoxes. The appeal of Akutagawa's story is predicated on precisely this desire to synthesize the disarticulated parts.

Kobayashi, however, would have us regard the paradox in a completely different fashion. The epigraph with which he opens "Gyakusetsu to iu mono ni tsuite" expresses this alternative: "Do not speculate with the intention of reaching a conclusion. That is the hidden essence of speculation."[84] In this sense, Kobayashi's veneration of the paradox parallels his glorification of the intellectually impenetrable materiality discussed in Chapter 1. By restoring each to an impenetrable whole, Kobayashi short-circuits modern man's hypertrophied capacity to dissect and interpret, and through this process restores man's capacity to feel.

In Kobayashi's reading Akutagawa is unable to embrace the true paradoxes of a holistic, dynamic reality, and it is for this reason that Kobayashi rejects him as the representative intellectual of the age. Although grappling with the immensity of the challenge presented to the rational mind by the paradox would have left Akutagawa quite properly at his wit's end, Kobayashi insists, this writer "has never lamented over this psychological frailty. For him the contemplation of a paradox has not been an endless flagellation. Instead, he has sanitized it. [For Akutagawa, paradox] was not a matter of intellectual passion; it was a twitching of his nerves."[85] In this way, based on Akutagawa's handling of the paradox, Kobayashi rejects his status as the modern intellectual.

This harsh denunciation of Akutagawa's reputation was almost certainly fueled as much by Kobayashi's awareness of how easily he himself could have followed Akutagawa's path as it was by purely literary and intellectual concerns. This awareness is suggested by Kobayashi's portrayal of his alter ego in the autobiographical story "Tako no jisatsu" (discussed in Chapter 2). Here he expressed his dissatisfaction with his own penchant for precisely the sort of analysis that had made Akutagawa famous: "Kenkichi felt the anger welling up in him as he realized his same old habit was once again rearing its ugly head—in spite of the fact that he would always end up mentally piecing together some sort of half-baked conclusion, still he would insist, for some odd reason, on skeptically picking everything apart and turning it over and over in his head before being satisfied."[86]

This aspect of his own personality was one that had only intensified due to the earthquake and his personal trials and tribulations. It also reflected his generation's growing dissatisfaction with Cartesian perspectivalism. Unlike the critics of Akutagawa introduced above, Kobayashi's solution as proposed in this essay entailed not a balancing of the modern intellect, not an amplification of it, not an ideological harnessing of it; Kobayashi proposed instead a complete reassessment of what it means to "know." In writing of his mode of knowing here and elsewhere, Kobayashi co-opted the very metaphor that he was rebelling against. He wrote of true knowledge as being possible only by the act of "seeing."

The Act of "Seeing"

Formulated in reaction to the faltering ocularcentric epistemology, Kobayashi's act of "seeing" shares much with the thought of others working in that same vein, and the idea might even owe something to the pioneering work of Henri Bergson. Like Nishida Kitarō, Kobayashi was almost certainly reading Bergson when he was still a student. Ōoka Shōhei, whom Kobayashi tutored for a time, claims that Kobayashi was speaking of Bergson as early as 1928.[87] This is not at all surprising for a student graduating from a French literature department in the very same year (1928) that Bergson won the Nobel Prize in Literature. Though by all accounts Kobayashi was reading French with ease by that time, he could also have perused the French philosopher in his native tongue: a Japanese translation of *Matter and Memory* (1896), by the aforementioned Takahashi Satomi, had been published in 1914.[88] That Bergson's philosophy was very much on his mind at that time is suggested by the title Kobayashi gave to a series of essays contributed to *Bungei shunjū* in 1930: "Ashiru to kame no ko" (Achilles and the Baby Tortoise), a reference to Bergson's beloved paradox, introduced above.[89] Though written much later in his career, there are also the 56 installments of Kobayashi's ultimately discontinued "Kansō" (Impressions), a study of Bergson published in the journal *Shinchō* between 1958 and 1963.[90]

The links between Kobayashi and Bergson are introduced here not so much in an effort to trace direct lines of influence as to suggest that Kobayashi, like Nishida, was participating in the wider discourse concerning the faltering but still dominant ocularcentric scientific paradigm. As this worldview stretched its tentacles even into non-scientific fields (history, literature), thinkers of a certain disposition reacted. Kobayashi was one such thinker. His particular understanding of the limitations of the scientific paradigm that held sway even in the literary circles of his time, and his reactions to them, are a central concern of this study. They will be revisited time and time again: Kobayashi's prioritizing of the particular over the universal will be part of the discussion of "Samazama naru ishō" in Chapter 4; his revalorization of time over space (introduced in Chapter 1 through Kobayashi's idea of memory) will be revisited in the analysis of his historical consciousness in Chapter 5; his distaste for "disarticulation," in addition to the discussion above, will be further explored in his writings on the war as introduced in Chapter 6.

The remainder of this chapter, however, is dedicated to examining the manner in which his attack on ocularcentrism took the form of an epistemology based on, ironically, the act of "seeing." His notion of "seeing" was, of course, not an affirmation of Cartesian perspectivalism, but rather his metaphor for an ideal encounter with the world that shared many traits with Bergson's intuition and Nishida's pure experience. In it we find the conflation of subject and object, the recorporealization of the cognitive subject, and an accent on the experience itself over any insights (that is, deployable knowledge) it may yield. All of these are attributes of the epistemological revolution promulgated by Bergson and Nishida as well.

The most memorable early usage of the metaphor of "seeing" in Kobayashi's work is found in this essay on Akutagawa. After vehemently rejecting the "intellect" that Akutagawa represented and that so many of his contemporaries had accepted, Kobayashi advocated his alternative epistemology. Here he associates it with the arts, but in the following years he would expand its domain to include all modes of knowing:

> What I believe is that all art can be exhaustively described with the single verb "to see." The most moving experience for the artist is seeing the world just as it is. . . . To see things just as they are is, in the end, nothing other than to view the object with the desirable humility of self-effacement. What we mean when we speak of the reality of a text is that which is transcribed by the passion of such moments.
>
> Akutagawa is an author who most definitely did not execute this act of seeing. For him life existed exclusively as a function of his nerves. He dissected life through the use of his nerves.[91]

Kobayashi's act of "seeing" is clearly not that which informs Cartesian perspectivalism. His emphasis on the need for "the desirable humility of self-effacement" (*nozomashii bōga no kenjō*), an act that erases the subject/object dichotomy so central to the Cartesian mode of knowing, indicates the extent of his diversion from that method. The passage also implies a surrender of a conscious agency (such as that exercised by Akutagawa) parsing reality into its component parts in hopes of gaining insight into its workings. Furthermore, Kobayashi's insistence that the "reality" (*genjitsusei*) of a text is the product of a fleeting moment of involuntary insight suggests that such "realities" are dynamic and ever changing.

"Seeing," to Kobayashi, is an involuntary, intuitive leap of the imagination. In the paragraphs that follow he expands on the nature of this act, portraying it in terms of the relationship between an artist's "destiny" and "muse": "Though one can manipulate the images one thinks up [*shisaku suru*], one cannot do a thing about those images that appear like a star on the horizon of our consciousness. From there one must then move forward by inventing theories and being invented by them. When I speak of the destiny [*shukumei*] of an author, I am referring to this spiritual destiny."[92]

Here Kobayashi contrasts the images that one "thinks up" with those that "appear" in our consciousness. The implication here, too, is that agency—volition—must be surrendered if we are to move beyond superficial intellectual manipulation into something grander: a flash of insight. The artist is left, then, with no choice but to grapple with abstract formulations ("theories," or *riron*) in its articulation.

Though it is an artist's destiny to struggle with abstract formulations of his insight, Kobayashi's act of "seeing" is by no means entirely a matter of theoretical musings. It is inextricably tied to what he terms the "muse" (*bishin*), a component of the natural world that gives "substance" (*jisshitsu*) to theory. These two currents, a theoretical "destiny" and a concrete "muse," pulse like "an alternating current" through the artist. Although the relationship between the two currents varies according to personal dispositions and artistic mediums, Kobayashi tells us, the writer is best served by moving from theory to substance.[93] In short, the trajectory is away from the abstract and ever toward the particular, a facet of Kobayashi's thought that has parallels in the philosophies of both Bergson and Nishida. Akutagawa Ryūnosuke's failing, Kobayashi concludes, was that he wandered aimlessly between these two poles.

Kobayashi's reading of Akutagawa in this early essay remains in the realm of the abstract. Though he does mention a number of specific works, nowhere does Kobayashi explicate precisely where Akutagawa's "nerves" inhibit his ability to "see." For a more concrete analysis of Akutagawa's fiction, we must turn to Kobayashi's 1941 essay "Rekishi to bungaku" (History and Literature), in which he compares the portrait of Nogi Maresuke (1849–1912) in Akutagawa's short story "Shōgun" (The General) to a biography of this same military man written by *Chicago Daily News* war correspondent Stanley Washburn.[94] Nogi, who served in both the Sino-Japanese War (1894–95) and Russo-Japanese War (1904–05), is best remembered for having led the bloody but ultimately successful seven-month siege of Port Arthur and for his ritual suicide (*junshi*), in which his wife accompanied him, after the death of the Emperor Meiji in 1912.[95] Writing of a military hero like Nogi, even if only peripherally, in 1941 meant Kobayashi had to keep Japan's wartime censorship in mind. Nevertheless, his comments reveal not only something further about his notion of "seeing," but also suggest a manner in which it is related to the Kobayashi quest, discussed in Chapter 1, to restore an impenetrable surface to materiality.

In "Rekishi to bungaku" Kobayashi writes that though he found Akutagawa's story interesting when he first read it as a student, he found it not at all so when he read it again later in life, because he could no longer appreciate the writer's attitude toward his subject:

> Although one can assume that the author had mixed emotions in his writing of "Shōgun," it is clear that he intended to object to the public's idea of Nogi the Hero by portraying instead Nogi the Man. This intention is obvious in the piece. Although the public was excited about this hero, Akutagawa believed that detached observation would reduce the hero to nothing but an ordinary man. To this end Akutagawa depicts the brutal, monomaniacal look in General Nogi's eyes as enemy spies are being executed, and portrays a scene in which the General is moved to tears by a silly play about armed robbery performed by the troops out in the field. However, this sort of dissection is, in the end, not so very different from a discussion of General Nogi's weight. The more the author forces his manipulations [*gikō*], the more General Nogi appears not as the ordinary man that the author intended, but rather as a caricature [*ponchi-e*].[96]

Kobayashi's characterization of the story is accurate. Akutagawa's satire of the beloved general, a national icon, was so sharp that in spite of the fact that he refrained from mentioning the general by name, the authorities insisted on inserting *fuseji*, meaningless characters, in an act of censorship of various "objectionable" sections of the story.[97]

More important to us here, however, is Kobayashi's appraisal of the method and effects of the story. In this critique of a specific Akutagawa work, we see Kobayashi identifying many concrete examples of his general complaints about this author and his method. What Kobayashi had identified as Akutagawa's tendency to "analytically break down reality into a stage and what goes on behind that stage" manifests itself in this story as the author's attempt to reveal the ordinary man behind the public's image of a hero. Kobayashi had faulted Akutagawa for his penchant for "paradoxical psychologies."[98] This manifests itself in "Shōgun" in a brutal Nogi witnessing executions juxtaposed with a childlike Nogi moved to tears by a sentimental play staged by the troops. This technique, the "dissection" of a whole into its component parts, is a product of the Cartesian thinking to which Kobayashi objects.

How, then, does Akutagawa's story compare with Washburn's book? In Kobayashi's eyes, Washburn's book is far superior:

> While the book is not a biography proper, but rather a series of reminiscences, I felt that the image [*menboku*] of the man called Nogi was vividly depicted. I imagine that there are probably many sorts of biographies written on General Nogi, but I felt that surely there are few in which the man is portrayed in the lifelike manner of this work. . . .
>
> Although Washburn's book is a simple recollection and not one that exercises a particularly observant eye, by no means does it overlook the monomaniacal look in General Nogi's eyes or his childlike simplicity. Washburn does write of how the General's face, which was like an iron mask when he was poring over a map or issuing orders to a subordinate, would turn joyous as that of a hand puppet [*ponchi ningyō*] when his poetry was praised. However, this book differs greatly from Akutagawa's work in that the author perceives the extraordinary tragedy that General Nogi, a man possessed of an extraordinary spiritual strength, had to perform, and he sees all aspects in light of this perception. The difference is that Washburn does not forget this fact and consequently fumble around with something like the "human nature" of General Nogi.[99]

The operant term in this passage is "image." The word in Japanese is *menboku* (or, alternatively, *menmoku*), which indicates one's public persona, one's reputation, or one's visage or countenance.[100] All of these meanings point to the surface of the man Nogi; they preclude precisely the sort of disarticulation that Cartesian perspectivalism relies upon. Kobayashi's "seeing," then, is a manner of perception that insists on both maintaining a certain distance and preserving the holistic unity of the whole. Only then can an intuitive appreciation of the whole be worked.

Not surprisingly, this ability to "see" that Kobayashi finds so lacking in Akutagawa is a distinguishing characteristic of the author Kobayashi most respects: Shiga Naoya. Furthermore, Shiga's ability to "see" is, to Kobayashi, predicated on an epistemology distinctly at odds with that promoted by the sciences, indebted as they are to the dominant strain of Cartesian thinking. In this schematic, Kobayashi contrasts "scientific" realism with Shiga's mode of "seeing":

> It goes without saying that the techniques of realism developed under the influence of the advances in science. Just as science consistently sees realities as primed for disassembly into their component parts, so too does the literature of realism view the world as ever ready to be dissected into elemental linguistic ingredients. This belief is an unwitting abuse of science; it is a deluded piece of wishful thinking.[101]

Here Kobayashi explicitly links the realism that constitutes the mainstream of his literary moment with the sciences and their proclivity for disarticulation. A stark contrast to this method is the holistic approach evinced by Shiga, an approach that travels in a trajectory toward the particular rather than the universals so beloved of science:

> People speak of the beauty of Shiga's depictions of nature. Such beauty can only be evoked by a writer in whom observation and emotional reaction move in perfect accord. For the thing observed to assume an immutable and singular aura of reality, it must be dyed in the emotion unique to the observer at that instant. In this act we find the healthy experience of the world that gave rise to the epic.[102]

The mode of observation that Kobayashi attributes here to Shiga is one he had explored in his earlier essay on this writer. In that piece he had explained it specifically through a visual metaphor that illuminates the nature of the act of "seeing" that Kobayashi identifies with Shiga:

> I am not afraid of any so-called keen eye [*keigan*]. What people mean when they speak of "keen eyes" are eyes that, rather than being able only to view a certain thing from a single angle, are able to look at things from a variety of perspectives. . . . I've never been flustered by a keen eye focused on me. At the very most a keen eye is able to recognize my lies. What horrifies me, though, are eyes that *see* without at all trying to *look*, eyes that do not need to decide an angle from which to view, eyes that defy our attempts to ascertain their standpoint. Shining at the core of all Shiga's works are such eyes.[103]

Clearly Kobayashi perceives the disarticulation of reality (Akutagawa's forte) as a legacy of the scientific worldview, and he compares it unfavorably with an "act of seeing" that transcends Cartesian perspectivalism. "Seeing" in this passage is clearly the exercise of an intuitive apprehension.

The approach Kobayashi is forging in his reading of Akutagawa entails first rendering the object an impenetrable materiality, a polished surface too slick to dissect. The perceiving subject, on the other hand, must nurture his or her "destiny," the insights that appear to him "like a star on the horizon of . . . consciousness." Once such distance has been reestablished (for in the post-earthquake world the categories have blurred), it is possible for the poles to merge in that holistic, largely involuntary act of seeing.

The Roots and Articulations of "Seeing"

Though Kobayashi's rebellion against Cartesian perspectivalism begins with the 1927 essay "Akutagawa Ryūnosuke no bishin to shukumei" and is refined through his later essays on Akutagawa and Shiga, the idea of "seeing" appears in a wide variety of contexts in Kobayashi's oeuvre. It was so integral to Kobayashi's critical method that he chose to feature it prominently in his 1949 essay "Watakushi no jinseikan" (My View of Life).[104] In this essay Kobayashi turns his attention to the meaning of the character *kan* (観) translated in the title as "view" but with an original meaning of "to see." He traces the Buddhist roots of the word, which he claims gives it its unique Japanese nuance:

> "Zen" means to "think" or "speculate." "Zenkan" means to see that which one has speculated on. So, Buddhist meditation is not simply an epistemology. Deep within man's consciousness, thinking and seeing must be the same. In order to attain a consciousness in which mind and body are in perfect accord [*shinshin sōō*], one must train in conflating the two.[105]

The exercise is that of "seeing" with one's mind as well as with one's eyes. This act, then, stands in opposition to the fully cerebral approach of a writer like Akutagawa, an approach that attempts to comprehend analytically. Kobayashi's "seeing" merges the interiority of thought with the exteriority of sight. It is both an ideologically neutral, physical act as well as an intuitive, non-analytical mode of comprehension.

Kobayashi further distinguishes his act of seeing from the usual sense of the word by quoting the famous swordsman and popular hero Miyamoto Musashi (1584?–1645) on the same subject. Summarizing Miyamoto's instructions to a swordsman, Kobayashi writes:

> When one is to do battle and fixes the eyes on the opponent, one must emphasize the eyes that see and weaken the eyes that look. According to Miyamoto, the eyes that look are our ordinary ones, those for common use. They

are the eyes that analytically and intellectually appraise the movements of the opponent. However, there are other eyes, eyes that intuit [*chokkaku suru*] the existence of the opponent in his entirety. . . . Musashi claims that eyes like these are such that "though the enemy draws near, he is seen as if far away." Our everyday eyes attempt to look; they are "infused with intention but untouched by the soul." There are, however, also eyes at work when the heart is not driven by such desires. . . . The desire to look clouds the vision. It is for this reason that Miyamoto admonishes us to emphasize the eyes that see and weaken the eyes that look.[106]

Through this invocation of Miyamoto Musashi, Kobayashi is emphasizing the need to "intuit" the significance of things in their "entirety," as opposed to the desire to analyze pieces of a whole. This section also raises the related issue of distance: "though the enemy draws near, he is seen as if far away." This maintenance of distance is essential if one is to resist the temptation to disarticulate phenomena and analyze components rather than the whole.[107]

Kobayashi's idea of "seeing" does indeed seem to draw heavily on the Buddhist, particularly Zen Buddhist, tradition. Kyoto school philosopher Nishitani Keiji points this out, and celebrates Kobayashi's reintroduction of the idea into Japan, going so far as to suggest that Bergson himself may have been indebted to that tradition.[108] Kobayashi does not, however, tie his epistemology to some uniquely Japanese or Asian tradition. In fact, scholars such as Yokota Shun'ichi have traced Kobayashi's formulation of this idea to the French Symbolist poet Jean Arthur Rimbaud, on whom Kobayashi published three essays, one of them preceding even his early essay on Akutagawa.[109] This claim is not without merit; as Martin Jay points out, literary movements in Europe straining against the restrictions of an ocularcentric naturalism in the 1920s also turned to Rimbaud as an inspiration for "self-conscious sensual derangement and the suppression of the mundane, rational ego."[110] Similarly motivated, Kobayashi naturally found Rimbaud inspirational, particularly for the latter elements. Kobayashi would himself later emphasize the impact this poet had had on him. In a much-quoted passage from his third essay on Rimbaud, published in 1947, Kobayashi described the initial encounter in the following way:

It was during the spring of my twenty-third year that I first encountered Rimbaud. I might mention that at the time I was meandering through Kanda. A man I did not recognize, coming the other way, suddenly knocked me to the ground. I was totally unprepared. I had never dreamed that such a powerful explosive could be contained in that beat-up little Mercure edition of *Une*

Saison un Enfer that I stumbled on in front of a bookstore. The detonator on this explosive was so sensitive that even my shaky language skills did not pose a problem. That little book exploded gloriously, and for a number of years thereafter I remained within the event known as "Rimbaud."[111]

The passage evocatively captures the type of literary encounter that Kobayashi always sought: an event (*jiken*) powerful in a visceral rather than cerebral sense.

Still, Kobayashi's essays on Rimbaud are more important for the texture they lend his conception of "seeing" than for the evidence they provide of some direct intellectual or literary influence. More than a method to be appropriated, Rimbaud provided inspiration, a vocabulary, and a fertile testing ground for Kobayashi's formation of a literary vision that would transcend the boundaries of Cartesian perspectivalism. Absolutely irreducible to a cogent analysis, Rimbaud's life and poetry served as a springboard for musings on alternative modes of knowing.

From his first essay on the poet, Kobayashi was experimenting with the idea of "seeing" as the largely involuntary and fortuitous synthesis of "destinies" and "muses." He who would achieve the genius of a Rimbaud, he writes, must first fill himself with intelligence and passion. Then, to create, he must "have his eyes wide open like the idiot or the sleepwalker. His eyes must be those of one lost in prayer. The reason for this is that when he attempts to confirm the face of his destiny, the muse slips away."[112] This appropriation and reconfiguration of the visual metaphor and the relinquishing of volition, two tropes that figure prominently in the essay on Akutagawa, are expounded here in the context of Rimbaud.

Our understanding of Kobayashi's concept of "seeing" is also enhanced by considering it in light of Rimbaud's famous "lettre du voyant" (Letter of the Seer, 1871), which Kobayashi translates in his final essay on the poet:

The poet makes himself *voyant* by *a long, immense, and calculated derailment of all the senses.* All the forms of love and suffering and madness—he seeks himself and exhausts in himself all the poisons, keeping only the quintessences. Unspeakable torture, in which he needs all the faith, all the superhuman strength, by which he becomes the great invalid, the great criminal, the great pariah, above all others—and the supreme Savant!—For he attains the *unknown*! Since he has cultivated his soul, which was rich to start with, more than anyone else! He reaches the unknown, and if, finally overwhelmed, he turns out to lose the meaning of his visions, at least he has seen them! Let him die in his surge through things unheard of and beyond naming: other horrible workers will come after him and begin at the horizons where he sank back![113]

It is easy to imagine how this romantic vision of the poet as seer would have appealed to Kobayashi during his university days: the painful loss of his father, the pressing financial concerns, and the tempestuous relationship with Hasegawa Yasuko—"all the forms of love and suffering and madness"—would have been easier to bear if viewed as nurturing his literary soul.

This passage includes ideas that Kobayashi incorporated in his epistemology, most significantly the belief that the greatest insights are, ultimately, an infinitely personal experience and largely incommunicable to others. Though the poet may "lose the meaning of his visions"—which is to say that they cannot be articulated in the universal language of reason—he nevertheless has the comfort of at least having seen them. By quoting this passage from Rimbaud, Kobayashi is asserting that it is the experience of "seeing" itself, rather than the insights gleaned from it, that is of the utmost importance. In this sense, too, Kobayashi sides with both Bergson, who derided meanings as but "artificial reconstructions" of the original insight, and Nishida, who found judgments "meager in content" in comparison to the "pure experience" itself.

Kobayashi explores the ramifications of Rimbaud's poetic practice most fully in this final essay, and the conclusions he draws apply as much to his own work as they do to Rimbaud's: "What he saw was so distant from the rest of us that no language he invented could communicate it to us. No matter what sense he turned to for help, he could not make us perceive as he did. . . . What he collided with was not the 'outside world' but rather the essence of the riddle that was his own humanity."[114] Perhaps more than any other expression of the act of "seeing," these lines reveal the intimately personal nature of the insight. To express it in terms easily understood by others would be to compromise its glorious specificity. The only task it is feasible to undertake, therefore, is an exploration of the subjectivity that had experienced that moment of clarity. The ultimate "riddle" faced by the seer, then, is that of his or her own humanity.

Kobayashi saw his own critical practice in much the same terms. In his own famous definition of the practice, Kobayashi wrote: "Criticism is the act of narrating the self; it is the act of using the literary work of another as the material with which to narrate the self."[115] This approach to critical praxis roots Kobayashi firmly in what might be called the Augustinian camp of the epistemological divide initiated by Descartes's *cogito ergo sum*. While this grounding of the self prompted some to look with confidence on the external world and map its contours, others found in it inspiration for self-reflection. (As discussed earlier in this chapter, Martin Jay describes this lineage as "identitarian reflexivity.") This turn to introspection is something that distinguished most of the reactions to Cartesian perspectivalism that emerged in the early twentieth century. Of Nishida Kitarō, for example, James W. Heisig writes: "all questions of logic and metaphysics had to answer to the fundamental question of illuminating the self."[116] The same might be said for Kobayashi Hideo. His "studies" of geniuses from Rimbaud and Dostoevsky to Motoori Norinaga and Mozart are, true to his own conception of critical practice, largely narrations of his own subjectivity in its responses and reactions to the stimuli provided by these artistic geniuses. In fact, Kobayashi's conflation of himself with the object of his criticism is so marked that his work has often been referred to as "I-criticism."

Criticism and the Narration of Self

Kobayashi's reaction to the faltering Cartesian perspectivalism of his age took the form of an embrace of critical practice as a means of exploring first and foremost the workings of one's own subjectivity. His dedication to the practice and proliferation of such criticism, based as it was on the act of "seeing," represents the birth of a genuinely new epistemology for Shōwa Japan. Critic Etō Jun writes:

> It is not that there were no critics before Kobayashi Hideo. The point is that there were no self-conscious [*jikakuteki*] critics before him. By "self-conscious" I mean being aware of the fact that the act of criticism is tied to questions of one's own existence. What existed before Kobayashi's appearance was a long history of healthy Enlightenment thought, and what emerged at the moment that Kobayashi fell silent was a new breed of Enlightenment thinker, weakened by their adoption of Kobayashi's lexicon. In short, Kobayashi invented a criticism and raised it to the level of artistic expression. At the same time, he destroyed Enlightenment thought.[117]

Etō is right to point out both the ultimately introverted nature of Kobayashi's project and, ironically, its ramifications for the entirety of critical discourse. Once he had introduced a literary or aesthetic mode of knowing as an alternative to the pursuit of the "disinterested, monologic, epistemic truth," as Jay describes the holy grail of ocularcentric thinking, the literary and intellectual system as a whole was irrevocably changed. The Enlightenment project with its pursuit of deployable knowledge at the expense of all else was no longer the single, undisputed epistemology; there were alternatives.

The shift worked by Kobayashi, however, was not without its dangers. Karatani Kōjin identifies what is perhaps the most significant of them: a lack of genuine "intercourse" (*kōtsū*, a translation of the German *Verkher*, a concept taken from Marx) with anything beyond the narrow confines of his own consciousness. Quoting from Kobayashi's "Marukusu no Gotatsu" (The Insight of Marx, 1931), Karatani Kōjin writes:

> "Marx began with an understanding of society and proceeded to understand the self. One might say that Dosteovsky, on the other hand, followed the reverse course. These two masters always appear to me as intertwined." While these two people may *appear* to be of equal value to Kobayashi, it is inconceivable that between them he would choose Marx. To Kobayashi a self-understanding—or, to put it another way, a process beginning with an analysis of one's own consciousness and only then moving to "materiality" or "society"—was for him the alpha and omega of criticism.[118]

Karatani goes on to make the point that while Kobayashi's readings of Western writers are often brilliant, and while this represents a genuine act of intercourse with the foreign, the system that emerges after Kobayashi's critical practice is instituted as system precludes just such fortuitous and genuine moments of intercourse with the unfamiliar. Karatani's critique is, of course, linked to the point noted above in the general discussion of reactions to Cartesian perspectivalism: the focus on the ultimately incommunicable particularity of intuitive insight, pure experience, or "seeing" is in constant danger of falling into solipsism.

Other writers shared Kobayashi's distrust of the worldview emerging from Cartesianism and managed to avoid this solipsism, though at a price. The most prominent example is Yasuda Yojūrō and other writers affiliated with the journals *Cogito* and *Nihon rōman-ha* (Japan Romantics). While Kobayashi had objected to the Cartesian disarticulation of phenomena, he did not explicitly launch a critique of this philosopher; the Japan Romantics, on the other hand, were quite consciously rethinking the subjectivity born of Descartes's famous dictum, as the title of their first journal suggests.[119] The explicit identification of this source of modern subjectivity led the Japan Romantics in a different direction. As Kevin Doak notes:

> The *Cogito* group saw Descartes's formula of the knowing subject as the epistemological and existential origin of all forms of modern identity and criticized it for excluding a Japanese identity grounded in native sensibilities. These writers saw the Cartesian Ego as an historically and culturally specific construct and sought to go beyond it to something akin to what Rabinow and Sullivan have more recently called "a reality before and behind the cultural world to which that world can be reduced."[120]

Kobayashi shared with the Romantics this nostalgia for "a reality before and behind the cultural world to which that world can be reduced." This yearning took the form of his quest for a stable materiality beneath the "endless clutter of things and events that have changed too quickly," discussed in Chapter 1. The difference, however, is that Kobayashi did not indulge this desire by positing a unique Japanese identity that would yield immediate access to it. Instead, he worked always at the level of the individual genius, and found inspiration in figures from both native and foreign traditions. His "I-criticism" is a reflection of this focus on the individual.

Yasuda and the Japan Romantics, in keeping with their belief that the Cartesian Ego was historically and culturally specific, worked instead to forge a collective subjectivity based on the "non-knowledge" (*muchi*) of the Japanese people. This epistemology was, as Doak notes, mobilized as "a functional equivalent (and therefore as a negation) of Western knowledge (*chisei*)."[121] While this trajectory parallels the development of Kobayashi's thinking in many respects, the crucial difference was that Yasuda and the Japan Romantics were thinking in collective terms (nation, ethnic unity, race), a fact that made it impossible for them to sustain what was initially an ironic vision of an alternate modernity. In the end, as Doak convincingly argues, "the tragic irony of the Romantic School gives way to farce and the triumph of myopia." Furthermore, in the case of Yasuda, "the emphasis on irony as a form of negative praxis proved impossible to reconcile with any concrete form of social or political intervention and was transformed from a promising critical practice to a latent desire for total culture and, finally, to an aesthetics of death as the ultimate form of totality."[122]

Though Kobayashi brushed up against a similar ideology, he was able to avoid being completely enveloped by it.[123] The reason he was so empowered is intimately linked to his fierce dedication to the machinations of the *individual* subjectivity. In his dedication to "I-criticism" Kobayashi may have suffered from a myopia of his own, but it was one that enabled him to rebel against the Cartesian modern world without succumbing entirely to the fascistic totalism of a thinker like Yasuda.

Not coincidentally, Kobayashi also shared with the Romantics a preference for the (poetic) critical essay over stories and novels. Though his interest in poetry was exercised in the form of critique and translation rather than in composition itself (at least in the conventional sense), Kobayashi's critical mode, like Yasuda's, was infused with poetic locutions and inspirations.[124] Kobayashi's gradual turn to criticism may be linked to two conditions of his literary and cultural moment. First, on a personal level, Kobayashi found himself after the earthquake in a commodified world that had so diminished what Benjamin termed the "aura" of a literary work that, even had Kobayashi been able to reproduce the Shiga-esque sensibility he so admired, his efforts would not have been read that way. The world around him had turned increasingly toward the subjectivity of someone like Hirotsu Kazuo, whose 1919 essay on Shiga had succeeded in penetrating beneath the harmonious surface of that writer's work to parse it into component parts, even while acknowledging the appeal of the whole. In addition to restoring his own Shiga-esque sensibilities, Kobayashi had to engender in the contemporary audience a mode of reading conducive to that worldview. This mission was best carried out in the genre of criticism.

A second condition that spurred Kobayashi deeper into criticism as opposed to other genres is a structural one. As theoretical and critical methodologies had increasingly encroached on the world of fiction, the only recourse must have seemed to lie in bringing the intimately literary and poetic into the genre of criticism. Kobayashi's epistemological revolution was, therefore, an "inside job," worked from within the borders of the genre most indebted to the intellect he was rebelling against. His notion of "seeing" as an intuitive alternative to the Cartesian perspectivalism so deeply embedded not only in criticism, but in fiction as well was the lever he used to challenge the status quo. Quite naturally this agenda first found articulation in the discourse pondering the significance of Akutagawa Ryūnosuke's suicide, a discourse that acknowledged the "impotence of the intellect" and sought alternatives.

FOUR

The Inescapable "Designs"

Through his early engagement with Shiga and Akutagawa, Kobayashi began to reconstitute the subjectivity/materiality system of the early Shōwa period. The next step in his development as a thinker and critic was to propogate this system. He pursued this mission through an engagement with the theory that most aggressively pursued the disarticulation of cultural phenomena into its component parts and ideological motivations: Marxism. Marxist literature and criticism dominated the Japanese world of letters through the late 1920s and into the early 1930s. The movement gained much of its momentum from the perception that it was the rightful offspring of the methods of the natural sciences (these, in turn, being based in epistemologies inspired by a visual metaphor for cognition, as discussed in the previous chapter). Kobayashi worked to curb the influence of Marxist thought by relentlessly problematizing its most basic assumptions. This campaign began with his award-winning essay of 1929, "Samazama naru ishō" (The Various Designs), and continued through 1937 in the form of his debate with Marxist critic Tosaka Jun (1900–45).[1]

"Samazama naru ishō" was a significant catalyst for the recalibration of the literary and critical world that occurred in 1930s Japan, the "conversion" (*tenkō*) of Marxists and the so-called "literary renaissance" (*bungei fukkō*). In this essay Kobayashi outlines and advocates a literary practice that apotheosizes the creative, imaginative reconstruction of a familiar realm. What is truly radical about this vision is its conflation of all discursive realms: the genius of Marx in his understanding of the world through the concept of dialectical materialism is utterly interchangeable with the brilliance demonstrated by Balzac in the panoply of *La Comédie Humaine*. The fact that the philosophical and historical insights of the former point to a radical social activism, whereas the aesthetic vision of the latter points to an obsession with the concrete realities of everyday life, was of no significance in Kobayashi's eyes. As visionaries able to break through the conventional paradigms of their chosen fields, these men were of a stripe, and both were worthy of admiration and emulation for that reason alone. This understanding of literary practice is closely related to Kobayashi's idea of "seeing." Both authors reveal an overriding concern with the act of almost mystical insight; neither paid heed to the veracity, instrumentality, or ideological ramifications of that insight.

This chapter introduces this vision of literary praxis, first as it was expressed by Kobayashi in "Samazama naru ishō," and then as it was transformed through its clash with the "scientific" Marxism of the day. Through his ongoing dialogue with this hegemonic discourse, Kobayashi's literary vision was elevated to a worldview that in many circles replaced Marxist thought. This escalation of its purview is what makes Kobayashi's vision and its legacy so important. His evolution from a literary critic in the narrow sense to the persuasive advocate of literary aestheticism (*bungaku shugi*, a term defined below)—an ideology substituted for Marxism—engendered a truly critical aesthetics. The ambivalence about Kobayashi's legacy, alluded to at the end of the previous chapter through the conflicting evaluations of his career offered by Karatani Kōjin and Etō Jun, has its roots here. On one hand, Kobayashi's critique of Marxist criticism and proletarian literature hastened the demise of the left-wing movements that offered the only resistance to the increasingly nationalistic, imperialistic national mood and governmental agenda. In certain understandings and configurations, Kobayashi's literary vision also inspired and lent legitimacy to repressive, fascistic tracts (some from his own hand) that buttressed the regime's imperialist program. On the other hand, however, Kobayashi's fierce dedication to literature as not apolitical but rather anti-political also promoted a genuinely critical praxis that held the potential as much for liberation as it did for sublimation into the national polity. Both of these potentials were rooted in his continued rebellion against Cartesian perspectivalism, represented in this period by the "scientific" methodology of Marxist criticism and proletarian literature. These were the paradigms against which Kobayashi created his conception of a proper praxis.

Marxism, the "Composite Symbol" of a Scientific Modernity

In that Kobayashi's literary mode of cognition filled a void left by the decline of Marxism, an understanding of the contours of this ideology and its functions in Japan serves as useful context. Marxism was integrated into Japanese intellectual life in three stages, according to Miriam Silverberg:

> The process began with the import of Marxism as an admixture undifferentiated from strains of syndicalism during the early years of Taishō. A second stage, of intense study of the works of Marx and Engels, followed. By the mid-1920s, intellectuals had completed the process of importation, translation, and study of European Marxist writings, which had begun after the First World War, and were eager to apply them within their own work. This led to the third stage, when an explosion of indigenous scholarly and literary writing on Japanese society and history informed by Marxism was published during the second half of the 1920s and the early 1930s.[2]

The third stage, which coincides with the emergence of Kobayashi Hideo, was indeed an "explosion." As Silverberg herself notes, "By 1930 . . . 23 percent of the articles in *Chūō kōron*, the leading magazine aimed at an apolitical mass audience, were written by Communist and non-Communist writers on the revolutionary left."[3] Jay Rubin offers a similar picture of the rise of Marxism-influenced literature at this time, estimating that in 1929 and 1930 proletarian works represented 29 percent of the literary texts published in *Chūō kōron* and another general magazine, *Kaizō*. In the following year, this figure rose to 44 percent.[4]

Many reasons have been proposed to explain this sudden and widespread embrace of Marxist doctrine. One significant cause was undoubtedly the coincidence of the importation of Marxist doctrine with a period of disturbing social upheaval that seemed to testify to its importance. Arima Tatsuo highlights this confluence:

> The chronic depressions conformed to Marxism's predictions. The labor-union movement became conspicuously active under the leadership of various brands of socialists. A series of strikes haunted the government. The rice riots brought down a cabinet. And there was formed for the first time a cabinet in September 1918 headed by a party leader rather than an oligarch. Agrarian discontent was general all over Japan. In order to survive, poverty-stricken families in the rural north sold their daughters into white slavery.

> All cities presented scenes of decadence. Precisely at the moment when political parties began to play a more important part in Japanese politics, they revealed their incompetence, seeming to represent only the interests of the capitalists and the landowners. Constant revelations of corruption irritated and discouraged those who might have stood with the parliamentary liberals to oppose the system's eventual disintegration, and many forsook the institution in disgusted despair.[5]

In short, the conditions of social strife were precisely those addressed by Marxism, and Japanese intellectuals jumped at the latest theories explaining it.[6] Robert Scalapino suggests that, in addition to the felicitous timing of its arrival in Japan, Marxism was quickly absorbed because it was easily digestible for Japanese thinkers in the 1920s. Having been trained in the German intellectual tradition, the context from which Marx himself emerged, the nodes of the discourse were already familiar to them.[7]

These sociopolitical motivations were balanced by more idiosyncratic incentives as well, particularly among the writers and critics associated with the movement. In addition to those inspired by a genuine humanitarian social agenda, some writers were drawn to Marxism as the latest "fad" or to the aura arising from its reputation as a dangerous (and later outlawed) foreign doctrine. Undoubtedly another attractive feature was the fact that employing Marxist theory made Japanese intellectuals part of a contemporaneous international discourse within which industrialized Japan could stand as an equal.[8] But perhaps the greatest factor making Marxism appealing to Japanese academics and writers in the 1920s was the authority of the scientific method to which it laid claim.

The importance of the idea of "science" in the discourse of the late 1920s and 1930s in Japan has been trenchantly argued by political scientist Maruyama Masao in his classic *Nihon no shisō* (Japanese Thought, 1961). It was, according to him and others, inextricably linked to Marxist analysis:

> Philosophical elements which, in modern Europe, each had their own lineage and history, and developed in a variety of logical combinations, were brought into the art world of Japan compressed into a single "scientific worldview." Marxism functioned as a composite symbol for that worldview. This fact is at the root of both the glory and the tragedy of the proletarian literary movement—or rather of all Shōwa literary history, which began with it.[9]

Maruyama's argument is that Marxist-oriented literary discourse represented such an unfamiliar, yet persuasive, type of analysis that with its introduction the entire constellation of thinking was altered. The ideological positions that were available after the arrival of Marxism, Maruyama explains, had to explicitly situate themselves among the nodes of science, politics, and literature. In the shifting alliances among these discourses, both the conceptual understanding and social significance of each was inevitably altered.[10]

An early, seminal essay that brought science into the literary realm through a Marxist perspective was Aono Suekichi's " 'Shirabeta' geijutsu" ("Investigative" Art, 1925). In this essay Aono laments the current state of Japanese literature: "No matter what anyone says, the Japanese novel up to this point has been a patchwork of impressions taken—some consciously but the majority unconsciously—from the author's daily life."[11] Aono is clearly thinking primarily of the I-novelists, and he goes on to spell out explicitly his dissatisfaction with these writers in the paragraphs that follow. The current practice of impressionistic literature is rooted, Aono tells us, in a strong tradition focused on the minutiae of everyday life, a fact that obstructs the sort of analytical approach he advocates:

> The shallow and misdirected interpretations that the naturalist movement of today offers concerning "reality," "life," and "the self" all point to that strong tradition. It is a tradition that always takes "the truth" to be a matter of an individual's narrow, arbitrary experience; it is a tradition content to believe that simply poking around in that experience will mystically and miraculously reveal something worthwhile. This tradition has resulted in what we see today: whimsical, directionless literature.[12]

What Aono advocates in place of such impressionistic writing is "investigative literature": "I believe that the best possible way to save the contemporary literary community is to adopt a deliberate, probing investigation of reality, and to employ the theories that this approach yields. . . . In a word, I want 'investigative' art. There are various ways of 'investigating.' The method of the scientific survey is, of course, among them."[13] Aono seems to be imagining a literature that yields instrumental knowledge, writing that points to modes of social intervention. This interpretation is supported by the models that Aono offers: Upton Sinclair's *The Jungle* (1906) and *King Coal* (1917).

In this essay, one of the most influential in the burgeoning Marxist literary movement, Aono introduces the concept of a scientific literature, by which he means novels portraying a thoroughly researched social milieu, a type of social realism. But perhaps more telling than the agenda he announces is the dismissal of what he sees as having come before. Aono would drive out from the literary world the intimately personal and the directly experienced. These things were an integral part of the "I-novel" tradition, and their value was all but indisputable in those circles. As discussed in Chapter 3 in the context of Masamune Hakuchō's critique of Akutagawa, many writers felt that an account of even the most trivial event, provided it was personally experienced and hence factual, was somehow "truer" than even the grandest of fictional narratives. Maruyama Masao attests to just how deeply embedded in the experiential this faith was; he refers to this period as one distinguished by "experience worship" (*jikkan shinkō*).[14] Aono's scornful dismissal of the possibility that personal experience might "mystically and miraculously reveal something worthwhile" struck at the core of the mainstream of Japan's literary world at the time. It is not hard to imagine that some of the appeal of Kobayashi's later alternative to Marxism was generated by his reintegration of the personal into the literary realm.

Philosopher and Marxist critic Tosaka Jun, one of the most subtle thinkers in Aono's line, furthered the infiltration into literature of a rigorous, analytical mode of analysis such as Marxism. Tosaka argued persuasively that the scientific method was indispensable to all criticism. In his 1933 essay "Kagaku to hihyō" (Science and Criticism), Tosaka defended criticism as a genre integral to all intellectual pursuits, even the field of science, where it was too often dismissed as arbitrary, derivative, and extraneous. It gained this poor reputation, Tosaka argues, simply because criticism has too often been merely "impressionistic." While he admits that criticism always starts from an impression, Tosaka insists that this is simply the beginning of the process:

> For criticism to possess objectivity and the concomitant universality and applicability (which are important characteristics for criticism and without which it is useless), the worldview to which it is connected must not be left out of reach; it must be ordered and shaped into a logical, scientific worldview. Only when an unmediated impression is both recognized as a product of part of a scientific worldview and teased out of that worldview does it qualify as objective criticism. These are also the conditions whereby criticism becomes systematic. Criticism with these qualifications is rightly called scientific criticism.[15]

A few short paragraphs later Tosaka goes on to write: "One can rightly say that in the intellectual history of recent years, the truly scientific worldview that has emerged is the Marxist worldview."[16]

As the above lines demonstrate, Tosaka identified the qualities that distinguish the method of the natural sciences—objectivity, universality, applicability—as being at the very heart of all critical practice. This epistemological paradigm, of course, arises from modernity's preferred mode of cognition, discussed in the preceding chapter as Cartesian perspectivalism; it is the tradition against which Kobayashi Hideo (along with Henri Bergson and Nishida Kitarō) rebelled. As with other Marxist thinkers, Tosaka also incorporated that other integral component of the Cartesian worldview: the unassailable distinction between perceiving subject and knowable object. "Criticism," Tosaka writes, "always functions as a catalyst for the progress of the object it critiques."[17] As argued above, this subject/object distinction was for Kobayashi but a preliminary state eventually overcome by a conflation of the poles through his intuitive act of "seeing."

One of the internal factors contributing to the decline of Marxist-oriented literature in Japan in the 1930s was its tendency toward formalism, an indiscriminate, mechanical application of the "formulas" of the analysis, a tendency noted by numerous scholars. Scalapino, for example, writes:

> Marxism, claiming to be science, ceased to employ scientific techniques in Japan at a very early point and merely applied ready-made foreign formulae to indigenous problems. The testing of hypotheses through field work, the objective collection of data, and the use of various measurements were largely ignored. "Pure theory" held sway on the one hand; legalistic-institutional studies on the other. Old myths—Marxist, *Kojiki*, or merely formalistic—were merely repeated in ritualistic fashion.[18]

Although such was never the case for Tosaka, he recognized this tendency among his peers. Writing again on the topic of science and criticism in his "Iwayuru hihyō no 'kagakusei' ni tsuite no kōsatsu" (Observations on the So-called "Scientific Nature" of Criticism, 1938), Tosaka states that he is troubled by "a confused piece of common sense making its way around the world today that holds that to be scientific means to be formulaic."[19] Tosaka's criticism was far too vibrant ever to be so classified, however. Nowhere is his magnanimity, and paradoxically his prejudice, more evident than where he writes of the ultimate purpose of literary criticism: "In short, what is the ultimate reason for the existence of criticism? . . . Here is what I think: in the case of literature, the purpose of its criticism is to confer an awareness of a literary mode of cognition."[20] Tosaka's willingness to concede that the literary arts may indeed represent a unique mode of cognition, an epistemology, distinct from all others reveals his perspective as truly critical. He is not, however, without his blind spots, for he refuses to recognize that such a mode may fall outside the borders of "scientific criticism" with all its objectivity, universality, and instrumentality. Such a literary mode of cognition is precisely what Kobayashi brought to the Japan of the 1920s and 1930s. While its basic contours were forged in his essay on Akutagawa Ryūnosuke, the work that marked his more formal debut in the literary world recalibrated the intellectual constellation of Shōwa Japan. That work was "Samazama naru ishō."

"The Various Designs": Objectivity, Universality, Practicality

Although Kobayashi himself spoke of "Akutagawa Ryūnosuke no bishin to shukumei" as his first critical essay, his debut in the literary world is generally traced to this 1929 essay, "Samazama naru ishō." In garnering him second prize in a contest sponsored by the magazine *Kaizō*, the essay made Kobayashi's name known to the literary world at large. First prize in that 1929 contest went to Miyamoto Kenji's "Haiboku no bungaku" (The Literature of Defeat), the Marxist critique of Akutagawa Ryūnosuke discussed in the preceding chapter. Miyamoto was only 21 years old at the time, still a student in the economics department at Tokyo Imperial University.

The decision to award first prize to Miyamoto had been difficult. Fukada Kyūya (1903–71), who had made Kobayashi's acquaintance through activities connected with the magazine *Bungaku*, was one of the judges for the contest. He would later write that though the editorial staff of *Kaizō* narrowed the entries down from several hundred to two (Miyamoto's and Kobayashi's), the judges "were confused as to which should be awarded first prize. We debated the issue along various lines but could not settle it. We decided to vote on it, and the result was three votes for each essay. We were once again thrown into confusion."[21] Fukada goes on to claim that what finally pushed the vote in favor of Miyamoto's essay was that it was more in keeping with the leftist atmosphere of the literary community of the time.[22] Indeed, the very month that Kobayashi's essay appeared in print saw the publication of such Marxist-oriented pieces as "Kikai to geijutsu no kōryū" (The Interaction of Technology and Art), by Itagaki Takao (1894–1966), "Gendai Nihon bungaku to geijutsu no musan kaikyū" (Contemporary Japanese Literature, Art, and the Proletariat), by Kurahara Korehito (1902–91), and "Geijutsu ni kansuru hashirigakiteki oboegaki" (A Scribbled Note concerning Art), by Nakano Shigeharu (1902–79).[23] Proletarian fiction was equally prominent that year, with Tokunaga Sunao (1899–1958) serializing *Taiyō no nai machi* (Street without Sunlight) and Kobayashi Takiji (1903–33) publishing *Kani kōsen* (Factory Ship). Being so at odds with the spirit of the times, it is no surprise that Kobayashi's essay lost out to a class-based critique of Akutagawa Ryūnosuke. Kobayashi himself, however, had remained undaunted by the trends and was supremely confident. When Fukada personally delivered the news of the decision, Kobayashi treated him to a beer and confessed that, convinced he would win the competition, he had already taken out a loan for the exact amount of the first prize purse.[24]

"Samazama naru ishō" was confusing to all who encountered it. Fukada Kyūya described the essay as being "of a new sort" (*shinpū*) and "abstruse" (*nankai*).[25] Nakamura Mitsuo, himself on the road to a career as a distinguished critic, writes of how it frustrated the contemporary expectations for the genre. Nakamura recalls how in the early Shōwa period critics were expected to serve as theoreticians of specific literary movements, ideologues around whom creative writers gathered for guidance. Kobayashi's essay, though, was such a radical deviation from this paradigm that nobody was quite sure what to make of it: "Being a youth under the influence of contemporary left-wing thought, I remember that on my first reading I had no idea what Kobayashi was talking about. . . . 'The Various Designs' was not at all understood by the literary community [*bundan*] of the time, which is to say that with this work Kobayashi was not recognized as a critic."[26] The fact that both Nakamura and Fukada, astute readers familiar with the literary trends both in Japan and abroad, found this essay puzzling yet important suggests something of the immensity of the challenge it presented to contemporary literary expectations.

Succinctly put, in "Samazama naru ishō" Kobayashi cedes the considerable cultural capital that had accrued to the image of science and instead champions a literary mode of cognition that is theoretically incompatible with it. Kobayashi does not oppose Marxist criticism on the grounds that its claims to objectivity and universality were suspect, an argument that would have been more easily understood by his contemporaries. Rather, he argues against the very *desirability* of that objectivity that, in his eyes, leads inevitably to formalism and dogmatism—mere "designs." The literary mode of cognition that he espouses in place of this scientific paradigm is one focused on a dynamic, incessantly creative praxis. This message is conveyed in "Samazama naru ishō" as much through the rhetoric as it is through the contents. As Paul Anderer has remarked: "As if to build a defense against determinism into his writing itself, Kobayashi rejected a neutral, rationalist idiom in favor of paradox and indirection. In trying to convey the reality of his encounter with a specific work or controversy, he moved with often sudden recognition toward the spiritual, magical aspects of cultural engagement."[27] The combination of an often dense poetic language with this unfamiliar perspective is the reason the essay both appealed to and confounded the literary community of the time.

Speaking for the entire generation of critics inspired by the "science" of Marxism, Tosaka Jun had called for objectivity, universality, and applicability in criticism. Without these, he claimed, the critical enterprise was useless. In the course of "Samazama naru ishō," Kobayashi dismantles all three of these pillars of scientific modernity. In some of the most often quoted lines of Kobayashi's immense oeuvre, he writes:

> People say, "It is easy to critique a man based on one's own preferences." However, holding a man up to a yardstick is an equally easy task. The real challenge lies in constantly maintaining vibrant tastes, a yardstick that is always changing. People think of a man's preferences as distinct from a yardstick, but this is nothing more than pure speculation, similar to conjectures that consider the mind and body as separate entities. . . . Without dynamic tastes, how might we maintain a vibrant yardstick? Still, the fact that the theoreticians tend to forget lies at the next step: it is possible to meticulously and endlessly theorize on our critical method only when we are comfortable with the stipulation that the pure, spiritual activity that is criticism can be divided into the categories of preferences and yardsticks. However, the fact is that no matter how thoroughly we interrogate our critical methods, that enterprise has no bearing on the question of whether the criticism actually moves people. Think of it this way: one might pin one's hopes for love on an analysis of the rhetoric of the love letter. But even should one attain love, only a fool would attribute it to that love-letter research. Or perhaps what this person has achieved is not love at all but something different altogether.[28]

Kobayashi is here rejecting critical objectivity, represented by the idea of an unchanging "yardstick." The statement contains an echo of the objection that he had first voiced in the Akutagawa essay: the personal preference/objective yardstick distinction implies a failure to have fully internalized abstractions or, to use Kobayashi's romantic term, to have captured one's "destiny." Fully digesting the principles behind the yardstick, and making them one's own, would have made them perfectly congruent with one's preferences. When critics beholden to a particular theory insist on this artificial distinction, they are in essence validating the superficial adoption and formulaic application of abstractions. This path leads inevitably to precisely the sort of facile manipulation of ideas that Kobayashi found so distasteful in the work of Akutagawa. As he did in his writing on Akutagawa, in "Samazama naru ishō" Kobayashi stresses the need to fully internalize abstractions: "no ideology [*kannengaku*] is such that it lays its foundations in the human consciousness. . . . A man's ideology is always entwined with his entire being. It is entwined with his destiny."[29] In other words, ideology is more than a matter of abstract thought; it is a matter of one's entire existence.

With remarks that resonate with ideas from the paragraph quoted above, Kobayashi then turns his attention from objectivity to a tenet equally sacred to modernity's epistemological paradigm: universality.

> I come across a boorish phrase posing pretentiously—"the universality of criticism." Since the days of old, what kind of artist ever set out after a monster like universality? Without exception they took aim at the particular [*kotai*]. They did not hope to relate a truth relevant to all ages and in all places; they simply hoped to relate, as sincerely and completely as possible, the specific truths. . . . Putting categorical or a priori truths aside, all human truths are guaranteed by the stamp of the human upon them. Why would you seek affirmation anywhere else? It is the same for literary criticism; there is no evidence to suggest any distinction. The best criticism is always the most idiosyncratic [*koseiteki*].[30]

This argument for the inversion of the conventional hierarchy placing universality above particularity is ultimately unassailable because it is not really an argument at all. Here and throughout the essay, Kobayashi presents his ideas as pronouncements; he has no choice but to proceed in this fashion. To logically defend his preferences for subjectivity over objectivity, and the idiosyncratic over the universal, would require him to resort to the very modes of discourse that he hopes to supplant, that is, sustained, abstract argument. What fuels Kobayashi's propositions is thus not logical argument, but rather his appeal to artistry. In the above passage this appeal takes the form of his conflation of the categories of criticism and art. In the lines quoted further above, it is the insistence that criticism be measured not by its usefulness or clarity, but rather by its ability to move us.

This emphasis on the artistry of criticism, its ability to arouse some emotional reaction in the reader, is a third way in which Kobayashi's vision diverged from the scientific paradigm adopted by his Marxist contemporaries. In addition to insisting on the objectivity and universality of criticism, Tosaka, for one, had contended that criticism must be practical (*jitsuyōteki*). By this he presumably meant that critical exploration and the delineation of the worldview underlying our impressions would enable us to better judge and intervene in the workings of the world. For Kobayashi, however, the pursuit of such instrumental knowledge was of no concern. His focus was on an enrichment of the human experience of the world, a refinement of the power to feel. This experience of the world is always an intimately personal one:

> No matter how pure an artist's work may be, it is not pure in the sense that water may be pure to the scientist. An artist's work is always rich in its embrace of a variety of hues and shadows. Due to this richness, no matter what ideas I may abstract from the work, there will be others that are left behind. Wandering behind the richness of the work, I come to believe that I have fully comprehended the author's philosophy. But, at precisely that moment, some new fragment of his thought will catch sight of me from an unexpected angle. Once I am spotted, the conclusion is preordained: the fragment is no longer simply a fragment. It expands rapidly to swallow the philosophy I had grasped but a moment before. The wandering I do amounts to an attempt to analytically grasp my own nature. When the confusion caused by my analysis ends, I hear it—the plaintive melody of the author's destiny that runs beneath the richness of any masterpiece. At that moment I am roused from the confusion of my dream, and my heart begins a narration in words that are my very own. I am awakened to the potential of my criticism.[31]

Though the language is overly dramatic, it is appropriate to the Romantic nature of the experience of art that Kobayashi is describing. Moreover, the point is clear: Kobayashi, as a critic, seeks that moment when a text or an idea overwhelms its reader through the simple fact that any interpretation that poses as definitive is ultimately grossly reductive of the original text. Kobayashi as reader prepares for this experience by a close and careful reading ("wandering behind the richness of the work"), but it is ultimately an almost mystical experience, and one beyond volition. Most importantly, it is a deeply personal experience, a fact that is underscored by the repetition of the word "I" (*watashi*) a full five times in a single sentence in the original.[32] Given the tendency to omit the first-person pronoun in Japanese, the frequency of the word is striking. Kobayashi's denunciation in this essay of the various schools of criticism is ultimately in hope of opening the self once again to this experience: "I have no right to object to the fact that literary critics arm themselves with various systems of thought. Still, I cannot help but think that while their armor may protect them, it is surely a very heavy weight to bear."[33]

"The Various Designs": Critical Praxis

Kobayashi's call to the literary community to throw off the heavy "armor" of critical "designs" is sometimes mistaken for an unequivocal rejection of abstract thought. For example, Edward Seidensticker, in one of the first essays on Kobayashi in the English language, claimed: "were one to commence indexing Kobayashi's collected works it would soon become apparent that 'concept, hostility to' is a useless heading, for it includes everything, even as does 'Kobayashi Hideo, collected works of.' A dislike of abstraction is everywhere. . . ."[34]

The statement is misleading. Kobayashi, in fact, accepted the role of abstraction and conceptual thinking in the artistic process (they were, indeed, the core of his idea of "destiny"), but he protested the manner in which they were raised to the level of static universals. This distinction is evident in the closing lines of "Samazama naru ishō": "I believe that here I have taken a stroll through the various designs of the Japanese literary world today, or at least through those that seem most important. I have certainly not attempted to degrade these designs in hopes of discovering something else. Rather, I have simply endeavored to believe in all these designs so as to not believe too much in any single one of them."[35]

Though the statement is somewhat disingenuous, for Kobayashi has indeed degraded the movements he discusses (Marxism, art for art's sake, modernism), the fact remains that Kobayashi expresses here and elsewhere a genuine respect for artists and thinkers who creatively articulate a genuinely original insight. It is the reification of such insights into "designs" of universal applicability that he abhors. Kobayashi's agenda as laid out in "Samazama naru ishō" calls for an abandonment of such static, abstract constructs in favor of an incessantly creative praxis as the core of all literature.

While Kobayashi had spoken in his earlier essay on Akutagawa of the act of "seeing," his vision here is delineated through a linguistic theory that serves as a metaphor for all creative practice. The importance of the linguistic metaphor is suggested by the fact that it appears in the opening lines of "Samazama naru ishō":

> For better or for worse, no issue in this world is easily resolved. Language, given to man along with consciousness so long ago, and our sole weapon in thought, continues to work the same magic it has for so very long. There are neither words so lofty they do not suggest the vulgar, nor words so vulgar they do not hint at the lofty. If, somehow, language were to discard the magic whereby it bewitches the hearts of man, it would be reduced to but a fleeting shadow.[36]

The parallel with Kobayashi's experience of reading, discussed above, is readily apparent. The "richness" of the text is here expressed at the level of language, with the excessive ambivalence of words (*kotoba*) giving them an undirected "magic." When Kobayashi returns to the issue of language a few pages later, it is to acknowledge again its ambivalent power:

> When the gods bestowed the natural world upon man, in their wisdom they let him discover it through the act of naming. Man's invention of the word "mankind" is as deserving of our respect as his invention of fire. However, people have discarded the internal logic whereby such words were invented, and they have abandoned themselves instead to the fabulous social practices that language, by its very nature, makes possible. Their reward has been the attainment of lively social relationships, but they have paid a price as well: language has usurped the rules and magic that man bestowed on it and, in the guise of the various designs, turned those rules and the magic against man to control him.[37]

The two sides of language, that which is "lofty" and that which is "vulgar," are here brought to the fore. The creation of language—words—Kobayashi contends, is a discovery equal in value even to that of fire. It forges the bonds by which a community can be just that. But the "magic" whereby language creates community also functions to restrict creativity. As we forget the contingent nature of linguistic constructs, they come to possess us, reducing our ability to see in anything but the established "designs."

Kobayashi outlines the challenge for the creative artist through this same linguistic metaphor. "The poet who would work the magic of language," Kobayashi writes, "begins with a realization of the structure of that magic." That structure is revealed in the process whereby children acquire their first language:

> A child learns from his mother that the ocean is blue. If in attempting to sketch the waters of the Shinagawa, this child felt the color of the waters be-

fore his eyes to be neither blue nor red nor any color in his pencil box, and if he should, in amazement, throw out his colored pencils, that child would be a genius. The world, though, has never seen the birth of such a prodigy. Does that mean, then, that the child grasps the concept "the ocean is blue"? No, a child living on the shores of Shinagawa Bay cannot conceive of the ocean apart from this bay. So, for the child, language points neither to a concept nor an object. The wandering of language between these two poles is an essential condition for the child's coming to maturity in this world. A person remains half child throughout his life. What, then, is that other half that makes the child an adult? People label it "reasoning" [*ronri*]. This is to say that children become adults by combining the communal practice of language with the communal nature of logic. The rejection of both these communal layers of language is the premise of a poet's practice.[38]

These passages on the nature of language and its relationship to thought are unique in the Japan of 1929. Quite clearly, Kobayashi recognizes the tenuous nature of the link between language and the reality it represents, and he traces the production of meaning to an utterance's location in a synchronic linguistic system (the "communal practice of language"). Kobayashi also seems to be reaching for the idea that reason or logic (*ronri*) is in some way both a product and producer of the linguistic system in which it operates. These ideas, though not explored by Kobayashi in a rigorously systematic manner, bear striking resemblance to the linguistic analysis of Ferdinand de Saussure.[39] And, not surprisingly, Kobayashi's literary vision based on this understanding of language anticipates in some ways the theoretical discourses that would later arise from Saussurean linguistics.

Maruyama Shizuka makes the claim that this introduction of linguistic theory into the realm of criticism is Kobayashi's first major accomplishment.[40] Kamei Hideo, too, takes these sections of "Samazama naru ishō" very seriously. In his provocative reading, Kamei argues that Kobayashi is most likely taking his cue from Marx's theory of the fetish of the commodity: just as the use-value of the commodity fades as the trade-value grows in a capitalist system, so too does the value of language as a constructive, *presentational* symbol depreciate in a world increasingly defined by journalism's strictly *representational* use of language. Kobayashi sets out to reverse, or at least stem, this trend.[41] For the purposes of this study, however, Kobayashi's linguistic theory is important chiefly for what it reveals about the subtly nuanced and radically literary nature of critical practice as he envisioned it.

Based on his realization that language (by which Kobayashi means not only vocabulary, of course, but rather something closer to "discourse" as it is used in critical circles today) is originally a presentation or construction of the world, Kobayashi expresses an appreciation of the geniuses who have created those language conventions. They have, in a very real sense, "invented" their worlds. By rejecting the established channels of interpreting the world, and once again acknowledging the ultimately impenetrable nature of materiality, great thinkers have taken the intuitive leap to "see" these things in dramatically new ways. This act is what Kobayashi posits as the core of the literary imagination; his various odes to genius all chronicle this reinvention of the world through a new language. Kobayashi did not systematically elucidate this vision. As was the case with his opposition to objectivity and universality, to have done so would have undermined the very argument he was making. Like his heroes, Kobayashi was reaching for a new literary "language" (discourse), and it was one that precluded deploying the conventions he was struggling to break free of.

This vision of language as constitutive of a discursive realm resonated with how Kobayashi wrote of artistic praxis, which he saw as an attempt to synthesize a deeply personal, abstract vision of the world (a "destiny") with the concrete realities before one's eyes (the "muse"). This synthesis takes place through the medium of language. Being fully interdependent, the three nodes come into being simultaneously, in the act of "seeing." This conception of artistic praxis, and the apotheosis of it, is what prompted Kobayashi to consider Balzac, Marx, and Dostoevsky as peers. In "Samazama naru ishō" Kobayashi sings the praises of Balzac for his ability to capture a unique vision of the world in his *Human Comedy*: "When Balzac saw the world just as it was [*aru ga mama*], this 'just as it was' took shape as his fundamental understanding of the human condition."[42] He then goes on to write:

> The logical connection between Balzac's unique theory and practice was certainly the same as that between Marx's unique formulations of the same. To take this one step further, in that both men strove to portray the basic character of the age in which they lived, and in that each desired nothing for the premise of their work but the vibrant reality [*ikiiki to shita genjitsu*] before their eyes, they were equals, with no difference between them. It is simply that each had a different destiny.[43]

This association of Karl Marx, philosopher extraordinaire and demigod to the literary community of the time, with Balzac, a bourgeois writer of mere fiction, was intended to do more than rankle the Marxist critics (though it was surely meant to do that as well). In presenting the accomplishment of Marx as the portrayal of "the basic character of the age in which [he] lived," Kobayashi was obviously not reading him as the philosopher who uncovered some transcendental, universal truth. Kobayashi was judging him on criteria usually reserved for literary figures: the degree to which they exercise their creative faculty in the articulation of an episteme. The effect of this characterization of Marx's achievement was heightened, of course, by Kobayashi's equating him with Balzac. Quite plainly, Kobayashi was co-opting Marx as a literary figure.

Kobayashi makes much the same move in a 1931 essay entitled "Marukusu no gotatsu" (The Insight of Marx), this time explicitly linking Marx's creativity to his use of language as the tool whereby the abstract and the concrete are fused:

> In order to capture the economic structure of this world in his dynamic vision, Marx promptly discarded the raw, living nature [*namanamashisa*] of the written word. For him it was sufficient to use the written word as [a] symbol of pure logic. His genius lies in having proven the precision of these symbols of pure logic entirely by using them to capture the raw, living nature of the actual economic system. In this manner he was able to avoid the vacuousness of universal theories.
>
> Now, there have also been those who promptly discarded the idea of the written word as a symbol of logic. There have been artistic geniuses who have trod this other path. Their genius lies in having proven the precision of their ambiguous language solely by tracing the raw, living contours of the corporeal body. In this manner they avoided the arbitrariness of a personal, insular language. For these men, too, reality was their touchstone.
>
> Marx began with a personal understanding of society and pushed through to an understanding of himself. And one might say that Dostoevsky, for example, took the opposite route. To my eyes the patterns exhibited by these two masters always appear intertwined.[44]

The frustrating rhetoric, with its juggling of words within sentences of parallel syntactical structure, is a hallmark of Kobayashi's prose in this period. His point, however, is clear: the tendency toward the abstract, whether it be in the form of a universal theory or an incommunicable personal vision, is tempered by its fusion with the concrete (an "actual economic system" or the "corporeal body"). This fusion takes place through the mediation of language, a unique form of which must be reinvented in order not to compromise the singularity of the vision.

In the expression of these ideas, Kobayashi is wrestling with a sophisticated conception of the relationship of language, theory, and reality that is far ahead of his time.[45] An important, distinguishing feature of it is Kobayashi's stubborn refusal to frame his insights within any context other than the aesthetic. The geniuses he identified were not part of a teleological progress of knowledge, nor were their insights considered for their ideological or political ramifications. His concern was strictly with the aesthetic, the literary, and for him this was a matter of incessant praxis, the creation of new languages capturing unique epistemes. Kobayashi notes that while the scholars of aesthetics may examine the structures of artistic movements to explain their emotional impact, or chart them in a history of art to explain the evolution of ideas, such work is of but secondary importance because it is the artist that must remain the focus of our attention, and the practitioner has a very different perspective:

> For the artist, art is neither the object of an emotion nor the object of speculation; it is a matter of praxis [*jissen*]. The completed work is for the artist simply a milestone; what is truly important to him is the act of walking. The feelings or motivations that the milestone inspires in the people who see it are of no concern to the artist. When the poet pens the final line of a poem, he has erected a memorial commemorating a battle, and nothing more. The moment it is erected, the monument is nothing more than that. If this corpse should live for all eternity, it does so simply because people through the generations relate to it. . . . The artist, however, must incessantly create new forms. What is important to the artist is not the new form, but the process whereby it is created. . . .[46]

In this exclusive focus on praxis, Kobayashi is proposing a worldview that is fully aesthetic in perspective. Ironically, in this unflagging dedication to the literary and artistic, he fulfills Tosaka Jun's prescription for literary criticism as cited above: "in the case of literature, the purpose of its criticism is to confer an awareness of a literary mode of cognition." Kobayashi's mode of cognition is precisely that.

Kobayashi's critique of Marxism (and, in fact, of all literary and ideological constructs) is, then, essentially a denunciation of the formalized, reproducible manifestations of the original insight, or what he refers to as a "design." Of Marxism, Kobayashi writes:

> Isn't it the case that the Marxist ideology in your heads is neither a praxis informed with theory nor a theory informed with praxis? Having taken shape as a commodity, isn't it now working the magic of a commodity itself? Marxism claims that commodities control the world. When Marxism, as a design, runs rampant in the human brain, it makes a splendid commodity.

What's more, this transfiguration has the power to make people forget the obvious fact that commodities control the world.[47]

These lines are an expression of why Kobayashi can accept Marx and his achievement but never embrace Marxism: once the remaking of the world has been accomplished through the fusing of an abstract vision and concrete realities through the medium of a creative language, the work of the literary imagination is done, and it is time to return the world to its impenetrable concreteness. With the world rendered uninterpretable once again, one then waits for a flash of insight to reveal it anew.

"Samazama naru ishō" rejected modern science's sacred tenets of universality and objectivity; it called for a mode of cognition that was extremely literary in orientation. Kobayashi's manifesto came at a time of heightened political and ideological agendas that had encroached on the literary world in the form of Marxist criticism and proletarian literature. As such, in spite of the fact that Kobayashi's agenda was, at least at this stage of his career, entirely literary in orientation, the vision had repercussions outside of this realm. In other words, with the appearance of Marxism as the "composite symbol" of an integrated, comprehensive, scientific worldview, any perspective that challenged the very premises of Marxism was immediately and automatically raised by that context to a similar stature. Kobayashi's thought was elevated to that point through his debate with Marxist theorist Tosaka Jun.

Literary Aestheticism

In the years that followed the publication of "Samazama naru ishō," Kobayashi worked diligently to establish himself as a critic. Much of what he wrote in the ensuing five years took the form of the *bungaku jihyō*, the monthly literary reviews published in newspapers and journals, and it was through these less ambitious works that Kobayashi's reputation was secured and his perspective gradually understood. In April 1932 Kobayashi also began lecturing in the newly established art department of Meiji University.[48]

Perhaps the most representative work of this period of Kobayashi's career is "Kokyō o ushinatta bungaku" (Literature That Has Lost Its Home, 1933), discussed in some detail in Chapter 1. The nostalgia for a "home," which Kobayashi defined as the source of powerful memories rooted in "solid objects and incidents," is a recurring theme during these years. A similar emotion runs through "Gendai bungaku no fuan" (The Anxiety of Modern Literature, 1932), as well, where the alienation from an intellectual "home" is described as the confusion and anxiety prompted by the younger generation's obsession with theories and abstract thought:

> Nothing, not a single thing, is clear. Today, more than ever before in the history of mankind, the phrase "new facts" is accorded the greatest importance. Our eyes are exhausted from pursuing these new facts, and they can no longer clearly distinguish any object or event—their colors are layered one upon the other and the borders between them merge. If we should steal a moment's rest and close our eyes in contemplation, wave upon wave of confused thoughts wash over our minds, flooding us with irresolvable contradictions. Any intellectual who does not admit feeling these contradictions is either an idiot or a liar.[49]

Kobayashi is describing a world flooded by commodities of all sorts—manufactured goods as well as information and ideological "designs." The solution that Kobayashi proposes in this essay is in keeping with the ideas he espoused in "Samazama naru ishō." Rather than cast about for a ready-made "design" through which to order our world, we must follow our own "destiny":

> For youth, all philosophies are nothing but a means of rationalizing their actions, and it is so very hard for them to grasp these abstract ideas in concrete terms. This phenomenon is understandable as the language of these philosophies is easily acquired while the facts they are to represent are complex. This deluded embrace of theory has spread its net everywhere, into the world of passions and every corner of the emotions, into feelings of love and hate, and even into every nook and cranny of our sensibilities. The riddles posed by life will not be solved no matter how long one examines society, reads books, or plays at political activism. One must look within the self. In my personal experience, limited as it may be, my errors have not been due to an overabundance of emotion. They have been caused by unexamined theories that do not take the world into account. What has obstructed my ability to see through to the true shape of things has not been my emotions; it has been my emotions as held captive by abstract concepts.[50]

The picture of the modern literary youth Kobayashi paints here suggests that the "designs" he had railed against three years before continued to hold sway. The tone of his writing reflects their persistence as well. Whereas his debut essay had been a bold manifesto, the essays from this period are irritated, anxious, almost desperate.

Kobayashi, however, refuses to compromise on his stand, and he acknowledges how this leaves him outside the mainstream of the literary community:

> I've never stepped on board that gaudy chariot sheathed in theory and speeding down the highway of literary abstractions. No, I've thrown stones at it instead. My choice has been to stroll down alleys of my own liking, stopping off here and there for a drink or two. With the very few people I do chance to meet along the way, I've wanted nothing more than to exchange a few heartfelt words.[51]

This image of a solitary figure making his way on the periphery is an apt one for Kobayashi in the years immediately following his debut. The "gaudy chariot . . . speeding down the highway of literary abstractions" was, of course, theory-based literature, especially Marxism. It would only be after this vehicle's collision with the authorities that his contemporaries joined Kobayashi in the back streets.

This collision came in the wake of the Manchurian Incident of 1931, when the pressure of hostilities abroad prompted the government to crack down on dissent on the home islands. Invoking the Peace Preservation Act (*chian iji hō*) with increasing frequency, various ministries began the repression of all left-wing organizations. A major campaign launched in March 1932 resulted in the arrest of over 400 Marxist literary figures, including the famous Nakano Shigeharu and Kurahara Korehito. In February of the next year, Kobayashi Takiji was beaten to death by members of the Tokkō (Special Higher Police), whose numbers had risen from 70 in 1928 to 380 in 1932 for the city of Tokyo alone.[52] The year 1933 also marked the ideological conversion (*tenkō*) of high-ranking Communist Party members Sano Manabu (1892–1953) and Nabeyama Sadachika (1901–79). This persecution of liberal (mostly Marxist) thinkers only intensified after the outbreak of full-scale war in China in July 1937.

It was during these years, particularly 1934–37, that Kobayashi engaged in a debate with Marxist critic Tosaka Jun. In the course of the exchange, at the prodding of Tosaka, Kobayashi reiterated and clarified his critique of modernity's scientific worldview. In Tosaka's critique of Kobayashi's method (or, more precisely, of a perceived lack thereof), the literary nature of Kobayashi's agenda was again brought to the fore. Most importantly, in the course of the dialogue, and in conjunction with the conversions of so many literary figures away from Marxism, Kobayashi's dynamic mode of praxis became, ironically, somehow formalized into a sort of "commodity," or "design," of its own. As such it entered into the marketplace of ideas in Japan in the late 1930s and early 1940s, reconfiguring the constellation of politics, literature, and science.

Though Kobayashi had addressed fundamental principles of the scientific method (universality, objectivity, practicality) in "Samazama naru ishō," he did not portray science itself, in its entirety, as a "design." He took the first step toward this position in 1931, with "Bungei hihyō no kagakusei ni kansuru ronsō" (The Debate on the Scientific Nature of Literary Criticism), and this argument reached full maturity with "Bungei hihyō no yukue" (The Direction of Literary Criticism), published in 1937.[53] In the latter Kobayashi put forth an argument much like that he had turned on Marxism: he lamented the disappearance of the creative origins of the endeavor as scientific practice evolves into nothing more than the development of technology. This sad fate came about because our education encourages us to take the various scientific discoveries of the past as a matter of faith, Kobayashi writes, and this "dulls our intellectual efforts and adventures."[54]

Kobayashi cites, as a record of the true spirit of scientific empiricism, the autobiography of Fukuzawa Yukichi (1834–1901), a man whose life coincides with the importation of Western science at the end of the Tokugawa period and the beginning of Meiji. Kobayashi summarizes the section in which Fukuzawa describes how he "scientifically" tested the old superstitions by stomping first on a piece of paper with the feudal lord's name on it, then on a votive tablet with the name of a deity, and eventually by throwing away the contents of the neighborhood shrines. Fukuzawa took great pleasure in proving to himself, through experimentation, that the old folks' stories of divine retribution were false.[55] In Kobayashi's eyes, this episode embodied what was admirable about the scientific spirit: the bold testing of stale, accepted truths. Kobayashi lamented the passing of this spirit and the nature of the poor descendant that stood in its place: "The belief in scientific method is, in a word, skewed. Science knows how to solve a problem but not how to formulate one."[56]

Related to this reconfiguration of scientific discourse was Kobayashi's defense of impressionistic criticism, a genre that Tosaka posited as the alternative and as not genuinely critical. While Kobayashi conceded that while the movement in Japan may have had serious shortcomings, he also insisted that any weaknesses were entirely a product of the unfortunate circumstances in which the genre had been imported from Europe. It arrived in Japan during a time of intellectual crisis for the critical community: the struggle of Shimamura Hōgetsu (1871–1918) and Hasegawa Tenkei (1876–1940) to come to grips with Japan's version of naturalism had lost all its vitality as naturalism itself waned and a critical vacuum arose. While authors experimented with various "isms" from Europe, the critics by default took refuge in impressionistic criticism, a genre that Kobayashi insisted they did not understand. This resulted in the genre's reputation in Japan as arbitrary and subjective, and hence not really criticism at all.[57]

The original European version of impressionistic criticism, however, was far different, Kobayashi tells us. In France it was developed by people such as Jules Lemaître (1853–1914) and Anatole France (1844–1924). In opposition to the one-dimensional, rationalist criticism of their time, these men attempted to discover a "societal criticism based on a free and flexible mode of reason. . . . Science, of course, rested at the very core of their education and, though what they proposed was often anti-scientific [*han kagakuteki*], there was nothing a-scientific [*hi kagakuteki*] about it."[58] With this comment it is clear that Kobayashi was associating his own critical inspirations with a tradition outside the Cartesian perspectivalism of modern science and, indeed, in active opposition to it. Kobayashi carried this banner in Japan. His refusal even to pay lip service to this hegemonic mode of discourse, turning instead to a critique of it, is what made it so hard for contemporaries to comprehend, much less accept. It was also at the heart of Tosaka's refusal to acknowledge Kobayashi's writings as legitimate critical practice.

Tosaka's most concerted attack on Kobayashi came in 1934, with the essay "Bungei hyōronka no ishiki" (The Consciousness of Literary Critics).[59] It was a time when government repression of Marxists was in full swing, and the avalanche of ideological conversions (*tenkō*) had already begun. The sense of urgency and the passion in Tosaka as he struggled to reaffirm a scientific, Marxist criticism at this juncture is palpable. His frustration was compounded by the fact that, close as he may have come, Tosaka could not quite comprehend the radically literary nature of Kobayashi's project. True to Marxist materialism, Tosaka denounced Kobayashi as one who "fears nothing more than the objective, material world":[60]

> But what is important for Kobayashi is himself, particularly his world of images, his world of "dreams," which serves as the fishbowl for this expensive goldfish. Who cares about the objective world? Seeing it through the glass of the fishbowl is plenty. Truth and reality exist exclusively within himself. Whether it be history, tradition, society, politics, or nature, according to him it is nothing but a perspective on paper, devoid of all real-world authority.[61]

From a Marxist perspective, Tosaka was right, of course, to focus on Kobayashi's refusal to address the "objective world." What perplexed Tosaka, however, was that Kobayashi could not be grouped with the idealists subscribing to some manifestation of false consciousness. Kobayashi's rejection of all "designs" made a critique from this angle impossible, as Tosaka as much as admits when he writes:

> Up until recently Kobayashi Hideo gave us the feeling that he had something close to a system. I have previously called this a "fear of the material" system. But, in fact, this was neither a method nor a system. It seems we would have to label it as nothing more than a simple exaggeration of idiosyncrasies. . . . What we saw previously was no system; it was nothing more than mere style.[62]

As these passages indicate, Tosaka was groping for an alternative to the standard Marxist critique of a work or author as narrowly class-based or rooted in a misguided ideological framework. These objections do not readily lend themselves to an analysis of Kobayashi's work. In fact, Tosaka's claim that for Kobayashi "truth and reality exist exclusively within himself," his professed inability to find within Kobayashi a "system" (design?), and his remark on Kobayashi's idiosyncrasies all suggest that Kobayashi was remaining true to the principles he espoused in "Samazama naru ishō." Kobayashi's messages were personal and particular, their format fluid, and their expression idiosyncratic.

Tosaka turned, therefore, to a critique of Kobayashi's conviction that the world (or at least our understanding of it) is, ultimately, largely a linguistic or rhetorical construct. Tosaka claimed that Kobayashi's work was essentially a matter of "style," that for him history, tradition, society, politics, and nature are "but a perspective on paper." In a very important sense, Tosaka was right. For Kobayashi, language is indeed the medium through which an amorphous sense of the world is fused with the concrete materialities of it. Where Tosaka erred, however, was in his judgment that discursive constructs are "devoid of all real world authority." The propaganda of the war years, to which Kobayashi would himself contribute in some way, is convincing evidence to the contrary.

Tosaka proceeded to circle around the discursive (as opposed to "real-world") foundations of Kobayashi's thought. Tosaka admitted to being charmed by Kobayashi's work, but in exploring the origins of this attraction concluded, "the reason that Kobayashi is admired rests not in the type of critic he is, but rather in the fact that he is an 'excessively literary' literary critic [*mottomo 'bungeiteki' bungei hihyō-ka*]."[63] The overall context makes it clear that Tosaka was using the word *bungeiteki* (literary) disparagingly, but the fact is that its connotation is negative only within Tosaka's strictly teleological Marxist perspective. A concrete example that Tosaka provides is Kobayashi's use of the paradox:

> I question whether or not Kobayashi's paradoxes have the qualifications of a paradox. The reason for this is that his paradoxes, while appearing to be real or true paradoxes, reveal themselves as being, in fact, nothing more than a simple rhetorical form. And so, what charms me about Kobayashi are actually not his paradoxes, but rather his paradoxical rhetoric.[64]

It is not surprising that Tosaka should latch onto this aspect of Kobayashi's style. To a Marxist, the identification of such paradoxes is an all-important first step in their dialectical resolution. In that Kobayashi's paradoxes do not move toward such resolutions, Tosaka dismisses them as inauthentic. He claims "for Kobayashi, the paradox takes exclusively the image of a 'dizziness' [*memai*] . . . Kobayashi makes that dizziness permanent."[65] Tosaka goes on to speculate how Kobayashi would respond to a suggestion to replace that dizziness with a dialectical analysis moving toward a resolution. "Kobayashi would probably say that dialectics would be fine, *as long as they are applied with real style* [*ki ga kiite iru*]. But he'd be sure to pass on the real thing: 'You mean dialectical materialism? You've got to be joking! How gauche [*yabo kusai*]!'"[66]

All of these comments by Tosaka, though they have negative connotations, are really a testimony to Kobayashi's masterful application of his literary imagination. The disruption of our conventional modes of understanding—the creation of "dizziness" through the use of paradox—is Kobayashi's method of undermining formalism and maintaining an authentically critical perspective. The incessant re-problematization of the paradigms of thought is not conducive to firm conclusions or a social agenda, two things that irritate Tosaka the most. But it is productive in the sense that it generates a critical consciousness ready to question things at their most basic levels, and from outside the teleological, scientific, Marxist framework.

In this sense, Kobayashi's strategy was precisely the sort of "literary mode of cognition" that Tosaka himself said is the proper basis of literary criticism. Its emergence as a paradigm opposed to Tosaka's science in so many fundamental ways rendered it virtually incomprehensible to him. Unable to appreciate literary rhetoric and the atmosphere created by style, a frustrated Tosaka concludes that Kobayashi is nothing but "a slick chatterbox" (*tassha na oshaberi*).[67] For better or worse, however, a "slick chatterbox" is often the most interesting person in the room—and even the most influential.

In one of his most famous essays from this period, "Handōki ni okeru bungaku to tetsugaku: bungaku shugi no sakkaku ni tsuite" (Literature and Philosophy in Reactionary Times: On the Illusion of Literary Aestheticism, 1934), Tosaka continues to struggle with the literary paradigm subverting the Marxist agenda.[68] He remains unwilling or unable to recognize the importance of the rhetorical force of a literary text, and insists instead on making literature strictly a matter of content:

> Writers and critics say that true literature springs from an examination of issues like life and desire, which serve as its backdrop or its core. If we take this thinking one step further, we realize that what we generally assume to be the essence of literature, that is, the text as a concrete object with a certain form that is recognizable as literature, is actually not that at all. The essence of literature is not really the text as so produced, but rather the ideas of life and desire, mentioned above, that comprise the background of the text. . . . If we focus simply on the form [*keishiki*] of the literary text, whether novel or poem, all we have are its formal attributes, as the word itself suggests. Even if we postulate that some content is composed from literary technique, it goes without saying that that alone does not constitute thought [*shisō*].[69]

Quite clearly, Tosaka continues to distinguish form and content, vehicle and message. His prioritizing of content and message, however, makes him ultimately blind to what Kobayashi's work represents.

Based on his insistence that literature be considered first and foremost in terms of its contents, and that these be tied to a social agenda rooted in a theoretical system, Tosaka proceeds to criticize the literary community (*bundan*) for what appears to him as a naive, narcissistic preoccupation with strictly literary matters. "Literature," Tosaka writes,

> remains always within the interior of "literature." Although there may occasionally be some interaction with other realms, in general it circles around the *bundan*, and is critiqued from this viewpoint. Eventually, not only literature, but all things get critiqued in a "literary fashion" from this perspective. If anyone should critique literature from outside the category "literature," well, it would be a blasphemy that would make one's hair stand on end.[70]

This insular naiveté, Tosaka goes on to argue, is a result of a "perversion" in which literary figures have conflated the concepts of "literature" and "life." Tosaka labels this misguided thought *bungaku shugi*, a neologism that means literally "literature-ism," but is perhaps better translated as "literary aestheticism." In Tosaka's eyes this critical perspective inverts the proper hierarchy of objective reality over literary representation, and subjugates material realities to the fictional whims of literature. Real-world issues are being evaluated purely in terms of literary aesthetics.

Quite surprisingly, Kobayashi embraces the label, turning it around to reveal Tosaka's blind spots more clearly than ever before. In "Bungei hihyō no yukue," Kobayashi admits that man is intimately interconnected with politics in his life, and that literature, in dealing with life, cannot avoid making a political statement of some sort. Kobayashi, though, will not subsume literature into a political framework; he insists instead on its value as an alternative worldview:

> The reason literary practice is made easy by adding a political perspective is, in principle, quite simple: it is because in so doing writers would be limiting the conceptual range of literature to its political nature, never questioning this. If this were the case, political criticism through the vehicle of literature would, of course, gain in vigor. But this is at most a superficial vigor. In other words, literature of this sort would be nothing but one political perspective being critiqued by another political perspective that has borrowed the label of literature. . . . However, literature cannot stop at the concrete standpoint of issuing a critique from a political standpoint. Literature presses further; it cannot abandon the ideal of *criticizing politicality itself*. It is this ideal more than any other that forms the essence of literary thought; it is what feeds the internal creativity of the writer's thinking.[71]

This statement was one of the very few times that Kobayashi acknowledged the inescapability of politics in modern life. It was also perhaps his most explicit declaration of an awareness of the enormous scope of his critical practice. Literary aestheticism has, in the course of the exchange with Tosaka, risen to a place of prominence in the realm of real-world power relations. For the first time since the Meiji Restoration of 1868, literature was characterized as an autonomous discursive realm wielding influence on a par with politics and science.

By making his debut in a literary world dominated by a Marxist perspective buttressed by its claims to scientific methodology, Kobayashi was forced to strike out in a drastically different direction if he was to carve out a realm wherein the "magic" of the literary encounter could survive. Critic Yamazaki Kōtarō describes the nature of the encounter concisely: "Philosophically Kobayashi was influenced very little by Marx. However, we can detect an exceedingly deep influence from the radical nature of Marx's thought, the manner in which he questioned things at their most basic level."[72] In short, the encounter with Marxism pushed Kobayashi to a genuinely critical attitude, even in the contemporary sense. This breakthrough changed the nature of literary criticism in modern Japan, allowing the genre to evolve beyond the borders of the monthly literary reviews (*bungaku jihyō*) and literary research.[73] Kobayashi himself came to see a certain construction of literary discourse as posing a challenge to the politically oriented, modern world order.

Conversion of, and within, the Discursive Realm

In *Nihon no shisō*, Maruyama Masao declared that the absence of any comprehensive intellectual history of Japan reveals the most important aspect of that history: Japan has never had a central intellectual tradition that might serve as the focal point around which to narrate or categorize the ideas and movements that have arisen over the ages.[74] What existed instead was a dynamic practice drawing on eclectic syntheses of various traditions, both imported and indigenous. As Maruyama and others have argued, the import of Marxism, backed as it was by the aura of "science," changed that fact.[75] For a time, at least, the world of the Japanese intellectual was overwhelmingly consumed with the analysis of all modes of cultural production according to a single, internally consistent, comprehensive framework.

The repression of the Japan Communist Party and Marxist thinkers of all stripes that began shortly after the Manchurian Incident of 1931 coincided with the emergence of an aversion to that framework. A wide variety of thinkers began to feel confined by the restraints of Marxism's hegemony in cultural life. Partly because the movement tended toward formalist applications, but also partly because of the tradition of eclectic thinking, writers began to feel constrained by what many perceived to be an overly reductive analytical framework. Kobayashi gave voice to that resistance more eloquently and more persistently than any other writer. What he was calling for in his rejection of slavish adherence to rigid "designs" was, in effect, a resurrection of the fluid, eclectic practice that had dominated in Japan for so long. His articulation of a literary mode of cognition that was conducive to a wide variety of creative practices across genres struck a chord with writers whose Marxist affiliation had been stretched to the breaking point, both by a repression of artistic freedom within the movement and by governmental persecution from without. In short, Kobayashi supplied a home for those committing ideological conversion (*tenkō*). Part of the appeal of this home was, to be sure, the safety it afforded in the face of government repression. But that was only part of the story. This literary home also provided liberation from a constricting subjectivity. It seems unlikely that without this appealing "movement" to which one could convert, far fewer Marxists would have renounced that affiliation.[76]

The converted believed they were turning to the very eclectic, decentered universe of interchangeable, philosophical elements to which they had once longed to bring order. Maruyama Masao describes *tenkō* as "an escape from the tensions of self-regulation imposed according to a theory (or formula); like the release of a tightly coiled spring, *tenkō* brought about an instantaneous return to a 'natural' world of inclusivity, blending, and conflation. . . ."[77] The destination, then, was not an alternative, ideologically based subjectivity but rather a "natural" state in which the converted were no longer bound by the restrictions of some artificially constructed theoretical position. Kobayashi provided a contemporary articulation of this subjectivity, an articulation that was neither inherently reactionary nor innately conservative, but rather was informed by a genuine appreciation of both Western and indigenous traditions and was conducive to powerful critical thinking.

The turn away from Marxism and toward Kobayashi's more inclusive, eclectic literary praxis fueled the "literary renaissance" (*bungei fukkō*) of the 1930s. Even the titles of the journals that appeared in this period reflect the shift. As publications such as *Nōmin* (The Peasant), *Puroretaria bungaku* (Proletarian Literature), and *Puroretaria bunka* (Proletarian Culture) folded one after the other, journals such as *Bungaku* (Literature), *Sakuhin* (Texts), and *Bungakukai* (The Literary World) emerged to take their place. The very first issue of *Bungaku* declared the journal's dedication to precisely that: literature, and with no modifiers or disclaimers. Kobayashi published translations from Rimbaud's *Une Saison en Enfer* in this journal. When it folded in 1930, many of the writers associated with it joined Kobayashi in launching *Sakuhin*, which continued to be published until April 1940. Still, the main journal appearing around this time, and the one to have the largest influence on the literary community, was *Bungakukai*. It was conceived as a "united front" against Marxist literature, driven largely by Kobayashi, who served as editor from January 1935 to June 1936. It continued to be published through most of the war years, closing only in April 1944 (it was revived in 1948). These journals moved to the center of the literary community in the vacuum left by the persecuted magazines that had published Marxist criticism and proletarian literature. As the titles suggest, they did not adopt a particular political ideology or, for that matter, even a specific literary stance. Rather, they reveled in a diversity of literary modes.[78]

Many of the *tenkō* writers paralleled the turn exhibited by the publishing world.[79] The most striking example is writer Hayashi Fusao, who began his career as a proletarian writer. After serving a jail sentence for political activities, however, Hayashi grandly announced: "I have made up my mind. I will stake my life on literature. The task of literature is noble and great. It is worth a man's staking his life on it. Or, it might be more proper to say, no literature worthy of the name can be created unless a man stakes his life on it."[80] The ability to speak of "literature" in such grand yet nebulous terms—it was not the literature of realism, naturalism, symbolism, and certainly not Marxism—was possible only because of the way Kobayashi had recalibrated the constellation of cultural discourse in the preceding few years. Hayashi's debt to Kobayashi is also apparent in the following statement, in which he speaks of literature as an all-encompassing activity centered on the creative imagination:

> It is really quite amazing how stupid novels by stupid authors—and this does not only apply to proletarian literature—do not move beyond the category of popularized introductions to issues in biology, psychology, sociology, or history. . . . This is not the fault of literature; it is the fault of writers. . . .
>
> *The Origin of Species* is an interesting book. But Maupassant is interesting, too, though in a different way. *Das Kapital* is fabulous. But to Marx himself there was no better reading than Shakespeare and Balzac. Now here is the point: do not be carried away by *Das Kapital*; instead write something that would impress its author.[81]

Just as Kobayashi had compared Marx to Balzac and Dostoevsky in his "Samazama naru ishō," Hayashi places him alongside Darwin and even throws Shakespeare into the mix. Hayashi's conversion brings him to an embrace of a grand critical praxis very much like Kobayashi's, one that celebrates all brands of genius for their ability to move readers. What is more, it is this ability to move readers rather than the direction in which they are moved that constitutes the essence of literature.

But conversion is never a simple thing. In his seminal work on the subject, originally published in 1933, A. D. Nock reveals some of the complexities in his discussion of how the appearance of institutionalized Judaism and Christianity changed the course of human consciousness. Nock argues that before these institutions made their mark on the world, paganism functioned primarily through myth and ritual. At this point, "the rites were actions efficient in themselves as rites and not as the expression of a theology and of a world order."[82] Put another way, "a man used Mithraism, but he did not belong to it body and soul."[83] Institutionalized Judaism and Christianity, however, were qualitatively different from these traditional practices in that they were matters of conviction, theology, and faith. These once alien factors exerted so powerful an influence on consciousness that paganism could not but evolve along similar lines. Nock writes: "Genuine conversion to paganism will appear in our inquiry only when Christianity had become so powerful that its rival was, so to speak, made an entity by opposition and contrast."[84] That is to say, as a by-product of its demand for a denunciation of paganism in its converts, Christianity posited the qualities of conviction, theology, and faith in what had once been a matter of myth and ritual.

Nock's analysis has many parallels in the Japan of the 1930s. With the adoption of "faith" in the scientific objectivity of Marxist analysis, what Maruyama called the "'natural' world of inclusivity, blending, and conflation" was no longer "natural." Adherence required an act of faith, and, paradoxical though it may seem, the eclectic literary praxis advocated by Kobayashi and embraced by writers like Hayashi Fusao acquired a theology all its own: literary aestheticism. Maruyama Masao suggests that Kobayashi himself may have realized this irony, and quotes a 1933 essay by him as evidence:

> It goes without saying that a scientific, socially concerned critical method was introduced into the criticism of our country by today's Marxist philosophy. This introduction was certainly not by pure coincidence, but all the same it was a shocking incident for our literary community. We were totally unprepared for it, and the repercussions of the importation turned out to be more important than the substance of the theory itself. Because of these extensive repercussions, both the people who introduced the methodology and those who embraced it have completely forgotten the fact that no similar methodology had ever existed in the critical tradition of our country. This situation is unique to Japan—another point that not a single critic has

pointed out. People are admonished for the bourgeois liberalism underpinning their criticism. The one so admonished has no memory of consciously writing liberal literary criticism, but once it is pointed out to him, he is soon taken with the idea of his liberal criticism. Such complicated buffoonery is being played out everywhere, and it can only be explained by taking into account the situation unique to Japan.[85]

In short, Marxism raised the stakes in all critical endeavors, and once this systematic, comprehensive mode of analysis had taken hold, all parallel approaches inevitably gravitated toward the same stature. Kobayashi's dynamic mode of literary praxis was no exception; the struggle to resist the allure of adhering to a "design" was always on the brink of itself falling into formalism.

Maruyama also writes of how the dance of science in the form of Marxism, literature, and politics eventually pushed literature into a closer relationship with politics.[86] In his analysis, it was the alienation of science from politics and the influence of literature in its place that led to the irrationality and fascism of the war.[87] The shifting alliances, however, can just as validly be portrayed as presenting an opportunity (ultimately missed, perhaps, but an opportunity nevertheless) for a thorough reformulation of the conception of politics through the infusion of the literary mode of cognition that Kobayashi had been nurturing. Though he routinely rejected the notion of conceiving of literature in any and all political terms, Kobayashi himself seems to have been aware that this stance was, ironically, of some political import. This realization is revealed in a 1934 roundtable discussion on the relationship between literature and politics that was published, not surprisingly, in the journal *Bungakukai*. After a rambling discussion, the aforementioned Hayashi Fusao asked those present to join him in summarizing their positions on the relationship between the two fields. The contrast between his opinion and Kobayashi's demonstrates not only how fluid and flexible Kobayashi was in his thinking, but also how easily that same literary paradigm in the hands of one like Hayashi could slip into a rigid, formalistic stance:

HAYASHI: If there is a writer at this very moment who gives no thought to the choice between politics and literature, that writer is a fool. If there is a politician who cannot publicly declare that he is practicing politics, that man is a fool. If there is a writer who cannot publicly declare that what he does is literature, that writer is a fool. That's the entirety of my conclusion.

KOBAYASHI: First of all, I believe that the concept of "politics" contained in the question of politics versus literature is much more serious than the politics that people conventionally discuss. It is very different from what the average man means when he prattles on about politics. For example, if the question of literature versus politics existed, say, at the time of the French Revolution, the word "politics" would mean something very different from the common-sense understanding of the word. [If we in Japan today are] using the word "politics" for its common-sense meaning, it would not have excited literary figures to the extent that it has. The word "politics" as we speak it today carries aspirations. The word "politics" would not be an issue for writers if it did not include a sense of these aspirations based on the grand realization that our current worldview is changing, and that mankind's happiness or misery depends on what emerges in its place. . . . And so, we must not tether our political consciousness so tightly and directly to practical problems in the manner of the proletarian writers, deciding what study circles need to be formed and what organizations should be started. . . . If we interpret politics entirely in terms of a practical awareness of practical problems like study circles and organizations, the entire political consciousness of the moment is bankrupt. . . .

HAYASHI: I don't know what you're talking about [*sore wa wakaran*].[88]

In his comments Kobayashi is acknowledging the shifting meanings of the word "politics" as it travels through time. He is also suggesting that at the current historical juncture, "politics" as a concept is on the verge of a radical transformation, and is perhaps absorbing attributes previously associated with the cultural and literary. Kobayashi was right: the literary and cultural realms were increasingly being tied to political agendas as more and more of the population was wrapped up in wartime mobilization efforts. These subtleties, however, were lost on Hayashi.

Marxist critic Aono Suekichi, also in attendance, was impressed with Kobayashi's comments, agreed with him, and even remarked how they represent Kobayashi "losing his virginity" (*dōtei o yabutta*) concerning politics.[89] Arakawa Ikuo, writing on this discussion in 1989, echoed this sentiment, claiming that with this statement Kobayashi attained the "socialized I" (*shakai-ka shita watakushi*) that he had written of in "Watakushi shōsetsu ron."[90] While this is overstating the case, it is possible to locate here a fine example of Kobayashi's awareness that his literary mode of cognition, formed in opposition to the composite discourse linking science, Marxist literature, and politics, had altered the entire discursive constellation. Politics, a central pillar of the opposition, had evolved beyond simply the matter of how best to administer the nation and had acquired something of a literary, or critical, perspective in its awakening consciousness to shifting worldviews. The challenge posed to politics by literary modes of cognition had resulted in an understanding of politics that could no longer be limited to an objective analysis of capital formation and distribution, class conflict, and the revolution of the proletariat. It must now account for "aspirations," an English word Kobayashi records in *katakana*. Kobayashi was calling for a literary (which in his vision was also a genuinely critical) reappraisal of the world's options for the future.

Hayashi's part of the exchange, however, showed how easily this literary mode of cognition could slip into a rigid formalism of its own. While at times Hayashi exercised a very creative and probing analysis of the world, here he cannot see beyond the charged "designs" of literature and politics. Nor will he tolerate anyone who can. Having committed himself to "literature," Hayashi is revealed here to be trapped in a static conception of it, and unwilling to negotiate with the changing conditions around him; though he has slipped the bonds of one "design" (Marxism), he has reified his conception of literature into another.

The pitfall that Hayashi succumbed to in this roundtable discussion is precisely that threatening Kobayashi himself at every step. Though his literary mode of cognition was formulated as resistance to the concepts of objectivity and universality as well as their manifestation in the "science" that is Marxism, the emergence of this comprehensive, systematic, and internally consistent intellectual framework altered the constellation of discursive practices in such a way that any alternative gravitated toward the status of "design." Where Kobayashi was able to authentically practice literature as he advocated it in "Samazama naru ishō," he produced constructive, liberating criticism and moving literature—and during a time when such things were indeed rare. His method, however, required battling the tendency to disarticulate phenomena in a Cartesian manner and to render the world once again distant, foreign, and whole. Only this would allow him to take the intuitive leap of understanding, and render the world new through a unique articulation of it. This move carried the ever-present danger of culminating in a simple reification of phenomena, and a tendency toward a celebration of passive acceptance of them. These dimensions of Kobayashi's thought are explored in the following two chapters. Chapter 5 focuses on his successes, Chapter 6 on his failures.

FIVE

A Nation and History of One

Through the enormous corpus of critical essays that Kobayashi Hideo produced in the mid-1930s he established himself as a leading critical voice for his generation. The decline of the hegemony of the Marxist literary paradigm (a decline hastened by Kobayashi himself), in particular, created a vacuum that "literary aestheticism" (*bungaku shugi*) was well positioned to fill. Kobayashi pushed this paradigm, promoting in all fields of intellectual inquiry his call for constant critical recalibrations, whether it be of the theoretical models one brings to a study or of the concrete modes of expression with which one represents the world. Kobayashi's unflagging dedication to vibrant praxis without regard for ideological consequences or the production of instrumental knowledge distinguishes his mode of cognition as thoroughly literary (or critical), as even the frustrated Tosaka Jun acknowledged.

The fact that Kobayashi remained largely true to that aesthetic vision throughout the war years has raised difficult questions in the postwar world. Critics who in 1946 addressed the relationship of literary figures to the imperialist state were convinced that any support for Japan's war effort could have been possible only through a betrayal of a literary subjectivity. An example of this belief is found in an early manifesto by three young, emerging critics who were instrumental in setting the tone for many analyses of wartime culture. In the essay that opens the first issue of *Bungaku jihyō* in January 1946, Ara Masahito, Odagiri Hideo, and Sasaki Kiichi wrote:

> There were writers and critics who . . . joined forces with the fascists. The greatest of these were the manufacturers and supporters of the literature of

the "Holy War." Like Judas, who betrayed Christ for just 30 pieces of silver, these men were driven by petty ambitions and a desire for trifling supplements to their daily lives. In exchange, they took the purity of literature and treated it like a prostitute, casting it with their own hands down into the filth.[1]

This conviction that literature and the pursuit of war are incompatible runs through most of the essays produced during the short-lived investigation of writers' involvement in the war effort.[2] However, much as these critics may have wished the two realms to be mutually exclusive, the career of Kobayashi Hideo reveals a far more complex relationship between them. This chapter documents areas in which Kobayashi's thoroughly literary orientation did indeed prompt him to resist the temptation to pursue the simplistic manipulations of history and reductive notions of cultural identity that buttressed Japan's military endeavors. Kobayashi produced some of the most beautiful prose of his career in resistance to these very things. The same orientation, however, also manifested itself in expressions on the opposite side of the ideological spectrum: literary aestheticism led Kobayashi to affirm the social controls of the wartime state and to find beauty in the destruction of war, as will be treated in Chapter 6.

The writings considered in this chapter appeared as Japan's position in the world changed radically during the expansion of its empire in the 1930s. The Manchurian Incident of September 1931 had led to the establishment of the puppet state Manchukuo in February 1933. Next came the Marco Polo Bridge Incident in July 1937. In April of the following year the National General Mobilization Law (*kokka sōdōin hō*) was passed, and with it the "incidents" were replaced with an all-out war against China. While Japan was thus expanding its empire in Asia, it was extricating itself from its previously cooperative relationships with the Western powers. Symbolic of this shift in policy was Japan's withdrawal from the League of Nations in February 1933, after that organization followed the recommendation of the Lytton Commission and voted to condemn Japan as the aggressor in China. Historian Kenneth Pyle interprets this sequence of events as pushing Japan into theretofore uncharted waters:

> The Manchurian Incident thus proved a turning point—a point at which Japan abandoned the general policy of cooperation with the [Western] powers, which had for the most part controlled its international behavior since 1868, and chose to pursue its own destiny in East Asia, to trust its own strength to protect and advance its interests. The leadership now spoke of an "Asian Monroe Doctrine," declaring Japan's responsibility for maintaining peace in Asia.[3]

This was a new role for Japan, and its conception was tied to the ways in which intellectuals were positing their relationship with the West. A commitment to forging its own destiny, to formulating an "Asian Monroe Doctrine," was conceivable only after a reconfiguration of the heretofore ingrained belief, buttressed by Marxist theory, that a singular history was unfolding with Western nations at the vanguard. This radical shift in the projected trajectory of Japan's future demanded a reassessment of its past.[4]

Kobayashi took part in this reassessment. His interest in history first manifested itself in 1936 with his decision to teach a seminar on Japanese cultural history (*bunkashi kenkyū*) at Meiji University. Kobayashi himself makes light of his decision to turn his attention from literature to history: "It had simply become unbearably boring teaching something I knew [that is, literature], so I requested permission to teach something with which I was unfamiliar. Permission was granted."[5] Though he displayed a rather flippant attitude and began inauspiciously, Kobayashi acknowledged the pressing importance of historical understanding for his age and immediately began to stamp his aesthetic vision on the field of history. In the opening lines of his 1941 essay "Rekishi to bungaku" (History and Literature), Kobayashi writes:

> During any period of history there seems to be a word that controls the intellectual world at the time and is largely idolized by it. At one time that word was "Buddha" [*hotoke*], and at another it was "the gods" [*kami*]. During the Tokugawa Period it was "the heavens" [*ten*], and in eighteenth-century France it was "reason" [*risei*]. Looking for that which functions in this way in contemporary times, the word "history" comes to mind. It has reached a point where people—even those who have not once asked, "What exactly is history?"—accept phrases like "historical fact" and "the inevitability of history" as possessing some sort of solemn aura. It seems to me that all of this is something that today we are taking completely on faith.[6]

As even this short excerpt suggests, Kobayashi would participate in this discourse by addressing it at its foundation, asking the question "What exactly is history?" Whereas some of his contemporaries worked to adjust the specifics of the historical narrative (often with the goal of rationalizing Japan's imperialism), and others forged a new conception of the relationship of the past to national culture (sometimes in ways that supported the national agenda), Kobayashi remained focused on sustaining a vibrant praxis in his engagement with the past. In so doing he remained resistant to the production of knowledge easily harnessed by wartime ideologues.

Intimately linked to the renewed interest in history was, of course, heightened awareness of national identity. While this issue had been a concern since Japan's opening to international discourse in the closing years of the Tokugawa period, the questions "what is Japan?" and "where does it fit into the world community?" were now being posed in a very new context. With Japan increasingly alienated from its former Western mentors, it was incumbent on thinkers to fashion a "Japan" that was something other than a "rogue" modern power. The Japan Romantic School (Nihon rōman-ha) pursued these questions most vigorously, creating a definition of "Japanese-ness" based on an epistemology that rejected the cognitive modes of empiricism and positivism that had flourished in modernity.

A nuanced understanding of Kobayashi Hideo's considerable accomplishment at this ideologically charged moment in history is predicated on an understanding of two trends in modern Japan's intellectual history: the attempt to rewrite history in a manner that presented Japan's aggression on the continent in a more positive light, and the quest to define "Japanese-ness" in a way that both accounted for its debt to Western cultures *and* construed it such that it was something other than a hybrid culture. Within the context of the issues and stakes in both these undertakings, Kobayashi's literary aestheticism is revealed as both a radical critique of modernity's positivism and as a stance subversive of the ideologies of the wartime state.

Grappling with Universals and Particulars to Define the Nation

The excavation of history in pursuit of national identity was certainly not a new project in 1930s Japan. It had occupied thinkers since residents of the archipelago first encountered the culture of the Asian mainland centuries before. The intensity of Japan's contacts with the West around the time of the Meiji Restoration, however, altered the contours of the project. The nature of "Japan" came to be conceived, in the Meiji period, in terms of a Spencerian social Darwinism.[7] Viewed within this belief in a universal pattern of development among nations, Japan in the early years of Meiji was clearly far behind the Western nations in terms of technological development. As Kenneth Pyle points out, two approaches emerged to respond to this difference. One, proposed by the Min'yūsha (Friends of the Nation), was wholesale adoption of Western culture. The other was that of the Seikyōsha (Society for Political Education), which "believed that only by maintaining a distinct cultural identity could Japanese feel equal to Westerners and recover their national pride. In their writings they sought to define Japan's uniqueness and to formulate an independent Japanese role in international society."[8] At the time, "international society" meant, of course, the community of Western powers.

These two factors, the Spencerian framework and the West as model, informed the Seikyōsha mission and virtually all of the early modern discourse on national identity. In a word, the Japanese had no recourse but to accept the "more culturally advanced" West as a universal standard, and to forge their national identity within the categories posited there. The task they set themselves was, essentially, the articulation of a self in a language not their own (in both the abstract and, as it turns out, literal senses). Though it would not be widely recognized for several decades, there was a fundamental philosophical issue at stake here: the nature and relationship of universals and particulars. As Naoki Sakai argues, as moderns we have inherited "the European legacy of a historical time that coincides with the transition, gradual or rapid, from particularity to universality, from abstract universality to concrete universality, and ultimately coincides with the process of increasing rationalization, of reason realizing itself."[9] The danger in this process arises from the fact that any universalism, whether abstract or concrete, is in fact nothing more than "a particular thinking itself as universalism."[10] In this sense, the transition toward universality represents not so much an evolutionary step to a higher stage as it does the conquest of the diverse range of idiosyncrasies through the apotheosis of one of them.

A concrete example of this universal/particular dynamic is the seminal study of the Japanese national character, *Bushido: The Soul of Japan* (1899), by Nitobe Inazō (1862–1933). In this book Nitobe offered, in English, a romanticized explanation of the samurai code of chivalry as the key to understanding Japan. His comments in the preface to the first edition explain his motivation for composing the work:

> About ten years ago, while spending a few days under the hospitable roof of the distinguished Belgian jurist, the lamented M. de Laveleye, our conversation turned during one of our rambles, to the subject of religion. "Do you mean to say," asked the venerable professor, "that you have no religious instruction in your schools?" On my replying in the negative, he suddenly halted in astonishment, and in a voice which I shall not easily forget, he repeated "No religion! How do you impart moral education?" The question stunned me at the time. I could give no ready answer, for the moral precepts

> I learned in my childhood days were not given in schools; and not until I began to analyze the different elements that formed my notions of right and wrong, did I find that it was Bushido that breathed them into my nostrils.[11]

M. de Laveleye's conviction that a moral code based on religion is a universal facet of culture is matched only by Nitobe's surprise that direct correlations were expected: "The question stunned me at the time." This encounter represents Nitobe's initiation into the language of universals, and his response, not surprisingly, is in the "universal language": Nitobe first wrote the work in English and published it in the United States. It was then published in Japan, in English, in the following year, with a Japanese translation appearing in 1908.[12]

A similar pattern can be detected in *The Book of Tea* (1906) by Okakura Tenshin (1862–1913), also originally written in English. Like Nitobe, Okakura frames his explanation of this Japanese aesthetic tradition in terms of a religion comparable to those in the West. He writes, for example, that rituals associated with tea are "a religion of aestheticism—Teaism," and shortly thereafter states that the "Philosophy of Tea is not mere aestheticism in the ordinary acceptance of the term, for it expresses conjointly with ethics and religion our whole point of view about man and nature."[13] This desire to establish a Japanese equivalent for the religion serving as the backbone of Western culture is also reflected in the very title of the book: *The Book of Tea* is an allusion to the books of the New Testament (for example, "The Book of John").[14] Okakura was one of the most subtle thinkers of his generation, and his less than fully serious tone in this work suggests that he recognized the contradictory nature of an attempt to express what is uniquely Japanese in terms of Western categories.[15] So many others who came before him, however, like Nitobe, found the attractions of universalist discourse sufficiently compelling to compromise even the most glorious of Japan's particularities by associating them with privileged categories of Western universalist discourse.[16]

In the 1930s, however, things changed. International relations being played out on the world stage were revealing the inconsistencies of the universal/particular dichotomy to anyone who bothered to pay attention. The League of Nations' condemnation of Japan for its act of aggression against China was the most visible example. The sacred nature of national borders—the "universal" principle on which the League of Nations based its condemnation of Japan—was clearly nothing more than a self-serving preservation of glorified particulars instituted during the powerful West's earlier partitioning of territories. To insist on the inviolability of national sovereignty as a universal principle of civilization, based as it was on arbitrarily drawn lines, was therefore patently absurd. The growth of this consciousness prompted a recalibration of the Meiji world of Western universals and Japanese particulars.

One such recalibration was worked by, essentially, repositioning Japan in the world and thereby foregrounding a different "universal," one more amenable to Japan's imperialist agenda. Although the slogan behind many of the changes in the Japan of the early and mid-Meiji period was "Escape Asia, Enter Europe" (*datsua nyūō*), the growing antagonisms between Japan and the Western powers prompted a reversal. In order to shed the shackles of Eurocentric universals, thinkers found it necessary in their formulation of a national identity to "Escape Europe, Enter Asia" (*datsuō nyūa*). Whereas earlier thinkers like Nitobe had accepted Western categories and worked to fit Japanese tradition and history into them, thinkers of this generation spoke in terms of Eastern alternatives to Western cultural categories. Japan was no longer working within a foreign paradigm; it was constructing an alternative running parallel to it.

A pioneer on this track was Okakura Tenshin. His *The Ideals of the East* (1904) opens with an oft-quoted line: "Asia is One."[17] As Najita and Harootunian point out, Okakura's definition of Asia's common inheritance as "love for the Ultimate and Universal" represented an attempt to "establish Asia's cultural equivalence to the claims of Western hegemony."[18] Most interesting is the fact that at this early stage in Japan's revision of history, the appeal was still to the "Universal." That Okakura should choose to establish Japan's unique position in Asia through an assertion of its role as inheritor and caretaker of Asian art, however, reveals the extent to which he was still beholden to the metanarratives of the West—the Orient had long been patronizingly admired for the detailed craftsmanship of its "quaint" arts. Though Okakura sought a means of linking Japan to something bigger in order to challenge Western supremacy, he was unable to completely sever his ties to Western categories.

The more radical break in this "Escape Europe, Enter Asia" lineage came with the innovators of the field of *tōyōshi* ("Oriental history"), a project within which Japan turned the objectifying gaze upon China. Stefan Tanaka describes the groundwork of this project as laid by Shiratori Kurakichi (1865–1942) in the 1910s and 1920s, and traces its trajectory through to its logical conclusions in the 1930s and

1940s by the many students he trained. Taking his cue from the German historian Leopold von Ranke, Shiratori believed that scientific positivism was the method by which a framework for history was to be built, followed by an exercise of the more creative, poetic abilities of the historian to imbue the work with the living spirit of the age being depicted.[19] In the generations that followed, however, this balance was lost, and the entirety of the historical effort came to be seen as science, pure and simple. This belief became so entrenched in the psyche of scholars of *tōyōshi* that a third-generation student went so far as to say the deep roots in positivism rendered the field devoid of theory.[20]

Tanaka's analysis goes on to demonstrate convincingly that this legacy had a two-pronged effect: in one sense it linked Japan to China and, in a second sense, it alienated the two. The link was established through an assertion of the primacy of Confucian thought to the identity of all Asian nations. What distinguished Japan from China, however, was the fact that Japan was the rightful heir to that legacy. Simply put, Shiratori argued that the Chinese had interpreted the Confucian canon too literally, and that it was Japan's imperial system that was most in keeping with the true spirit of Confucius. Joined by other scholars working along similar lines, Shiratori's *tōyōshi* historians succeeded in parlaying this into a justification for Japanese leadership in Asia.[21]

The history of this history reveals it as having deployed the universal/particular dichotomy inherited from the West, albeit within a new context. By instituting an Asian universal, Confucianism, the *tōyōshi* historians were able to discursively establish an identity for a geocultural realm centered on Japan and China. In the hands of these historians, the "privileged" methods of modernity's positivist science were marshaled to argue that Japan more perfectly embodied that universal, with China representing no more than a particular manifestation at an earlier stage of the dialectical progression. While these thinkers succeeded in wrenching from the West the prerogative of defining universals, their adoption of the historical method, not surprisingly, brought with it a replication of the oppressive, hierarchical systems of international relationships. More radical critiques of the historical narratives underpinning national identities and the world order—critiques that would question the very positivist paradigm—were left to others, including the Japan Romantic School.

Irony Reified: The Japan Romantic School

Ironically, the approach of the *tōyōshi* historians emerged from the ethos of the Taishō era, a period distinguished by its faith in universal discourses. Their adoption of scientific positivism in their historical project was based on the assumption that this cognitive mode was applicable across cultural, linguistic, and national borders. This ethos changed as Shōwa progressed. Najita and Harootunian describe the shift: "Whereas an earlier cosmopolitanism promoted the ideal of cultural diversity and equivalence based on the principle of a common humanity, which served also to restrain excessive claims to exceptionalism, the new culturalism of the 1930s proposed that Japan was appointed to lead the world to a higher level of cultural synthesis that surpassed Western modernism itself."[22]

Leading this charge to a "higher level" was the Japan Romantic School, which pursued an understanding of history and cultural identity through the application of very different cognitive methods. Chapter 3 introduced a rupture in Western philosophy rooted in Descartes's *cogito ergo sum*. On the one hand, this produced a "Galilean" tradition that accepted Descartes's belief that the reasoning abilities of the subject were guaranteed by God; thinkers in this tradition pursued an understanding of the world through empirical, analytical methods. The positivism of the *tōyōshi* historians places them in this camp, firmly rooted in the Cartesian perspectivalism of the modern world. On the other hand, however, an "Augustinian" tradition also arose, which pursued Descartes's proclamation by exploring the subject (the thinking "I") and its modes of musing. This is a lineage that includes French philosopher Henri Bergson, whose thought inspired in Japan both Nishida Kitarō and Kobayashi Hideo. It also inspired the Japan Romantic School.

Although their inspiration was the German Romantics rather than Bergson and French literature, the members of this group also traced their roots to the Augustinian side of this fracture. As Kevin Doak notes, this is evident in the title of their first magazine, *Cogito*. Najita and Harootunian offer a similar characterization, portraying the movement as a reaction to literary naturalism, based as it was on an acritical privileging of an "I" observing the world.[23] As such, like Kobayashi Hideo, the Japan Romantic School represents a challenge to certain central pillars of modernity. Though the fascistic tracts of some of their members have discouraged scholars from a careful consideration of these thinkers, the group nevertheless warrants investigation for their contributions to the critique of modern subjectivity and the role history played in its formation.[24]

Many of the issues and solutions that the group identified can be seen in a short essay by Japan Romantic School poet Hagiwara Sakutarō (1886–1942): "Nihon e no kaiki " (Return to Japan, 1937). Hagiwara writes of how post-Meiji Japanese worked tirelessly to build a Western utopia only to find upon its completion that it had been a disappointing illusion all along. At this point attention turned back to Japan where, Hagiwara writes,

> the now discredited image of the West has steam engines rolling, electric trams running, and tacky buildings standing on every corner, each of them nothing but a clumsy replica. We have lost everything. And yet there is nothing so certain as the fact that, at the same time, we are traditional Japanese, and in our veins pulses the two-thousand-year history of our ancestors. Thus, to that extent, we have not lost a single thing.[25]

Hagiwara is asserting that although on the surface Japan is no longer Japan, the potential for rehabilitation exists. The seeds for this rehabilitation lie, not surprisingly, in "the two-thousand-year history of our ancestors." Hagiwara, like many of his contemporaries, turns to history for a national identity.

While the *tōyōshi* historians had mined history for a relatively straightforward construction of a Confucian identity for Japan, to Hagiwara and the Japan Romantic School it was not such a simple matter. They saw the past as no longer so easily accessible. Summarizing the movement as a whole, Doak writes that in the group's concern for ethnic identity "it soon became clear that the difference between indigenous culture and the West remained only as a memory that now had to be produced."[26] Hagiwara's proposal for this production takes the forgotten nature of this memory into account:

> I once wrote this in a lyric poem:
>
> I have not lost a thing
> And yet I have lost everything
>
> Truly today, from the midst of the emptiness in which culture has collapsed, the single song that we poets can sing is none other than that of the nihilistic drifter, a song given rhythm with contradictions such as these. A is not A; A is not not-A [*A wa A ni arazu. A wa hi A ni arazu*]. In the Japan of today this dialectical formula lives on as the rhythmical lyricism of the everyday emotions of the poet.[27]

The first half of Hagiwara's formula, "A is not A," is essentially a rejection of essences: Japan (as it is naively conceived) is not (truly)

Japan, or conversely (what you see before your eyes as a Westernized) Japan is not (truly) Japan. The second half of the formula opens the gate for a rehabilitation of "contingent essences," if such a thing is conceivable: (what is naively conceived of as) Japan is not (necessarily) not Japan. Similarly, there is no reason why what appears as a Westernized Japan must be rejected for being not-Japan.

It is a tortured argument to be sure, but one that allows for a clearing of the slate in preparation for the conscious construction of a new Japanese identity. That Hagiwara sees post-Meiji history as leading to the point where the slates have been cleared is evident in the following lines. Hagiwara notes how it is the very intellectuals once so enamored of the West who are now concerned with things Japanese:

> Certain people of superficial opinions look at this phenomenon and call it the defeat of the intellectuals, proclaiming it a "cowardly retreat" in our war. However, we have never in the past retreated. On the contrary, we have struck out at the enemy siege, attacking recklessly. Then, when at last we succeeded in breaking through, we stepped out onto a vast, open plain of nothingness [*kyomu*]. Now, in this place *there are no images of any kind.* All that one finds here are the clouds and sky, our shadows on the earth, and a starved, abandoned feeling.[28]

To Hagiwara, and to many in the Japan Romantic School, the mid-1930s were a time of infinite possibility. History had pushed Japan to a point where nothing existed as a given, and yet all remained as potential. It was a time when the "starved, abandoned feeling" could generate images at will upon the "vast, open plain of nothingness."

Hagiwara's "Return to Japan" articulates a stance held by many members of the Japan Romantic School. In spite of the fact that these writers realized that an indigenous culture could exist only as an artificial construct (their "dreams of difference," as Doak calls it), still it was to history and tradition that they turned for their raw materials and inspiration: "The Japanese romantics made clear . . . the artificial nature of 'ethnicity' or 'culture' in modern Japan and, hence, the need to consciously produce within the context of the modern world what will appear as native, traditional, and pure."[29] This was what the leader of the group, Yasuda Yojūrō (1910–81) referred to with the phrase "Japan as irony" (*ironī to shite no Nihon*).

The importance of irony as a mediating force in the clash of conflicting ideologies is well recognized. The assumption is that the nationalistic, ethnocentric tendencies of a strong national identity are muted by recognition that unique cultures and traditions possess no transcendent essence but are, rather, rhetorical constructs. The Japan Romantic School, however, suggests that this is not always the case: in their case the ironic construction of a tenuous identity evolved into an entrenched identity based on irony as a dominant, cognitive trope. The tension of the historical moment and the public nature of the discourse changed the ironic to the absolute, much as Hayashi Fusao's embrace of literature as a liberated praxis quickly slid into a formalism that brooked no consideration of its relationship with politics.

Doak traces this shift in Yasuda's thought, quoting a 1940 essay: "The basis of the Japan Romantic School has become a realism called Japan as irony, or the irony of a free Japan that has simultaneously maintained destruction and construction."[30] Here the emphasis is no longer on irony as a mediating force muting claims to the real, but rather on irony as a reified mode of realism. Considering the shifting contours of the concept of the "real" throughout history, it is not surprising that even irony, something usually employed to undermine claims to absolute reality, should be called into its service.

Hashikawa Bunzō reads the seeds of this claim to realism in the very start of the Japan Romantic School, their advertisement in the magazine *Cogito*: "I think it is significant both that the Japan Romantic School was conscious of itself as being the successor to a certain type of 'realism,' and that they virtually never abandoned this as a polemic weapon. . . . In short, one can conceive of a subject position for realism in the mediation of a mutual denial of 'Japan as irony' and 'the Japan Romantic School as irony.'"[31] Hashikawa sees the Japan Romantic School as committed to somehow teasing out reality through the technique of juxtaposing ironic tropes. The creation of a subject position through a double negation (the "mutual denial of 'Japan as irony' and 'the Japan Romantic School as irony'") functions in the same manner as the Hagiwara formula discussed above. As a vehicle for analysis such formulas are nothing but perplexing. However, they are also the only means available for escape from the stifling paradigms of modernity, inscribed as they are on our consciousness through the medium of the language (in the broadest sense) that has evolved hand-in-hand with these paradigms. To do more than reproduce Western historical discourse with a Japanese equivalent, the Romantics had to reinvent a human relationship with the past. This new relationship required a new language, a literary language that made full use of the antinomies that Hagiwara advocated and that Hashikawa identified as present from the school's inception.

Alan Tansman has identified and explored the integral role that language plays in Yasuda's work, arguing that the *kotodama*, or "spirit of the Japanese language," that Yasuda explicitly describes in some essays is implicitly invoked in all his best work. His release of this *kotodama* takes many forms, the most important of which are punning and the transgression of conventional genre boundaries. As Tansman notes, Yasuda's famous "Nihon no hashi" (Japanese Bridges, 1936) includes repeated "riffing" on the homonyms of *hashi* (bridge, edge, chopstick), and, in terms of genre, is in fact a "melange of historical treatise, serious and fanciful etymological investigation, cultural polemic, nationalist myth-building, and intense poetic evocation."[32] Through this infinitely literary reconfiguration of the modern world, Yasuda was able, at least for a moment, to propose a challenge to the universalist discourse of modernity more radical than that of the *tōyōshi* historians. Kobayashi Hideo worked in a similarly literary manner, his literary aestheticism functioning at times as a mode of resistance to the transparently self-serving tracts of nationalistic histories and even to the reification of literature or irony into a formal design, or literary universal.

The Very "Stuff" of History

Scholars writing on Kobayashi Hideo often see his sudden interest in history as a turning point in the evolution of this once cosmopolitan critic. Although the word *tenkō* (conversion) used in its strictest sense refers to the writers, thinkers, and activists who denounced Marxism in the 1930s, the label is also sometimes more loosely applied to include individuals whose change of ideological direction, while perhaps not as dramatically enacted or explicitly expressed, followed the same pattern of movement from the Westernized, liberal positions that characterize the Taishō period to the conservative or even reactionary stances assumed by intellectuals during Japan's years at war. It is in this more general sense of the word that some scholars and critics have claimed that Kobayashi Hideo's wartime writings on history and the Japanese literary tradition represent an instance of *tenkō*.

The most sustained argument for viewing Kobayashi's work during the war years as a conversion is presented by Kitagawa Tōru, who sees Kobayashi's early interest in poetry, particularly that of Rimbaud, Nakahara Chūya (1907–37), and Tominaga Tarō (1901–25), as leading to a belief in the revolutionary potential of poetic language.[33] Kitagawa finds evidence of this in texts such as "Samazama naru ishō," particularly the section dedicated to outlining the role that language plays in the formation of both individual subjectivities and communal life.[34]

Comparing this early poetic orientation with Kobayashi's stance in his wartime essays, Kitagawa writes that

> one would have to say that the "muse" [*shishin*] within Kobayashi had undergone an obvious transformation. I have claimed time and again that the "muse" of this writer, wrapped as he was in an extreme state of self-consciousness, existed in opposition to the status quo that existed external to Kobayashi's consciousness. At this juncture, however, Kobayashi's "muses"—language, history, society, and the corporeal body—were regrettably reified as elements of a nature that "enveloped [him], allowing not a drop of water to seep through." The moment Kobayashi arrived at a literary resignation to "sadly taking into his heart" these naturalized elements, his "muse" could no longer survive.[35]

Kitagawa is arguing here that at this point in his career Kobayashi's emphasis on critical praxis, the incessant reinvention of the most basic categories of thought, came to a halt, and that he began working strictly within the borders of contemporary discourses. While Kitagawa is right to problematize Kobayashi's tendency toward resignation to the concrete realities of the world around him (an issue to which I return in Chapter 6), this reductive reading effaces two important elements of the essays from this period. First, Kobayashi did produce some of modern Japan's finest prose-poetry in the form of the essays later collected in *Mujō to iu koto* (The Fact of Evanescence, 1946). If this feat was made possible only by killing his "muse," Kobayashi was better off with it dead. Second, in his desire to keep the truly literary sharply distinguished from the frighteningly fascist, Kitagawa fails to recognize how all of Kobayashi's wartime essays are fully informed by the literary stance he had espoused up to that time. We may be far more comfortable denouncing the fascistic pronouncements as an aberration from a career dedicated to literature (as did Odagiri Hideo in the manifesto cited at this chapter's opening), but the fact of the matter is that in some important ways the two are intricately linked in Kobayashi's vision. As this chapter and the next chronicle, Kobayashi's literary orientation made him both subversive of the formulaic, ideological propaganda disseminated in the guise of history and literature *and* complicit in the formation of a subjectivity conducive to acts of aggression.

Evidence that the "muse" continued to live in Kobayashi, and that he continued to wield the "vibrant yardstick" of literary aestheticism, is found in his various wartime writings on history. While the *tōyōshi* historians were embedded deeply within the universal/particular chimera of modernity, and the Japan Romantics were experimenting with irony as an alternative trope, Kobayashi applied to history the very arguments he had leveled against the "design" of Marxism. He found such approaches to history plagued by the same problem he had found in modern literature and criticism: the surrender to formalistic approaches that had come to obscure the world and to numb our ability to revel in its wonders. In the 1939 essay "Rekishi no katsugan" (A Keen Eye for History), Kobayashi wrote:

> A living eye [*katsugan*] for history—I think this was most evident among the scholars who boldly endeavored to forge history anew during the Meiji period, when the hearts of this nation's people were first drawn toward the positivist fields that had come in from the West. After this, I believe, that the living eye for history gradually clouded over. Most historians continue to fall into decline over one of two paths: they lose the keenness of their vision as their feet slowly sink in the quagmire of historical source materials, or they lose their understanding of what constitutes keen observation as their hearts are stolen by the convenience of historical methodologies such as the materialist view of history [*yuibutsu shikan*].[36]

As in his writing on literature and criticism, Kobayashi praises the creative formation or adaptation of an idea—an act wherein abstract thinking is merged with concrete realities through the mediation of language—and denounces both the privileging of objectivity (the "quagmire of historical source materials") and the dependence on static "designs" (such as the materialist view of history).

As he had done in "Samazama naru ishō," Kobayashi acknowledges the connection between language and understanding. In the earlier essay he had insisted that while the initial act of naming constitutes an invention on a par with the discovery of fire, he also notes how language used mechanically obfuscates the reality it was once meant to evoke. The same is true, of course, for the vocabulary of history, and the example Kobayashi offers is the tired use of abstract labels such as "feudal":

> [The mainstream historians] say that it is only natural that ideas such as those expressed in the *Hagakure* should emerge under a feudal system. . . . But what these modern historians understand about this word "feudalism" has absolutely no connection to the people of the Tokugawa period. They believed in ethics, not something called "feudal ethics." Historians say that

> the feudal system constrained human freedoms. However, can we allow historians to overlook the very shocking freedom that Yamamoto Jōchō achieved under these constraints?[37]

The point here is that an interpretation of the age, and by extension all that occurred in it, as "feudal" does an injustice to the singularity of the accomplishments of individuals living therein. Seeing the authorship of the *Hagakure* as "only natural" obscures the creative use of the intellect that produced it. In that such creativity is the centerpiece of Kobayashi's literary aestheticism, it comes as no surprise that he seeks to displace the historical interpretation and understanding that would compromise it.

Kobayashi's objection to such formalism and uninspired articulation is based on his belief that they diminish the human experience:

> Without man there is no history. This is surely an incontestable truth. And yet, for some odd reason, we must remind ourselves each and every day to open our eyes wide to this truth and rescue it. Not only the materialist view of history, but all of modernity's rationalist theories of history happen to have a tendency to completely forget this simple truth. It is not forgotten out of carelessness—I would contend that, in fact, these approaches contain a mechanism whereby this truth is skillfully erased from our memories. . . . It reaches the point that as long as one has a theory of history, one no longer needs history itself.[38]

This sentiment, like many of Kobayashi's feelings about contemporary historical methods, corresponds to those in his critique of literature and philosophy. His point is that the writer, whether of literature, philosophy, or history, is the ultimate source of the discourse. Good history, like good literature, requires a writer to look deep within and forge a unique narrative that links his vision with the historical materials at hand. To adopt an established method, or "design," is to forget that the historian is the source of history. It is to surrender one's unique "destiny."

The method that Kobayashi advocated for the rehabilitation of historical inquiry was a variation of the act of "seeing." This literary mode of cognition was one that required, first and foremost, a reassertion of distance between the perceiving subject and the perceived object. In a post-earthquake world filled with commodities, each of them mechanically reproducible and exceedingly susceptible to both physical and intellectual disarticulation, reassertion of this distance was required in order to circumvent the temptations to pull things close and interpret. As argued in Chapter 2, Kobayashi did this by rhetorically restoring to things a surface so unified and clean that it could be accepted at face value rather than excavated for meanings hidden consciously or unconsciously by the author. In the case of the literature of his hero Shiga Naoya, Kobayashi had reacted to Hirotsu Kazuo's dissection by advocating a mode of reading that posited Shiga's works as a painting hung on the wall, to be admired in stunned silence as its beauty deprives us of a critical language to describe it.[39] In the late 1930s and early 1940s Kobayashi championed this epistemology in the realm of history. Metaphorically—and sometimes even almost literally—he substituted for history an impenetrable piece of materiality, immune to Cartesian disarticulation and dissection but conducive to intuitive, emotional appreciation.

To short-circuit the interpretive disposition, however, Kobayashi first had to re-establish a psychological distance between the present and the past. He first accomplished this by emphasizing the "pastness" of the past, an attribute evident in the utter singularity of the historical event: "'History repeats itself' is a favorite adage of historians, but we recognize the fact that once something has occurred, it is irretrievably lost. We feel this in our bones [*kimo ni meijite shōchi shite iru*]."[40] In addition to establishing a respectful distance, this fact renders history immune to any scientific approach. By foregrounding the particularity of an event, Kobayashi inoculated it against incorporation into universal categories such as "feudalism." This distance was widened by Kobayashi's refusal to recognize a temporal link between the singular events of the past and the present moment. In "Rekishi ni tsuite" (Concerning History, 1938), for example, Kobayashi argued that all concepts of time are, ultimately, human inventions, and that the measure of time based on natural phenomena is not universally applicable.[41] In "Mujō to iu koto" he claimed that "the bloodless idea that time stretches from the past to the future like a piece of taffy [*ame*]" is "the grandest illusion of our time."[42] He also rejected the idea of history as linked by the chain of causality.[43] All of this serves to distance the historian further from the past; the gulf between the two is immense. This unbridgeable gap precludes the possibility of reconstructing history through research and reason.

A second means by which Kobayashi rendered the past unknowable to the analytical modern mind was by rhetorically restoring an awareness of it as materiality, an act not unlike his portrayal of Shiga's literature as a painting. As he argued in "Rekishi ni tsuite," our only links to the past exist in the form of historical materials. To Kobayashi these are not to be analyzed for their veracity or parsed for hidden meanings. Rather, they are to serve as concrete agents transmitting a vision of the past to the historian; they are like talismans. "We do not recognize a history where there are no documents (*shiryō*). Furthermore, this documentation is, in its most basic form, entirely material (*busshitsu*)."[44] And on the next page: "History is myth, myth forced to accept to a greater or lesser extent the limitations placed on it by the materiality (*busshitsusei*) of historical documents."[45] This materiality serves as almost a conduit to the past for the historian: "a man who takes the roof tile of an ancient temple in his hand has two personalities: with one he measures the weight of that tile, while with the other, he draws a mental image of the human figure behind it."[46] The historical "document" of the roof tile is readily recognizable as consisting of materiality, but Kobayashi attributes a similar nature to the written word and, as argued below, the staged performance as well.

A better sense of this sensibility emerged in Kobayashi's 1950 dialogue (*taidan*) with friend and ceramics connoisseur Aoyama Jirō. The men held forth on the topic "Eyes Trained on Form" (*katachi o miru me*), and lamented the way modern audiences are unable to appreciate form. In the case of dramatic performances, for example, people focus on the plot line, but both men agree this attention is misplaced:

KOBAYASHI: Take the lines delivered in a kabuki play. They're not a conceptual use of language, they're form.

AOYAMA: That's right, form. That's exactly what they are.

KOBAYASHI: The point is that the lines don't *mean* anything. But people just can't seem to grasp the fact that there is no meaning there. . . . They're too busy trying to understand. Modern man believes that the only ones to whom the sense of form means anything are the collectors of antiques. But if you really think about it, you'll see that the form is really also there in man's philosophical thought. . . . In other words, non-positivistic thought reaches its pinnacle in form.[47]

To insist that language, the most exquisite semiotic system, is without referents or connotations is Kobayashi's way of pulling us back to the surface of things in order to stem the interminable slide into ever more abstract interpretations. In place of meaning, a focus on form offers a chance to recover something of a dormant sensibility:

KOBAYASHI: Now, form, this is something that can't be grasped cerebrally. Form is something grasped by the most advanced, refined sensibility. It just requires a kind of training, like the training of the tongue [to distinguish delicate flavors]. As with swimming, it's not something you can really teach—you just toss somebody in the ocean and, in the course of their splashing around, they learn to swim. This sort of thing requires a tactile sense from the entire body; it's not the sort of thing that can be grasped through the brain.[48]

This refined sensibility is precisely what he would require of the historian. It is predicated on a respect for the distance between subject and object, a distance that is maintained through attention to the "form" or materiality of that object. As these lines suggest, for Kobayashi the materiality that he insists is the most basic quality of all historical documents is not so much a quality innate to the object as an attitude or sensibility nurtured by the writer.[49]

With history distanced from the would-be historian through his emphasis on its irretrievable "pastness" and the intellectually impenetrable materiality of its documents, Kobayashi then turned his attention to what remained of the historical project: the subject. As with his view of fiction and criticism, Kobayashi saw the perceiving subject and his/her experience as the essence of the encounter with the past. In fact, the historical drive is itself entirely a matter of a subject's reaction to the flow of time: "History never repeats itself. It is precisely for this reason that we are loath to let it go [*oshimu*]. History resembles an enormous resentment [*urami*] held by mankind. I believe that the line running through history is our sense of reluctance to part with it, certainly not some chain of causality."[50]

It is this sense of irretrievable loss that Kobayashi established at the core of his historical method. More than the modern theories of historical progress, which rely on rational investigation to give us an understanding of history, it is the sentiment expressed in the opening passage of the famous *Heike monogatari* (The Tale of the Heike, ca. early twelfth century)—"The proud do not endure, they are like a dream on a spring night"—that suggests the proper attitude toward what has come before.[51] The attitude is one of a personal longing for what is irretrievably lost. The historical attitude that Kobayashi invoked with these lines is that of the classical Japanese aesthetic concept of *mujō* (transience or evanescence) and the melancholy inspired by this awareness of the ephemeral nature of life. It is no coincidence that Kobayashi's essays on the Japanese classics, discussed below, were collected under the title *Mujō to iu koto* (The Fact of Evanescence).

Kobayashi offers a synthesizing image for his vision of the historian's attitude and approach, an image that, though overly sentimental (or perhaps that is the point), combines all the elements of his historical project:

> It will be clear if you imagine a mother who has lost her child in death, and consider her attitude toward the historical fact of that child's death. For the mother, surely, the historical fact is not simply the time, place, reasons, and conditions surrounding the event of the death. Unless these are accompanied by a feeling that an irreplaceable life has been irretrievably lost, the event does not generate meaning as a historical fact. Without this feeling, no matter how detailed an explanation of the circumstances of the child's death is achieved, it will not lead to an image of the child's face flitting before one's eyes.[52]

Kobayashi had, in fact, introduced this image in his first essay on history, "Rekishi ni tsuite":

> If we think carefully about what occurs in a mother's heart as she sits with some trifling articles once used by her beloved child . . . we can grasp the basic wisdom needed for the historical project. The wisdom is not some primary, cognitive mode for approaching historical facts. It is, rather, a basic technique, for in this approach we are not looking at given historical facts but rather *making* them with the inspiration provided by the materials at hand. In the application of this wisdom, the historical fact is neither an objective nor subjective thing. While this sort of wisdom may be epistemologically vague, when we can act on it we attain a certainty as unquestionable as the fact that we are alive.[53]

Kobayashi's emphasis on the distance separating us from the past is evident here in two ways. First, the mother realizes keenly that the child is gone; she, more than anyone, recognizes the unbridgeable chasm opened up by the death. The second element of distance arises in the inverted nature of the image that Kobayashi projects. As Kamei Hideo points out, rather than a mother faced with the death of a child, the historical project is more easily likened to a child faced with the death of a parent. This arrangement, Kamei insists, would better represent the sadness experienced by the historian struggling against the collective amnesia of the present.[54] Kobayashi's inversion of the expected chronology, however, matches his project perfectly: whereas a parent's death strikes us as being in the natural order of things, a child predeceasing its parents defies rational explanation. The image is so powerful that Yasuda Yojūrō makes it a central motif in his "Nihon no hashi."[55] The death of the child cannot be "understood"; it can only be felt.

The image of the mother who has lost her child embodies other aspects of Kobayashi's vision for history. The reluctance to part with the past is there in the mother's longing for the time when the child was still alive, and this prompts a connection between them that is direct, an understanding that is not mediated by abstract thought or generalizations. It is inspired by "articles once used by her beloved child" (*aiji no sasayaka na ihin*). This materiality is what sparks the "recollection" (*omoidasu koto*) of the past, this word substituting for "seeing" in Kobayashi's writings on history. As Aeba Takao points out, to Kobayashi the historical fact "is seen from what is essentially the emotional realm of an autonomous individual, and exists solely in the reality of those emotions."[56]

In summary, then, Kobayashi posited a history that is irreparably severed from the present and therefore beyond reconstruction through rational means. This fact leads us to a longing for the past, an emotion that prompts us to "recollect" it in the present. The motivation is an essentially emotional one, which means that history begins with a particular individual's sensibilities (rather than a theory or method); its object is similarly specific (an individual or moment, rather than a group or period). As such the practice of history becomes the practice of literary aestheticism, an exercise or appreciation of individual creativity as inspired by the mysteries suggested by the historical material.

Kobayashi's theory of history was, at every turn, antithetical to the project of creating the type of national identity that could fuel the usual varieties of nationalism and imperialism. His rejection of a positivist or even a shared ironic approach to history in favor of an emotional one that is deeply personal prevented his discourse from developing either a communal aspect or a forward momentum. The specificity of the person at either end of the project was also conceived in a manner that discourages, from the very start, the abstractions and generalizations that generated national identities. Therefore, while Kitagawa Tōru saw in these writings a new and regrettable surrender to reified exteriority, Kobayashi's writing had always relied on such, and his wartime essays are, in fact, entirely consistent with his earlier work. Furthermore, and most importantly, what Kitagawa saw as surrender to a reified history and society was not innately reactionary. In fact, it was precisely Kobayashi's stubborn insistence on the impenetrable materiality of history that infused his resistance to a metanarrative casting Japan as the nation destined for supremacy in Asia and perhaps the rest of the world, a metanarrative constructed by and motivating for the *tōyōshi* historians and eventually overwhelming the Japan Romantic project as well.

The Very "Stuff" of the Nation

Just as his focus on particularity and materiality kept Kobayashi aloof from the production of nationalistic historical narratives justifying its imperialism, so too did it prevent him from contributing to the construction of a national identity. In an essay entitled "'Nihonteki na mono' no mondai" (The Question of 'Things Japanese'"), originally published in the Tokyo *Asahi shinbun* in April 1937, Kobayashi attacked the simplistic manner in which so many writers were attempting to construct a national identity based on the discovery of things quintessentially Japanese.[57] Kobayashi scoffs at the efforts to formulate an abstraction, claiming that it was only in an articulation of the specific that the concept had any connection to the world: "Attempting to talk about ethnicity [*minzokusei*] or tradition [*dentō*] is nothing but empty theorizing unless the writer has his own particular literary image of what these things are."[58] These same sentiments are echoed later in the essay:

> Surely there is nothing a writer can accomplish by relying on the signboards of Japanism [*Nihonshugi*] and patriotism [*aikokushugi*]. No masterpiece of national literature has ever once succeeded thanks to feelings of nationalism. The literary concept of "things Japanese" produces nothing of any real consequence outside of the question of whether or not the writer is able to formulate a unique image of what is quintessentially Japanese. The whole issue is not so much reactionary as it is paradoxical.[59]

"Paradoxical" is indeed the word for it. By pulling the issue of national identity into the world of literary aestheticism, Kobayashi was insisting that articulations of it conform to his insistence on personal, idiosyncratic visions that, the moment they are formulated, are no longer anything but another "design." Kobayashi's call in "Samazama naru ishō" for a rejection of the communal aspects of language for liberated critical praxis is used here to deflate the entire project whereby a national identity is constructed. In that any vision of what constitutes "Japanese-ness" must be intimately personal and nothing more than a fleeting exercise in seeing, it cannot be propagated as a communal myth.

The same is true for an investigation of tradition. In his 1941 essay "Dentō" (Tradition), Kobayashi outlined the process whereby one may revive (*kaifuku suru*) classic works of literature. What he advocated was, initially, an exhaustive analysis of the historical conditions of their production. This endeavor is ultimately doomed, Kobayashi claimed, but is valuable nevertheless because it makes us painfully aware that the power of a classic is beyond rational explanation. The inevitable failure of such positivistic analyses reveals the classics as inexplicably perfect works of art; by resisting interpretation they exhibit "the immutable archetypal form" (*ugokashigatai kihan no katachi*).[60] To speak of an "immutable form" is to assert the "wholeness" of each classic; it is to render it a materiality that is meaningless when disassembled into components.

This emphasis on materiality, on the "immutable form," was Kobayashi's technique for resurrecting the "lost home" he nostalgically depicted in his essay "Kokyō o ushinatta bungaku" (discussed in Chapter 1). With the proliferation of commodities and the concomitant loss of the "aura" that had once emanated from the irreplaceable work of art, the human experience of the world had changed. Kobayashi had detected remnants of it in his youth, before the Great Kantō Earthquake had altered the system of materiality-subjectivity. As the hands of the clock could not be turned back, and as technological advance was unstoppable, Kobayashi was left with no choice but to rhetorically resuscitate that relationship with things, a relationship that had originally been dictated by the corporeal realities of the world. By force of will Kobayashi returned the objects of his attention to pieces of precious, irreplaceable, and wondrous matter.

This attitude toward history, tradition, and the Japanese classics inspired, and was in turn fed by, Kobayashi's infatuation with ancient ceramics and antiques. Though he was first introduced to this world as a student, it was only in the late 1930s that he became "possessed" by them (*Kitsune ga tsuita*).[61] In these years, and particularly during the war, Kobayashi would dedicate a considerable amount of his time to seeking out, buying, selling, and talking about such precious artifacts. The art of trading in antiques, at least as Kobayashi understood and practiced it, served as a perfect metaphor for the mode of interacting with the world that he sought to revive.

Kobayashi appreciated antiques for their resistance to intellectual understanding and their appeal entirely to the visual and tactile senses. Like the roof tile of the ancient temple that his imagined historian would take in hand, Kobayashi considered ancient ceramics to be historical "documents" that were meant not to be read but to serve as a conduit of history. They do not represent history, they *are* history, as John Treat says of the artifacts that litter Ibuse Masuji's literature.[62] Kobayashi expressed this aspect of the antique:

> The word "antique" oozes an indescribable musty sort of odor. People choose to refer to them as "works of ancient art" in order to contain this smell. The word "antique," though, is saturated with man's fondness for ceramics, it is heavy with the weight of a history of desire. "Works of ancient art" is a euphemism just too flimsy to carry these meanings. [Modern intellectuals], however, very rarely realize this fact because what they do is appreciate art rather than dabble in antiques. They rarely stop to think about the difference between the two, or consider what they gain by belittling the dealing in antiques and opting instead for the appreciation of art. Antiques are meant to be dabbled with, art to be appreciated.[63]

This expression of the mood surrounding the antique contains the ingredients of Kobayashi's vision for the historical project as well. Like the positivist historian, the modern intellectual appreciating art engages it cerebrally. To Kobayashi, however, the antique is encountered through the senses; it has a "musty sort of odor" and is meant to be handled. Kobayashi repeats the idiom *kottō o ijiru*, translated here as "dabbling in antiques." The verb *ijiru* suggests both the acts of poking and prodding the artifact as well as the acts of buying and selling. Everywhere the abstract encounter of art ("appreciation") is replaced with a corporeal contact, making the antique indeed an object of "desire" (rather than understanding) and the medium through which the past appears before one's eyes. Shown a seal from a port at the southern end of the Korean peninsula, and dating back to the Nara period (710–784), Kobayashi "felt his heart pound as he spun fragments of dreams of Japan's interaction with Korea."[64]

Shirasu Masako, a long-time acquaintance of Kobayashi who shared his love of antiques, attests to the fact that through his obsession with antiques Kobayashi confirmed and refined his intuitive mode of cognition: "It is all a matter of suffering through the encounter with something that cannot be dissected through reason. Kobayashi said this all the time. He said that when looking at antiquities, one had to discard all preconceived notions, dispense with all knowledge, and empty the heart. He would declare that to be successful, one had to polish the intuition."[65] As had always been the case with Kobayashi, this mode of cognition was the only way he could conceive of rehabilitating the human emotions numbed by the flood of abstractions in the modern world:

> It is not my intention to defend dabbling in antiques. That would be as foolish as defending womanizing. But this is how I feel about it—in this day and age, when it is all but impossible to live a consistently tasteful life that incorporates beauty in our everyday activities, people are backed into a world where art is enjoyed entirely on a conceptual level. This trend may be irreversible. Still, I find it absurd that the enjoyment of this world where art is accessible only through abstractions should be thought of more highly than womanizing. The absurdity of relegating beauty to something to be enjoyed conceptually can only be fully realized if we experience the full range of human emotions—joy, anger, melancholy, and pleasure—that are aroused by a concrete interaction with beauty through that black magic known as "dabbling in antiques." What a deplorable state we are in![66]

Kobayashi is nostalgically alluding to an age where beauty was incorporated into our everyday lives in a corporeal sense. By this he means a time before commodities—countless and infinitely replaceable—ruled the world. He portrays this as a time full of healthy human emotions and desires, a time when our interaction with materiality was unmediated by conceptual thinking and as physical as the pursuit of sex through "womanizing" (*onna dōraku*). Kobayashi longs for a world where things—real, corporeal things—still aroused the emotions that make us human.

What invests the antique with such power is its absolute singularity. In a world permeated with mechanical reproductions, the antique alone retains an undeniable "thingness." It is the antithesis to the commodities that flood the market. It is also anathema to any universal category of beauty, for its worth resides more in its singularity than in its embodiment of an abstract, universal aesthetic value.

In an ironic twist, the antique's existence as the anti-commodity makes it simultaneously the most sought-after commodity. Kobayashi accommodated the marketplace in his engagement with antiques. As Shirasu remarks, "Kobayashi loved *buying* antiques."[67] The reason was that the formidable prices sustained in a market rife with forgeries demanded he fully invest himself in the act of "seeing." In his essay "Shingan" (The Original and the Forgery, 1951) he tells the story of his purchase of a scroll inscribed with the calligraphy of the poet Ryōkan (1758–1831). When a friend reveals to him that it is a forgery, Kobayashi snatches up a sword, slices the scroll to pieces, balls up the shredded remains, and tosses them into the hallway.[68] This anecdote represents the inextricable link in Kobayashi's thought between the singularity of an object and its beauty. Though even the forgery may very well have been one of a kind, it is not the specific one of a kind that Kobayashi had thought it to be, and the fact that he had purchased it reflected his inability to "see." When Aoyama Jirō raises some doubts about the authenticity of a bowl in Kobayashi's collection, Kobayashi is beside himself, experiencing the sort of human emotions aroused only by genuine interaction with materiality. Throughout the night he gets up time after time to turn on the light and look again at this antique. Deciding that "if the bowl is bad, then so am I, and there is no middle ground," Kobayashi takes it to a professional appraiser the very next day. This time his taste is confirmed. Surprisingly, knowing now that his intuition had been correct, Kobayashi is no longer interested in the object. He leaves it at the dealer's for resale.[69]

"Dabbling in antiques" provided Kobayashi with precisely the sort of passionate interaction with the world that he felt slipping away as technology altered the very nature of materiality. The absolute, unreproducible "thingness" of an ancient artifact made it possible to interact with it without the mediation of universal categories and abstractions. Kobayashi sought to restore the literary text to the same level of materiality and uniqueness. When he turned to the medieval classics of the Japanese canon during the war years, Kobayashi reproduced this premodern cognitive mode in his readings. In the essay "Dentō," he rejected the idea of interpreting temporally distant texts. Instead, he wrote, they should be "appreciated." Though this is the word he had used disparagingly to describe the modern intellectual's relationship to art, here Kobayashi connotes the term positively. Here he employs it to refer to an approach that parallels his attitude toward antiques. "While appreciation seems at first glance to be a refusal to act," Kobayashi writes, "this is not actually the case. Appreciation is the act of imitation [*mohō*], made conscious and purified."[70] This act of imitation is what Kobayashi attempted in the essays that comprise *Mujō to iu koto*.

Channeling the Past: "The Fact of Evanescence"

Shirasu Masako draws a link between the above discussion of antiques and Kobayashi's writing: "Beautiful objects compel a person to silence. Kobayashi was a writer who always composed with a focus on this fact; it made no difference whether he was dealing with antiques, literature, or painting."[71] This statement is particularly true for the wartime essays later collected under the title *Mujō to iu koto*: the self-portraits included in the essays portray a Kobayashi fallen silent, and the essays themselves are terse. "Mujō to iu koto," the title essay, and "Taema," the other essay considered here, run to only three pages each. The collection as a whole, but these two essays in particular, are masterworks of prose poetry. More than any other essay from Kobayashi during this period, they disprove Kitagawa Tōru's claim that the war years represent the death of his muse.

While to some extent Kobayashi does weave into these essays allusions to the arguments he had been making since the late 1920s, for the most part here he "practices what he preaches." Phrased in the vocabulary Kobayashi himself used in "Akutagawa Ryūnosuke no bishin to shukumei" and "Samazama naru ishō," Kobayashi fuses his "destiny" (his abstract vision of incessant, critical praxis) with his "muse" (the texts he addresses as artifacts ultimately immune to interpretation). The objects of his attention in the two essays analyzed here, the *Ichigon hōdanshō* (Brief Sayings of the Great Teachers, ca. early fourteenth century) and the *nō* play "Taema" (ca. early fifteenth century), are taken as "the material with which to narrate the self."[72] One might describe Kobayashi's approach to them as one that sought most of all to avoid a disarticulation of them, opting instead to consider them in their "immutable forms." One might also say that Kobayashi acted on the claim he made in "Dentō"; "appreciation is the act of imitation [*mohō*], made conscious and purified," he wrote there, and in these essays he indeed strove to achieve in his criticism an effect similar to that evoked by the works he engaged.

In "Mujō to iu koto" Kobayashi took his inspiration from a piece of classical literature that deals with *mujō*, transience or evanescence, and the essay recreates that sentiment. The first paragraph of the essay lifts lines from *Ichigon hōdanshō*:

> Someone related the story of a young woman at the Shintō shrine on Mount Hiei who falsely pretended to be a medium. Late one night, when the sounds of people had quieted down, she sat before the Jūzenshi Shrine and, beating on a drum, she cried out in a fervent voice, "It makes no difference any more. Please, oh please!" When someone insisted that she reveal what this meant, she replied, "When I think of the process of life and death and the evanescence of all things, nothing in the world makes any difference. So I say, 'Please save me in the life to come.'"

This is a section from *Brief Sayings of the Great Teachers*. When I first read it, it stuck in my mind as a fine piece of writing, but the other day I went to Mount Hiei, and while wandering aimlessly in the area of the Sannō Gongen, looking at the green leaves, the stone fences, and the rest, suddenly this short passage flashed into my mind as if I were examining a fragment of a horizontal picture scroll of the period, and the different phrases of the text spread in my mind exactly as if I were following the course of the slender but strong lines of an old picture. This was the first time I had had such an experience, and I was extremely shaken. Even while I was eating *soba* at Sakamoto a while later, the strange feeling persisted. What was I feeling or thinking at the time, I wondered? It baffles me even now. Of course, one could say that I simply had a mild hallucination. That would be a convenient way of disposing of the matter, but somehow I do not feel I can trust such convenient evasions. I wonder why? To tell the truth, I have begun to write this before I am really sure of what it is I want to say.[73]

At one level Kobayashi is encountering the "historical document," the *Ichigon hōdanshō*, in its materiality: it appears before his eyes as "a fragment of a horizontal picture scroll" and his eyes peruse not the words but rather "the slender but strong lines of an old picture." Furthermore, Kobayashi does not attempt to explicitly explain or interpret the meaning of the section he sees. He recollects it, not in terms of the ideas represented therein, but as "object." This impression is heightened by the fact that the excerpt from *Ichigon hōdanshō* is reproduced verbatim, the stilted classical language resisting an easy comprehension on the part of modern readers.

The act of recollection narrated here is clearly an example of Kobayashi's act of "seeing," discussed in Chapter 2: the experience comes unexpectedly (he was "wandering aimlessly"), physically affects him ("I was extremely shaken"), and lasts but an instant. Also, the experience itself takes priority over whatever may have been learned by it; sitting down later to write of it, Kobayashi is still not sure what to make of the experience. Kobayashi is narrating in this passage what Rimbaud had described as the experience of the "voyant": "He reaches the unknown, and if, finally overwhelmed, he turns out to lose the meaning of his visions, at least he has seen them!"[74] Kobayashi has certainly been overwhelmed by his vision. His confession of having begun the essay without knowing what it is he wanted to say is the mark of one working at the boundaries of the powers of expression. Kamei Hideo has called this section a depiction of the "pure experience" of Nishida Kitarō, and comments on its resemblance to a religious revelation.[75] The religious overtones are indeed strong, heightened by the fact that Kobayashi is struck by this vision while "on the mountaintop"—and that of Mount Hiei, no less, the mountain associated more with religious lore than any other in Japan.

Next Kobayashi narrates a failed attempt to attain the same immediacy of experience through the application of more conventional intellectual means:

> *Brief Sayings of the Great Teachers* was a favorite book of Kenkō's, and this section would by no means strike us as inferior if it were added to his *Essays in Idleness* [*Tsurezuregusa*, 1330–31]. Now, with this same section of the text before my eyes, I can think of nothing but this trivial point. As before, it strikes me as an example of excellent prose. But the beauty that so moved me—where has it gone? Perhaps it has not disappeared but remains right before my eyes. Perhaps it is that particular state of body and mind appropriate for grasping it that has disappeared, and I know not the technique to regain it. This childish doubt launches me into a labyrinth, and I do not put up any resistance because I am unable to find anything of a suspicious nature in the condition, which can only be called the germination of aesthetics. In no way, however, do I arrive at an aesthetics.[76]

Kobayashi here attempts to recreate the experience through an analysis of the text. The best he can do is compare it to *Tsurezuregusa*, and this he finds trivial in comparison to the beauty he experienced in the original encounter. It becomes clear in these lines that any understanding or knowledge to which his latter analysis might lead is but poor consolation for the loss of that original, unmediated revelation of beauty. Having been pushed beyond the point of being able to explain it rationally (launched into the "labyrinth") has in a sense wiped the slate clean. Without a "design" to explain the experience, a new aesthetic is born. Kobayashi is quick to add his disclaimer, of course: "In no way, however, do I arrive at an aesthetics." He would remain in the state of wonder rather than render it a formalized pattern.

These early passages from the essay are performative. Critic Etō Jun claims that all of the essays in this collection are "a type of *nō* drama attempted in the genre of modern criticism, the work of classical literature essentially a mask that Kobayashi attaches to his own face."[77] This feat would be in keeping with Kobayashi's own objectives: in "Dentō," he had said that the classics should be appreciated through the act of imitation. In "Mujō to iu koto," Kobayashi did this by adopting the perspective of the very text he was working from; it is an essay describing an evanescent experience of a text dealing with evanescence. Kobayashi's failed attempt to reproduce the original experience, his admission that he "know[s] not the technique to regain it," places the recollection in the irretrievable past. Just as the young woman from the *Ichigon hōdanshō* laments the transience of this world, Kobayashi is here writing an elegy to the passing of his recollection of the text. This rhetorical reproduction of the literal content of the original text serves in place of an analytical explication of it. This is what has prompted critics to argue that these essays are better thought of as "poems" than criticism.[78]

There is a second type of imitation in the text, a type of self-reflexivity in the essay that enriches its performative nature. This is the overlapping of Kobayashi, the writer of the essay, and the young woman presented in the quote he offers.[79] Kobayashi's attempt to revive the classics by embodying them is a form of spirit-possession (*monogurui*) not unlike that demonstrated by the young woman. Furthermore, just as her act of devotion is no less valid because she is merely pretending to be a medium, neither is Kobayashi's accomplishment diminished by the fact that his authentic moment is actually an artificial, rhetorical recreation of such. The point is that the appreciation of the classics, or of tradition or history, lies not in explicating the meaning represented therein but rather in an imitation of "the immutable archetypal form," as Kobayashi had referred to it in "'Nihonteki na mono' no mondai." Kobayashi does this by rhetorically recreating the sense of evanescence of the *Ichigon hōdanshō* and simultaneously recreating the subject position of the woman represented there. This self-reflexivity allows Kobayashi to revel fully in his own self-consciousness, and it is a technique he had praised in André Gide's *The Counterfeiters* years earlier.[80]

The remainder of the essay is less performative than this first half, serving instead to inculcate in the reader a state of mind conducive to a vision like Kobayashi's. In his recollection of the text, Kobayashi writes, he experienced "a time of fullness" (*michitarita jikan*), a moment "brimming with proof that I am alive, and in which each and every thing was clear to me."[81] This experience was possible precisely because of the attitude with which the project was approached, an attitude at which Kobayashi arrived gradually:

> The more I examined it, the more history appeared to me as an immutable form. It was not something that could be shaken by some new interpretation of it. . . . The more I gave myself over to this idea, the more beautiful I found history to be. . . . Only that which remains unperturbed, resisting interpretation, is beautiful. This . . . is the most deeply hidden secret of our interpretation-inundated time.[82]

Kobayashi has shifted from a performative recreation of an aesthetic experience to a more general statement concerning the conditions whereby it had become possible. The statement is predicated on our restoring the object of our attention to an uncompromised wholeness, positing by an act of will an uninterpretable nature on that which we would have move us.

This ability to be deeply and genuinely moved by beauty was the experience Kobayashi had spent virtually his entire career attempting to resuscitate. In the closing paragraphs of the essay he implied that, indeed, it is that alone that makes us human. Toward this end, Kobayashi introduced an anecdote involving Nobel laureate Kawabata Yasunari (1899–1972):

> I remember how one day a certain thought suddenly occurred to me, and I expressed it to Kawabata Yasunari, who just happened to be at my side at the time. He smiled but did not respond. "A living man is really quite a poor substitute. Do we ever know, whether it is another or even oneself, what he is thinking or what he will say and do? He is worthy of neither appreciation nor observation. Now the dead man is something altogether different. Isn't he both clear and strong? He has the form of a real human being. And so I guess a living man is but a type of animal in the process of becoming human.[83]

This passage reflects Kobayashi's anxiety concerning the modern world, where things and people change so rapidly that there is no opportunity for quiet reflection. History, however, the realm of the "clear and strong" dead, contains the key to restoring something of the human in the living. Edward Seidensticker was quite rightly taken with these lines, finding the inclusion of the eerie Kawabata an almost novelistic touch: "One can see the two of them, the elegantly loquacious sage expounding a theory of history and historiography, an injunction against turning documents and analysis against the quiet and perfect dead, and the novelist, so fascinated with death that it was almost his only subject, silently smiling."[84]

Kobayashi then continues his theory of historiography, and assures us that our salvation lies within it:

> I was quite taken with my idea of man as a sort of animal, but it developed no further. The dead, and the dead alone, appear in history; one sees in it only the faces of solid men, the beautiful shapes of the unmoving. Some say that in a recollection everything looks beautiful, but their understanding of this phenomenon is mistaken. It is not that we tend to embellish the past; it is because history permits us no superfluous thoughts. Recollection [*omoide*] will save us from our animal-like state. It is not enough to simply remember [*kioku suru*]; we must recollect. Isn't the reason so many historians remain mired in an animalistic state that their heads are full of memories [*kioku*], and they cannot empty their hearts long enough to simply recall the past?[85]

History, if we will but abandon the attempt to catalog and classify, interpret and analyze, will resuscitate within us the capacity to be authentically moved by beauty.

"Mujō to iu koto" is hence essentially a reiteration, now in poetic diction, of a key concept in Kobayashi's attitude toward history: the recognition and lamentation of the pastness of the past. The structure of the essay is both performative and persuasive. Kobayashi moves from imitation to innovation. All of these aspects of this essay suggest that rather than surrendering to the pure exteriority of his subjects (the accusation made by Kitagawa), Kobayashi was indeed exercising his "muse" in the poetic presentation of his critical vision.

Sliding on the Surface: "Taema"

"Mujō to iu koto" lent its name to the postwar compilation of Kobayashi's essays on the medieval classics, but this essay, "Taema," was actually published two months before it, in April 1942. While "Mujō to iu koto" had "performed" evanescence so that the reader might feel once more a sense of awe and beauty emanating from the past, "Taema" is a dramatization of another key feature of Kobayashi's historical vision: the need to resist the temptations of complex, cerebral explanations and turn instead to the basics for salvation. Here, too, Kobayashi incorporates an impenetrable materiality into his reading of the source text he borrows "as the material with which to narrate the self." Whereas in the essay discussed above, Kobayashi conflated himself with the young female medium on Mount Hiei, the essay is related only to that one small section of the medieval text he treats.[86] "Taema," on the other hand, brilliantly captures, imitates, and transcribes the essence of the entire *nō* play that inspired it.

The play "Taema" is almost certainly by master playwright Zeami himself.[87] It is performed as either a fourth- or fifth-category play.[88] Although so many plays deal at least peripherally with the matter of Buddhist salvation, "Taema" makes it an explicit theme at all levels. The play asks the question: "How are we to be saved?" The resounding answer, echoed implicitly in the imagery as well as explicitly in song, is surely why Kobayashi chose to write on this play: to be saved, the play teaches us, we must not be confused by the myriad of sutras, we must return to seeing things in their most basic, original, and material forms.

This message is conveyed at a number of levels. Most concretely, the play enacts two visitations. In act one, the traveling priest (the *waki*) encounters an old nun (the *shite*) who eventually reveals herself to be the *bodhisattva* Kannon, who once appeared in this very place to Princess Chūjōhime; in act two, the priest is visited by Princess Chūjōhime (the *nochijite*), now herself a *bodhisattva*. She attained this state when her prayer was answered: "May Amida Buddha come / in a holy living form / graciously to welcome me / that I might worship him / from my heart in one devotion."[89] The play both tells the story of this divine visitation *and* reproduces it, as not one but two ethereal forms appear before the monk. In this sense, as Thomas Hare writes, "the form of the drama is made to imitate its content."[90] Both focus on visitation, and it is the concrete manifestation of a *bodhisattva* that saves those involved.

There is also the repetition of the sentiment that so much of Buddhism is just too complicated for the average human to comprehend. The mysterious nun in the first act mentions "80,000 creeds and practices"; Chūjōhime and the chorus in act two sing: "For the sake of all the world, / well expounded are these laws / otherwise too recondite for man. / As these teachings seem, indeed, too profound for comprehension, / so believing in them is too / difficult for us, we hear."[91] The solution to this overwhelming complexity is twofold. Chūjōhime advises us to "just depend on him," Amida. Perhaps more significantly, however, as she sings these words she rolls up the sutra she has had before her, literally turning a complex series of signifiers (the sutra) into an object (the scroll). She hands this material item to the monk, who takes it, does not read it but bows to it reverently, and puts it in his bosom.[92] The teaching is received as an object, a piece of materiality, and without any attempt to interpret what the words inside might represent. The message is one Kobayashi himself had been preaching for years: believe, and find solace in the materiality itself rather than step into the labyrinth of speculation on what it may all mean.

The call to return to the basics, the origin, is present at the level of imagery as well. The site of the visitations is known for the dyeing of threads made from the lotus root. Throughout the Buddhist canon, the lotus, a beautiful flower emerging from muddy waters, is a metaphor for enlightened souls who emerge from our sullied world. In the play "Taema" we are called to turn our attention away from the multicolored hues in which the lotus is dyed and attend instead to its origins as a plain white root, pure and simple. This reminder parallels the call to withdraw from the complex teachings that have accrued to Buddhist truth and return to the simple faith at its roots: "What is more, this very pond / is Somedono's / well known for multicolored dyes / as the multitudes who go / here and there to offer prayers. / So there are ten thousand teachings / which we do not know but pray / with our single faith / like a pure white thread that makes / me say so single-heartedly / 'Holy Lord Amida!'"[93] The monk has received this message to concentrate on the pure white root (the simple call to Amida) rather than the complexly colored extremities of the Pure Land faith. This story is Kobayashi's; he, too, had wandered in the myriad intellectual designs before discovering his salvation in a focus on concrete form and impenetrable materiality. It is perhaps no coincidence that while most traveling monks in the *nō* repertoire are off to see strange and distant lands, this one, like Kobayashi, is trying to find his way home.[94]

In his essay named for this play, Kobayashi does not, of course, attempt to tease this interpretation out of the text. It would serve only to undermine the message. Instead, Kobayashi replicates the message, transcribing it into the language of a "critical" prose-poem. As was the case with "Mujō to iu koto," Kobayashi opens the essay with the depiction of a skillful act of recollection:

> I saw Manzaburō perform *Taema* on the Umewaka *nō* stage.
>
> Under stars, through the last of the snow, I was walking a night road. Why did the dream-shattering sound of flute and drum linger on in my ears? Had not the dream been shattered? White sleeves waving, gold crown glittering, the maiden Chūjōhime still danced before my eyes. It was not the lingering aftermath of pleasure. It was utterly different. What was it, what shall I call it, two white feet starting up to the sound of the flute? Zeami quite clearly had a name for it: Taema. Do I believe in him, Zeami, the man, the poet? The question came to me, and startled me.[95]

Read in conjunction with "Mujō to iu koto," the first thing that strikes the reader about this essay is the temporal coordinates they share. Both essays work at a three-step remove: a foundational encounter with a literary text or dramatic performance, the "recollection" of it, and finally the narration and evocation of that recollection in the essay. In other words, "Taema" is Kobayashi's reflection on his recollection of his experience of the play.

This tortured perspective serves two purposes. First, by writing of his recollection of the play rather than the real-time experience of it, Kobayashi was able to distill the narrative, an experience that unfolds over time, to a single composite impression. This remove, therefore, is a rhetorical technique that sustains (or creates) the uncompromised "wholeness" of the original experience. Second, by refraining from writing from within the recollection itself, Kobayashi was able to allude to an experience that is, by nature, so personal as to be incommunicable. In "Mujō to iu koto," he had described it simply as "a time of fullness," here it is the play recalled in its concrete form: "the music is like a cry, the dance is little more than a walk, and the song is like ordinary prayer. It is enough. What else is needed? . . . I felt as if I were being subdued by a simple, persistent flow of sound and form."[96] The presentation of the recollection from a point at which it is no longer in process serves to keep it looming as a calm and comforting presence over the remainder of the essay.

Having alluded to that "pure experience" of the play, Kobayashi then moves to generate from within the experience the conditions that made it possible:

> Staff in hand, wearing a gray-violet cloak, an old nun appeared at the passage to the stage. There were only glimpses of brown eyes and nose beneath a pure white cowl, but in them was a strange, unearthly quality. I could not turn my eyes away. It was not as if I had glimpses of a Nō mask, but somehow as if the forms of two or three dead kittens, perhaps, were showing through a kerchief. I did not know why such an image should have come to me. As I had expected, the old woman did not do or say much of anything. I could not hear the muffled voice very distinctly, but the point seemed to be that intoning the holy name does as well as anything. Her main purpose, it seemed, was to have priests and audience observe the mask. The corpse of kittens—a ridiculous simile.[97]

Having been moved to a reverie by the experience of the play, Kobayashi is prepared for a flash of intuitive insight, which comes in the form of this narrowing of his attentions to the mask worn by the nun in the first act. This mask becomes a synecdoche for both the play and the vision of Zeami, the grandmaster of *nō*. In a move he repeated elsewhere, Kobayashi employed a "feint" that underscores the singularity of the materiality that he will focus on. In "Mujō to iu koto" this feint took the form of a pro forma comparison of the *Ichigon hōdanshō* with Kenkō's *Tsurezuregusa*, a comparison that yielded nothing but the impression that Kobayashi's experience on the mountain was beyond comparison and reproduction. Here in "Taema," the feint is the attempt to capture his impression of the mask by likening it to the "corpse of kittens . . . showing through a kerchief." Even this forced comparison, somehow like a Zen *kōan*, cannot express the impression. Kobayashi himself dismisses it as a "ridiculous simile."

With this stroke, the impression of the mask as an object of perfect singularity was strengthened. It is also significant that in this passage the impenetrable surface of the mask takes priority over the language that emits from behind it. Kobayashi was insisting that we remain at the surface of the play, both in the literal sense of focusing on the materiality of the mask and in the figurative sense of not trying to interpret the play's hidden meanings.

Kobayashi was fascinated by the mask, so much so that he could not tear his eyes away from it. The image continued to haunt him as he made his way to the lobby at intermission, where he viewed the faces of the people around him in terms of that impenetrable and therefore beautiful mask:

> In this area there are plenty of faces gathered, but there didn't seem to be a single one so interesting that it kept my attention. Each one held a bored and uneasy expression, and there was no telling what sort of idiotic face I was exposing to the people around me as I thought this. None could be held responsible for the expression on their face, and yet people proudly read each other's expressions. How comical and hopeless it all is. When had we fallen into this annoying, unreliable state? Surely it was not so long ago. The stage right before our eyes tells us that until just recently there were lives in which it was more important to wear a mask than don one's clothes.
>
> With the cry "Remove the mask, reveal the face beneath it!" modern civilization set off wildly without knowing where it was going. Rousseau did not confess a single thing in his *Confessions*. And hasn't the womanly pettiness scattered throughout that book—something that neither Rousseau himself nor his readers noticed—gradually spread to all corners?[98]

In these passages the synecdochic mask becomes the fragment of the whole that overwhelms the subject. Through this mask Kobayashi expresses his despair over the endless series of digressions that paralyze modern man as he attempts to read behind the surfaces of people's faces. The mask, in contrast, is uninterpretable materiality, perfect surface. Of the mask, Kobayashi writes: "Things hovered about the lovely form and went no further. Nothing was permitted inside that solemnly contrived mask. There, without a doubt, was Zeami's 'flower.'"[99]

Kobayashi tied his praise of impenetrable form over systems of representation to Zeami's achievement. In Zeami's art, the *nō* drama, Kobayashi insisted, "There is a beautiful 'flower,' but there is no such thing as the beauty of the 'flower.'"[100] The "flower" (*hana*) is, of course, a reference to the metaphor by which Zeami spoke of the pinnacle of artistic achievement. The movement is away from the abstract ("beauty," the meaning of an expression) to the concrete ("a beautiful flower," the surface of the mask). Kobayashi's point is that it is only by encountering a concrete materiality, and by refusing to delve behind it, that a true aesthetic encounter is possible. On the outside chance that we might have missed the point, Kobayashi closed the essay with yet another feint: "I walked the night road, looking at stars and snow. Where are the snows of yesteryear—no, I must not fall into that sort of thing. I looked again at the stars, and the snow."[101] Kobayashi closed by redirecting our attention once again to the concrete, the material. And the stars and snow are all the more beautiful for having any interpretation of them swept aside.

Like "Mujō to iu koto," this essay is a grandly performative prose-poem. The intertextual play between the essay's rhetoric and its subject matter, the multiplicity of "I"s in the text, and the challenge to genre borders included in both of these essays demonstrate that Kobayashi's obsession with materiality in history and tradition did not extinguish the "muse" within him; rather it fed and nourished his ability to experience beauty and his ability to lead his readers toward the same experience. These essays show Kobayashi not calling for vibrant literary praxis, but instead practicing it. Though like many of his contemporaries during the war years he turned to the Japanese classics and history, his insistence on the intimately personal, ultimately incommunicable encounter with them allowed—in fact made necessary—the avoidance of reductive theories of national identity and communal historical myths. This feat was possible because Kobayashi stayed true to his practice of literary aestheticism. His view of history, tradition, and the Japanese classics reconstitute the contours of these discourses in such a way as to render them antithetical to the centripetal pull toward national essences. In short, he turns the raw materials of nationalism into the poetry of the individual.

SIX

"The People Cope in Silence"

In Chapter 5 I argued that, contrary to the opinion of certain critics, Kobayashi Hideo's turning to history and the classics of Japanese literature during the war years represented neither a conversion (*tenkō*) from a liberal to a reactionary stance, nor a contribution to the discourse of national identity spurring on Japan's imperialist agenda on the continent. On the contrary, his unflagging efforts to resist the language of universals in favor of a celebration of the radical singularity of both the perceiving subject and the object of attention pulled historical and cultural discourse into a realm antithetical to both of these—that is, the realm of literary aestheticism (*bungaku shugi*). In this realm, the gelling of a particular insight—its attaining the status of "design"—so detracted from its artistic value that Kobayashi considered it trite and formalistic. Kobayashi insisted instead on a continuous, personal reconstruction of history and tradition. This precluded the possibility of these discourses being co-opted into a production of some myth of national community. There was, as Honda Shūgo testified, a heady feeling of freedom in the type of discourse that Kobayashi was championing.[1]

During the years 1937 to 1942, the same period in which he wrote the essays on history and tradition, Kobayashi was also writing about the escalating hostilities with China, the colonization efforts there, and Japan's entry into the Pacific War. This was a subject new to Kobayashi, and one very different from the topics he had addressed up to that time. The war and colonization of China were "real" in a sense that literature, philosophy, and history were not, and these subjects brushed more closely against issues of life and death. In spite of this vastly different subject matter, Kobayashi remained true to his vision.

Viewing the realities of a war in progress through the lens of his literary aestheticsm, however, brought to the fore the limits of his aesthetic practice. Of particular significance was Kobayashi's penchant for reifying the object of his attention in order to make possible the intuitive appreciation of its latent beauty. This dimension of his thinking is evident as early as his first essay dealing explicitly with the conflict in China, written as the hostilities rapidly escalated following the Marco Polo Bridge Incident of July 1937:

> Though one feels an idle confusion when one's concept-filled head collides with the harsh fact of war, it is best not to confuse this with a critique of the war. There is but one method by which to regain one's senses: give up the nasty habit so popular these days of making predictions about the fate of mankind and reflect on your very own life under the present circumstances. This should make you realize that now that the war has begun, your precious life is no longer your own. As long as you take your life from Japan and there is a war in progress, you are not free to do with your life as you please—even should it be in the name of mankind. This is a harsh fact. Now, the harsh fact of war can only be faced with another harsh fact: regardless of what the future may hold, as long as the people [*kokumin*], working as a unit of war, cannot change the fact of that war, they must accept it and resolve themselves to deal with the present. Any other type of resolution is mistaken.[2]

Quite clearly, the freedom that Honda found in Kobayashi's essays on history is lacking here. While Kobayashi had freed the discourse of history from the ideology of nation-building, he offered none of that same freedom to the life of the individual in wartime. At such a juncture, Kobayashi unequivocally informs the reader that "your precious life is no longer your own." This conclusion stems from his perceiving the fact of the war as yet another sort of materiality that must not be subjected to endless intellectual speculation if it is to be appreciated for what it is. While Kobayashi's overall vision for the arts and knowledge is a powerful and persuasive one—and he remains true to that vision in writing about Japanese aggression on the continent—it leads him here to impulsively condone the existing state of military aggression and violence.

As argued in Chapter 5, and restated above, Kobayashi's writings on history and tradition do not represent a conversion from a liberal to conservative or reactionary position. The same is true for his writings on the colonization of China and the war. It is difficult to reconcile the fact that the former (that is, his writings on history and tradition) represent a dissenting, subversive voice at a time when a reductionist construction of national identity was fueling imperialism, with the realization that the latter demonstrated at times a heartless, unconditional support of oppression and brutality. Still, neither dimension of Kobayashi's writings during the war represents a deviation from the core of his vision; both are fully consistent with his earlier writings on literature and philosophy. This chapter argues that this attitude is inherent in Kobayashi's aesthetic vision, and one cannot but acknowledge that a radically literary mode of cognition offers both a liberating form of praxis *and* empowerment for horrifying acts of violence.

This chapter will explore how the subjectivity constructed through Kobayashi's unique epistemological paradigm—a subjectivity completely consistent with that which he had espoused up to this point, and one that made possible the recovery of artistic human sensibilities that appeared to be quickly disappearing in the age of mechanical reproduction and the commodification of culture—led naturally to a specific sort of fascistic discourse. By revealing how an ideology of individual creativity exercised through creative praxis was, simultaneously, an ideology urging men to surrender their lives acritically in a time of war, this chapter documents the inextricable links between subjectivity's ability to be deeply moved by beauty and its capacity not only to condone, but actually to revel in, acts of violence, between the deification of the individual and the erasure of human agency.

"Touring" the Continent

Between 1938 and 1943 Kobayashi made six trips to the continent, writing travel sketches based on his experiences during the first two.[3] He made the initial trip in February of 1938 in the capacity of special correspondent for the magazine *Bungei shunjū*. The main purpose of this trip was to deliver to Corporal Hino Ashihei (1907–60), stationed in Hangzhou, the Akutagawa Prize for his novella *Funnyōtan* (A Tale of Excrement, 1937). Kobayashi's second trip was from October to December of that same year. This time he was accompanied by sculptor Okada Harukichi, but not in any official capacity. Together they visited the Korean peninsula, Manchuria, and northern China. The travel sketches I discuss below were based largely on Kobayashi's experiences during these two trips.

The remainder of his forays on the continent were for an assortment of official, semi-official, and private purposes. In August 1940, for example, Kobayashi joined the Literary Home Front Movement (Bungei jūgo undō) contingent touring Korea and China, delivering a lecture entitled "Bungaku to jibun" (Literature and I) in various cities there. Having attended the first two meetings of the Greater East Asian Writers' Conference (Daitōa bungakusha taikai), one of which was held on the continent, Kobayashi was involved in planning the third. This was the impetus for his final trip to the conti-nent, which took place in 1943.

The travel sketches are for the most part rather bland observations of sites and scenery, combined with accounts of Kobayashi's daily activities. The tone is not at all what one would expect from a special correspondent or distinguished literary critic touring the expanding Japanese empire.[4] Kobayashi did not, for the most part, reflect on Japan's "Asian Monroe Doctrine," nor did he speculate on the effect that the colonization was having on the people and former nations of the continent. In many parts of these essays Kobayashi sounds like nothing more than a tourist making the rounds of the sights. In "Manshū no inshō" (Impressions of Manchuria, 1939), for example, Kobayashi writes:

> To tell the truth, there was really no specific purpose for this trip. Standing on the deck of the ferry as it entered the port of Pusan at dawn, Hayashi Fusao, who was along, chuckled. With a perplexed look on his face, he said, "Imagine, seeing Chōsen [Korea] for the first time at the age of 36!" I was probably gazing at the mountains of Pusan with a similar feeling, and one that didn't leave me during the entire trip. I was shown, day after day, sights that I was seeing for the first time in my life. In the process, an attitude gradually gelled: I wouldn't really do anything except follow my childlike curiosity and enjoy myself as much as time and stamina would allow. That's the way it worked out. Back home now, I'm dead tired.[5]

This image is an odd one. Kobayashi joins Hayashi on the deck of the ferry at the crack of dawn not in fear of missing that initial sighting of the colonies, but rather simply out of excitement at traveling abroad for the first time. Though there are times when Kobayashi does speculate on the war with China (examined below), the passage quoted above effectively captures the tone of most of these travelogues—Kobayashi seems largely unable to move beyond the tourist's "childlike curiosity" and appetite for nonstop sightseeing and pleasure.

This attitude is represented in other places as well. As mentioned above, Kobayashi's first trip was ostensibly for the purpose of awarding the Akutagawa Prize to Corporal Hino Ashihei. In "Kōshū," (Hangzhou, 1938), Kobayashi briefly describes the perfunctory ceremony during which the presentation was made, and then describes the way he spent the afternoon:

In the afternoon, Hino, Private First Class "N," and I bought a two-liter bottle of *sake* and, for a snack, some canned seaweed rolls that looked like the national flag [*hinomaru*]. We hired a Chinaman's [*Shinajin*] skiff, and took a spin around the lake. Everywhere the water was shallow and we could see the seaweed waving below the surface in the same colors that we see when we peer at them over the railing of a veranda. Hino said that because of the shallowness, the lake was always just like a mirror. That was easy to believe. One did not even have the lapping of waves to lull one to sleep at night. When the lights were turned off, all the stars in the sky glittered on the surface of the lake. There was nothing other than the faint croaking of the frogs and the occasional splash of a carp leaping from the water.[6]

They spent the afternoon seeing the sights and sipping the *sake*. The talk turned briefly to the war, but Hino's reticence to speak of it quickly brought the conversation back to literary topics. This description of the pleasure cruise, too, strengthens the feeling that Kobayashi was there more for a vacation than to see the writer Hino Ashihei in action or to gather material on the latest developments in the colonies to report back to the readers of *Bungei shunjū*.

Like any tourist, Kobayashi came home with a humorous anecdote about encounters with the natives. This one concerns the pilot of the skiff:

Since we had only brought along a single two-liter bottle of *sake*, we drank sparingly. Still, there was soon only a little left. Every time we went up onto an island, the pilot of the skiff would follow behind carrying the bottle. Judging from the rate at which the *sake* was disappearing, it would seem that he was a drinker. After checking that there was a final cupful left in the bottle, I handed it to him to carry. When we got back to the boat he showed us the now empty bottle, and asked to keep it. Through mime, I accused him of drinking the *sake* but, with a shocked look on his face, he protested vehemently in a shrill voice. The whole picture was so ridiculous that I didn't get angry. As I expected, he was drunk, and soon stripped to the waist as he poled the skiff. We moved at a snail's pace. He had a yellow, scrawny physique. All the Chinese soldiers are like that.[7]

This description is, in fact, the only one of a specific Chinese national in all of these essays. Like the typical tourist, Kobayashi stuck close to his fellow expatriates and had only this superficial, patronizing encounter with a native to show for his time on the continent.

In addition to setting off on his travels intending to "enjoy [himself] as much as time and stamina would allow" and limiting his interaction with the natives to servants, Kobayashi's tourist attitude was reflected in his disdain for the local culture, which he universally found inferior to that of his homeland. In "Soshū" (Suzhou, 1938) he describes his visits to a number of temples and gardens in the area only to conclude that they "are better called overgrown plots than gardens."[8] Having heard that the Lion Grove (Shishirin) was the most well maintained garden in the area, Kobayashi paid a visit, only to conclude: "The materials they have used in making the garden are, indeed, rocks, but to those of us who know the garden at Ryōanji, this garden had nothing to offer."[9] Kobayashi had a similar reaction to the temples that once hosted Saichō, Kūkai, and Dōgen, three of the most important figures in Japanese religious history:

> There is no doubting the fact that the [legendary] elegance is nowhere to be found. The temples are in general new, the grand ancient ones having all turned to ash at the bottom of the lakes. The new ones have an impressive facade, but are all flimsy structures. Eyes accustomed to viewing the ancient temples of Japan don't detect the slightest trace of beauty here. The Buddhist statues . . . have life-like skin and red lips; the smirks on their faces are so lewd they send shivers down the spine.[10]

In his description of these sites there was no attempt to grasp the reasons behind the loss of the ancient temples; there was only a visceral repulsion at what seemed tawdry by the standards of his homeland.

I offer a final episode in this vein from "Soshū." Kobayashi relates a visit to a temple in an area famous for producing ink rubbings taken from the calligraphy engraved in a stone (*ishizuri*). Having reached the temple, Kobayashi was shocked by the dilapidated state of the temple's famous bell tower. It is through his description of the inside of the Hall of the Buddha that we discover why the temple had fallen into such a state of disrepair.

> The inside of the Hall of the Buddha was, in essence, an ink rubbings factory. They had ripped up the stone floor and built a fire. At first I wondered why, but then noticed that they had suspended bamboo poles over the fire and were drying the rubbings by hanging them there like diapers. Because of the heat, the child in charge of this was stripped bare. There was, of course, a big commotion around the stone monument carved with the famous poem by Zhang Ji. The stone was a new one; the old one had broken into pieces, and the fragments had been plastered into the wall. The characters were almost illegible. These craftsmen were most likely experiencing a rush of business like never before as the orders came pouring in—a hundred copies for this squadron and two hundred for that. With shirtsleeves rolled up and covered in sweat, one of the craftsmen was dabbing on the ink and

gently tapping at the paper on the stone. A crack had formed between the monument and the gravestone in which it was set. The whole thing shook as he tapped away, and was ready to crumble at any moment.[11]

Kobayashi did not seem to connect the disappointing fact that the temple was being neglected with his observation that it was in fact the Japanese Imperial Army's demands for the ink rubbings that had turned it into a factory. He neither lamented the negative impact of the colonizing army's presence nor rationalized it. Instead, he completely ignored this larger context.

In these records of his travels on the continent, Kobayashi Hideo was flatly transcribing "scenery" divorced from any historical or cultural context. For this reason he sounds more like a tourist than the sharp-tongued, highly opinionated critic that animates virtually all his other writings. These essays reveal the limits of the subjectivity that Kobayashi had constructed. His epistemology is predicated upon a self-consciousness not only severed, but even distanced from exteriority. This serves as a precondition for the empathetic, intuitive leap to an appreciation of an object. The problem here is that in looking at the distanced "landscape" of China and Korea, Kobayashi was unable to muster the empathy needed to make that leap. Therefore, the polarized consciousness and materiality of his paradigm remained separated by an unbridgeable gap, and Kobayashi was left able to do nothing but record that exteriority as landscape.

The People as Landscape

This inability to muster the empathy needed to appreciate, at whatever level or in whatever manner, the situation around him is most evident in Kobayashi's depiction of the people in this landscape. The aforementioned description of the drunken "Chinaman" piloting the skiff begins to seem vivid and even sympathetic in comparison to the impersonal nature of his musings on the other people whose paths he crossed. These depictions take one of two shapes: they are either one-dimensional portraits of almost wooden characters, or vapid, romanticized generalizations about the simple life led by the masses.

In "Kōshū" Kobayashi writes of two monks he encountered on one of his many temple-viewing excursions:

Both of them seemed plump due to the layers of grimy clothes they wore as they sat facing each other across a table. Turning the pages of a sutra, they murmured something softly. I approached and brazenly stared at their faces.

Still, their expression did not change. Nothing could catch their attention, least of all some tourist, as they had entered some divine realm of concentration. Or perhaps they had merely lost all sensitivity to such things; I don't know which. Either way, I felt right at home and so walked around them as if I were inspecting wooden statues. One seemed to be a nun. In front of her sat an empty box of imported cigarettes, and a single stick of incense stood inside it.[12]

One is reminded of stories describing tourists torturing the stoic sentries at London's Buckingham Palace. As had been his practice, Kobayashi emphasizes the materiality, the rational impenetrability, of his subject matter. Where this had been a prelude to some intuitive appreciation of the same, the technique was very effective. Here, however, Kobayashi lacked the empathy required to understand these monks in any way. To him they remained materiality in a quite literal sense: they were "wooden statues."

Although the individuals who appear in these essays are portrayed either with caricatures (the pilot of the skiff) or as inanimate parts of the landscape (the "wooden" monks), "the people" in a collective sense are depicted in a romanticized and reductive manner. At this level, too, it is apparent that Kobayashi was distancing himself from the masses as materiality (or landscape) and was unable, or unwilling, to make the intuitive leap of appreciation. The result is that those portrayed are, in spite of their extraordinary circumstances, robbed of what makes them individuals—or even humans.

We see this not only in the manner that Kobayashi depicts the Chinese as a group (which I discuss below), but also in the way he portrays the colonizing Japanese. This is evident in Kobayashi's description of the Japanese youths he encountered in a training camp for the Manchurian-Mongolian Colonization Volunteer Youth Corp (Man-Mō takushoku shōnen giyūtai). The camp, newly established and facing its first winter, was populated by some 1,400 boys between the ages of sixteen and eighteen. Kobayashi was shocked by how ill-equipped the boys were, lacking sufficient housing and even basic winter coats and shoes to keep them warm. His initial reaction was this: "What they have here is not training; it is privation, plain and simple."[13]

Though Etō Jun claims that this indicates a feeling of "righteous indignation" on the part of Kobayashi Hideo, the following passages would seem to suggest otherwise.[14] This concern for the hard lives the boys led in the service of the Empire was soon replaced by a different conclusion reached through Kobayashi's intuitive mode of "seeing." Kobayashi relates how he had at first been unable to read the boys' faces due to their myriad expressions, but eventually got to the core of it:

> There had been nothing complex in the faces of the youths. It had been my heart that was jaded as I looked at them. Their faces had been the wide-open faces of children . . . .
>
> The youths did not have an adult's determination to overcome adversity. However, in its place they had that youthful energy that does not recognize adversity as adversity. They did not have the ability to live through hope but, as consolation, neither did they have the ability to conjure up abstractions such as "hopelessness." I was deeply moved the moment I recognized this innocence in the faces of these youths. In short, their rebelliousness and submissiveness were all part of their innocence. In this sense it was the youths pulling along their leaders, rather than the other way around. "Privation is another form of training." The youths, in their innocence, knew nothing of this sort of adult romanticism.[15]

True to his literary mode of cognition, Kobayashi rejected the trite conclusion that most would reach on viewing this scene—that hard-luck circumstances had placed these children in an almost unbearable situation of privation. Instead, Kobayashi borrowed them as a tool with which to narrate his own consciousness. In a variation of his standard diatribe against viewing the world through the lens of abstractions, Kobayashi banished the conception of "hopelessness" from the children to portray them as authentically engaged with the realities of their material existence. He saw them as living in precisely the sort of "home" he himself never knew, a "home" rooted in "countless strong impressions from a concrete environment."[16]

A second group that Kobayashi portrayed in this manner is the colonizers as a whole. In this portrayal as well, Kobayashi "saw" the colonizers in a reductive characterization that erased the suffering they endured and inflicted. On visiting a colony settlement called Mizuho, Kobayashi was entertained by the village head, a man named Hayashi Kyōhei. Hayashi regaled him with tales of the wild early days of the settlement, including the time when "rebels" fired 28 bullets through one of his windows. Kobayashi shrugged this off, claiming "the exceedingly ordinary peace that I see now before my eyes is what really impressed me."[17] From this, Kobayashi leapt to the conclusion of this particular essay: "Having come to Manchuria, I felt for the first time that I was seeing Japanese living robust lives in a perfectly straightforward manner [*atarimae ni*]."[18] The group was obviously living the existence that Kobayashi associated with the spiritual "home" (*kokyō*) of that earlier essay. It was a romantic vision, and not without its own appeal, but it was visible only by effacing the oppressive conditions that made it a necessity.

In an oft-quoted passage from "Soshū," Kobayashi paints a picture of life along a street near a temple. There, a man selling sugarcane splashed filthy buckets of water over his product to keep it looking fresh. He crushed some of the sugarcane into a sweet juice with a primitive press, which he operated by sitting down on the raised lever. The juice dribbled down a shallow trench dug in the wooden press, and dripped into a small cup. The beverages were for sale and sat lined up on the counter. While the man worked, he traded snatches of a song with the owner of an identical shop across the street. The same scene was duplicated farther down the road.

Critic Etō Jun interprets this passage in much the same manner as he read Kobayashi's attitude toward the Japanese youths in the training camp. Quoting Aono Suekichi, Etō labels this passage "oppositional."[19] Kamei Hideo, in a similar vein, reads this scene as evidence that, quite possibly for the first time in his life, Kobayashi was really seeing the everyday life of everyday people. He goes on to suggest that in painting this peaceful picture, Kobayashi was making a subtle statement: any political or social condition that would destroy this serenity is evil.[20] As in the passages cited above, however, it soon becomes apparent that Kobayashi was in fact celebrating the immediacy of these people's experience of their surroundings, and in order to do so he effaced any self-consciousness from their minds.

This becomes clear in the paragraph following the scene described above, where Kobayashi has an experience reminiscent of Proust and his madeleines in *Remembrance of Things Past*. Kobayashi, however, does not need to ingest a thing:

> Seeing the cups filled with the yellowish juice lined up on the damp counters suddenly revived in me the taste of the tangerine juice I used to drink at the shops in the evening bazaar as a child. This surprised me. As I walked on, I turned a little sentimental, mulling over something I couldn't quite put my finger on. To aspire to nothing more than what daily life [*seikatsu*] has to offer, a life in which one simply lives sincerely, a life in which one never hypothesizes about how it will all turn out—in the end that's what it all comes down to. This mode of existence is stronger than any other and, in the face of it, all abstractions crumble. Is this idea a depressing one? Depressing? What could one possibly mean by such a ridiculous thing![21]

Clearly Kobayashi is not lamenting the hardships represented here. Rather, he is reveling in the "sincerity" of the lives represented, lives lived dealing with pressing, concrete concerns that bridge no thought of anything else. In this world materiality does not lend itself to speculation or interpretation; it has an unassailable immediacy that brooks very little manipulation of it. Life simply is what it is. While the appeal of the image is undeniable, it is important to remember that it emerges entirely from a position alien to such conditions. Kobayashi's romanticized portrait of these sugarcane juice vendors was largely a reaction to the anxieties of a man living in the modern world and nostalgic for "the good old days."

In these sections of his travel sketches, we see Kobayashi working the same method he had applied in the masterful prose poems of *Mujō to iu koto*. Remaining true to this vision, Kobayashi never lapsed into grand metanarratives of Japan's national identity or its glorious destiny in Asia. At times the prose is not without a certain stark, poignant beauty of its own. But this beauty comes at a cost. Compare the two paragraphs below. The first depicts the scientific method he so despised, the second the ease with which his own cognitive mode could produce a virtually identical result.

In his 1938 essay "Rekishi ni tsuite," Kobayashi ridiculed the scientific worldview, one in which the sacred subject/object dichotomy is not simply a precondition for the intuitive leap of understanding; it is an inviolable distinction. Kobayashi characterized this subject position in the following manner:

> We open the tiny window known as the intellect, and then merely stand there with our arms folded. We can do nothing more than apprehend [the world]. Peeping through the window, we find objective truths. Rather than claiming that we have found truth, it would be better to say that through the opening of the window we have but properly posed a question to nature.[22]

Kobayashi is objecting to the scientific approach on the grounds that its insistence on sustained objectivity (the view from the window) limits the sort of insight one might have. One can merely "look," not "see." In this worldview, laments Kobayashi, "there is not a single route whereby one can leap right into the bosom of the object."[23]

Compare this to these short paragraphs in "Kōshū yori Nankin" (From Hangzhou to Nanjing, 1938). Kobayashi is discussing the flood of people in Nanjing proper after displaced people were released from certain sections where they had been quarantined:

> Looking down from my window on the second floor, in the square right beneath my eyes, there is a shantytown where one can see people exhibiting extraordinary stoicism as they take what is essentially their first steps in life.

Shantytowns are an odd thing—people piece together houses from planks, zinc plates, sheets of tin, straw mats, broken beds, split doors, ragged cloth, and other unimaginable materials.

I spent every morning sitting at my table gazing blankly at the various aspects of this living situation. It was not that there was anything particularly interesting going on but, it being right below my window, my eyes just naturally settled there, and the time I spent watching went by uneventfully.[24]

The metaphor from the first quote is literally enacted by Kobayashi in the second. Kobayashi roundly criticized the passive, uninvolved stance of the objective observer standing by the window, arms folded, unwilling or unable to do more than look at what was unfolding beneath him. And yet, in the second quote, we see Kobayashi himself, safe at his table in his second-floor room, unable or unwilling to do more than "gaze blankly" at the shantytown below, a shantytown created by Japan's imperialist agenda (the Nanjing Massacre having occurred the previous year). His insistence on an initial exaggeration of the autonomy of, and distance between, his own self-consciousness and the materiality has gelled in that state. Lacking any empathy for the refugees below, he, too, was left without "a single route whereby [he] can leap right into the bosom of the object."

Literary Estrangement

What was the source of Kobayashi's inability to muster the empathy required by his intuitive appreciation? In the case of the Japanese youths and the colonizers on the continent, it would seem that Kobayashi's reductionist, romanticized portrayal was inspired by their spartan living conditions, a fact that allowed him the opportunity to portray them as having escaped the propensity for the abstract thought and reasoning that numbs our ability to recognize or authentically engage the concrete realities of our world. More importantly, though, Kobayashi was unable to muster even such romanticized dreams for the Chinese suffering under Japan's imperialist drive, as his writing on the displaced people of Nanjing demonstrates. It is his dismissal of these people as part of the landscape, or as beings without self-awareness, that made his approval of the war in China possible.

In "Manshū no inshō," Kobayashi reveals why he feels so distanced from the Chinese people: his estrangement is entirely literary. Kobayashi's point is so surprising that it warrants quotation at length. In the passage translated below, Kobayashi is describing his first few days spent in the city of Harbin, a city that serves as home to many Russian expatriates:

> While I was a student, Japanese literature was being heavily influenced by the literature of Russia. What supplied the strongest, most fertile material for the literary dreams of my adolescence were the translated novels of the nineteenth-century Russian writers. Now, I don't understand Russian nor have I ever been to Russia, and yet I experienced something quite mysterious gazing at the Russians in Manchuria. For example, as I was strolling down Kitaiskaya Avenue in Harbin, the faces of the beggar, the driver, the barmaid, and the hotel bellhop all brought back the names of characters from the Russian novels I once adored. I did not do this intentionally; it is just that I was simply incapable of looking at these faces without this childlike association. . . .
>
> As I slipped ten cents to the old man helping me on with my overcoat, I patted him on the back. Then, to myself I mumbled, "Yes, I know you well, old man. Chekhov wrote about a man just like you, and I read that story time and time again." Certain people might laugh this off as a writer's sentimentality. But what would the facts of the world be like without this sort of sentiment? It is exceedingly doubtful that a foreign diplomat well versed in the contemporary Russian political situation really knows the Russian people better than I, one who has avidly read their literature.[25]

This passage establishes Kobayashi's affinity with the Russian people; a seed of empathy had been planted through the literature he had read. Additionally, though the point may be exaggerated, Kobayashi was right about the manner in which familiarity with a country's literary tradition instills a certain kind of knowledge of its people. Literature helps put a human face on what might otherwise be a cold, inhumane analysis of political situations.

It is, however, in the next paragraph of the essay that the limits of this perspective emerge:

> With this I noticed something. Today the Japanese are haunted by a pressing need to come to a new understanding of the Chinese. In this context there arises an unexpected hurdle in the fact that China is totally lacking in a modern literature that gives new expression to Chinese ethnicity [*minzokusei*]. . . . To some minimal degree Lu Xun has shown us, in a familiar mode of expression, a literature that penetrates deeply, though somewhat narrowly, into the Chinese heart. Still, it is much harder for me to pick out Ah Q's face in the streets of Beijing than Mishkin's face on the streets of Harbin. Looking at the flocks of thousands of refugees in the ruins of the war in central China, I ask myself whether I could understand them. With expressions from the "Mulberries Tender" section of *The Book of Songs* being the only thing that comes to mind, it is unlikely.[26]

Here it becomes apparent that what kept Kobayashi standing in the window looking down on the "flocks" (*mure*) of refugees from above rather than intuiting the suffering that defined their existence below was his lack of literary affinity with them. He attributed his lack of empathy to a perceived failure of Chinese literature to create fictional characters through which he could appreciate the real-world Chinese. Because Chinese literature had failed to inspire him, Kobayashi was unable to move beyond seeing the Chinese as pure materiality in the form of "wooden statues" or as beings apparently lacking in self-consciousness.

Again, this was a direct result of the subjectivity Kobayashi had himself so carefully nurtured. On the one hand, he glorified the autonomous individual, particularly the person of singular vision, and detested the human tendency to ingest acritically the visions, or "designs," of others. This aspect of Kobayashi's thought dominated the essays on history and culture, as discussed in Chapter 5. Kobayashi continued to speak of the individual in these terms, even with the war raging all around him. Touring the continent in 1940 as part of the Literary Home Front Movement, Kobayashi presented a lecture entitled "Bungaku to jibun" (Literature and I) to audiences, including military personnel, in various cities there. Kobayashi spoke of the sacred nature of the individual in this lecture, stating:

> A realization that there is no true path through this world other than that in which one acquires knowledge for oneself [*jitoku*]—this is the resolution that a writer makes. Some may call this the philosophy of individualism [*kojin shugi shisō*]. But if you think that by merely identifying my point with such labels, you've understood me, then you had best think again. They say that the philosophy of individualism is no longer in vogue, but this doesn't change the fact that, popular or not, the question of how man should live is something that requires effort from each and every person.[27]

Kobayashi is so emphatic here about the importance of the individual's vision that he even goes so far as to call for the individual to think critically about the concept of individualism itself. Later in this same paragraph Kobayashi encourages members of the audience to think for themselves not only about "justice" and "humanity," but even about Japan's "grand mission" (*daishimei*).[28] At first glance, this seems an assertion of the integrity of the individual in the face of the national agenda.

This belief in the autonomy of the individual and the sacred nature of pure interiority is, however, problematic. Kobayashi states it best himself: "The world of the 'I' is, of course, the world that I directly experience myself. This world is a small one."[29] Kobayashi's limited personal world was one that did not include a familiarity with, or an appreciation of, Chinese literature. Additionally, his deification of the individual's vision allowed for neither recognition of its limitations nor the means for employing abstractions in supplementing it. Consequently, there was no potential for empathy, and China and the Chinese were relegated to the status of an unknowable materiality beyond the scope of his intuition. The autonomy and singularity of Kobayashi's self-consciousness, therefore, contained the potential both for the dissenting, liberating voice of his essays on history and the cold, inhumane projection of the colonized Chinese and China.

"The People Have Coped in Silence": Essays on the War

As disturbing as one may find Kobayashi's essays on China and the Chinese, there are statements in his writing on the war itself that far surpass them in their power to shock even readers mesmerized by the beauty of the essays in *Mujō to iu koto*. The most distinguishing feature of these texts is Kobayashi's incessant insistence on the unprecedented nature, or "newness," of the war and our consequent inability to explain it rationally. In "Giwaku II" (Doubts II, 1939) Kobayashi writes:

> Waging a great military campaign without a declaration of war in a country never visited or seen by the majority of our nation's people; establishing political sovereignty and simultaneously pursuing both the construction of culture and the development of resources; on the domestic front, instituting spiritual mobilization and economic controls. Never, since the beginning of history, has there been a nation of people who have experienced anything like this. We understand this fully, and still the single most distinctive feature of the China War is, oddly enough, how difficult it is for us to grasp the fact that it is something completely unprecedented.[30]

This "newness" (*atarashisa*) of the situation was such that it represented to Kobayashi the perfect example of the limits of human reason and analysis. The only person who had come to terms with this, wrote Kobayashi, was a former prime minister who, in spite of great criticism from those around him, had refused to say more of the affair than that it was "complex and bizarre" (*fukuzatsu kaiki*).[31]

Kobayashi's assertion is only partially convincing. The aspects of the China War that Kobayashi insisted are unique do not seem so at all. Almost any act of imperialist aggression shares most, if not all, of the facets that Kobayashi enumerates here. There were, however, other aspects of the war that did indeed render it "complex and bizarre," and one wonders if Kobayashi did not actually have these in mind while holding himself in check for fear of censorship.

Surely what distinguished the war in China, particularly during the early years, was the unpredictable manner in which the hostilities escalated. Historian Kenneth Pyle suggests that this escalation was largely the result of "the fragmented nature of decision-making in the Japanese government, which at that time lacked a strong, central controlling leadership able to exercise its will over all factions of the administration, and able to coordinate and develop prudent and balanced policy goals."[32] This confused leadership made possible the insubordinate exploits of the Kwantung Army and prompted the unpredictable outbursts of ultranationalist right-wing factions within the military, outbursts such as Inoue Nisshō's Blood League Incident and the February 26 Uprising of the Imperial Way Faction (Kōdōha). These factors certainly contributed to the constant "newness" of the situation and explain the firmness of Kobayashi's conviction that the war as a whole was beyond man's powers to explain rationally.

Of course, not everyone agreed with Kobayashi on this point. Intellectuals of all stripes sought to come to an understanding of the war and either coherently to condemn or justify both Japan's imperialism in China and its eventual confrontation with the West. Philosopher Nishitani Keiji's contribution to the infamous 1942 "Symposium on Overcoming the Modern" (*kindai no chōkoku*) is in many ways representative of attempts to justify Japan's war philosophically, and it serves as a useful counterpoint for grasping Kobayashi's writing on the topic.[33] Nishitani's strained generalizations about Western culture, the facile deployment of concepts from Buddhist philosophy, and the tortured nature of the logic in this essay make Kobayashi's disgust with such discourse easy to understand, and one cannot help but sympathize with Kobayashi's wish that such thinkers would forgo the urge to explain what is clearly beyond their power to understand. Still, Nishitani's essay is important for the manner in which it exhibits some of the features of Japanese fascism identified by Maruyama Masao, including a propogation of racial myths and national essences as well as an internal "logic" that forgoes reason in favor of a fluid intuitive reaction to developments.[34] In a comparison of the attitudes of Nishitani and Kobayashi toward the war, we find that they both drew on this "logic" outlined by Maruyama.

Nishitani, in his essay entitled "'Kindai no chōkoku' shiron" (A Personal Theory on "Overcoming the Modern," 1942), struggles to put the war in a historical context. He maintains that the modern world is threatened by the fragmented cultural legacy of the early modern period, a legacy that includes three mutually exclusive pillars: 1) the religious Reformation, which is centered on God; 2) Renaissance humanism, which is centered on man; and 3) the scientific worldview, which is centered on nature.[35] What is needed to heal this fracture, Nishitani writes, is a religiosity (*shūkyōsei*) that can transcend and encompass all three of these pillars.

This religiosity, he tells us, lies in "what might be called a position of subjective nothingness" (*shutaiteki mu no tachiba*).[36] This erasure of the subject position in the attainment of nothingness resolves the contradictions inherent in modernity because it "includes both an absolute denial and an absolute transcendence of the body and its natural world, as well as of the spirit [*kokoro*] and its world of culture."[37] Nishitani is, of course, building on work done by his teacher Nishida Kitarō, and attempting to slip out of the Western philosophical discourse centered on presence. Nishitani's explanation of the attainment of this "subjective nothingness" is reminiscent of Nishida's reworking of Buddhist philosophy in his concept of "pure experience," a subject touched on in an earlier chapter. However, whereas Nishida focuses on the experience itself, the instant wherein the subject/object division is, for a fleeting moment, transcended, Nishitani moves one step further.

Unlike Nishida, Nishitani posits the position of subjective nothingness as a sustainable state, a belief that allows him to assert that

> the absolute denial of everything, including both culture and science, can lead directly to an absolute affirmation. A subjectivity that creates culture or practices science has not yet realized the position of a subjective nothingness. However, it is possible for an actualized position of subjective nothingness to be immanent in a subjectivity that creates culture and practices science. It could maintain its transcendental status, and would be immanent there as a true subjectivity.[38]

Having proposed his "subjective nothingness" as the cure for our fragmented modern world, Nishitani then goes on to reassert it as a qualitatively different sort of presence. First denying subjectivity, Nishitani rehabilitates it as a true subjectivity.

Nishitani works the same circular logic in his rationalization of Japan's military aggression. Late in the same essay he claims that the situation must be one in which the nation is manifesting that aspect of itself that is a fundamental denial of self. This being the case, in that it would be a nation carrying the universal spirit, it could [rightly] assert its authority as the leading nation of the present time. In short, its self-denial makes possible a proper self-assertion.[39]

This self-assertion, of course, takes the form of Japanese aggression on the continent and the war with the Allied Forces.

Such circular logic owes much to Japan's long tradition of Buddhist philosophy.[40] It is also a manifestation of a certain trope quite prevalent at the time. As discussed in Chapter 5, Hagiwara Sakutarō reverted to it in "Nihon e no kaiki," most notably in his insistence that Japan be conceived of in terms of the antinomy "A is not A; A is not not-A." Also discussed there was Japan Romantic School writer Yasuda Yojūrō, whose concept of "Japan as irony" served not so much to mute the pull of the nation as to reaffirm it.[41] Kobayashi Hideo's essays on the war, too, draw on this trope, though his deployment of it is somewhat less formulaic.[42] As noted above, Kobayashi rejected the possibility of achieving an understanding of the war, and in fact believed the very desire to understand was born of nothing more than an inability or unwillingness to accept its "newness." In 1940 Kobayashi, repeating his belief that the China War represents a unique historical contingency, wrote:

We are unable to remain calm when faced with the newness of this sort of incident. Every one of us is feeling an anxiety; not only do we feel it, we find we cannot bear it. We try to somehow escape from the uncertainty as quickly as possible. We try to comfort ourselves by interpreting the new event in old ways. This is something we all do unconsciously.[43]

This statement represents Kobayashi's first half of the equation to which many turned in these years of crisis. As in all of his essays on the war, the dominant mode is that of a negation, or denial, of that which is usually taken for granted. Here this takes the form of a denial of both the possibility and the appropriateness of a rational understanding of the war.

Kobayashi is particularly critical of attempts to understand the war by placing it in a historical context, such as Nishitani was to do in 1942. Paradoxically, Kobayashi tells us that it is history itself that teaches us to ignore history:

History teaches us, in a broad sense, what to expect of the future. But, at the same time, it teaches us how very dangerous a specific prediction can be. Those who acquire from history an attitude that allows them to sit themselves down in the future and look back at the present have missed the greatest lesson that history has to teach us. The greatest moral to be learned is that the people who make history are those who do not blindly believe in predictions for the future, but rather have a vital attachment to the present, and the present alone.[44]

In support of this point, made again elsewhere, Kobayashi pointed to two of the nation's greatest military leaders, Toyotomi Hideyoshi and Oda Nobunaga. Kobayashi recounts in some detail Hideyoshi's grand scheme for a conquest of the Korean peninsula and his ultimate failure. In keeping with his point above, Kobayashi attributed this failure to Hideyoshi's falling victim to the human predilection for predicting the future or judging the present based on what one has learned from the past:

His mistaken calculations were due to the fact that the situation he faced was absolutely new. In dealing with this new situation, Hideyoshi's abundance of knowledge did him no good. Not only did it not do him any good, it became, in fact, an enormous obstacle in his judgment of the situation. In other words, what caused him to err in his judgment was precisely that accurate knowledge that he had gleaned from his vast experience.[45]

The man Kobayashi contrasts with Hideyoshi is, not surprisingly, Oda Nobunaga, perhaps the most reckless and ruthless warrior in Japanese history. Kobayashi recounts the well-known story of the Battle at Okehazama in 1560, in which Nobunaga faced the larger army of Imagawa Yoshimoto. In spite of the fact that all military theory suggested that Nobunaga try to wait out the siege, he rallied his troops and, in broad daylight, boldly charged the enemy. If Nobunaga had a theory, Kobayashi concludes, it was "to be suspicious of all silly, imperfect theories."[46] Kobayashi voiced the same sentiment elsewhere in these words: "While there may be strategies for times of emergency [*hijōji*], there is no such thing as a philosophy for them."[47]

It is not hard to understand the appeal of this insistence that reason, philosophy, or thought of any kind is completely insufficient in a time of war, especially one that the prime minister himself could describe only as "complex and bizarre." If even a prominent thinker like Nishitani Keiji was forced to employ the type of tortured, circular logic evident in his essay, then it seems that the rational faculty was indeed most decidedly *not* up to the task. As is true of the initial negation in the other examples of this fascist trope, Kobayashi's negation, that of the validity of conventional reasoning, is at first glance a seemingly logical direction in which to proceed.

The problem, however, lay in the direction that Kobayashi took from here. Like the fascistic discourse of the thinkers mentioned above, Kobayashi paradoxically reaffirmed that which he had negated, and in the process reduced man to an almost animal-like condition in which blind instinct takes over. This move is most obvious in a particularly bombastic statement that Kobayashi made on a number of occasions. It is a statement of surrender in the guise of conquest, and is one of the most oft-quoted lines from Kobayashi's writings on the war. As the intellectuals and authorities failed to recognize that their theories and reasoning were completely insufficient to the task, Kobayashi found the ideal expression of his attitude toward the war embodied in the common man:

> The people of this nation have coped with the war in silence [*kokumin wa damatte jihen ni shōshita*]. The fact that they have coped in silence is a defining characteristic of our war with China. . . . The wisdom whereby the people have responded unerringly and effectively at this juncture has not yet taken shape as a new philosophical expression [*shisō hyōgen*]. This is because in conforming itself to the newness and the difficulty of the situation, this wisdom has not had the leisure to assume some disingenuous form of expression. As a critic I relish the work of sniffing out this wisdom scattered about the landscape. Everything else is trivial.[48]

To Kobayashi this silent coping, this refusal to exercise wisdom, constitutes "wisdom" in and of itself.

Kobayashi takes to extremes this validation of the legitimacy of any action in the name of "coping," going even to the point where he would threaten his own livelihood in its name. On the grounds that such is necessary in coping with the war, Kobayashi expresses his full support even of censorship and thought control. He goes so far as to claim that these should be pursued more vigorously than they had been to date.

> In the past I believed it was only natural [that] a formerly unprecedented control was exercised by the authorities over thinkers and writers. I feel the same way today. This type of passive thought control is rather easy, and so the authorities have managed to show themselves in their best light. Things will not be so easy when they move to a more active type of thought control. Their worrying themselves over how to make this proceed smoothly does nothing but cause problems. Isn't this the reason they are so ineffective? I fully support active controls. Without these, the passive forms of thought control will be, ultimately, worthless. It does far more damage than good when the authorities struggle and rack their brains over some sort of direc-

tion for, or theory of, national policy in order to appease the writers and thinkers.[49]

Kobayashi's belief in "coping" as the legitimizer of any action prompts him to advocate more stringent control over the very literature he himself produces.

What is left of Kobayashi's ideal for a man at war is nothing but primal, undirected action. The almost animal-like nature is evident in the following lines:

> If one would exercise doubt, then never has there been a time when there have existed more seeds of doubt than the present. Everything is suspicious. Why is it that in spite of this people seem ready to believe the shreds of dubious abstractions and the tattered rags of ideology? Doubt everything that is suspicious! Then you will be able to see the movement of things in their naked state, the movement that mocks the human spirit. You can see your egotism, your patriotism, which is as certain as your sexual desire. This is all that is left. A time when you must rebuild from these—that is what we call a "time of emergency" [*hijōji*].[50]

In these lines Kobayashi is, essentially, displacing reason as a controlling factor for human action and substituting in its stead "egotism" and "patriotism" fueled by libidinal desires.

This irrational, unplanned assertion of libidinal drives is linked to Kobayashi's overall aesthetic vision. Kobayashi himself suggested this is so, though in a somewhat ambiguous manner. On his return from his first trip to China, the trip that inspired many of his travel sketches, Kobayashi indicated that he felt his vision vindicated by the chaos of the war in China. Reflecting on how the trip has affected him, he writes: "Of course the way I think about things has not changed as a consequence of my going to China. . . . It was a wonderful feeling to see that the mode of thought I have maintained all by myself in one corner of the *bundan* is so very deeply rooted."[51]

This "mode of thought" is, of course, based in Kobayashi's rejection of abstractions and his insistence on the radical autonomy of the individual. This ultimately led Kobayashi to reject any and all attempts to explain the confusing reality around him in the universal language of reason (nothing but a "design") and to affirm the unbridled assertion of the individual ego. Perhaps most frightening, Kobayashi did not link this instinctual mode of existence to any larger agenda; he posited it neither as an innately Japanese characteristic nor as a product of Japan's history, but as natural to all men everywhere.

"Overcoming the Modern"

As I have argued from the beginning of this study, Kobayashi was driven by nostalgia for a fading mode of authentically experiencing a world of hard and fast materiality. Only this mode of experience could stem the disconcerting slide into ever more cerebral abstractions, and reinvigorate atrophied elements of the human sensibilities. Under the banner of literary aestheticism, Kobayashi in effect "colonized" the realms of literature and philosophy and, in the late 1930s and early 1940s, international politics and war as well. His appreciation of the war was, essentially, based on his rejection of "designs" in favor of a lively, creative praxis; in the war's unpredictable nature and ad hoc policies he found the entire world around him abandoning sterile abstractions and simply "seeing" the world for what it was. The war was praxis unmediated by self-conscious questioning and doubt. As such, he found it beautiful.

It was this thoroughgoing aestheticism that spawned the divergence of thought between thinkers like Nishitani and himself. This difference emerged in the aforementioned "Symposium on Overcoming the Modern." Kobayashi's presence at this symposium was confusing. On the one hand, the theme itself was one that had concerned him for many years, and he was one of the three people most active in organizing the event.[52] In spite of this fact, however, it seems that Kobayashi participated only reluctantly in the project. Of the thirteen participants, Kobayashi was the only one who did not submit a written contribution at any time.[53] In addition, during the discussions (particularly on the first day) Kobayashi was rather reticent, speaking out only rarely and only minimally engaging any of the others in a sustained debate.[54] Kobayashi's reluctance to participate fully is understandable. Surely he was disappointed with the nature of the essays. Nishitani's essay, as mentioned above, represented precisely the sort of tortured logic that Kobayashi detested. Other essays were equally disappointing in that they reified the very paradigms of modernity that they ostensibly sought to "overcome."[55] In short, Kobayashi's approval of how "the people of this nation have coped with the war in silence" and the concept behind this was, from the very start, at odds with the nature of a gathering of intellectuals. The incessant speculation and explanation diminished the direct, aesthetic appreciation that he had of the war.

When Kobayashi did speak out, at the start of the second day, it was in an attempt to steer the discourse toward lines more acceptable to him. He began by saying, "I do not like general theories [*ippanron*] and so will, for your reference, speak from my personal experience."[56] He then launched into an explanation of true literary appreciation and how it required a view of history as static rather than dynamic.[57] This statement was a reaffirmation of Kobayashi's belief, introduced in Chapter 5, in the historical event as inaccessible to reason.

At this point in Kobayashi's monologue, Kawakami Tetsutarō interrupted Kobayashi, and the following exchange occurred:

KAWAKAMI: I'm sure that's important, too, but there really isn't any need to call this "history," is there?

KOBAYASHI: Well, if not "history," what would you call it?

KAWAKAMI: A more universal sort of anthropology or something . . .

KOBAYASHI: Or perhaps a certain *aesthetics* . . .[58]

This is precisely the point. Even during the war years, when he claimed that "should the time come to take up a gun, I will gladly die for the nation," Kobayashi's concern was always aesthetics. This is the reason that his vision ultimately deviated from the paradigm adhered to by Nishitani and the others seeking to break through the impasse of modernity through an examination of the meanings of the war. Nishitani sought to understand the war, Kobayashi only to appreciate it. Nishitani's motivation was what drove him to reaffirm, in different form, that which he initially denied. Kobayashi's aesthetics was not a matter of understanding; it was enough to "see," and this required only the negation of the ultimately confusing rational faculty.

This fundamental difference prompted Nishitani to interrupt the exchange between Kobayashi and Kawakami. Kobayashi and Nishitani circled around a number of points, and were, in the final analysis, talking about completely different things, as Kobayashi pointed out.[59] The fundamental difference between their assertions lay in their ultimate focus. While Kobayashi, as he himself suggested above, was thinking in terms of the aesthetic, Nishitani was seeking progress. Nishitani expressed this difference by rejecting Kobayashi's approach to the classics and their creators, and suggesting his own equivalent: "Rather than being gazed at for their physicality [*sō*] or shape, they should be made our own. As someone said long ago, 'Do not follow the ancients, follow what the ancients followed.' "[60]

Nishitani was thinking teleologically; he believed that there is some transcendental truth out there to "get," and that thought could lead him to it. Kobayashi, on the other, was interested in the aesthetic appreciation of the polar opposite of that transcendental truth: the singular and the specific. Kobayashi was attempting to identify and nurture the point where self-consciousness merged with materiality through an intuitive leap. He was pursuing that fleeting moment he had described as "a time of fullness" and "brimming with proof that I am alive, and in which each and every thing was clear to me."[61]

The essays examined in this chapter reveal a very different manifestation of Kobayashi's aesthetics. He had always privileged the singular vision of the individual, an act whereby one conflated a deeply personal consciousness with a fully autonomous aspect of materiality. Bringing this epistemology to the subjects of history, culture, and tradition generated an aura of individual artistic freedom that was anathema to wartime's reductive theories of national identity. Kobayashi was largely consistent in this glorification of the individual even when writing both about his travels in China and the war there, as well as in his essays on the military conflict with the Allied Powers. Here, however, a different dimension of the subjectivity Kobayashi had constructed comes to the fore; here we see the individual whose "precious life is no longer [his/her] own."

It was, in fact, the particular subjectivity constructed by Kobayashi that formed the root of this fascistic ideology. It did so in three ways. First, Kobayashi's epistemology was predicated upon a self-consciousness not only distanced, but even severed, from an exterior materiality. Although this was a precondition for a subsequent empathetic, intuitive appreciation of an object, it was no guarantee that such an appreciation would indeed be forthcoming. Kobayashi's appreciation was not indiscriminate, and where personal inclination, historical circumstance, or aesthetic alienation prevented the leap of intuition, that same distance separating interiority and exteriority served as an impenetrable barrier to understanding or empathy of any kind. It was this aspect of Kobayashi's vision that prevented him from "seeing" the thousands of nameless Chinese and Japanese suffering and dying on the battlefields. As the conditions for an intuitive understanding of them were lacking, they remained part of an unfathomable exteriority, a feature of the landscape.

The second manner in which Kobayashi's particular subjectivity led to a fascistic attitude toward the war is evident when the gap between the individual and exteriority *is* bridgeable (again, whether for reasons of personal inclination, historical circumstance, or literary affinity). Here Kobayashi's epistemological method allowed for a moving aesthetic appreciation. As he had made clear since "Samazama naru ishō" in 1929, accessing the full potential of such experience is impossible when an individual is committed to a particular ideology or "design." Such thinking pushes what could be an intuitive appreciation into a realm of volitional, intellectual interpretation and analysis, a shift that ultimately diminishes the powerfully emotional encounter with the world available through intuition. Conformity to this paradigm was, essentially, the only consistent critical measure that Kobayashi employed in his career. The question was always this: Is the object (book, author, critical piece, philosophical discourse) under consideration "creative" in the sense that it merged a singular subjectivity with the concrete specifics of a particular piece of materiality?

This floating, flexible subjectivity as Kobayashi constructed it provided, therefore, only two possible responses: utter indifference or unconditional appreciation. Whereas the plight of the Chinese under siege elicited the former, the act of war itself prompted the latter. The situation of war appealed to Kobayashi for the direct experience it offered. In its confusion and ever-changing nature Kobayashi found a world that, in its unpredictability, was always beyond the mediation of the intellectual abstraction. In this extended crisis situation (*hijōji*, literally "conditions ever changing"), events were so volatile that a reasoned plan could not be put into effect, and both soldiers on the front line and the military commanders behind them were forced to act intuitively. They were forced to constantly reformulate their apprehension of the situation, exercising the type of vibrant, intuitive cognition that Kobayashi championed in the literary realm. In addition, as any critique of the war would require a sustained, rational argument based on universal principles (activities deleterious to the ability to appreciate beauty and creativity), Kobayashi's brand of subjectivity was inherently incapable of seeing the war in terms other than aesthetic. This prompted his appreciation of the war as "beautiful."

A third and final way in which Kobayashi's construction of subjectivity determined his reaction to the war stems from the relationship he posited between subjectivity and materiality. The act of "seeing" in which the two are conflated, the pinnacle of the aesthetic experience, dictates that the energy be focused on how one can move beyond the confines of a consciousness of self (*jiishiki*) to the certainty of an intuitive understanding of materiality. In Kobayashi's world this translated, paradoxically, to a reification of consciousness, represented by his idea of the author's "destiny" (*shukumei*), as well as a reification of pure exteriority, as demonstrated in his obsession with the impenetrability of materiality. While Kobayashi had early in his career recognized the fact that one's experience of materiality shapes consciousness, after his early experiments in fiction, he ceased to consider the fact that an individual may, to some extent, control that influence. In Kobayashi's vision an individual's destiny, like materiality, exists as a static given.

This refusal to turn an analytical eye on consciousness, or interiority, ultimately undermines the freedom of that consciousness. By surrendering oneself to a personal destiny, one relinquishes whatever control an individual may possibly exercise over consciousness. This aspect of Kobayashi's thought is evident in his essay "Mujō to iu koto," which I discussed in the previous chapter. There Kobayashi relates the experience that inspired the topic of the essay: a fleeting apprehension of a section of an ancient text: "the other day I went to Mount Hiei, and while wandering aimlessly in the area of the Sannō Gongen, looking at the green leaves, the stone fences, and the rest, suddenly this short passage flashed into my mind as if I were examining a fragment of a horizontal picture scroll of the period. . . ."[62] This section, like all of Kobayashi's narrations of intuitive insight, is presented as having occurred spontaneously, without volition. While this encounter with materiality is, of course, all a rhetorical construct, there are real-world implications. In that this paradigm of understanding represents the ideal of Kobayashi's vision and the subjectivity toward which he strives, it inculcates a real-world erasure of the intentionality it rhetorically obscures.

All of this is to say that while the preparation and maintenance of a self-consciousness conducive to the act of appreciation requires the exercise of a certain type of volition, in Kobayashi's mind the act itself must occur spontaneously. His act of intuitive appreciation is, for this reason and in this respect, a passive act, one in which the rhetorical surrender of control over consciousness translates into a passive acceptance and affirmation of materiality. Therefore, though he stated explicitly that "Literature exists for peace; it does not exist for the sake of war," Kobayashi turned his literary attention time and again over the next five years to the topic of war.[63] The reification of a consciousness divorced, at least in the first stage, from materiality was, essentially, a surrender of control over both these poles. With evidence of the war all around him, Kobayashi could not but exercise his aesthetic appreciation of it in spite of the fact that he explicitly denied the compatibility of the two.

EPILOGUE

Literary Aestheticism in the Postwar World

The ambiguity of Kobayashi's legacy is an important reason to continue the examination of his oeuvre. He forged a radically literary mode of cognition through battle with the universalist discourse of modernity as it appeared in the form of Marxist theory. Kobayashi was largely responsible for replacing this worldview with literary aestheticism (*bungaku shugi*). Through this cognitive mode, he was not only successful in instilling a lively critical consciousness in the thinkers who would succeed him, he was also able to write some of the most rhetorically complex and deeply moving prose-poems of his era. Not least, Kobayashi invented a means of restoring something of that most intimately human experience of the world—the authentic encounter with the work of art—that was on the brink of extinction in the mechanically reproducible, commodified culture of our modern world.

Kobayashi's essays on the colonies and the war are an integral component of this legacy. The inability to empathize with foreign people, the celebration of the violence of war as an exercise of intuition, and the glorification of a silent acquiescence are as much a product of the subjectivity he forged as are the haunting atmospheres of the essays in *Mujō to iu koto*. To be capable of invoking unmediated beauty, it seems, is to be capable of unleashing untamed instincts.

The ambivalence of this legacy is most clearly evident in Kobayashi's "Sensō to heiwa," a short poetic reflection on a photograph he saw in the newspaper on New Year's Day in 1942. As he would soon do in *Mujō to iu koto*, Kobayashi here deftly reproduces in the connection of the reader to his text the very same relationship that he depicts *within* the text. In "Taema" Kobayashi's synecdochal use of the impenetrable mask to represent his authentic experience of the *nō* play elicits a similar suspension of analysis on the part of the reader perusing his essay. We are seduced into simply reveling in the eerie beauty of it. "War and Peace" is a reverie on the camera's frigid, unflinching attention to surface appearances, and Kobayashi rhetorically reproduces this attitude toward the object of representation in the reader of his essay.

The photograph inspiring the essay is an aerial view of the U.S. Naval Fleet being bombed at Pearl Harbor.

War and Peace

On the morning of January first I was looking at the newspaper photograph of the Imperial Navy's bombing of Pearl Harbor. The large print declaring "A Shining Moment in History: The Annihilation of the U.S. Pacific Fleet" danced before my eyes, but the all-important photograph itself appeared calm and quiet. Seven vessels, all looking like model ships, were lined up neatly, giving off small clouds of white smoke and spewing something that looked like ink from a squid. "Don't be fooled by appearances—this photo, more than anything else, is an honest representation of a scorching hell engulfing some thousands of men." I kept repeating this to myself, but to no avail. No man has ever taken a photograph as shocking as this. The more I remind myself of this fact, the more settled I feel, and my imagination stubbornly refuses to be again engaged. I imagine that all the people who saw this photo experienced, like myself, a certain confusion over the fact that there was really nothing shocking about this presumably shocking photo.

It suddenly struck me that millions of people were, like me, looking at this photo at the very same moment. Compared to the certainty of this idea, the photograph before my eyes seemed almost incomprehensible. I pondered this as I sat on a chair on the porch, all the while unable to tear my eyes from the photo.

The sky was perfectly clear and the sea stretching out beneath my eyes glistened. A fishing boat sailed along, leaving a white wake on the dark blue sea. If it was a torpedo moving across the water rather than that fishing boat, that wake would be its trail. And still the sea would rise and fall as before, and its beauty would not have changed. This little idea flashed across my mind leaving a pure white wake in the deep blue of my brain. It was this very same sun that shone over Pearl Harbor and this very same cold, blue saltwater that, when the torpedoes hit their targets, sent out the ripples that physicists have so carefully observed. That scene must have appeared beautiful to the eyes of the brave soldiers on the bombers. There can be no doubt about it—the true appearance of the light and the ocean surely etched itself on the hearts of these men who had purged themselves of all idle thoughts and evil intentions. Surely it is a sight they will always remember. Imagining all this somehow gave me great pleasure. The sun shines, and the ocean is blue—this is always the case, both in war and in peace. This thought was like a prayer, and it struck me as being an act of deep meditation.

I again began looking at the photograph on my lap. This must have been just the way they saw it. In what manner other than this could it appear to the soldiers who circled calmly around the heads of the enemy? Isn't it the case that the heartless camera sees with the vision of people who have transcended a concern with life and death? This is because the will to battle destroys all useless thoughts. Their bird's eye view is identical to that of the camera. Otherwise, how could their bombs have struck home?

I recalled a line from, I believe, the Lotus Sutra. Though I didn't remember the exact wording, it was something to the effect that what may appear to all living things as an apocalypse appears in the eyes of the Buddha as paradise. This is surely not intended as a metaphor. Our spirit is weak and we cannot but take it as such, but isn't it in fact quite literally true? Don't they say that the man on the battlefield attains the vision of the Buddha? We can imagine how he completely escapes from all the preconceived notions of everyday life and sees with eyes that are extraordinarily clear. They are not much fond of telling war stories on their return from the battlefield. They must find it disgusting how, in the good name of inspiring bravery in the people, there is such a flood of literature and literary reporting on the war and so much encouragement of useless ideas and loquacity on the extraordinary nature of the war.

I continued to think as I looked at the photograph. It seemed to gradually reveal to me its true meaning. Isn't everything perfectly clear, perfectly obvious? Theory and literature about the war cannot cloud the eyes of he who does battle. Wasn't this what Tolstoy ultimately arrived at through his bold observations in *War and Peace*? Wasn't it the horrifying philosophy wherein war and peace are the same? Once the idea of a criminal psychology occurred to modern man, he promptly produced that odd concept of a psychology of war. War does not occur because of the existence of hawks; it occurs because life itself is a battle.[1]

All of the classic Kobayashi rhetorical techniques are here. In imitation of the photograph itself, Kobayashi pulls us up high over the ships ablaze, preventing us from pulling them close and noticing the carnage below. To accomplish this distance, he employs his feint, first inviting us to consider the "scorching hell engulfing some thousands of men," which he then promptly dismisses in favor of calling our attention, explicitly, to the singularity of the object we are examining. The photo is rendered as impenetrable materiality, and language becomes irrelevant. Our relationship to the photo mirrors that of the bomber/photographer to the scene below: there is "seeing" without effort and without judgment or interpretation. Kobayashi convinces us to accept the surface of the scene in much the same way that the camera passively records it. Here, from this distance and with this refusal to interpret—to look for meaning—the burning ships and the dying sailors are no more important than the sun and the ocean and the waves. In fact they are just as natural. War and peace are one.

Kobayashi's poetry almost lulls us into believing it.

Kobayashi fell gradually silent in the last years of the war, publishing only one piece in 1945. Perhaps his quiet was an act of solidarity with the people he had praised for having "coped with the war in silence." Perhaps it was a natural reaction to the "beauty" he found in the war—Kobayashi's response to art had always gravitated toward silence.

In June 1946, the editorial board of the journal *Shin Nihon bungaku* (New Japanese Literature) published a manifesto that shocked the literary world. It was itself a declaration of war, in a sense, on the writers who had been complicit in the war effort. Not one to equivocate, Odagiri Hideo, in whose name the article was published, leveled accusations and, more importantly, he named names. Kobayashi Hideo was one of them.[2] Many of these writers never recovered professionally. Kobayashi most certainly did, and went on to serve until his death as the grand dean of Japanese letters.

Kobayashi's quick re-emergence was no doubt due to the fact that the postwar literary community soon realized that in spite of the fascist statements Kobayashi had issued during the war, he was really not guilty of any of the offenses that Odagiri and his colleagues listed. The names of those deemed complicit were preceded by the following accusations:

> It is not for us to engage in that "collective repentance of the hundred million," which is a stupid idea. As you are all well aware, claiming that responsibility is shared by each and every one of us obscures the fact that some of us bear a greater, more direct responsibility. Were there no writers directly responsible for the degradation [*daraku*] of Japanese literature, none who served to lead us into that degraded state? Were there no writers who, in spite of their role as the very soul of the people, became megaphones for the invasion authorities, driving the people on in the war? Were there none who employed deception and flattery in shamelessly prostituting themselves to those in control? None who blazed this trail for others to follow? Did no writer jump for joy at his windfall when the Special Higher Police [Tokkō keisatsu], military police [*kenpei*], or other authority silenced some-

> one critical of him? Did no writer sell out a literary rival by tipping off the thought police with an anonymous report of communist or liberal inclinations? Were there no writers whose crude humanism caused them to misunderstand the war, to dress this imperialist endeavor in the guise of a battle for the sake of humanity, and in so doing inspire our malleable youths to dedicate themselves to the war? Furthermore, were there no writers who, though only accepting the war with resignation as a turn of events beyond their control, became the primary force prompting a similar acceptance in the younger generation of writers?
>
> There were all of these. We list the names of the major offenders below.[3]

Kobayashi had certainly not contributed to the "degradation" of literature; in fact, in many ways he had been the boldest defender of a genuinely literary mode throughout the war, and it was what had kept him aloof from the reductive diatribes about national identity and imperial mission. Kobayashi had not assumed a fawning posture toward the authorities. He never couched his words of support for the war in a metanarrative amenable to usage as propaganda. In short, Kobayashi's "pardon" was almost certainly granted because he had remained true to his bold vision of creative literary praxis.

A genuinely literary man, Kobayashi had resisted the temptations to pen formulaic propaganda to fuel the war effort. A genuinely literary man, Kobayashi had written some of the most moving words on, and convincing arguments for, the carnage and oppression.

Reference Matter

Notes

Prologue

1. Lentricchia, "Last Will and Testament of an Ex-Literary Critic," 60.

2. Lentricchia, *Criticism and Social Change*, 2.

3. Ibid., 60. Emphasis in the original.

4. "Dirty Harry" is, of course, a reference to the 1971 film of the same name starring Clint Eastwood as a no-nonsense San Francisco policeman capable of handling even the "dirtiest" of cases. The moniker was first attached to Lentricchia by Maureen Corregan in a 1984 *Village Voice* review. See the summary of Lentricchia's career in Tinari, "Being Frank."

5. Lentricchia, "Last Will and Testament," 59.

6. Ibid., 65–66.

7. Mellen, "Homeward Bound," 7.

8. Altman, "Life and Letters," 7.

9. See, for example, Lentricchia and McAuliffe, *Crimes of Art and Terror*, particularly the widely-reproduced "Groundzeroland," where he explores the dynamics of art, violence, commodification, and patriotism.

10. Sontag, "Against Interpretation," 7. Emphasis in the original.

11. Ibid., 5–7.

12. Ibid., 11. Ellipses in the original.

13. Ibid., 13–14.

14. Quoted in Rollyson, *Reading Susan Sontag*, 70.

Introduction

1. Seidensticker, "Kobayashi Hideo," 157.

2. Sontag, "Against Interpretation," 14. Emphasis in the original.

3. Lentricchia, "Last Will and Testament," 59; Sontag, "Against Interpretation," 14.

4. Odagiri Hideo, "Bungaku ni okeru sensō sekinin no tsuikyū," 65.

5. The essay "Jinsei shakudanka Ranbō" was later renamed "Ranbō I."

6. Karatani and Nakagami, *Kobayashi Hideo o koete*, 13; Keene, *Dawn to the West (Poetry, Drama, Criticism*; hereafter *Dawn to the West* II), 582.

7. Etō, "Modern Japanese Literary Criticism," 181. The six critics are Nakamura Mitsuo, Etō Jun, Hayashi Fusao, Hirano Ken, Yamamoto Kenkichi, and Kawakami Tetsutarō.

8. See, for example, the short essay by friend and rival Nakahara Chūya, "Kobayashi Hideo ron" (1927), 96–97.

9. See Honda, "Kobayashi Hideo ron," reproduced with minor revisions in Honda, *Kobayashi Hideo ron*, 17–98. The earlier work was done by writers such as Inoue Yoshio, Tosaka Jun, Nakano Shigeharu, Kubokawa Tsurujirō and Hanada Kiyoteru. For a detailed account of this lineage of Kobayashi studies, see Midori Matsui's dissertation, "Beyond the Failure of Modernism," 6–9.

10. Most notably Maruyama Masao, Yoshimoto Takaaki, and Karatani Kōjin. See Matsui, "Beyond the Failure of Modernism," 6–9.

11. Yoshida, "Shūrokubun kaisetsu," 334. Nakamura's essay can be found in the May 1958 edition of the journal *Bungakukai*, but see also his *Ronkō Kobayashi Hideo*, particularly 157.

12. Though it did not greatly affect the overall discourse, a similar statement was actually made as early as 1931 by Sakamoto Etsurō. See Shimizu, "Kobayashi Hideo kenkyū annai," 350.

13. Hirata, "Criticism in Poetry."

14. Etō, *Kobayashi Hideo*. For this psychological portrait, Etō draws on unpublished material as well as personal accounts by Ōoka Shōhei (1909–1988) and Kawakami Tetsutarō (1902–1980), two close friends of Kobayashi.

15. A recent example, and one of the few English-language essays on Kobayashi, is Hirata, "Criticism in Poetry," mentioned above. Taking its lead from questions posed in Etō's study, Hirata's essay is itself a Kobayashi-esque sort of poetic reverie sliding easily between Kobayashi Hideo, French symbolist poets, and Western literary theorists such as Foucault, Lacan, and Žižek. Expanding on the biographical side of Etō's approach are three books written by Kobayashi's younger sister, Takamizawa Junko: *Ani Kobayashi Hideo to no taiwa*; *Ani Kobayashi Hideo*; and *Ningen no oikata shinikata: ani Kobayashi Hideo no ashiato*. The second of these includes a wealth of biographical information, particularly about Kobayashi's earliest years, and is now available in English: *My Brother Hideo Kobayashi*. It should be noted that Takamizawa's works are aimed at a general audience and are therefore anecdotal as opposed to Etō's more sophisticated psychoanalytical approach.

16. Yoshida, "Shūrokubun kaisetsu," 334.

17. *Motoori Norinaga* was serialized in *Shinchō* from June 1965 to December 1976, and published as a single volume in October 1977. A two-part supplement was added in the January and February 1979 editions of *Shinchō*.

18. See, for example, the five essays on *Motoori Norinaga* collected in *Kobayashi Hideo o yomu*.

19. See Kitagawa, *Shishin to shukumei: Kobayashi Hideo ron*; Nozaki, *Norinaga to Kobayashi Hideo*; Moriwaki, *Kobayashi Hideo to Beruguson*; and Yamazaki, *Kobayashi Hideo to Beruguson*.

20. Kamei, *Kobayashi Hideo ron*; Aeba, *Kobayashi Hideo to sono jidai*.

21. Yoshida, "Shūrokubun kaisetsu," 326.

22. Seidensticker, "Kobayashi Hideo," in Shively, ed., *Tradition and Modernization in Japanese Culture*, 420. This essay is hereafter referred to as "Kobayashi Hideo" (I). The other two essays are the aforementioned "Kobayashi Hideo" (II), and "The Death of Kobayashi Hideo."

23. Keene, *Dawn to the West* II, 593.

24. Anderer, "Introduction," in *Literature of the Lost Home*, 15.

25. Particularly helpful are the complete translations: "Multiple Designs" (Samazama naru ishō, 1929), "The Anxiety of Modern Literature" (Gendai bungaku no fuan, 1932), "Literature of the Lost Home" (Kokyō o ushinatta bungaku, 1933), "Chaos in the Literary World" (Bungakukai no konran, 1934), and "Discourse on Fiction of the Self" (Watakushi shōsetsu ron, 1935). The translated excerpts (37 in all), offered without introductory comments, are rather less accessible.

26. Hirata, "Home and History."

27. The full-length study is Königsberg, *Der junge Kobayashi Hideo, Leben und Werk eines japanischen Literaturkritikers der Moderne*; the English essay is "Kobayashi Hideo's 'Return to Japan'." Another trenchant critique of Kobayashi, although not as readily accessible, is Matsui's dissertation, "Beyond the Failure of Modernism." Matsui's work was been particularly helpful to me in formulating my reading of Kobayashi's wartime essays.

28. Königsberg, "Kobayashi Hideo's 'Return to Japan'," 167. This deferential tone is evident in most Japanese-language studies and in virtually all work done outside of the mainstream of the Japanese academy. See, for example, Ninomiya, who publishes on Kobayashi in French as well as Japanese: *La Pensée de Kobayashi Hideo* and *Kobayashi Hideo no koto*. Hirata's work also falls squarely in this vein. As compelling as I find Hirata's reading of the wartime essay "Mujō to iu koto," his defense of Kobayashi's wartime record based solely on a passage in the 1933 "Kokyō o ushinatta bungaku" (Literature That Has Lost Its Home) leaves something to be desired. See Hirata's "Home and History," particularly 257. A Japanese-language version of some of Hirata's work on Kobayashi is available in Hirakawa, ed., *Ikoku e no shōkei to sokoku e no kaiki*. I might also list here the brief introduction to Kobayashi, written by Leith Morton, included in *My Brother Hideo Kobayashi*.

Chapter One

1. These biographical details are based largely on information from Yoshida and Horiuchi, *Shoshi Kobayashi Hideo*.

2. Autobiographical information here and below comes mainly from the following two sources: Yoshida, "Nenpu," and Takamizawa, *Ani Kobayashi*

Hideo. The latter work is now also available in English: *My Brother Hideo Kobayashi*, trans. James Wada (hereafter Wada).

3. Etō, *Kobayashi Hideo*, 9–17. Shima makes much the same claim in *Kobayashi Hideo: aku o yurusu kami o yuruseru ka*, 7.

4. See Takamizawa, *Ani Kobayashi Hideo*, 61; cf. Wada, 35.

5. "Ponkin no warai" was later renamed "Onna to ponkin" (The Woman and Ponkin).

6. Hatano, "Hatachi no Kobayashi Hideo," 262–63.

7. Ibid., 64.

8. Etō, *Kobayashi Hideo*, 20.

9. Takamizawa, *Ani Kobayashi Hideo*, 94, 102; cf. Wada, 56, 62.

10. Takamizawa, *Ani Kobayashi Hideo*, 29; cf. Wada, 15; Saitō, "Wakai koro no Kobayashi Hideo to sono shūhen," 98.

11. Takamizawa, *Ani Kobayashi Hideo*, 73; cf. Wada, 43.

12. Keene, *Dawn to the West* II, 582.

13. For details on the Great Kantō Earthquake, see Seidensticker, *Low City, High City*, especially 3–9, and Uranishi, "Kantō daishinsai to bungaku."

14. Matsumoto, "Tōkyō moyu: tensai jinsai fukugōtai," 6.

15. Yokomitsu, quoted in Hirano, "Shōwa," 328–29. This translation is a slightly modified version of that provided by Iwamoto in "Aspects of the Proletarian Literary Movement in Japan," 157.

16. Washburn, *The Dilemma of the Modern in Japanese Fiction*, 1.

17. Ibid., 2.

18. Ibid.

19. For an objection to Harootunian's foregrounding of capitalism at the expense of all else, particularly the state, see Andrew Barshay's review of *Overcome by Modernity* in *Journal of Japanese Studies*, 151.

20. Harootunian, *Overcome by Modernity*, 23. He is here quoting from Žižek, *Tarrying with the Negative*, 209.

21. Harootunian, *Overcome by Modernity*, xi–xvi.

22. Though this narrative might be traced back to Kobayashi Hideo's "Watakushi shōsetsu ron" (Discourse on the I-Novel, 1935), such prewar analyses focus on the *literary* ramifications of the selfhood constructed in the I-novel (*watakushi shōsetsu*). It was in the postwar period that the narrative came to center on issues of subjectivity itself, with literary texts serving as source material. A leading proponent of this narrative is critic Nakamura Mitsuo. See his *Fūzoku shōsetsu ron* and *Nihon no kindai shōsetsu*. In addition to the influence of Nakamura's work in Japan, this general approach has inspired a number of English-language studies as well, most notably Arima, *The Failure of Freedom*, and Walker, *The Japanese Novel of the Meiji Period and the Ideal of Individualism*. For an important challenge to this perspective, see Strong, "Downgrading the 'Kindai Jiga.'"

23. Karatani, *Nihon kindai bungaku no kigen*; translated as *Origins of Modern Japanese Literature*, translations edited by Brett de Bary. For a contextualization of this book and its author, and a critique of Karatani's problematic rela-

tionship with history, see the review written by John Whittier Treat for the *Journal of Japanese Studies.*

24. Ibid., 66–67; translation from de Bary, ed., *Origins of Modern Japanese Literature*, 61.

25. Harootunian, *Overcome by Modernity*, 97.

26. Ibid., 216.

27. Though the infatuation with materiality is less marked in Watsuji, he did address it (even pre-earthquake) in its relationship to the human spirit. See his "Gūzō saikō." For the importance of this essay in the evolution of Watsuji's thought, see LaFleur, "A Turning in Taishō."

28. Harootunian, *Overcome by Modernity*, xxv.

29. Ibid., 30–31. In his study of the Japan Romantic school, Kevin Doak also notes the centrality of memory: "The immediate problem facing the later romantics was how to produce a memory that belonged irretrievably to an earlier generation" (*Dreams of Difference*, xix).

30. See Culler's summary of this in *On Deconstruction*, 86–87.

31. Kobayashi, "Kokyō o ushinatta bungaku," 31–32. The translation is mine, but I am here and elsewhere indebted to the translations provided in Anderer's *Literature of the Lost Home*. Anderer's translation of these lines appears on 48–49.

32. Kobayashi, "Kokyō o ushinatta bungaku," 31; cf. Anderer, *Literature of the Lost Home*, 48. Hirata provides an interesting reading of this section of the essay in his "Home and History," particularly 234–36.

33. Kobayashi, "Kokyō o ushinatta bungaku," 33; cf. Anderer, *Literature of the Lost Home*, 49–50.

34. Kobayashi, "Kokyō o ushinatta bungaku," 32; cf. Anderer, *Literature of the Lost Home*, 49.

35. See Lippit's chapter on Akutagawa in *Topographies of Japanese Modernism*. As Lippit convincingly argues, Akutagawa's later unraveling and eventual suicide were also inextricably tied to literary developments. The importance of Akutagawa to the development of Kobayashi's method is explored in Chapter 3.

36. Takahashi, "Shirakaba," 35.

37. For the loss of that issue of *Bungei shunjū*, see Komori, "Kigen no gensetsu," 132. Circulation statistics are from Keene, *Dawn to the West* II, 549. The most extensive English-language study of the publishing world during this period is Mack, "The Value of Literature."

38. Shiozawa, *Zasshi 100-nen no ayumi: 1874–1990*, 63–64.

39. See Komori, "Kigen no gensetsu," 132.

40. Kōno, *Shomotsu no kindai*, 159; quoted in Komori, "Kigen no gensetsu," 132–33.

41. Shiozawa, *Zasshi 100-nen no ayumi*, 75.

42. Noma, *Watashi no hansei*; quoted in Shiozawa, *Zasshi 100-nen no ayumi*, 73.

43. Quoted in Shiozawa, *Zasshi 100-nen no ayumi*, 78.

44. Keene, *Dawn to the West* II, 549.

45. Shiozawa, *Zasshi 100-nen no ayumi*, 76–77.

46. Satō, *Taikutsu tokuhon*, 166–67. Quoted in, and translated by, Keene, *Dawn to the West* II, 575.

47. Benjamin, "The Work of Art in the Age of Mechanical Reproduction," 222.

48. Ibid., 223.

49. Ibid., 233–34.

50. Shiozawa, *Zasshi 100-nen no ayumi*, 76.

51. Keene, *Dawn to the West* II, 579.

52. See Iwamoto, "Aspects of the Proletarian Literary Movement in Japan," esp. 159–61.

53. The relationship of Marxist criticism and the aesthetic experience is considered in more depth in Chapter 4.

54. Akutagawa, "Aru ahō no isshō," 307. Translated by Jay Rubin. For the full translation, see "The Life of a Stupid Man" in *Ryūnosuke Akutagawa*, 187.

55. Lippit, *Topographies of Japanese Modernism*, 52.

56. For a detailed analysis of Akutagawa's ambivalent relationship to the foreign authors he encountered in Maruzen, see Cavanaugh, "Portrait of the Writer as a Young Reader."

57. Kobayashi Hideo, "Tako no jisatsu," 348–49.

58. The influence of Christianity is, for example, particularly evident in the work of Kitamura Tōkoku (1868–94) and Shimazaki Tōson (1872–1943). See Walker, *The Japanese Novel of the Meiji Period*, 66–75, 128–33. For the issue as it pertains to the Naturalists and the Shirakaba group, see Arima, *The Failure of Freedom*, 89–90, 114. Anderer, in his study of Shirakaba member Arishima Takeo (1878–1923), goes so far as to say that Arishima "looked to literature as a replacement for religion." See Anderer, *Other Worlds*, 56.

59. Hibbett, "Akutagawa Ryūnosuke and the Negative Ideal," 447.

60. It should be noted that this devaluation of literature was unique neither to Japan nor to this historical moment. As Peter Kornicki indicates, a shift from intensive reading to extensive reading was also a concern in Europe during the growth of commercial publishing, as well as in Japan during the Tokugawa period. See his *The Book in Japan*, especially 37–38, 258–69. Like the "crisis of modernity," the devaluation of literature occurs cyclically.

61. The modernist dimension of Kobayashi's fiction is explored in Chapter 2; its relationship to his critical stance is examined in Chapter 3.

62. The term "performative essay" refers to those works that embody, as opposed to espouse, his aesthetic views. The distinction, of course, is but one of convenience, as all of his writings are performative in varying manners and degrees. Nevertheless, considering the vast number of proclamations Kobayashi made about what literature *should* be, he provided surprisingly few examples. The finest performative essays are perhaps the six written during the war years and included in the collection *Mujō to iu koto* (The Fact of Evanescence). A number of these are analyzed in Chapter 5.

63. Kobayashi, "Dentō," 229–30.

64. Nelson, "Soliciting Self-Knowledge," 709.

65. See Christy, "Representing the Rural." For a study of Yanagi Sōetsu, the ethnographer whose perspective matched Kobayashi's most closely, see Brandt, "Objects of Desire."

66. Kobayashi, "Kottō," in *KHZ* 9:87. Kobayashi does not explicitly mention the name of the acquaintance, but all indications are that it was Aoyama. See Okamoto, "Sakka kaidai," 52.

67. Kobayashi's infatuation with ancient ceramics and other antiquities, and the manner in which this interest informs the performative essays in *Mujō to iu koto*, is discussed in detail in Chapter 5. His writings on the war in China and then in the Pacific are the subject of Chapter 6.

68. Sakaguchi, "Kyōso no bungaku," 328.

Chapter Two

1. Karatani, *Nihon kindai bungaku no kigen*, 66–67; translation from de Bary, ed., *Origins of Modern Japanese Literature*, 61.

2. Harootunian, *Overcome by Modernity*, 30–31.

3. A word about periodization is in order here. Strictly speaking, the labels Meiji, Taishō, and Shōwa refer to the imperial reigns lasting from 1868–1912, 1912–26, and 1926–89 respectively. In that my subject is literary and cultural history, however, I use these labels from political history rather loosely to refer to the periods in which a particular ethos held sway. Temporally, of course, these moods overlap. My definition of the Taishō period is perhaps the most idiosyncratic. I see the "literary Taishō" period as beginning and ending with the magazine *Shirakaba*, which began publication in 1910 (Meiji 43) and ceased publication in 1923 (Taishō 12) due to damages inflicted on its facilities by the earthquake.

4. Katō, for example, writes: "Industrial production was almost doubled during the period between 1914 and 1919. The average profit rate for industry, which in the first half of 1914 was 40.8 percent, rose during the three-year period 1917–1919 to 55.2 percent. During this time, in areas like shipping, ship-building, and mining, the profit rate even rose as high as 160 to 200 percent" ("Taishō Democracy as the Pre-Stage for Japanese Militarism," 218).

5. Indicative of the relatively tranquil social conditions is the number of labor and tenancy disputes, both of which recorded a sharp upswing only once the blush of the wartime economy faded. Though the rice riots of August 1918 were the largest popular demonstration prior to 1960, the general social atmosphere was one of relative calm until after the earthquake. For a concise overview of the period, see "Crisis of Political Community," in Pyle, *The Making of Modern Japan*, 159–80.

6. For an introduction to this debate, see Rodd, "Yosano Akiko and the Taishō Debate over the 'New Woman.'"

7. Harootunian, "A Sense of an Ending and the Problem of Taishō," 15.

8. Ibid., 14.

9. Ibid., 17.

10. Karatani, "The Discursive Space of Modern Japan," 299.

11. Ibid., 302. In these lines Karatani alludes to a distinction central to his work, and one that informs this study. Rather than work with the more common self/other or subject/object dichotomies, Karatani uses the words "interiority" (*naibusei*, or alternatively, *naimensei*) and "exteriority" (*gaibusei*). Though in his usage, "exteriority" can refer to anything from the public consciousness (as opposed to personal) to foreign nations (in opposition to Japan), in this study I concentrate on materiality (*busshitsusei*) as the element of exteriority most operative in the formation of this system of subjectivity. Karatani's conception of interiority/exteriority is most fully elucidated in *Nihon kindai bungaku no kigen*, particularly Chapter 1, "Fūkei no hakken" [The Discovery of Landscape], 5–43, and Chapter 2, "Naimen no hakken" [The Discovery of Interiority], 45–83. English translations are available in de Bary, ed., *Origins of Modern Japanese Literature*.

12. See Rubin, *Injurious to Public Morals*, especially Chapter 8, "The Government Moves Right," 108–14. On the Local Improvement Movement (Chihō kairyō undō), a major government program intended to co-opt citizen groups into the national agenda, see Pyle, "The Technology of Japanese Nationalism." On the various ways in which structures put in place at this time would later help sustain the war effort, see Fujii, *Heitachi no sensō*, and Yoshimi, *Kusa no ne no fashizumu*, particularly 70–110.

13. Rubin, *Injurious to Public Morals*, 145–224. Rubin is careful to point out that a critical reaction to the High Treason Incident was hampered as much by a lack of reliable information as it was by any political naiveté or indifference.

14. The most outstanding exception is undoubtedly Ishikawa Takuboku (1886–1912). His "Jidai Heisoku no genjō" (The Impasse of Our Age), published posthumously in 1913 though written in 1910, exhorts writers to turn their skepticism toward the state, which he explicitly labels an enemy. Rubin provides a thoughtful reading of this essay and other works by Takuboku in *Injurious to Public Morals*, 175–84.

15. Rubin, *Injurious to Public Morals*, 94.

16. My reading of the Shirakaba school is partly based on Honda, *"Shirakaba"-ha no bungaku*; Ara Masahito and Nishida Katsu, "Taishō bungaku (I)"; Arima, "The Shirakaba-ha: The Tyranny of Art," in *The Failure of Freedom*, 99–127; and Usui, "Taishō."

17. Quoted in Honda, *"Shirakaba"-ha no bungaku*, 58.

18. Quoted in Ara and Nishida, "Taishō bungaku (I)," 21.

19. Akutagawa, "Haguruma." Translation by Jay Rubin, in "Spinning Wheels," 221. Shiga's masterpiece is available in English as *A Dark Night's Passing*, trans. Edwin McClellan.

20. Keene, *Dawn to the West* I, 584.

21. Honda, *"Shirakaba"-ha no bungaku*, 61.

22. The essay is "Shizenshugi zenpa no chōryō" (1916). Cited in Ikimatsu, *Taishōki no shisō to bunka*, 108.

23. See Kohl et al., *The White Birch School (Shirakaba-ha) of Japanese Literature*, 16.

24. Mushanokōji, "Momoiro no shitsu," 29.

25. Shiga, "Horibata no sumai," 198–99.

26. Usui, "Taishō," 243–51. Also, on Mushanokōji's "New Villages" movement, see Keene, *Dawn to the West* I, 451–53; on Arishima, see Anderer, *Other Worlds*, 22.

27. Though critical of the Shirakaba group's political naiveté, even Tatsuo Arima begrudgingly admits that these writers "freed education from state utilitarianism." See Arima, *The Failure of Freedom*, 126.

28. Shimaki's borrowing of the name Kensaku from Shiga is noted in Keene, *Dawn to the West* I, 899, footnote 7. On Kobayashi Takiji's admiration for Shiga, see Arima, *The Failure of Freedom*, 107.

29. Usui, "Taishō," 192.

30. The extremes might be represented by two works appearing during the same year (1910) that the magazine *Shirakaba* was first published: the autobiographical *Ie* (The Household), by naturalist Shimazaki Tōson (1872–1943), and the fantastic and sensual "Shisei" (The Tattooer), by Tanizaki Jun'ichirō (1886–1965).

31. Hirotsu, "Shiga Naoya ron," 294.

32. Ibid., 293.

33. Sontag, "Against Interpretation," 11. Ellipses in the original.

34. Ibid., 13–14; Hirotsu, "Shiga Naoya ron," 292.

35. Hirotsu, "Shiga Naoya ron," 295.

36. Ibid., 297.

37. Ibid., 301, 302.

38. Kobayashi, "Watakushi shōsetsu ron." An English translation of this essay, under the title "Discourse on Fiction of the Self," is available in Anderer, *Literature of the Lost Home*, 67–93. This essay represents a refinement of ideas Kobayashi began to develop in "Watakushi shōsetsu ni tsuite" (1933).

39. Nakamura Mitsuo has acknowledged Kobayashi's thorough understanding of, and deep engagement with, Western literature as demonstrated in this essay. See his *Ronkō Kobayashi Hideo*, 143–52, particularly 149–50. Kuwabara Takeo makes much the same claim in *Nihon no meicho*, 222. On the immense impact of this essay on subsequent interpretations of the "I-novel" genre, see Fowler, *The Rhetoric of Confession*, 51–58.

40. Kobayashi, "Watakushi shōsetsu ron," 124; cf. Anderer, *Literature of the Lost Home*, 72.

41. Kobayashi, "Watakushi shōsetsu ron," 123; cf. Anderer, *Literature of the Lost Home*, 71.

42. Kobayashi, "Watakushi shōsetsu ron," 122; cf. Anderer, *Literature of the Lost Home*, 69.

43. Kobayashi, "Watakushi shōsetsu ron," 130; cf. Anderer, *Literature of the Lost Home*, 78.

44. Kobayashi, "Watakushi shōsetsu ron," 126; translation by William F. Sibley, in *The Shiga Hero*, 1; cf. Anderer, *Literature of the Lost Home*, 74.

45. See Etō, *Kobayashi Hideo*, 32; Yoshida, "Nenpu," 244. Etō mistakenly refers to the 1929 essay as "Shiga Naoya ron."

46. Anderer provides translated excerpts from both of Kobayashi's Shiga essays. See his *Literature of the Lost Home*, 104–7. Seidensticker also quotes them at length. See "Kobayashi Hideo" (I), 425–28.

47. Kobayashi, "Shiga Naoya," 18.

48. Ibid., 23. The original passage is from Shiga Naoya, "Wakai," 281. A translation of the story can be found in Starrs, *An Artless Art*, 176–238, with this section falling on 204–5.

49. On the autobiographical and self-reflexive nature of the story, see Goossen, "Shiga Naoya," 331–47, esp. 338–40.

50. Kobayashi, "Shiga Naoya," 23.

51. Ibid., 20.

52. Ibid. The story, "Ko o nusumu hanashi" can be found in *Shiga Naoya shū*, 246–54, with the pertinent sections on pages 250 and 252. The story is translated as "The Kidnapping" by Sibley in *The Shiga Hero*, 158–75.

53. Shiga, "Wakai," 293–94. The translation is from Starrs, *An Artless Art*, 230.

54. See Shiga, *An'ya kōro*; cf. *A Dark Night's Passing*, trans. Edwin McClellan.

55. Kobayashi, "Shiga Naoya," 18–19.

56. Kobayashi, "Shiga Naoya," 20. See also my discussion of "Kokyō o ushinatta bungaku" in Chapter 1.

57. Ibid., 26.

58. Ibid., 16.

59. Ibid., 18. Shiga's works continue to strike many in the same way today. An example is the aforementioned study by Roy Starrs. As the very title, *An Artless Art: The Zen Aesthetic of Shiga Naoya*, suggests, Starrs turns to the classical Japanese arts associated with Zen to explain the interrelationship of the aesthetic, moral, psychological, and spiritual dimensions of Shiga's work (8–11). In her nuanced analysis of Shiga's style, Sharalyn Orbaugh comes to similar conclusions. She claims Shiga's texts work in ways similar to *waka*, *hokku*, *renga*, and *nō*, and that at their moments of climax "barriers of space and time between reader, narrator, and character often break down, encouraging a simultaneous and equally intense experience of that moment on the part of all the consciousnesses involved" ("Extending the Limits of Possibility," particularly 365 and 367).

60. Kobayashi, "Shiga Naoya," 100–101. Kobayashi's mention of readers rambling on like art connoisseurs is almost certainly an allusion to Hirotsu. See Hirotsu, "Shiga Naoya ron," 302.

61. Tansman, "Images of Repose and Violence in Three Japanese Writers," 110.

62. Ibid., 138–39.

63. See the chapter on Walter Benjamin in Lilla, *The Reckless Mind*. Lilla's analysis of Benjamin's correspondence leads him to state: "Benjamin's correspondence shows that throughout his life he was fascinated with these right-

wing theorists of myth, eroticism, power, dreams, and imagination—though it must be added that he was always repelled by their politics once he understood them." Ibid., 92.

64. Benjamin, "The Work of Art in the Age of Mechanical Reproduction," 218.

65. Ibid., 239.

66. Kobayashi, *Kindai kaiga*. These essays were revised and made available in a single volume from publisher Jinbun shōin later in 1958. The award was the Noma bungeishō. In a supplemental note to the volume, Kobayashi insists that the work is not the product of research but rather is an "impressionistic essay" (*kansōbun*) based on the *emotions* he experienced seeing the paintings. There is no hint of irony in the proud announcement of his decision to include *reproductions* of the paintings in the book. See ibid., 275.

67. See *Mōtsaruto* in *KHZ* 8:65–164. Kobayashi claims to have begun the work while traveling in China in 1943 and 1944. This manuscript was, however, destroyed, and he began anew after the war. The central essay was first published at the end of 1946. See the bibliographical material in *KHZ* 15:380.

68. Tansman, "Images of Repose and Violence," 114–15.

69. Kamei, writing in 1972, claims he did not have access to it (*Kobayashi Hideo ron*, 91). The same is true for Etō (*Kobayashi Hideo*, 6).

70. This information is included in a brief editors' introduction for the story's republication in the aforementioned edition of *Shinchō*, 344.

71. Aeba, *Kobayashi Hideo to sono jidai*, 24. Though not completed until 1937, Shiga began serializing the novel in the magazine *Kaizō* in January 1921.

72. Yoshida, "Nenpu," 243.

73. Kobayashi's sister Takamizawa Junko attests to the autobiographical nature of the story. Takamizawa notes that a young woman in the story, Yaeko, was closely modeled on their childhood friend Yoshiko, and even claims that Kobayashi based some of the story's dialogue on things Yoshiko had actually said. See Takamizawa, *Ani Kobayashi Hideo*, 70–71; cf. Wada, 41.

74. This affinity is pointed out in Kawakami, "Watashi no shi to shinjitsu," quoted in Aeba, *Kobayashi Hideo to sono jidai*, 22. Aeba also asserts the overall influence of Shiga on this story. See 26.

75. On this trait in Shiga's personality and writing, see Usui, "Taishō," 188.

76. Kobayashi, "Tako no jisatsu," 347, 347, 349, 350, 351.

77. Ibid., 345.

78. Ibid., 349.

79. Ibid., 345.

80. Ibid., 346. *The Origins of Love and Understanding* refers to *Ai to ninshiki to no shuppatsu* (1917 and 1921), a popular collection of philosophical musings by Kurata Hyakuzō (1891–1943), a writer at one point in his career associated with the Shirakaba group. The 1921 edition became, Thomas Rimer writes, "a kind of Bible" for young educated Japanese. See Rimer, "Kurata Hyakuzō and *The Origins of Love and Understanding*," 22.

81. Kobayashi, "Tako no jisatsu," 355–56.

82. For an alternative reading of the story that highlights the significance of this scene, see Nagafuji, *Kobayashi Hideo no shūkyōteki tamashii*, 32–38, particularly 36.

83. Kobayashi, "Tako no jisatsu," 356.

84. See, for example, Ōoka, "Kaisetsu," in *KHZ* 2:391 and Kawakami, "Watashi no shi to shinjitsu," quoted in Aeba, *Kobayashi Hideo to sono jidai*, 22. Though they qualify their statements, similar assertions are made by both Etō, *Kobayashi Hideo*, 8, and Kamei, *Kobayashi Hideo ron*, 92–93.

85. Unami points this out in "'Hitotsu no nōzui' ron," 67.

86. Kobayashi, "Hitotsu no nōzui," 13.

87. Ibid., 14. The town is initially referred to simply as "M," but later in the story the location is fully spelled out as Manazuru, a port city near Yugawara. See 19.

88. Ibid., 12.

89. Ibid., 13.

90. Ibid., 11.

91. Ibid., 16.

92. Ibid.

93. Ibid., 19.

94. Kobayashi, "Shiga Naoya ron," 107–8.

95. Kobayashi, "Hitotsu no nōzui," 16. Emphasis mine.

96. Ibid., 17.

97. Ibid., 18.

98. Kobayashi, "Shiga Naoya ron," 109; cf. Anderer, *Literature of the Lost Home*, 106.

99. Kobayashi, "Hitotsu no nōzui," 19.

100. On this dimension of Yokomitsu's work, see Washburn, "Translator's Postscript," in *Shanghai*, 219–40, particularly 231–38. Also helpful is Keene, *Yokomitsu Riichi: Modernist*.

101. Kobayashi, "Hitotsu no nōzui," 14.

102. The opening paragraphs of the story are equally cinematic. See Kamei, *Kobayashi Hideo ron*, 93.

103. In his "Shinkankaku ron" (A Theory of Neo-Perceptionalism, 1925), a manifesto of sorts, Yokomitsu explicitly mentions the inclusive nature of his approach: "I recognize the fact that Futurism, Cubism, Expressionism, Dadaism, Symbolism, Constructivism, and a part of Realism [*nyojitsu-ha*] are all connected to the Neo-Perceptionist school." See "Shinkankaku ron," 95.

104. Kobayashi, "Hitotsu no nōzui," 19. The almost surrealistic atmosphere of this passage becomes the dominant tone in a story Kobayashi published seven months later, "Ponkin no warai" (Ponkin's Smile, 1925). Revised and retitled, this story is now available as "Onna to Ponkin" (The Woman and Ponkin).

105. Kobayashi, "Hitotsu no nōzui," 20.

106. This point is made by Yoshida, "Kobayashi Hideo chosaku kaidai," 33.

107. In addition to virtually any of Yokomitsu's early works, see Neo-Perceptionist writer Kon Tōkō's "Gunkan" (The Warship, 1924), published in

the first issue of *Bungei jidai*. As Dennis Keene writes: "The opening pages describe the drawing office of a huge shipyard in terms of the tools used in it rather than of the people who use those tools, since 'man is revealed through objects in the world' " (*Yokomitsu Riichi: Modernist*, 92).

108. See Usui, "Taishō," 290.

109. See Keene, *Dawn to the West* I, 649.

110. Hayama Yoshiki, "Semento-daru no naka no tegami," 108–9. A translation by Ivan Morris is available: "Letter Found in a Cement Barrel."

111. To this list of writers and movements concerned with materiality, Yoshida Hiroo would also add the poets Takahashi Shinkichi (1901–87) and Kitagawa Fuyuhiko (1900–90). See "Kobayashi Hideo chosaku kaidai," 33. Certain post-earthquake works by Tanizaki Jun'ichirō (1886–1965) can also be read from this perspective. An example is *Tade kuu mushi*, which Tanizaki began serializing in 1928. This novel presents a protagonist increasingly obsessed with both the human-like puppets of *bunraku* and the puppet-like human O-hisa. In *In'ei raisan*, his paean to traditional Japanese culture written in 1933 and 1934, Tanizaki renders materiality once again fully inanimate in order to indulge in the aesthetic reveries that mark that work. What distinguishes Tanizaki's corner of this discourse is, of course, the playful irony infused in every statement. See *Tade kuu mushi*, available in an English translation by Seidensticker under the title *Some Prefer Nettles*; *In'ei raisan* is also available in English under the title *In Praise of Shadows*.

Chapter Three

1. Kobayashi, "Shiga Naoya ron," in *KHZ* 4:100–101.

2. On the importance of Kobayashi's extended flirtation with prose fiction in the "I-novel" tradition, see Königsberg, "Kobayashi Hideo's 'Return to Japan.' " particularly 177–80.

3. Kobayashi, "Akutagawa Ryūnosuke no bishin to shukumei." Kobayashi's claim that this essay is his first critical work was made in a later addition to the essay. Some date the addition to 1939 (Aeba, *Kobayashi Hideo to sono jidai*, 65) and others 1949 (Yoshida, "Shoshi," 351). The excerpt translated by Anderer is, in fact, this latter addition, and was not written or published in 1927 as mistakenly noted there (*Literature of the Lost Home*, 101).

4. Lippit, *Topographies of Japanese Modernism*, 42–43.

5. Aeba, *Kobayashi Hideo to sono jidai*, 65.

6. Kamei, *Kobayashi Hideo ron*, 100.

7. Jay, *Downcast Eyes*, 10.

8. Benjamin, "The Work of Art in the Age of Mechanical Reproduction," particularly 232–37.

9. Jay, *Downcast Eyes*, 24. He is summarizing Hans Jonas, "The Nobility of Sight: A Study in the Phenomenology of the Senses."

10. Jay, *Downcast Eyes*, 25.

11. Ibid., 26.

12. Ibid., 26–30.

13. Ibid., 69–70.

14. Ibid., 70. Eric Matthews also parses Descartes's contribution to philosophy along these lines, calling the former the "Galilean" dimension, and finding its successors in Locke, Leibniz, Spinoza, Kant, and Comte. The latter aspect of Cartesianism he labels "Augustinian," a strain most prominent in twentieth-century French philosophy. See Matthews, *Twentieth-Century French Philosophy*, 5–8.

15. See, for example, Zola's "Preface" to the second edition of *Thérèse Raquin*, where he defends the novel against charges of pornography on the grounds that his concerns are scientific. See "Preface to the Second Edition (1868)" in Zola, *Thérèse Raquin*, 21–27.

16. The seminal work in this evolution is undoubtedly Futabatei Shimei's *Ukigumo* (The Drifting Cloud, 1887–89). In the space of this one short novel (159 pages in English translation), Futabatei moves from an ironic, playful, and polyglossic narrative to a serious, narrowly defined monoglossia. The end of the novel is overwhelmingly the narration of Bunzō, the protagonist, brooding in his small room—an example of how ocularcentrism can easily turn from a disinterested gaze directed outward to an unflinching look into the self. An English translation is available in Ryan, *Japan's First Modern Novel*, 195–356. Ryan's commentary on this work and her companion volume, *The Development of Realism in the Fiction of Tsubouchi Shōyō*, are a good introduction to the issues involved. For the issue of language and the importance of *genbun itchi*, see Fowler, *The Rhetoric of Confession*.

17. Cf. Karatani, *Nihon kindai bungaku no kigen*, particularly "Naimen no hakken," 45–83; translated as "The Discovery of Interiority" in de Bary, ed., *Origins of Modern Japanese Literature*, 45–75.

18. Jay, *Downcast Eyes*, 113.

19. Ibid., 113–47.

20. Washburn, *The Dilemma of the Modern in Japanese Fiction*, 227.

21. Usui, "Taishō," 1:256.

22. Lippit, *Topographies of Japanese Modernism*, 42.

23. Washburn, *The Dilemma of the Modern in Japanese Fiction*, 231. The story is available in an English translation by Jay Rubin, "Spinning Gears," in Akutagawa, *Ryūnosuke Akutagawa: Rashōmon and Seventeen Other Stories*.

24. Jay, *Downcast Eyes*, 187.

25. Ibid., 151.

26. Matthews, *Twentieth-Century French Philosophy*, 13.

27. Bergson, *Mélanges*, 1148; quoted and translated by Lacey, *Bergson*, 26. I rely heavily on this volume by Lacey for my understanding of Bergson.

28. Bergson, *Creative Evolution*, 323; quoted in Jay, *Downcast Eyes*, 199.

29. Bergson, *Matter and Memory*, 192.

30. Bergson, *An Introduction to Metaphysics*, 12.

31. Ibid., 1. Emphasis in the original. Jay quotes this section from its reprint in *The Creative Mind*. See Jay, *Downcast Eyes*, 201.

32. Jay, *Downcast Eyes*, 202.

33. Bergson, "An Introduction to Metaphysics," 10.

34. Ibid., 11.

35. Kobayashi, "Dentō," 230.

36. Aeba, *Kobayashi Hideo to sono jidai*, 31. "Materiality" is a central concern of Chapter 1 of this study.

37. Ibid., 33. Mori Arimasa was a scholar of French literature and philosophy who eventually retired from his post at Tokyo Imperial University to take up permanent residence in France. Miki Kiyoshi, as Aeba points out, represents a particularly interesting case. Although best known for his research in Marxist venues and his opposition to an increasingly repressive government during the 1930s and 1940s, Miki also worked along Bergsonian lines, writing a treatise on aspects of self-realization in the writings of the thirteenth-century Buddhist thinker Shinran. See Aeba, *Kobayashi Hideo to sono jidai*, 34–35.

38. By far the most balanced and cogent English-language overview of Nishida's philosophy is Heisig, *Philosophers of Nothingness*. For explorations of the relationship of Nishida's thought and the wartime Japanese state, see Heisig and Maraldo, eds., *Rude Awakenings*, particularly Ueda, "Nishida, Nationalism, and the War in Question," 77–106; Yusa, "Nishida and Totalitarianism," 107–31; and Agustín, "The Return of the Past: Tradition and the Political Microcosm in the Later Nishida," 132–48. Any examination of Nishida's legacy that seeks to move beyond the scope of philosophy in its most narrow sense must also consider the following two essays: Faure, "The Kyoto School and Reverse Orientalism," and Sharf, " The Zen of Japanese Nationalism."

39. Kamei, *Kobayashi Hideo ron*, 104. Ōoka's statement, alluded to here, is from his "Kobayashi Hideo no sedai."

40. On Nishida's German and English influences, see Clarke's "Introduction" to Nishitani Keiji, *Nishida Kitarō*, particularly viii–ix.

41. See, for example, "Beruguson no tetsugakuteki hōhōron" (An Essay on Bergson's Philosophical Method, 1910). Yusa claims this was the first full-length article to introduce Bergson in Japanese. See Yusa, *Zen and Philosophy*, 124. Nishida also wrote "Beruguson no junsui jizoku" [Bergson's Pure Duration, 1911]. The line in which Nishida acknowledges his debt to Bergson is from "Yukeru Bergson," January 7, 1941, *Asahi shinbun*. Cited and translated in Yusa, *Zen and Philosophy*, 97.

42. Nishida, *Zen no kenkyū*, 46. Translation by Abe and Ives, *An Inquiry into the Good*, 26.

43. This similarity is pointed out by Nishitani (1900–90) in *Nishida Kitarō*, 66–67 and 80. Although Nishitani does point out some areas in which the thinking of these two men diverges, for the most part he sees them as working along similar lines.

44. Nishida, *Zen no kenkyū*, 13; translation by Abe and Ives, *An Inquiry into the Good*, 3–4.

45. Nishida, *Zen no kenkyū*, 47. I make a slight adjustment to the translation offered by Abe and Ives, *An Inquiry into the Good*, 27, rendering *tenchi yuitsu no genjitsu* as "the utter singularity of the realities of the universe" rather than their "the single actuality of the universe."

46. Nishida, *Zen no kenkyū*, 20; translation from Abe and Ives, *An Inquiry into the Good*, 9.

47. Takahashi's review is introduced in Yusa, *Zen and Philosophy*, 129.

48. Heisig, *Philosophers of Nothingness*, 55.

49. Lippit, *Topographies of Japanese Modernism*, 39.

50. For a list of these magazines and the titles of the essays they carried, see Yoshida, ed., *Akutagawa Ryūnosuke kenkyū*, 379–81.

51. This famous line can be found in "Aru kyūyū e okuru shuki," a letter that Akutagawa wrote to his friend Kume Masao (1891–1952) shortly before the suicide. See *ARZ*, 16:3–8. For English excerpts, see "A Note to a Certain Old Friend," translated by Beongcheon Yu in *The Essential Akutagawa*, 205–6.

52. Inoue, "Akutagawa Ryūnosuke to Shiga Naoya," 184. In the final line of this quote Inoue is alluding to a line from Akutagawa's "Shuju no kotoba" (Words of a Dwarf, 1923). In one the two sections, titled "Reason" (*risei*), Akutagawa had written: "What reason taught me was, essentially, the impotence of reason." See "Shuju no kotoba," 260.

53. Kume, "'Watakushi' shōsetsu to 'shinkyō' shōsetsu" (1925); quoted in Fowler, *The Rhetoric of Confession*, 47.

54. Masamune, "Akutagawa Ryūnosuke," 53. An English translation of Akutagawa's story is available in *Ryūnosuke Akutagawa*, 38–41.

55. Masamune, "Akutagawa Ryūnosuke," 53.

56. For "Jigokuhen," see ibid., 60–75. An English translation of "Jigokuhen" is available in *Ryunosuke Akutagawa*, 42–73.

57. Masamune, "Akutagawa Ryūnosuke," 55.

58. Kataoka, "Shinkankaku-ha wa kaku shuchō suru," quoted in Hasegawa, ed., *Kindai bungaku ronsō jiten*, 182.

59. Kataoka, "Sakka to shite no Akutagawa-shi," 59.

60. Ibid., 57.

61. Ibid., 60. The essays by both Kataoka and Hakuchō seem to be based very heavily on Akutagawa's earlier works. It is hard to imagine Kataoka finding a "balanced, moderate expression" or Hakuchō a lack of personal investment in the psychotic illusions of the autobiographical "Haguruma" (Spinning Gears, 1927).

62. Kataoka, "Sakka to shite no Akutagawa-shi," 59.

63. This essay bested "Samazama naru ishō" for the Kaizō prize.

64. Ibid., 98.

65. Ibid., 99.

66. Ibid., 104.

67. For another contemporary Marxist reading of this writer, see Aono, "Akutagawa Ryūnosuke to shinjidai" (1927), 82–85.

68. Kubota, "Akutagawa Ryūnosuke no jisatsu to sono jidai," 281.

69. Kobayashi, "Ranbō I," 142. This essay, Kobayashi's first on Rimbaud, was originally his graduation thesis, submitted in 1926 under the title "Jinsei setsudanka Aruchuru Ranbō" (Arthur Rimbaud, Man Severed from Life). The translation of the lines from Rimbaud is from Symons, *The Symbolist Movement in Literature*, 39.

70. Awazu, *Kobayashi Hideo ron*, 27; quoted in Königsberg, "Kobayashi Hideo's 'Return to Japan,'" 178.

71. Shimizu points out Kobayashi's debt to Symons's book. See *Kobayashi Hideo*, 62–63. Kawakami Tetsutarō, a close friend of Kobayashi, would later attest to the fact that he, Kobayashi, and Nakahara Chūya all devoured the book in Iwano Hōmei's 1899 translation and peppered their conversations with certain key words and concepts. See *Kobayashi Hideo*, 62.

72. Information on this journal is from Aoyama, "Daichōwa."

73. Takamizawa, *Ani Kobayashi Hideo*, 117; cf. Wada, 72.

74. Kobayashi, "Akutagawa Ryūnosuke no bishin to shukumei," 35.

75. Ibid., 39; cf. Anderer, *Literature of the Lost Home*, 101.

76. Kobayashi, "Akutagawa Ryūnosuke no bishin to shukumei," 36.

77. The protagonist of the autobiographical story "Haguruma," for example, claims "I have no conscience at all—least of all an artistic conscience. All I have is nerves." See *Ryūnosuke Akutagawa: Rashōmon and Seventeen Other Stories*, 214. As translator Jay Rubin points out in his footnote, Akutagawa made similar claims in many places, including *Shuju no kotoba*. See 264–65.

78. Kobayashi, "Akutagawa Ryūnosuke no bishin to shukumei," 36–37. Kobayashi offers the same example of a genuine paradox in "Gyakusetsu to iu mono ni tsuite," 213.

79. Kobayashi, "Akutagawa Ryūnosuke no bishin to shukumei," 36.

80. For "Yabu no naka," see *ARZ*, 8:113–27. *Akutagawa Ryūnosuke shū*, 166–70. An English translation is available: "In a Bamboo Grove," in Akutagawa, *Ryūnosuke Akutagawa: Rashōmon and Seventeen Other Stories*.

81. Kobayashi, "Akutagawa Ryūnosuke no bishin to shukumei," 36.

82. Ibid., 38.

83. Kobayashi, "Gyakusetsu to iu mono ni tsuite," 213.

84. Ibid., 210.

85. Kobayashi, "Akutagawa Ryūnosuke no bishin to shukumei," 37. As with the critics discussed above, it seems that Kobayashi is not thinking of Akutagawa's later works: stories like "Haguruma" are nothing if not lamentations over his "psychological frailty." The reason Kobayashi and so many other critics commenting on Akutagawa's suicide ignored the later works with their tortured psychology is most likely that these works were bracketed off from those that showcased his intellect. Put another way, the later works were products of the implosion of the rational mind and as such were the *result* rather than the cause of the failing of the intellect.

86. Kobayashi, "Tako no jisatsu," 345.

87. Referred to in Kamei, *Kobayashi Hideo ron*, 17.

88. On this translation, which included a foreword by Nishida, see Aeba, *Kobayashi Hideo to sono jidai*, 32. As mentioned above, Takahashi Satomi had written a critique of Nishida's *Zen no kenkyū*.

89. Yamazaki, *Kobayashi Hideo to Berukuson*, 76.

90. As Yamazaki notes, these essays are problematic in Kobayashi studies. In spite of the fact that they represent a significant investment of time and energy on Kobayashi's part, he left the series incomplete and later refused

to have them collected and published as a separate volume. They were also left out of his collected works, again by Kobayashi's request. See Yamazaki, *Kobayashi Hideo to Berukuson*, 66–75.

91. Kobayashi, "Akutagawa Ryūnosuke no bishin to shukumei," 37–38.

92. Ibid., 38. Kobayashi would offer a very similar explanation for Rimbaud's genius in his 1947 essay on the poet: "For Rimbaud, poetry was neither the conscious construction of a certain autonomous, harmonious image nor a surrender to the unconscious. It was the narration of what he had seen. It was the attainment of an unquestionable and certain external entity." See "Rimbaud III," 165.

93. Kobayashi, "Akutagawa Ryūnosuke no bishin to shukumei," 39.

94. Washburn had actually been sent to report on the Russians.

95. For an example of the respect that Nogi commanded across a broad spectrum of society, see *Kokoro* (1914) by Natsume Sōseki (1867–1916). Sensei, a central figure throughout the novel, though a Westernized, progressive thinker like Sōseki himself, is moved more by the suicide of Nogi than by the death of the Meiji Emperor himself. Natsume, *Kokoro*, 246.

96. Kobayashi, "Rekishi to bungaku," 212–13.

97. The censorship of "Shōgun" is mentioned in Norman, "Introduction," 12. Norman also provides an English translation of the story in the same book, 135–67. For the original Japanese language version, see Akutagawa, "Shōgun."

98. Kobayashi, "Akutagawa Ryūnosuke no bishin to shukumei," 36.

99. Kobayashi, "Rekishi to bungaku," 212–13.

100. Shinmura, ed., *Kōjien*, third edition (Tokyo: Iwanami shoten, 1985).

101. Kobayashi, "Shiga Naoya ron," 108.

102. Ibid., 109.

103. Kobayashi, "Shiga Naoya," 23–24.

104. This piece was originally a lecture delivered in the fall of 1948. In the following year it was published in three parts in the magazines *Hihyō*, *Bungakukai*, and *Shinchō*. After final editing and the addition of some material at the end of the essay, it was published as a separate volume in August 1949. My discussion is based on the *zenshū* version, *KHZ* 9:11–59.

105. Kobayashi, "Watakushi no jinseikan," 14.

106. Ibid., 33–34. In this essay Kobayashi juxtaposes two related Chinese characters: 見る and 観る (another reading of the character *kan* in the essay's title). Both are read *miru* and mean "to see." The first, however, is used in the sense of "to examine" or "to inspect," while the second emphasizes perception in an acritical, intuitive sense, as suggested by the word *chokkaku*, "intuition." To maintain this distinction in English translation, I render the first, wherever possible, as "to look" and the second as "to see."

107. Cf. my discussion of Walter Benjamin in Chapter 1. Benjamin identifies the collapse of subject/object distance as a distinguishing factor in the changing sense perceptions in the age of mechanical reproduction.

108. Nishitani, "'Watakushi no jinseikan' o yomu." I am inclined to agree, however, with Robert Sharf's argument that much of the Zen worldview

championed by Nishida Kitarō and Nishitani Keiji is, in fact, more accurately seen as a product of their struggle to formulate a unique Japanese contribution to world religions and philosophy by excavating and foregrounding isolated fragments from the indigenous tradition that are absent in the West. See Sharf, "The Zen of Japanese Nationalism."

109. Yokota, "Kobayashi Hideo no mondai," 75–76. Kobayashi's first essay on this French poet was a revised version of his university graduation thesis. It was first published in 1926 under the title "Jinsei shakudanka Aruchuru Ranbō" and later retitled simply "Rimbaud I." The second, known as "Rimbaud II," was originally published in 1930 under the title "Yokogao" (Profiles). "Ranbō no mondai" (The Question of Rimbaud) is the third. It was written as a preface to a new edition of Kobayashi's translations of the poet, which appeared in 1947.

110. Jay, *Downcast Eyes*, 238.

111. Kobayashi, "Ranbō III," 152. For an alternative translation, see Anderer, *Literature of the Lost Home*, 100.

112. Kobayashi, "Ranbō I," 138.

113. Translation, from the original French, by Frohock, *Rimbaud's Poetic Practice*, 235. Quoted in Kobayashi, "Ranbō III," 165. Emphasis from the English translation.

114. Kobayashi, "Ranbō III," 172–73.

115. Kobayashi, "Ashiru to kame no ko II," 46. The original Japanese reads: "hihyō suru to wa jiko o kataru koto de aru. Tanin no sakuhin o dashi ni tsukatte, jiko o kataru koto de aru."

116. Heisig, *Philosophers of Nothingness*, 65.

117. Etō, *Kobayashi Hideo*, 5.

118. Karatani, "Kōtsū ni tsuite" (On Intercourse, 1978), 178. The quoted lines are from Kobayashi, "Marukusu no gotatsu," 109.

119. See Saegusa, "Cogito," 159–60.

120. Doak, *Dreams of Difference*, xxxii; quoting from Rabinow and Sullivan, "The Interpretive Turn," 9.

121. Doak, *Dreams of Difference*, 19.

122. Ibid., xli.

123. This issue is dealt with in some detail in Chapter 6.

124. In addition to his essays on Rimbaud, discussed above, Kobayashi also wrote on Baudelaire. See "'Aku no hana' ichimen" (One Aspect of *Fleurs du Mal*, 1927). He also wrote a number of essays on his friends, the poets Nakahara Chūya (1907–37) and Tominaga Tarō (1901–25), most of which are collected in the second volume of the *KHZ*. As for poetry translations, the most well known is Kobayashi's Japanese rendering of Rimbaud's *Une Saison un Enfer*, "Jigoku no kisetsu."

Chapter Four

1. For a concise summary of the nodes of contention of this debate, and a complete list of the essays involved, see Matsugi, "Tosaka Jun," 113.

2. Silverberg, *Changing Song*, 45. In addition to the works cited below, Beckmann and Okubo, *The Japanese Communist Party, 1922–1945*, and Hasegawa, *Kindai nihon bungaku hyōronshi* inform my understanding of the history of Marxism in Japan.

3. Silverberg, *Changing Song*, 48.

4. Rubin, *Injurious to Public Morals*, 247. In this regard Rubin cites Yamada Seizaburō, *Puroretaria bungaku shi*, 2:269.

5. Arima, *The Failure of Freedom*, 174–75. Arima goes on to argue, however, that what ultimately prompted intellectuals to seize Marxism to explain these conditions was the redemption it promised from the irrelevance writers had brought upon themselves by their hopelessly naive political indifference: "Marxism resurrected the eighteenth-century image of man from the abyss into which the romantics in their enthusiasm for individual sentiment had driven it" (175).

6. Hirano makes a similar argument. See his "Shōwa," 319–20.

7. Scalapino, *The Japanese Communist Movement*, 329.

8. These motivations are introduced in Iwamoto, "Aspects of the Proletarian Literary Movement in Japan," 159–61. On the final point, Iwamoto is drawing on articles by Scalapino, the major thrust of which is incorporated in *The Japanese Communist Movement*, 329.

9. Maruyama, *Nihon no shisō*, 83. Though concerned more with political theory than the literary arts, Scalapino makes a similar claim. See *The Japanese Communist Movement*, 329. My analysis in this chapter is heavily indebted to this work by Maruyama.

10. Maruyama, *Nihon no shisō*, 67–122.

11. Aono, "'Shirabeta' geijutsu," 69; cf. the discussion and translated excerpts in Shea, *Leftwing Literature in Japan*.

12. Aono, "'Shirabeta' geijutsu," 69–70.

13. Ibid.

14. Maruyama, *Nihon no shisō*, 53–55.

15. Tosaka, "Kagaku to hihyō," 32.

16. Ibid., 36.

17. Ibid., 34.

18. Scalapino, *The Japanese Communist Movement*, 337. Maruyama makes a similar claim, using the term "political formalism" (*seijiteki zushiki shugi*). See *Nihon no shisō*, 88.

19. Tosaka, "Iwayuru hihyō no 'kagakusei' ni tsuite no kōsatsu," 157.

20. Ibid., 159.

21. Fukada, "Kobayashi Hideo kun no koto," 39.

22. Ibid., 39.

23. See Nakamura, *Ronkō Kobayashi Hideo*, 133. As Nakamura points out, strictly speaking, Itagaki's essay was more modernist in tone. Still, his concern with the relationship of industrialization and the arts was shared by the Marxist critics.

24. Fukada, "Kobayashi Hideo kun no koto," 39.

25. Ibid.

26. Nakamura, *Ronkō Kobayashi Hideo,* 134–35. Nakamura claims that it was only with Kobayashi's "Ashiru to kame no ko" series of essays, published in the following year, that his ideas took on sufficient concreteness to be recognized as "criticism."

27. "Introduction," in Anderer, *Literature of the Lost Home,* 7.

28. Kobayashi, "Samazama naru ishō," 12; cf. Anderer, *Literature of the Lost Home,* 20.

29. Kobayashi, "Samazama naru ishō," 16; cf. Anderer, *Literature of the Lost Home,* 23.

30. Kobayashi, "Samazama naru ishō," 13; cf. Anderer, *Literature of the Lost Home,* 21.

31. Kobayashi, "Samazama naru ishō," 14; cf. Anderer, *Literature of the Lost Home,* 22. In his 1941 essay entitled "Dentō" (Tradition), Kobayashi would offer a very similar account of his experience in researching Dostoevsky. See my discussion of this passage in Chapter 1.

32. The original Japanese reads: "Kono toki *watashi* no sōzentaru yume wa yami, *watashi* no kokoro wa *watashi* no kotoba o katarihajimeru, kono toki *watashi* wa *watashi* no hihyō no kanō o satoru no de aru." The repetition of the *watashi* indeed makes for tortured, tedious prose. Emphasis is mine.

33. Kobayashi, "Samazama naru ishō," 14–15; cf. Anderer, *Literature of the Lost Home,* 22.

34. Seidensticker, "Kobayashi Hideo" II, 158.

35. Kobayashi, "Samazama naru ishō," 27; cf. Anderer, *Literature of the Lost Home,* 34.

36. Kobayashi, "Samazama naru ishō," 11; cf. Anderer, *Literature of the Lost Home,* 19.

37. Kobayashi, "Samazama naru ishō," 20; cf. Anderer, *Literature of the Lost Home,* 27.

38. Kobayashi, "Samazama naru ishō," 20–21; cf. Anderer, *Literature of the Lost Home,* 27–28.

39. See Saussure, *Course in General Linguistics.* The first edition of this work was published in 1915. For an exploration of the resemblance of Kobayashi's theory of language to ideas found in Saussure, see the discussion of Watanabe Hiroshi's essay "Kobayashi Hideo to kotoba no mondai" in Hosoya, "Kobayashi Hideo ni okeru kotoba no mondai," 54.

40. Maruyama, *Hajimari no ishiki,* as cited in Kamei, *Kobayashi Hideo ron,* 9.

41. Kamei, *Kobayashi Hideo ron,* 7–51.

42. Ibid., 25.

43. Kobayashi, "Samazama naru ishō," 25; cf. Anderer, *Literature of the Lost Home,* 32.

44. Kobayashi, "Marukusu no gotatsu," 108–9.

45. A contemporary theorist who worked in a very similar paradigm was Richard Rorty, particularly in *Contingency, Irony, and Solidarity.* Many of the ideas in Kobayashi's work resonate with what Rorty argues in Chapter 1, "The Contingency of Language," 3–22.

46. Kobayashi, "Samazama naru ishō," 20; cf. Anderer, *Literature of the Lost Home*, 27.

47. Kobayashi, "Samazama naru ishō," 25–26; cf. Anderer, *Literature of the Lost Home*, 33.

48. See Yoshida, "Nenpu," 246.

49. Kobayashi, "Gendai bungaku no fuan," 148; cf. Anderer, *Literature of the Lost Home*, 38.

50. Kobayashi, "Gendai bungaku no fuan," 150; cf. Anderer, *Literature of the Lost Home*, 40.

51. Kobayashi, "Gendai bungaku no fuan," 145; cf. Anderer, *Literature of the Lost Home*, 35.

52. Rubin, *Injurious to Public Morals*, 249. This book is the best English-language account of the government repression of socialist and liberal thinkers. See, especially, Chapters 15 and 16, 246–78.

53. See Kobayashi, "Bungei hihyō no kagakusei ni kansuru ronsō." Anderer translates two short sections from this essay in *Literature of the Lost Home*, 120–21, and a number of pages from "Bungei hihyō no yukue," 146–50.

54. Kobayashi, "Bungei hihyō no yukue," 176.

55. Ibid., 176–77. For an English translation of the fascinating story of Fukuzawa's life, see *The Autobiography of Yukichi Fukuzawa*. The incidents that Kobayashi refers to here appear on pages 16–17.

56. Kobayashi, "Bungei hihyō no yukue," 177.

57. Ibid., 167.

58. Ibid.

59. This essay was originally published in the magazine *Kaizō* under the title "Bungei hihyōka no ideorogī" (The Ideology of Literary Critics). It appears in volume 4 of the *Tosaka Jun zenshû* under the revised title.

60. Tosaka, "Bungei hyōronka no ishiki," 108.

61. Ibid., 109.

62. Tosaka, "Bungei hyōron no hōhō ni tsuite," 185.

63. Tosaka, "Bungei hyōronka no ishiki," 105.

64. Ibid., 105–6.

65. Ibid., 109–10.

66. Ibid., 110. Emphasis in the original.

67. Ibid., 106.

68. This essay was later included in a collection of Tosaka's writings from the time, *Nihon ideorogī ron* (Japanese Ideology), published in 1935.

69. Tosaka, "Handōki ni okeru bungaku to tetsugaku," 266–67.

70. Ibid., 271.

71. Kobayashi, "Bungei hihyō no yukue," 179. Emphasis mine.

72. Yamazaki, *Kobayashi Hideo to Berukuson*, 133.

73. Ibid., 140.

74. Maruyama, *Nihon no shisō*, 5.

75. Ibid., 67–122. Germaine A. Hoston employs a similar argument in her analysis of the *tenkō* phenomenon. See her *"Ikkoku Shakai-shugi,"* especially 171.

76. Honda claims that over 95 percent of the proletarian writers committed *tenkō*. See "Tenkō bungaku to watakushi shōsetsu," 180.

77. Ibid., 15.

78. Information on these journals comes from *Kindai bungaku zasshi jiten*.

79. For an exploration of the creative potentials of the *tenkō* and contemporaneous "return to Japan" (*Nihon e no kaiki*) movements, with a focus on Hayashi Fusao and Hagiwara Sakutarō, see my "From Ideological Literature to a Literary Ideology."

80. Quoted in Keene, *Dawn to the West* I, 890–91.

81. Hayashi, "Sakka no tame," 200.

82. Nock, *Conversion*, 13.

83. Ibid., 14.

84. Ibid., 15.

85. Maruyama, *Nihon no shisō*, 77–78. Maruyama is quoting from the original version of this essay ("Hihyō ni tsuite"), published in the first issue of the journal *Bungaku*, issued in April 1933. The version included in the *Shinchōsha zenshū* differs slightly. See "Bungei hihyō ni tsuite," 237–38.

86. Maruyama, *Nihon no shisō*, 84.

87. Ibid., 119–21.

88. "Seiji to bungaku ni kansuru zadankai," 20–21.

89. Ibid., 21.

90. Arakawa, *Shōwa shisōshi*, 198–99. I discuss Kobayashi's "Watakushi shōsetsu ron" in Chapter 2.

Chapter Five

1. Ara, Odagiri, and Sasaki, "Hakkan no kotoba," 1.

2. See also Odagiri, "Bungaku ni okeru sensō sekinin," 64–65.

3. Pyle, *The Making of Modern Japan*, 191.

4. For an introduction to some of these thinkers, see Rimer, ed., *Culture and Identity*, particularly the chapters on ethnologist Origuchi Shinobu (1887–1953), Marxist theoretician and poet Nakano Shigeharu (1902–79), Communist Party officials Sano Manabu (1892–1953) and Nabeyama Sadachika (1901–79), and philosopher Kuki Shūzō (1888–1941).

5. Kobayashi, "Rekishi no katsugan," 189.

6. Ibid., 200.

7. The influence of the philosophy of Herbert Spencer on Meiji thinkers can be attributed largely to the enthusiasm for Spencer's ideas exhibited by Ernest Fenollosa (1853–1908). Fenollosa, who had founded a Spencer club at Harvard, held the first chair in philosophy at Tokyo University and apparently included works by Spencer in many of his classes. See Pyle, *The New Generation in Meiji Japan*, 60.

8. Ibid., 5.

9. Sakai, "Modernity and Its Critique," 97.

10. Ibid., 98.

11. Nitobe, *Bushido: The Soul of Japan*, xi–xii.

12. This information is included in the "Translator's Preface" (to yet another Japanese version): Nitobe, *Bushidō*, trans. Yanaihara Tadao, 3.

13. Okakura, *The Book of Tea*, 29.

14. I thank Professor Karatani Kōjin for pointing this out.

15. Okakura's other definition of Japan's national identity, *The Ideals of the East* (1903), can be read as an attempt to slip out of the paradoxes of this discourse. I discuss this book below.

16. One example is Min'yūsha historian Takegoshi Yosaburō's 1896 best-selling history of Japan, in which he suggests that *hiragana*, an indigenous phonetic orthography in use by the tenth century, was directly inspired by the Phoenicians! See Inoue, *Hōryūji e no seishinshi*, 78. Inoue includes many other similar examples here and in his *Tsukurareta Katsura rikyū no shinwa*.

17. Okakura, *The Ideals of the East*, 1.

18. Najita and Harootunian, "Japan's Revolt against the West," 715.

19. Tanaka, *Japan's Orient*, 58–59 and 63–64.

20. Ibid., 26.

21. Ibid., 151.

22. Najita and Harootunian, "Japan's Revolt against the West," 712.

23. See Najita and Harootunian, "Japan's Revolt against the West," 755.

24. For a history of the criticism directed at the group, see Hashikawa, *Nihon rōman-ha hihan josetsu*, particularly Part 1, "Mondai no teiki," 3–16. This study, originally published in 1965, was one of the earliest to break the taboo against serious consideration of writers considered fascist. Another was Kawakami et al., *Kindai no chōkoku*.

25. Hagiwara, "Nihon e no kaiki," 162.

26. Doak, *Dreams of Difference*, xv.

27. Hagiwara, "Nihon e no kaiki," 162–63.

28. Ibid., 163. Emphasis mine.

29. Doak, *Dreams of Difference*, xviii.

30. Ibid., 19. The essay he is quoting is Yasuda's "Waga kuni ni okeru rōman shugi no gaikan" (An Outline of Romanticism in Our Country).

31. Hashikawa, *Nihon roman-ha hihan josetsu*, 39–40.

32. Tansman, "Bridges to Nowhere," 45.

33. Matsui, in "Beyond the Failure of Modernism," employs a similar perspective, along with a cross-cultural comparative aspect.

34. Kitagawa, *Shishin to shukumei*, 272. The section of "Designs" that Kitagawa refers to is found in *KHZ* 1:20–21. I deal with this section but interpret it differently in Chapter 4.

35. Kitagawa, *Shishin to shukumei*, 270. The phrases that Kitagawa includes in quotation marks (other than the word "muse," which figures most prominently in Kobayashi's essay on Akutagawa) are from Kobayashi's 1942 essay "Bungaku to jibun" (Literature and Me), which I discuss in Chapter 6.

36. Kobayashi, "Rekishi no katsugan," 191.

37. Kobayashi, "Rekishi to bungaku," 220–21. The *Hagakure*, more properly known as *Hagakure kikigaki* (Transcription of "Veiled in the Leaves," 1716), was recorded by Tashiro Tsuramoto, a student of samurai-turned-priest Yama-

moto Jōchō (1659–1719). It is a lengthy compilation of anecdotes about, and advice for, a proper samurai lifestyle. Kathyrn Sparling notes that the book gained popularity in the 1930s as an example of the Japanese spirit (*yamato damashii*), and continued to sell well throughout the Second World War. See Sparling, "Translator's Note," 8.

38. Kobayashi, "Rekishi to bungaku," 205.

39. Kobayashi, "Shiga Naoya," 100–101.

40. Kobayashi, "Rekishi to bungaku," 206.

41. See Kobayashi, "Rekishi ni tsuite," 17–18.

42. Kobayashi, "Mujō to iu koto," 19.

43. Kobayashi, "Rekishi to bungaku," 206.

44. Kobayashi, "Rekishi ni tsuite," 13.

45. Ibid., 14.

46. Ibid., 13.

47. Kobayashi and Aoyama, "Katachi o miru me," 102–3.

48. Ibid., 101.

49. For a discussion of a similar attitude in a writer of fiction, see Treat, "Ibuse Masuji and the Materiality of History," 274.

50. Kobayashi, "Rekishi to bungaku," 206. Igarashi Yoshikuni translates the word *urami* with the French *ressentiment,* claiming that Kobayashi is alluding to a similar sentiment expressed by Nietzsche. See his dissertation: "Imagining History," 14.

51. Kobayashi, "Rekishi to bungaku," 209–10. Translation by McCullough, *The Tale of the Heike*, 23.

52. Kobayashi, "Rekishi to bungaku," 206–7.

53. Kobayashi, "Rekishi ni tsuite," 16.

54. Kamei, *Kobayashi Hideo ron*, 306.

55. See Tansman, "Bridges to Nowhere," 67–69.

56. Aeba, *Kobayashi Hideo to sono jidai*, 178.

57. Kobayashi mentions two by name: Ōmori Gitarō and Mukōzaka Etsurō.

58. Kobayashi, "'Nihonteki na mono' no mondai," 193.

59. Ibid., 194.

60. Kobayashi, "Dentō," 232.

61. Kobayashi, "Shingan" (The Original and the Forgery), 87.

62. Treat, "Ibuse Masuji and the Material of History," 272.

63. Kobayashi, "Kottō," 88.

64. Kobayashi, "Shingan," 101.

65. Shirasu, "'Bi' o miru me," 275.

66. Kobayashi, "Kottō," 91

67. Shirasu, "'Bi' o miru me," 272. Emphasis mine.

68. Kobayashi, "Shingan," 92–93.

69. Ibid., 96.

70. Kobayashi, "Dentō," 232.

71. Shirasu, "'Bi' o miru me," 272.

72. Kobayashi, "Ashiru to kame no ko II," 46.

73. Kobayashi, "Mujō to iu koto," 17. The translation, except for the final line, is from Keene, *Dawn to the West* II, 605–6.

74. Quoted in Kobayashi, "Ranbō III," 165; translation from the original French by Frohock, *Rimbaud's Poetic Practice*, 235.

75. See Kamei, *Kobayashi Hideo ron*, 329 and 331.

76. Kobayashi, "Mujō to iu koto," 17–18. Translation mine.

77. Etō, *Kobayashi Hideo*, 238.

78. See, for example, Nakamura, *Ronkō Kobayashi Hideo*, 157. Nakamura also makes the point, quite rightly, that this poetic dimension, rather than detracting from the critical force of the essay, actually adds to it (163).

79. Both Etō and Kamei make this observation. See Etō, *Kobayashi Hideo*, 239, and Kamei, *Kobayashi Hideo ron*, 327–29. Kamei pursues this line of thinking to a greater extent than does Etō, and the following discussion owes more to Kamei.

80. Kobayashi, "Watakushi shōsetsu ron," 136–37.

81. Kobayashi, "Mujō to iu koto," 18.

82. Ibid., 18–19.

83. Ibid., 19.

84. Seidensticker, "Kobayashi Hideo," 169–70.

85. Kobayashi, "Mujō to iu koto," 19.

86. Yoshimoto Takaaki makes this point. See "Kobayashi Hideo: *Mujō to iu koto*," 100.

87. See Sanari Kentarō's notes to Zeami, *Taema*, 3:1839. Thomas Hare lists it as a "work that can be considered Zeami's" (*Zeami's Style*, 45).

88. Sanari Kentarō's notes in Zeami, *Taema*, 3:1839.

89. Zeami, *Taema*, 3:1847. The translation is from Kenneth Yasuda, *Masterworks of the Nō Theater*, 449. I have also consulted a second translation by Thomas Rimer.

90. Hare, *Zeami's Style*, 164.

91. Zeami, *Taema*, 3:1842 and 3:1853; translation by Yasuda, *Masterworks of the Nō Theater*, 442 and 458.

92. Zeami, *Taema*, 3:1853; translation by Yasuda, *Masterworks of the Nō Theater*, 458–59. Sanari's stage directions have the rolling of the sutra scroll done by the monk rather than by Chūjōhime.

93. Zeami, *Taema*, 3:1845; translation by Yasuda, *Masterworks of the Nō Theater*, 446.

94. Zeami, *Taema*, 3:1841; translation by Yasuda, *Masterworks of the Nō Theater*, 441.

95. Kobayashi, "Taema," 13; translation by Seidensticker in "Kobayashi Hideo," 180. Seidensticker offers a full translation in his essay. "Manzaburō" is a reference to the famous Umewaka Manzaburō (1868–1946). Manzaburō was so accomplished an actor that Sakamoto Setchō, who saw him perform this play in 1918, wrote: "though I was only looking at his feet, . . . this, too, was most splendid." Quoted in Yasuda, *Masterworks of the Nō Theater*, 438.

96. Kobayashi, "Taema," 13; translation by Seidensticker, in "Kobayashi Hideo," 181.

97. Kobayashi, "Taema," 14; translation by Seidensticker, in "Kobayashi Hideo," 181.

98. Kobayashi, "Taema," 14–15. Translation mine; cf. Seidensticker, in "Kobayashi Hideo," 181–82.

99. Kobayashi, "Taema," 15; translation by Seidensticker, in "Kobayashi Hideo," 182.

100. Kobayashi, "Taema," 15; cf. Seidensticker, in "Kobayashi Hideo," 182.

101. Kobayashi, "Taema," 16; translation by Seidensticker, in "Kobayashi Hideo," 182.

Chapter Six

1. Honda, *Kobayashi Hideo ron*, 17.
2. Kobayashi, "Sensō ni tsuite," 289.
3. See Yoshida, "Nenpu," 252–56.
4. For a very different evaluation of Kobayashi's travel writings from China, see Fogel, *The Literature of Travel in the Japanese Rediscovery of China*, 287–90.
5. Kobayashi, "Manshū no inshō," 11.
6. Kobayashi, "Kōshū," 312.
7. Ibid., 314.
8. Kobayashi, "Soshū," 342.
9. Ibid.
10. Kobayashi, "Kōshū," 318.
11. Kobayashi, "Soshū," 344–45.
12. Kobayashi, "Kōshū," 316.
13. Kobayashi, "Manshū no inshō," 26.
14. Etō, *Kobayashi Hideo*, 212.
15. Kobayashi, "Manshū no inshō," 26.
16. Kobayashi, "Kokyō o ushinatta bungaku," 31.
17. Kobayashi, "Manshū no inshō," 26.
18. Ibid., 29.
19. Etō, *Kobayashi Hideo*, 211.
20. See Kamei, *Kobayashi Hideo ron*, 281–82.
21. Kobayashi, "Soshū," 340.
22. Kobayashi, "Rekishi ni tsuite," 18–19.
23. Ibid., 19.
24. Kobayashi, "Kōshū yori Nankin," 332.
25. Kobayashi, "Manshū no inshō," 13.
26. Ibid., 14. The story by Lu Xun is "Ah Q zhengzhuan" (The True Story of Ah Q, 1921). I have consulted the English translation of this story by Gladys Young and Yang Hsien-ye. Mishkin is the protagonist of Dostoevsky's *The Idiot*. *The Book of Songs* (*Shi jing*; Japanese *Shikyō*) is China's oldest poetry collection, and famous for the difficulty of its verse.
27. Kobayashi, "Bungaku to jibun," 151.
28. Ibid.

29. Ibid., 150.

30. Kobayashi, "Giwaku II," 63. Here, and in many of the quotations that follow, I translate Kobayashi's *jihen*, literally "incident," as "the China War." The euphemism "incident" was, apparently, adopted solely due to the fact that there was never a formal declaration of war. In all other aspects, however, it was certainly just that. Kobayashi wrote two essays that originally carried the title "Giwaku" (Doubts). The first was published in the magazine *Chūō kōron* in April 1939, and has since come to be known as "Giwaku I." The second, the essay I discuss here, was published in *Bungei shunjū* in August of the same year. This essay is referred to here and elsewhere as "Giwaku II."

31. Kobayashi Hideo, "Kamikaze to iu kotoba ni tsuite" (The Word "Kamikaze," 1939), 71. This essay was originally a three-part newspaper editorial published in the *Asahi shinbun*. On the first day it carried the heading "Kamikaze to iu kotoba—rekishi no gūzen to Nihonjin no kokoro" (The Word Kamikaze: Historical Contingencies and the Japanese Soul).

32. Pyle, *The Making of Modern Japan*, 191.

33. Nishitani's sentiments share much with those expressed by Hayashi Fusao (1903–75) and Kamei Katsuichirō (1907–66), for example.

34. Maruyama, *Thought and Behavior in Japanese Politics*, 35, 53. Maruyama's characterization is supported by his introduction of the thought of Blood League (Ketsumeidan) leader Inoue Nisshō (given name Akira, 1886–1967). During the 1930s Inoue engineered various political assassinations in the name of patriotism. At his trial in 1932 he stated: "It is more correct to say that I have no systematized ideas. I transcend reason and act completely upon intuition." See Maruyama, 53.

35. Nishitani, "'Kindai no chōkoku' shiron," 20.

36. Ibid., 25.

37. Ibid.

38. Ibid.

39. Ibid., 34.

40. For an extremely lucid and fascinating introduction to circular logic in Buddhism, see LaFleur, *The Karma of Words*.

41. To this list one might add the aforementioned Inoue Nisshō, who insisted that "since ultimate denial is the same as genuine affirmation, destruction is itself construction, and the two are one and inseparable." See Maruyama, *Thought and Behavior in Japanese Politics*, 53.

42. See Kamei, *Kobayashi Hideo ron*, 322. Kamei's argument, which focuses on Kobayashi's radical doubt rather than on the rejection of reason, finds in Kobayashi's thought a trajectory that might be seen as circular. By turning doubt on itself, Kamei writes, Kobayashi essentially canceled it out and achieved a sort of affirmation. Aeba Takao reaches a similar conclusion. Aeba explicitly links Kobayashi's thought to that of Hagiwara, Yasuda, and Sakaguchi Ango (1906–55), seeing a certain irony at work in the writings of all these authors.

43. Kobayashi, "Jihen no atarashisa" (The Newness of the Incident), 122.

44. Kobayashi, "Sensō ni tsuite," 291.

45. Kobayashi, "Jihen no atarashisa," 126–27.

46. Ibid., 132.

47. Kobayashi, "Shina yori kaerite," 349.

48. Kobayashi, "Giwaku II," 68. Kobayashi first made the statement "the people of this nation have coped with the war in silence" (*kokumin wa damatte jihen ni shōshita*) six months before in "Manshū no inshō," 17.

49. Kobayashi, "Shina yori kaerite," 348–49. Kobayashi was himself censored, and he claimed not to be bothered by the fact in the least. See "Jūgun kisha no kansō" (Reflections on Being a War Correspondent, 1938), 353.

50. Kobayashi, "Kamikaze to iu kotoba ni tsuite," 75–76.

51. Kobayashi, "Shina yori kaerite," 352.

52. The other two planners were Kamei Katsuichirō and Kawakami Tetsutarō. See Kamei, *Kobayashi Hideo ron*, 317–18.

53. The only form in which a record of this symposium is currently available is that edited by Takeuchi Yoshimi and published by Fuzanbō. This edition includes only eleven of the twelve original, written contributions. Suzuki Shigetaka, whose essay was printed with the others in the magazine *Bungakukai* in October 1942, later withdrew his contribution. It was not published in the hardcover transcription of this symposium that appeared in 1943, nor is it included in the Takeuchi edition. Also, to be precise, both Nakamura Mitsuo's contribution and Kawakami Tetsutarō's summary were not included in the original magazine publication. These were added later for the book publications.

54. I base this claim on the published transcript of the symposium, and acknowledge the fact that it may not accurately represent the oral contributions of the participants.

55. Nakamura Mitsuo's essay, written after the symposium itself and so able to benefit from hindsight, points out the many ways in which the thinkers remained either fully immersed in modernity or were unable to come to an acceptable understanding of what constitutes the very modernity they were rebelling against. See his "'Kindai' e no giwaku" (Doubts concerning "Modernity"), 150–64.

56. Kobayashi, in Kawakami et al., *Kindai no chōkoku*, 217.

57. Ibid., 220.

58. Ibid. Italics mine.

59. Ibid., 225.

60. Ibid., 224.

61. Kobayashi, "Mujō to iu koto," 18.

62. Ibid., 17. Translation by Keene, *Dawn to the West* II, 605–6.

63. Kobayashi, "Sensō ni tsuite," 288.

Epilogue

1. Kobayashi, "Sensō to heiwa," 166–68. The translation is complete. I am indebted to the abridged translation in Seidensticker, "Kobayashi Hideo" (II), 179–80.

2. Odagiri, "Bungaku ni okeru sensō sekinin," 64–65. The other writers listed were: Yokomitsu Riichi, Yoshikawa Eiji, Yasuda Yojūrō, Satō Haruo, Mushanokōji Saneatsu, Kikuchi Kan, Kume Masao, Nakamura Murao, Takamura Kōtarō, Noguchi Yonejirō, Saijō Yaso, Saitō Ryū, Saitō Mokichi, Iwata Toyoo (a.k.a. Shishi Bunroku), Hino Ashihei, Kawakami Tetsutarō, Kamei Katsuichirō, Hayashi Fusao, Asano Akira, Nakagawa Yoichi, Ozaki Shirō, Togawa Sadao, Fujita Tokutarō, and Yamada Yoshio.

3. Ibid. The nebulous phrase "the collective repentance of the hundred million" (*ichioku sōzange*) had been proposed by Prime Minister Higashikuni Naruhiko as the most effective manner of dealing with the defeat.

Works Cited

Abbreviations

ARZ *Akutagawa Ryūnosuke zenshū* (Complete Works of Akutagawa Ryūnosuke). 24 vols. Tokyo: Iwanami shoten, 1997.

KHZ Kobayashi Hideo. *Kobayashi Hideo zenshū* (Collected Works of Kobayashi Hideo). 15 vols. Tokyo: Shinchōsha, 1978–79.

Works Cited

Abe Masao. "Introduction." In Nishida Kitarō, *An Inquiry into the Good*, trans. Masao Abe and Christopher Ives. New Haven, CT: Yale University Press, 1990, vii–xxvi.

Aeba Takao. *Kobayashi Hideo to sono jidai*. Tokyo: Bungei shunjū, 1986.

Agustín, Jacinto Z. "The Return of the Past: Tradition and the Political Microcosm in the Later Nishida." In *Rude Awakenings: Zen, the Kyoto School, and the Question of Nationalism*, ed. James W. Heisig and John C. Maraldo. Honolulu, HI: University of Hawai'i Press, 1995, 132–48.

Akutagawa Ryūnosuke. "Aru ahō no isshō." In *ARZ*, 16:37–67.

——. "Aru kyūyū e okuru shuki." In *ARZ*, 16:3–8. Trans. Beongcheon Yu as "A Note to a Certain Old Friend," in *The Essential Akutagawa*, ed. Seiji M. Lippit. New York: Marsilio Publishers, 1999, 205–6.

——. "Haguruma." In *ARZ*, 15:40–85.

——. "Jigokuhen." In *ARZ*, 3:156–201.

——. "Kumo no ito." In *ARZ*, 3:208–14.

——. *Ryūnosuke Akutagawa: Rashōmon and Seventeen Other Stories*, trans. Jay Rubin with an introduction by Haruki Murakami. London: Penguin Classics, 2006.

——. "Shōgun." In *ARZ*, 8:157–87.

———. "Shuju no kotoba." In *Aru ahō no isshō, shuju no kotoba*. Tokyo: Kadokawa shoten, 1983, 194–280.

———. "Yabu no naka." In *ARZ*, 8:113–27.

Altman, Meryl. "Life and Letters." *Lingua Franca* 7, no. 1 (December/January 1997): 7.

Anderer, Paul. *Literature of the Lost Home: Kobayashi Hideo, Literary Criticism, 1924–1939*. Stanford, CA: Stanford University Press, 1995.

———. *Other Worlds: Arishima Takeo and the Bounds of Modern Japanese Fiction*. New York: Columbia University Press, 1984.

Aono Suekichi. "Akutagawa Ryūnosuke to shinjidai." In *Akutagawa Ryūnosuke kenkyū*, ed. Yoshida Seiichi. Tokyo: Chikuma shobō, 1958, 82–85.

———. " 'Shirabeta' geijutsu." In *Hirabayashi Hatsunosuke, Aono Suekichi, Kurahara Korehito, Nakano Shigeharu shū*, vol. 78 of *Gendai Nihon bungaku zenshū*. Tokyo: Chikuma shobō, 1957, 69–71.

Aoyama Takayuki. "Daichōwa." *Kindai bungaku zasshi jiten*, special issue of *Kokubungaku: kaishaku to kanshō* 30, no. 13 (October 1965): 197–98.

Ara Masahito and Nishida Katsu. "Taishō bungaku (I): jindōshugi to shakaishugi." In *Kōza Nihon bungakushi*, ed. Odagiri Hideo. Tokyo: Ōtsuki shoten, 1957, 7–70.

Ara Masahito, Odagiri Hideo, and Sasaki Kiichi. "Hakkan no kotoba." In *Bungaku jihyō* 1, no. 1 (January 1946); reprinted in *Fukkokuban bungaku jihyō*. Tokyo: Fuji shuppan, 1986.

Arakawa, Ikuo. *Shōwa shisōshi: kuraku kagayakeru 1930-nendai*. Tokyo: Asahi sensho, 1989.

Arima, Tatsuo. *The Failure of Freedom: A Portrait of Modern Japanese Intellectuals*. Cambridge, MA: Harvard University Press, 1969.

Awazu Norio. *Kobayashi Hideo ron*. Tokyo: Chūō kōronsha, 1981.

Barshay, Andrew. Review of *Overcome by Modernity: History, Culture, and Community in Interwar Japan* by Harry Harootunian. *Journal of Japanese Studies* 28, no. 1 (Winter 2002): 146–51.

Beckmann, George M. and Okubo Genji. *The Japanese Communist Party, 1922–1945*. Stanford, CA: Stanford University Press, 1969.

Benjamin, Walter. "The Work of Art in the Age of Mechanical Reproduction," trans. Harry Zohn. In *Illuminations: Essays and Reflections*, ed. Hannah Arendt. New York: Schocken Books, 1968, 217–51.

Bergson, Henri. *An Introduction to Metaphysics*, trans. T. E. Hulme. New York: Putnam's Sons, 1912.

———. *Creative Evolution*, trans. Arthur Mitchell. New York: Modern Library, 1944.

———. *Matter and Memory*, trans. N. M. Paul and W. S. Palmer. New York: Zone Books, 1991.

———. *Mélanges*. Paris: Presses Universitaires de France, 1972.

Brandt, Kim. "Objects of Desire: Japanese Collectors and Colonial Korea." In *positions: east asia cultures critique* 8, no. 3 (Winter 2000): 711–46.

Cavanaugh, Carole. "Portrait of the Writer as a Young Reader: Akutagawa Ryūnosuke in Maruzen Bookstore." In *Studies in Modern Japanese Literature*, ed. Dennis Washburn and Alan Tansman. Ann Arbor, MI: Center for Japanese Studies, University of Michigan, 1997, 151–74.

Christy, Alan S. "Representing the Rural: Place as Method in the Formation of Japanese Native Ethnology, 1910–1945." Ph.D. diss., University of Chicago, 1997.

Clarke, D. S., Jr. "Introduction." In Nishitani Keiji, *Nishida Kitarō*, by Nishitani Keiji, trans. Yamamoto Seisaku and James W. Heisig. Berkeley, CA: University of California Press, 1991, vii–xxii.

Culler, Jonathan. *On Deconstruction: Theory and Criticism After Structuralism*. Ithaca, NY: Cornell University Press, 1982.

de Bary, Brett, ed. and trans. *Origins of Modern Japanese Literature*, by Karatani Kōjin. Durham, NC: Duke University Press, 1993.

Doak, Kevin Michael. *Dreams of Difference: The Japan Romantic School and the Crisis of Modernity*. Berkeley, CA: University of California Press, 1994.

Dorsey, James. "From Ideological Literature to a Literary Ideology: 'Conversion' in Wartime Japan." In *Converting Cultures: Religion, Ideology and Transformations of Modernity*, ed. Dennis Washburn and A. Kevin Reinhart. Leiden and Boston: Brill, 2007, 465–83.

Dostoevsky, Fyodor. *Notes from the Underground, The Grand Inquisitor*, trans. Ralph E. Matlaw. New York: E. P. Dutton, 1960.

Etō Jun. *Kobayashi Hideo*. Vol. 3, *Etō Jun chosakushū*. Tokyo: Kōdansha, 1971.

——. "Modern Japanese Literary Criticism." *Japan Quarterly* 12, no. 2 (April–June 1965): 177–86.

Faure, Bernard. "The Kyoto School and Reverse Orientalism." In *Japan in Traditional and Postmodern Perspectives*, ed. Charles Wei-Hsun Fu and Steven Heine. Albany, NY: State University of New York Press, 1995, 245–81.

Fogel, Joshua A. *The Literature of Travel in the Japanese Rediscovery of China: 1862–1945*. Stanford, CA: Stanford University Press, 1996.

Fowler, Edward. *The Rhetoric of Confession: "Shishōsetsu" in Early Twentieth-Century Fiction*. Berkeley, CA: University of California Press, 1988.

Frohock, W. M. *Rimbaud's Poetic Practice: Image and Theme in the Major Poems*. Cambridge, MA: Harvard University Press, 1963.

Fujii Tadatoshi. *Heitachi no sensō: tegami, nikki, taikenki o yomitoku*. Tokyo: Asahi shinbunsha, 2000.

Fukada Kyūya. "Kobayashi Hideo kun no koto." In *KHZ* 15:38–40.

Fukuzawa Yukichi. *The Autobiography of Yukichi Fukuzawa*, trans. Eiichi Kiyooka. New York: Columbia University Press, 1966.

Futabatei, Shimei. *Ukigumo*. In *Futabatei Shimei shū*, vol. 4 of *Nihon kindai bungaku taikei*, ed. Hata Yūzō and Yasui Ryōhei. Tokyo: Kadokawa shoten, 1971, 37–220.

Futabatei Shimei. *Ukigumo* (English translation). In *Japan's First Modern Novel: Ukigumo of Futabatei Shimei*, trans. Marleigh Grayer Ryan. New York: Columbia University Press, 1967, 192–356.

Goossen, Ted. "Shiga Naoya." In *Modern Japanese Writers*, ed. Jay Rubin. New York: Charles Scribner's Sons, 2000, 331–47.

Hagiwara Sakutarō. "Nihon e no kaiki." In *Shōwa hihyō taikei*. Tokyo: Banchō shobō, 1968, 2:161–64.

Hare, Thomas Blenman. *Zeami's Style: The Noh Plays of Zeami Motokiyo*. Stanford, CA: Stanford University Press, 1986.

Harootunian, H. D. *Overcome by Modernity: History, Culture, and Community in Interwar Japan*. Princeton, NJ: Princeton University Press, 2000.

——. "A Sense of an Ending and the Problem of Taishō." In *Japan in Crisis: Essays on Taishō Democracy*, ed. Bernard S. Silberman and H. D. Harootunian. Princeton, NJ: Princeton University Press, 1974, 3–28.

Hasegawa Izumi. *Kindai bungaku ronsō jiten*. Tokyo: Shibundō, 1962.

——. *Kindai nihon bungaku hyōronshi*. Tokyo: Yūseido shuppan, 1959.

Hashikawa Bunzō. *Nihon rōman-ha hihan josetsu*. In *Hashikawa Bunzō chosakushū*. Tokyo: Chikuma shobō, 1985, 1:3–89.

Hatano Kanji. "Hatachi no Kobayashi Hideo." *Shinchō* 80, no. 5 (April 1983): 261–64.

Hayama Yoshiki. "Semento-daru no naka no tegami." In *Nihon puroretaria bungakushū*. Tokyo: Nihon shuppansha, 1985, 8:30–32.

——. "Letter Found in a Cement Barrel." In *Modern Japanese Stories: An Anthology*, ed. Ivan Morris. Rutland, VT and Tokyo: Charles E. Tuttle, 1962, 204–10.

Hayashi Fusao. "Sakka no tame." In *Shōwa hihyō taikei*. Tokyo: Banchō shobō, 1968, 1:197–202.

Heisig, James W. *Philosophers of Nothingness: An Essay on the Kyoto School*. Honolulu, HI: University of Hawai'i Press, 2001.

Heisig, James W. and John C. Maraldo, eds. *Rude Awakenings: Zen, the Kyoto School, and the Question of Nationalism*. Honolulu, HI: University of Hawai'i Press, 1995.

Hibbett, Howard. "Akutagawa Ryūnosuke and the Negative Ideal." In *Personality in Japanese History*, ed. Albert M. Craig and Donald Shively. Berkeley, CA: University of California Press, 1970, 425–51.

Hirakawa Sukehirō, ed. *Ikoku e no shōkei to sokoku e no kaiki*. Tokyo: Meiji shoin, 2000.

Hirata, Hosea. "Criticism in Poetry: Kobayashi Hideo as Poet Manqué." In *Discourses of Seduction: History, Evil, Desire, and Modern Japanese Literature*. Cambridge, MA: Harvard University Asia Center, 2005, 207–30.

——. "Home and History: Kobayashi Hideo and Other Visionaries of the Past." In *Discourses of Seduction: History, Evil, Desire, and Modern Japanese Literature*. Cambridge, MA: Harvard University Asia Center, 2005, 231–58.

——. "Kobayashi Hideo no ushinawareta kokyō." In *Ikoku e no shōkei to sokoku e no kaiki*, ed. Hirakawa Sukehirō. Tokyo: Meiji shoin, 2000, 185–207.

Hirano Ken. "Shōwa." In *Gendai Nihon bungakushi*, ed. Nakamura Mitsuo, Usui Yoshimi, Hirano Ken, supplementary volume 1 of *Gendai Nihon bungaku zenshū*. Tokyo: Chikuma shobō, 1959, 305–476.

Hirotsu Kazuo. "Shiga Naoya ron." In *Hirotsu Kazuo zenshū*, ed. Shiga Naoya et al. Tokyo: Chūō kōronsha, 1974, 8:292–302.

Honda Shūgo. *Kobayashi Hideo ron*. Tokyo: Kawade shobō, 1949.

——. *"Shirakaba"-ha no bungaku*. Tokyo: Shinchōsha, 1960.

——. "Tenkō bungaku to watakushi shōsetsu." In *Tenkō bungaku ron*. Tokyo: Miraisha, 1974, 179–82.

Hosoya Hiroshi. "Kobayashi Hideo ni okeru kotoba no mondai." In *Nihon bungaku kenkyū shiryō sōsho: Kobayashi Hideo*. Tokyo: Yūseidō shuppan, 1977, 50–61.

Hoston, Germaine A. "*Ikkoku Shakai-shugi*: Sano Manabu and the Limits of Marxism as Cultural Criticism." In *Culture and Identity: Japanese Intellectuals during the Interwar Years*, ed. J. Thomas Rimer. Princeton, NJ: Princeton University Press, 1990, 168–86.

Ichigon hōdanshō, ed. Yanase Kazuo. Osaka: Izumi shoin, 1983.

Igarashi Yoshikuni. "Imagining History: Discourses of Cultural Politics in Japan, 1930's and 1960's." Ph. D. diss., University of Chicago, 1994.

Ikimatsu Keizō. *Taishōki no shisō to bunka*. Tokyo: Aoki shoten, 1971.

Inoue Shōichi. *Hōryūji e no seishinshi*. Tokyo: Kōbundō, 1994.

——. *Tsukurareta Katsura rikyū no shinwa*. Tokyo: Kōbundō, 1986.

Inoue Yoshio. "Akutagawa Ryūnosuke to Shiga Naoya." In *Shōwa hihyō taikei*. Tokyo: Banchō shobō, 1968–78, 1:184–97.

Ishikawa Takuboku. "Jidai heisoku no genjō." In *Yosano Hiroshi, Yosano Akiko, Ishikawa Takuboku, Kitahara Hakushū shū*, vol. 15 of *Gendai Nihon bungaku zenshū*. Tokyo: Chikuma shobō, 1954, 205–10.

Iwamoto, Yoshio. "Aspects of the Proletarian Literary Movement in Japan." In *Japan in Crisis: Essays on Taishō Democracy*, ed. Bernard S. Silberman and H. D. Harootunian. Princeton, NJ: Princeton University Press, 1974, 156–82.

Jay, Martin. *Downcast Eyes: The Denigration of Vision in Twentieth-Century French Thought*. Berkeley, CA: University of California Press, 1993.

Kamei Hideo. *Kobayashi Hideo ron*. Tokyo: Hanawa shobō, 1972.

Karatani Kōjin. "The Discursive Space of Modern Japan." In *Japan in the World*, ed. Masao Miyoshi and H. D. Harootunian. Durham, NC: Duke University Press, 1993, 288–315.

——. "Kōtsū ni tsuite." In *Kobayashi Hideo o "yomu,"* ed. Ōe Kenzaburō. Tokyo: Gendai kikakushitsu, 1981, 50–61.

——. *Nihon kindai bungaku no kigen*. Tokyo: Kōdansha, 1988.

Karatani Kōjin and Nakagami Kenji. *Kobayashi Hideo o koete*. Tokyo: Kawade shobō shinsha, 1979.

Kataoka Teppei. "Sakka to shite no Akutagawa-shi." In *Akutagawa Ryūnosuke kenkyū*, ed. Yoshida Seiichi. Tokyo: Chikuma shobō, 1958, 57–63.

Katō Shūichi. "Taishō Democracy as the Pre-Stage for Japanese Militarism." In *Japan in Crisis: Essays on Taishō Democracy*, ed. Bernard S. Silberman and H. D. Harootunian. Princeton, NJ: Princeton University Press, 1974, 217–36.

Kawakami Tetsutarō et al. *Kindai no chōkoku*, ed. Takeuchi Yoshimi. Tokyo: Fuzanbō, 1979.

Keene, Dennis. *Yokomitsu Riichi: Modernist*. New York: Columbia University Press, 1980.

Keene, Donald. *Dawn to the West: Japanese Literature in the Modern Era (Fiction)*. New York: Henry Holt and Company, 1984.

——. *Dawn to the West: Japanese Literature in the Modern Era (Poetry, Drama, Criticism)*. New York: Holt, Rinehart and Winston, 1984.

Kindai bungaku zasshi jiten, special issue of *Kokubungaku: kaishaku to kanshō* 30, no. 13 (October 1965).

Kitagawa Tōru. *Shishin to shukumei: Kobayashi Hideo ron*. Tokyo: Ozawa shoten, 1982.

Kobayashi Hideo. "Akutagawa Ryūnosuke no bishin to shukumei." In *KHZ* 2:35–40.

——. "'Aku no hana' ichimen." In *KHZ* 2:41–51.

——. "Ashiru to kame no ko II." In *KHZ* 1:39–48.

——. "Bungaku to jibun." In *KHZ* 7:140–55.

——. "Bungei hihyō ni tsuite." In *KHZ* 1:237–38.

——. "Bungei hihyō no kagakusei ni kansuru ronsō." In *KHZ* 1:124–34.

——. "Bungei hihyō no yukue." In *KHZ* 3:166–81.

——. "Dentō." In *KHZ* 7:224–34.

——. "Gendai bungaku no fuan." In *KHZ* 1:45–154.

——. "Giwaku II." In *KHZ* 7:60–68.

——. "Gyakusetsu to iu mono ni tsuite." In *KHZ* 1:210–14.

——. "Heike monogatari." In *KHZ* 8:20–23.

——. "Hitorā no 'waga tōsō.'" In *KHZ* 7:133.

——. "Hitotsu no nōzui." In *KHZ* 2:11–20.

——. "Jigoku no kisetsu." In *KHZ* 2:193–230.

——. "Jihen no atarashisa." In *KHZ* 7:121–32.

——. "Jūgun kisha no kansō." In *KHZ* 4:353–56.

——. "Kamikaze to iu kotoba ni tsuite." In *KHZ* 7:70–76.

——. *Kindai kaiga*. In *KHZ* 11:25–275.

——. "Kokyō o ushinatta bungaku." In *KHZ* 3:29–37.

——. "Kōshū." In *KHZ* 4:307–21.

——. "Kōshū yori Nankin." In *KHZ* 4:322–37.

——. "Kottō." In *KHZ* 9:87–91.

——. "Manshū no inshō." In *KHZ* 7:11–29.

——. "Marukusu no gotatsu." In *KHZ* 1:100–110.

——. "Mōtsaruto." In *KHZ* 8:65–164.

——. *Motoori Norinaga*. In *KHZ* 13:11–473.

——. "Mujō to iu koto." In *KHZ* 8:17–19.

——. "Nakahara Chūya no omoide." In *KHZ*, 2:121–27.
——. "'Nihonteki na mono' no mondai." In *KHZ* 4:189–95.
——. "Onna to ponkin." In *KHZ* 2:21–27.
——. "Ranbō I." In *KHZ* 2:135–46.
——. "Ranbō II." In *KHZ* 2:147–51.
——. "Ranbō III." In *KHZ* 2:152–77.
——. "Rekishi ni tsuite." In *KHZ* 5: 10–21.
——. "Rekishi no katsugan." In *KHZ* 7:189–91.
——. "Rekishi to bungaku." In *KHZ* 7:200–23.
——. "Samazama naru ishō." In *KHZ* 1:11–27.
——. "Sensō ni tsuite." In *KHZ* 4:286–92.
——. "Sensō to heiwa." In *KHZ* 7:166–68.
——. "Shiga Naoya." In *KHZ* 4:13–27.
——. "Shiga Naoya ron." In *KHZ* 4:100–118.
——. "Shina yori kaerite." In *KHZ* 4:347–52.
——. "Shingan." In *KHZ* 9:92–103.
——. "Soshū." In *KHZ* 4:338–46.
——. "Taema." In *KHZ* 8:13–16.
——. "Tako no jisatsu." *Shinchō* 80, no. 5 (April 1983): 344–56.
——. "Tominaga Tarō." In *KHZ* 2:105–6.
——. "Tominaga Tarō no omoide." In *KHZ* 2:107–8.
——. "Tsurezuregusa." In *KHZ* 8:24–26.
——. "Watakushi no jinseikan." In *KHZ* 9:11–59.
——. "Watakushi shōsetsu ni tsuite." In *KHZ* 3:46–49.
——. "Watakushi shōsetsu ron." In *KHZ* 3:119–45.

Kobayashi Hideo and Aoyama Jirō. "Katachi o miru me." In *Kyūyū kōkan: Kobayashi Hideo taidanshū*. Tokyo: Kyūryūdō, 1980, 179–202.

Kobayashi Hideo, Hayashi Fusao, et al. "Seiji to bungaku ni kansuru zadankai." *Bungakukai* 1, no. 3 (August 1934): 2–24.

Kohl, Stephen, Yoko Matsuoka McClain, and Ryoko Toyama McClellan. *The White Birch School (Shirakaba-ha) of Japanese Literature: Some Sketches and Commentary*. Asian Studies Committee Occasional Paper Series, no. 2. Eugene, OR: University of Oregon Press, 1975.

Komori Yōichi. "Kigen no gensetsu: 'Nihon kindai bungaku kenkyū' to iu sōchi." In *Naiha suru chi: shintai, kotoba, kenryoku o aminaosu*, ed. Kurihara Akira. Tokyo: Tōkyō Daigaku shuppankai, 2000, 125–75.

Königsberg, Matthew. *Der junge Kobayashi Hideo, Leben und Werk eines japanischen Literaturkritikers der Moderne*. Hamburg: Gesellschaft für Natur und Völkerkunde Ostasiens, 1993.

——. "Kobayashi Hideo's 'Return to Japan.'" In *Return to Japan from 'Pilgrimage' to the West*, ed. Yooichi Nagashima. Aarhus: Aarhus University Press, 2001, 166–87.

Kōno Kensuke. *Shomotsu no kindai: media no bungakushi*. Tokyo: Chikuma shobō, 1992.

Kornicki, Peter. *The Book in Japan: A Cultural History from the Beginnings to the Nineteenth Century*. Leiden: Brill, 1998.

Kubota Michitarō. "Akutagawa Ryūnosuke no jisatsu to sono jidai: sakuhin no hyōka to kanren shite." In *Akutagawa Ryūnosuke I*, ed. Kikuchi Hiroshi. Tokyo: Kokusho kankōkai, 1994, 280–89.

Kuwabara Takeo. *Nihon no meicho: kindai no shisō*. Tokyo: Chūō kōronsha, 1962.

Lacey, A. R. *Bergson*. London: Routledge, 1989.

LaFleur, William R. *The Karma of Words: Buddhism and the Literary Arts in Medieval Japan*. Berkeley, CA: University of California Press, 1983.

———. "A Turning in Taishō: Asia and Europe in the Early Writings of Watsuji Tetsurō." In *Culture and Identity: Japanese Intellectuals During the Interwar Years*, ed. J. Thomas Rimer. Princeton, NJ: Princeton University Press, 1990, 234–56.

Lentricchia, Frank. *Criticism and Social Change*. Chicago, IL: University of Chicago Press, 1983.

———. "Last Will and Testament of an Ex-Literary Critic." *Lingua Franca* 6, no. 6 (September/October 1996): 59–67.

Lentricchia, Frank and Jody McAuliffe. *Crimes of Art and Terror*. Chicago, IL and London: University of Chicago Press, 2003.

Lilla, Mark. *The Reckless Mind: Intellectuals in Politics*. New York: New York Review of Books, 2003.

Lippit, Seiji M. *Topographies of Japanese Modernism*. New York: Columbia University Press, 2002.

Lu Hsun [Lu Xun]. "The True Story of Ah Q." In *Selected Works of Lu Hsun*, vol. 1, trans. Gladys Young and Yang Hsien-ye. Peking: Foreign Languages Press, 1956, 76–135.

Mack, Edward Thomas. "The Value of Literature: Cultural Authority in Interwar Japan." Ph.D. dissertation, Harvard University, 2002.

Maruyama Masao. *Thought and Behavior in Japanese Politics*, ed. Ivan Morris. London: Oxford University Press, 1969.

———. *Nihon no shisō*. Tokyo: Iwanami shoten, 1961.

Marx, Karl. "Preface" to *A Contribution to the Critique of Political Economy*. In *Marx: Later Political Writings*, ed. Terrell Carver. Cambridge Texts in the History of Political Thought Series. Cambridge, UK: Cambridge University Press, 1996, 158–62.

Masamune Hakuchō. "Akutagawa Ryūnosuke." In *Akutagawa Ryūnosuke kenkyū*, ed. Yoshida Seiichi. Tokyo: Chikuma shobō, 1958, 49–56.

Matsugi Hiroshi. "Tosaka Jun." In *Kobayashi Hideo hikkei*, ed. Yoshida Hiroo, special issue of *Kokubungaku* 18 (February 1983): 113.

Matsui, Midori. "Beyond the Failure of Modernism: Contradictions in the Poetics and Politics of T. S. Eliot and Kobayashi Hideo." Ph.D. diss., Princeton University, 1996.

Matsumoto Masao. "Tōkyō moyu: tensai jinsai fukugōtai." In *Dokyumento Shōwa gojūnenshi: Taishō kara Shōwa e*, ed. Matsumoto Masao. Tokyo: Chōbunsha, 1974, 1–22.

Matthews, Eric. *Twentieth-Century French Philosophy*. Oxford, UK: Oxford University Press, 1996.

Mellen, Joan. "Homeward Bound." *Lingua Franca* 7, no. 2 (February 1997): 7.

Miyamoto Kenji. "Haiboku no bungaku." In *Shōwa hihyō taikei*. Tokyo: Banchō shobō, 1968–78, 1:93–109.

Moriwaki Yoshiaki. *Kobayashi Hideo to Beruguson*. Tokyo: JCA shuppan, 1982.

Morton, Leith. "Introduction." In Takamizawa Junko, *My Brother Hideo Kobayashi*. Sydney: Wild Peony Pty Ltd., 2001, iii–x.

Mushanokōji Saneatsu. "Momoiro no shitsu." In *Mushanokōji Saneatsu zenshū*. Tokyo: Shinchōsha, 1955, 14:7–29.

Najita, Tetsuo, and H. D. Harootunian. "Japan's Revolt against the West: Political and Cultural Criticism in the Twentieth Century." In *The Cambridge History of Japan: Volume 6, The Twentieth Century*, ed. Peter Duus. Cambridge, UK: Cambridge University Press, 1988, 711–74.

Nagafuji Takeshi. *Kobayashi Hideo no shūkyōteki tamashii*. Tokyo: Nihon kyōbunsha, 1990.

Nakahara Chūya. "Kobayashi Hideo ron." In *Kobayashi Hideo*, ed. Abe Yoshio and Yoshida Hiroo, vol. 14 of *Gunzō Nihon no sakka*. Tokyo: Shōgakukan, 1991, 96–97.

Nakamura Mitsuo. *Fūzoku shōsetsu ron*. Tokyo: Kawade shobō, 1950.

——. "'Kindai' e no giwaku." In Kawakami Tetsutarō et al., *Kindai no chōkoku*, ed. Takeuchi Yoshimi. Tokyo: Fuzanbō, 1979.

——. *Nihon no kindai shōsetsu*. Tokyo: Iwanami shoten, 1954.

——. *Ronkō Kobayashi Hideo*. Tokyo: Chikuma shobō, 1975.

Natsume Sōseki. *Kokoro*, trans. Edwin McClellan. Chicago, IL: Henry Regnery Company, 1957.

Nelson, Cary. "Soliciting Self-Knowledge: The Rhetoric of Susan Sontag's Criticism." *Critical Inquiry* 6, no. 4. (Summer 1980): 707–26.

Ninomiya Masayuki. *Kobayashi Hideo no koto*. Tokyo: Iwanami shoten, 2000.

——. *La Pensée de Kobayashi Hideo: Un Intellectuel Japonais au tournant de l'histoire*. Paris: Librairie Droz, 1995.

Nishida Kitarō. *An Inquiry into the Good*, trans. Masao Abe and Christopher Ives. New Haven, CT: Yale University Press, 1990.

——. "Beruguson no junsui jizoku." In *Nishida Kitarō zenshū*. Tokyo: Iwanami shoten, 1947, 1:327–33.

——. "Beruguson no tetsugakuteki hōhōron." In *Nishida Kitarō zenshū*. Tokyo: Iwanami shoten, 1947, 1:317–26.

——. "Jikaku ni okeru chokkaku to hansei." In *Nishida Kitarō zenshū*. Tokyo: Iwanami shoten, 1947, 2:3–350.

——. *Zen no kenkyū*. In *Nishida Kitarō zenshū*. Tokyo: Iwanami shoten, 1947, 1:3–200.

Nishitani Keiji. "'Kindai no chōkoku' shiron." In Kawakami Tetsutarō et al., *Kindai no chōkoku*, ed. Takeuchi Yoshimi. Tokyo: Fuzanbō, 1979.

——. *Nishida Kitarō*, trans. Yamamoto Seisaku and James W. Heisig. Berkeley, CA: University of California Press, 1991.

——. "'Watashi no jinseikan' o yomu." In *KHZ* 15:22–23.

Nitobe Inazō. *Bushido: The Soul of Japan*. Rutland, VT: Charles E. Tuttle, 1969. Japanese trans. Yanaihara Tadao, *Bushidō*. Tokyo: Iwanami shoten, 1974.

Nock, A. D. *Conversion: The Old and the New in Religion from Alexander the Great to Augustine of Hippo*. Baltimore, MD: Johns Hopkins University Press, 1998.

Noma Seiji. *Watashi no hansei*. Tokyo: Chikura shobō, 1936.

Norman, W. H. H. "Introduction." In *Hell Screen ("Jigoku Hen") and Other Stories by Ryunosuke Akutagawa*, trans. W. H. H. Norman. Tokyo: Hokuseido Press, 1948, 1–14.

——. "The General" (translation of, and introduction to, Akutagawa Ryūnosuke's "Shōgun."). In *Hell Screen ("Jigoku hen") and Other Stories*. Tokyo: Hokuseido Press, 1948, 135–67.

Nozaki Morihide. *Norinaga to Kobayashi Hideo*. Tokyo: Meicho kankōkai, 1982.

Odagiri Hideo. "Bungaku ni okeru sensō sekinin no tsuikyū." In *Shin Nihon bungaku* 3, no. 3 (June 1946): 64–65.

Ōe Kenzaburō, ed. *Kobayashi Hideo o "yomu."* Tokyo: Gendai kikakushitsu, 1981.

Okakura Kakuzo (Tenshin). *The Book of Tea*. Tokyo: Kodansha International, 1989.

——. *The Ideals of the East, with Special Reference to the Art of Japan*. London: John Murray, 1920.

Okamoto Takuji. "Sakka kaidai." In *Spirit Kobayashi Hideo: sakka to sakuhin*. Tokyo: Yūseido, 1986, 5–57.

Ōoka Shōhei. "Kaisetsu." In *KHZ* 2:387–95

——. "Kobayashi Hideo no sedai." In *Ōoka Shōhei zenshū*. Tokyo: Iwanami shoten, 1983, 12:434–44.

Orbaugh, Sharalyn. "Extending the Limits of Possibility: Style and Structure in Modern Japanese Fiction." In *The Distant Isle*, ed. Thomas Hare, Robert Borgen, and Sharalyn Orbaugh. Ann Arbor, MI: Center for Japanese Studies, University of Michigan, 1996, 337–70.

Pyle, Kenneth B. *The Making of Modern Japan*. 2d ed. Lexington, MA: D. C. Heath, 1996.

——. *The New Generation in Meiji Japan: Problems of Cultural Identity, 1885–1895*. Stanford, CA: Stanford University Press, 1969.

——. "The Technology of Japanese Nationalism: The Local Improvement Movement, 1900–1918." *Journal of Asian Studies* 33, no. 1 (November 1973): 51–66.

Rabinow, Paul and William Sullivan. "The Interpretive Turn: Emergence of an Approach." In *Interpretive Social Science: A Second Look*, ed. Paul Rabinow and William M. Sullivan. Berkeley, CA: University of California Press, 1987, 1–24.

Rimer, J. Thomas, ed. *Culture and Identity: Japanese Intellectuals during the Interwar Years*. Princeton, NJ: Princeton University Press, 1990.

Rimer, J. Thomas. "Kurata Hyakuzō and *The Origins of Love and Understanding*." In *Culture and Identity: Japanese Intellectuals during the Interwar Years*, ed. J. Thomas Rimer. Princeton, NJ: Princeton University Press, 1990, 22–36.

Rodd, Laurel Rasplica. "Yosano Akiko and the Taishō Debate over the 'New Woman.'" In *Recreating Japanese Women, 1600–1945*, ed. Gail Lee Bernstein. Berkeley, CA: University of California Press, 1991, 175–98.

Rollyson, Carl. *Reading Susan Sontag: A Critical Introduction to Her Work*. Chicago, IL: Ivan R. Dee, 2001.

Rorty, Richard. *Contingency, Irony, and Solidarity*. Cambridge, UK: Cambridge University Press, 1989.

Rubin, Jay. *Injurious to Public Morals: Writers and the Meiji State*. Seattle, WA: University of Washington Press, 1984.

Ryan, Marleigh Grayer. *Japan's First Modern Novel: "Ukigumo" of Futabatei Shimei*. New York: Columbia University Press, 1965. Reprint edition, Ann Arbor, MI: Center for Japanese Studies, University of Michigan, 1990.

——. *The Development of Realism in the Fiction of Tsubouchi Shōyō*. Seattle, WA: University of Washington Press, 1975.

Saegusa Yasutaka. "Cogito." In *Kindai bungaku zasshi jiten*, a special issue of *Kokubungaku: kaishaku to kanshō* 30, no. 13 (October 1965): 161–62.

Saitō Torao. "Wakai koro no Kobayashi Hideo to sono shūhen." In *Bungei tokuhon: Kobayashi Hideo*. Tokyo: Kawade shobō shinsha, 1983.

Sakaguchi Ango. "Kyōso no bungaku." In *Teihon Sakaguchi Ango zenshū*, ed. Okuno Takeo. Tokyo: Tōjusha, 1968, 7:319–31.

Sakai, Naoki. "Modernity and Its Critique: The Problem of Universalism and Particularism." In *Postmodernism and Japan*, ed. Masao Miyoshi and H. D. Harootunian. Durham, NC: Duke University Press, 1989, 93–122.

Satō Haruo, *Taikutsu tokuhon*, vol. 1. Tokyo: Fuzanbō, 1978.

Saussure, Ferdinand de. *Course in General Linguistics*. New York: McGraw-Hill Book Company, 1959.

Scalapino, Robert A. *The Japanese Communist Movement, 1920–1966*. Berkeley, CA: University of California Press, 1967.

Seidensticker, Edward. "The Death of Kobayashi Hideo: The End of an Era." *Japan Quarterly* 30, no. 3 (July–September 1983): 270–73.

——. "Kobayashi Hideo" (I). In *Tradition and Modernization in Japanese Culture*, ed. Donald H. Shively. Princeton, NJ: Princeton University Press, 1971, 419–61.

——. "Kobayashi Hideo" (II). In *This Country, Japan*. Tokyo: Kodansha International, 1979, 149–87.

——. *Low City, High City: Tokyo from Edo to the Earthquake*. New York: Alfred A. Knopf, 1983.

Sharf, Robert H. "The Zen of Japanese Nationalism." In *Curators of the Buddha: The Study of Buddhism under Colonialism*, ed. Donald S. Lopez, Jr. Chicago, IL: University of Chicago Press, 1995, 107–60.

Shea, George Tyson. *Leftwing Literature in Japan: A Brief History of the Proletarian Literary Movement*. Tokyo: Hōsei University Press, 1964.

Shiga Naoya. *A Dark Night's Passing*, trans. Edwin McClellan. Tokyo: Kodansha International, 1976.

——. *An'ya kōro*. Vol. 5 of *Shiga Naoya zenshū*. Tokyo: Iwanami shoten, 1973.

——. "Horibata no sumai." In *Shiga Naoya zenshū*. Tokyo: Iwanami shoten, 1973, 3:189–99.

——. "Kinosaki nite" In *Kinosaki nite*. Tokyo: Kadokawa shoten, 1986, 46–53. Trans. Edward Seidensticker as "At Kinosaki," in *Modern Japanese Literature*, ed. Donald Keene. New York: Grove Press, 1956, 272–77.

——. "Ko o nusumu hanashi." In *Shiga Naoya shū*, vol. 20 of *Gendai Nihon bungaku zenshū*. Tokyo: Chikuma shobō, 1959, 246–54.

——. "Reconciliation," trans. Roy Starrs. In *An Artless Art: The Zen Aesthetic of Shiga Naoya*. Richmond, UK: Curzon, 1998, 176–238.

——. "The Kidnapping," trans. William F. Sibley. In *The Shiga Hero*. Chicago, IL: University of Chicago Press, 1979, 158–75.

——. "Wakai." In *Shiga Naoya shū*, vol. 20 of *Gendai Nihon bungaku zenshū*, 267–98.

Shima Hiroyuki. *Kobayashi Hideo: aku o yurusu kami o yuruseru ka*. Tokyo: Shinchōsha, 1994.

Shimazaki Tōson. *Ie*. Tokyo: Iwanami shoten, 1969.

Shimizu Takayoshi. "Kobayashi Hideo kenkyū annai." In *Kobayashi Hideo*, ed. Shimizu Takayoshi, vol. 16 of *Kanshō Nihon gendai bungaku*. Tokyo: Kadokawa shoten, 1981, 343–63.

Shimizu Takayoshi, ed. *Kobayashi Hideo*. Vol. 16 of *Kanshō Nihon gendai bungaku*. Tokyo: Kadokawa shoten, 1981.

Shinmura Izuru, ed. *Kōjien*, third edition. Tokyo: Iwanami shoten, 1985.

Shiozawa Minobu. *Zasshi 100-nen no ayumi: 1874–1990 jidai to tomo ni tanjō shi seisui suru nagare o yomu*. Tokyo: Gurīn arō shuppansha, 1994.

Shirasu Masako. "'Bi' o miru me." In *Shinchō* 80, no. 5 (April 1983): 272–76.

Sibley, William F. *The Shiga Hero*. Chicago, IL: University of Chicago Press, 1979.

Silverberg, Miriam. *Changing Song: The Marxist Manifestos of Nakano Shigeharu*. Princeton, NJ: Princeton University Press, 1990.

Sontag, Susan. "Against Interpretation." In *Against Interpretation and Other Essays*. New York: Delta Books, 1966, 3–14.

Sparling, Kathyrn. "Translator's Note." In *Mishima on Hagakure: The Samurai Ethic in Modern Japan*. Harmondsworth, UK: Penguin Books, 1977, vii–x.

Starrs, Roy. *An Artless Art: The Zen Aesthetic of Shiga Naoya*. Richmond, UK: Curzon, 1998.

Strong, Kenneth L. C. "Downgrading the 'Kindai Jiga': Reflections on Tōson's *Hakai* and Subsequent Trends in Modern Literature." In *Studies in Japanese Culture*, ed. Japan P.E.N. Club. Tokyo: Japan P.E.N. Club, 1973, 1:406–11.

Symons, Arthur. *The Symbolist Movement in Literature*. New York: E. P. Dutton and Co., 1958.

Takahashi Shintarō. "Shirakaba." In *Kindai bungaku zasshi jiten*, special issue of *Kokubungaku: kaishaku to kanshō* 30, no. 13 (October 1965): 34–36.

Takamizawa Junko. *Ani Kobayashi Hideo to no taiwa*. Tokyo: Kōdansha, 1970.

——. *Ani Kobayashi Hideo*. Tokyo: Shinchōsha, 1985.

——. *My Brother Hideo Kobayashi*. Trans. James Wada. Sydney: Wild Peony Pty Ltd., 2001.

——. *Ningen no oikata shinikata: ani Kobayashi Hideo no ashiato*. Tokyo: Kairyūsha, 1995.

The Tale of the Heike. Trans. by Helen Craig McCullough. Stanford, CA: Stanford University Press, 1988.

Tanaka, Stefan. *Japan's Orient: Rendering Pasts into History*. Berkeley, CA: University of California Press, 1993.

Tanizaki Jun'ichirō. *Tade kuu mushi*. Tokyo: Iwanami shoten, 1970. Trans. Edward Seidensticker as *Some Prefer Nettles*. New York: Vintage International, 1983.

——. *In'ei raisan*. Tokyo: Chūō kōronsha, 1975. Trans. Thomas J. Harper and Edward Seidensticker as *In Praise of Shadows*. New Haven, CT: Leete's Island Books, 1977.

——. "Shisei." In *Tanizaki Jun'ichirō shū*, vol. 18 of *Gendai Nihon bungaku zenshū*. Tokyo: Chikuma shobō, 1954, 348–51.

Tansman, Alan. "Bridges to Nowhere: Yasuda Yojūrō's Language of Violence and Desire." In *Harvard Journal of Asiatic Studies* 56, no. 1 (June 1996): 35–75.

——. "Images of Repose and Violence in Three Japanese Writers." *Journal of Japanese Studies* 28, no. 1 (Winter 2002): 109–39.

Tinari, Philip. "Being Frank." *The Duke Magazine* 88, no. 5, (July–August 2002). Online edition. http://www.dukemagazine.duke.edu/dukemag/issues/070802/frank2.html. Accessed 24 August 2007.

Tosaka Jun. "Bungei hyōronka no ishiki." In *Tosaka Jun zenshū*. Tokyo: Keisō shobō, 1967, 4:105–13.

——. "Bungei hyōron no hōhō ni tsuite." In *Tosaka Jun zenshū*. Tokyo: Keisō shobō, 1967, 4:180–86.

——. "Handōki ni okeru bungaku to tetsugaku: bungaku shugi no sakkaku ni tsuite." In *Tosaka Jun zenshū*. Tokyo: Keisō shobō, 1967, 2:175–81.

——. "Iwayuru hihyō no 'kagakusei' ni tsuite no kōsatsu." In *Shōwa hihyō taikei*. Tokyo: Banchō shobō, 1968, 2:152–60.

——. "Kagaku to hihyō." In *Tosaka Jun zenshū*. Tokyo: Keisō shobō, 1967, 4:32–37.

——. *Nihon ideorogī ron*. Tokyo: Iwanami shoten, 1977.

Treat, John Whittier. "Ibuse Masuji and the Materiality of History." In *Studies in Modern Japanese Literature: Essays and Translations in Honor of Edwin McClellan*, ed. Dennis Washburn and Alan Tansman. Ann Arbor, MI: Center for Japanese Studies, University of Michigan, 1997, 261–83.

——. Review of *Origins of Modern Japanese Literature*, ed. Brett de Bary. In *Journal of Japanese Studies* 21, no. 2 (Summer 1995): 440–47.

Ueda Shizuteru. "Nishida, Nationalism, and the War in Question." In *Rude Awakenings: Zen, the Kyoto School, and the Question of Nationalism*, ed. James W. Heisig and John C. Maraldo. Honolulu, HI: University of Hawai'i Press, 1995, 77–106.

Unami Akira. "Hitotsu no nōzui ron." In *Kobayashi Hideo no sekai*, special issue of *Kokubungaku: kaishaku to kanshō* 57, no. 6 (June 1992): 67–69.

Uranishi Kazuhiko. "Kantō daishinsai to bungaku." In *Kindai bundan jikenshi*, special issue of *Kokubungaku: kaishaku to kyōzai no kenkyū* 34, no. 4 (March 1989): 94–100.

Usui Yoshimi. "Taishō." In *Gendai Nihon bungakushi*, ed. Nakamura Mitsuo, Usui Yoshimi, Hirano Ken, supplementary volume 1 of *Gendai Nihon bungaku zenshū*. Tokyo: Chikuma shobō, 1959, 153–303.

Walker, Janet A. *The Japanese Novel of the Meiji Period and the Ideal of Individualism*. Princeton, NJ: Princeton University Press, 1979.

Watsuji Tetsurō. "Gūzō saikō." In *Watsuji Tetsurō zenshū*. Tokyo: Iwanami shoten, 1963, 17:3–284.

Washburn, Dennis C. *The Dilemma of the Modern in Japanese Fiction*. New Haven, CT: Yale University Press, 1995.

——. "Translator's Postscript." In Yokomitsu Riichi, *Shanghai*. Michigan Monograph Series in Japanese Studies, no. 33. Ann Arbor, MI: Center for Japanese Studies, University of Michigan, 2001, 219–40.

Washburn, Stanley. *Nogi: A Man against the Background of a Great War*. New York: Henry Holt and Company, 1913.

Yamada Seisaburō. *Puroretaria bungakushi*. 2 vols. Tokyo: Rironsha, 1954.

Yamazaki Kōtarō. *Kobayashi Hideo to Berukuson: "Kansō" o yomu*. Tokyo: Sairyūsha, 1991.

Yasuda, Kenneth. "Taema." In *Masterworks of the Nō Theater*. Bloomington, IN: Indiana University Press, 1989, 437–59.

Yasuda Yojūrō. "Nihon no hashi." In *Yasuda Yojūrō senshū*. Tokyo: Kōdansha, 1971, 2:19–47.

Yokomitsu Riichi. "Atama narabi ni hara." In *Yokomitsu Riichi zenshū*. Tokyo: Kawade shobō, 1987, 1:396–403.

——. *Shanhai*. In *Yokomitsu Riichi zenshū*. Tokyo: Kawade shobō, 1987, 3:3–246.

——. "Shinkankaku ron." In *Yokomitsu Riichi*, vol. 14 of *Kanshō Nihon gendai bungaku*. Tokyo: Kadokawa shoten, 1981, 89–109.

Yokota Shun'ichi. "Kobayashi Hideo no mondai." In *Nihon bungaku kenkyū shiryō sōsho: Kobayashi Hideo*. Tokyo: Yūseidō, 1977, 72–86.

Yoshida Hiroo. "Kobayashi Hideo chosaku kaidai: 'Hitotsu no nōzui.'" In *Kobayashi Hideo hikkei*, ed. Yoshida Hiroo, special issue of *Kokubungaku* 18 (February 1983): 31–33.

——. "Nenpu." In *KHZ* 15:241–74.

——. "Shoshi." In *KHZ* 15: 275–403.

——. "Shūrokubun kaisetsu: Kobayashi Hideo e no apurōchi." In *Kobayashi Hideo*, ed. Abe Yoshio and Yoshida Hiroo, vol. 14 of *Gunzō Nihon no sakka*. Tokyo: Shōgakukan, 1991, 326–35.

Yoshida Hiroo and Horiuchi Tatsuo. *Shoshi Kobayashi Hideo*. Tokyo: Tosho shinbun sōsho, 1967.

Yoshida Seiichi, ed. *Akutagawa Ryūnosuke kenkyū*. Tokyo: Chikuma shobō, 1958.

Yoshimi Yoshiaki. *Kusa no ne no fashizumu: Nihon minshū no sensō taiken*. Tokyo: Tōkyō Daigaku shuppankai, 1996.

Yoshimoto Takaaki. "Kobayashi Hideo: *Mujō to iu koto*," In *Nihon kindai bungaku no meisaku*. Tokyo: Mainichi shinbunsha, 2001, 99–105.

Yu, Beongcheon. *Akutagawa: An Introduction*. Detroit, MI: Wayne State University Press, 1972.

Yusa, Michiko. *Zen and Philosophy: An Intellectual Biography of Nishida Kitarō*. Honolulu, HI: University of Hawai'i Press, 2002.

——. "Nishida and Totalitarianism: A Philosopher's Resistance." In *Rude Awakenings: Zen, the Kyoto School, and the Question of Nationalism*, ed. James W. Heisig and John C. Maraldo. Honolulu, HI: University of Hawai'i Press, 1995, 107–31.

Zeami Motokiyo. "Taema." In *Yōkyoku taikan*, ed. Sanari Kentarō. Tokyo: Meiji shoin, 1965, 3:1839–56. Trans. Thomas Rimer as "Taema" in *Monumenta Nipponica* 25, no. 3–4 (1970): 431–45.

Žižek, Slavoj. *Tarrying with the Negative*. Durham, NC: Duke University Press, 1993.

Zola, Émile. "Preface to the Second Edition (1868)" in Émile Zola, *Thérèse Raquin*, translated by Leonard Tancock. London: Penguin Books, 1962, 21–27.

Index

Harvard East Asian Monographs
(*out-of-print)

*1. Liang Fang-chung, *The Single-Whip Method of Taxation in China*
*2. Harold C. Hinton, *The Grain Tribute System of China, 1845–1911*
3. Ellsworth C. Carlson, *The Kaiping Mines, 1877–1912*
*4. Chao Kuo-chün, *Agrarian Policies of Mainland China: A Documentary Study, 1949–1956*
*5. Edgar Snow, *Random Notes on Red China, 1936–1945*
*6. Edwin George Beal, Jr., *The Origin of Likin, 1835–1864*
7. Chao Kuo-chün, *Economic Planning and Organization in Mainland China: A Documentary Study, 1949–1957*
*8. John K. Fairbank, *Ching Documents: An Introductory Syllabus*
*9. Helen Yin and Yi-chang Yin, *Economic Statistics of Mainland China, 1949–1957*
10. Wolfgang Franke, *The Reform and Abolition of the Traditional Chinese Examination System*
11. Albert Feuerwerker and S. Cheng, *Chinese Communist Studies of Modern Chinese History*
12. C. John Stanley, *Late Ching Finance: Hu Kuang-yung as an Innovator*
13. S. M. Meng, *The Tsungli Yamen: Its Organization and Functions*
*14. Ssu-yü Teng, *Historiography of the Taiping Rebellion*
15. Chun-Jo Liu, *Controversies in Modern Chinese Intellectual History: An Analytic Bibliography of Periodical Articles, Mainly of the May Fourth and Post-May Fourth Era*
*16. Edward J. M. Rhoads, *The Chinese Red Army, 1927–1963: An Annotated Bibliography*
*17. Andrew J. Nathan, *A History of the China International Famine Relief Commission*
*18. Frank H. H. King (ed.) and Prescott Clarke, *A Research Guide to China-Coast Newspapers, 1822–1911*
*19. Ellis Joffe, *Party and Army: Professionalism and Political Control in the Chinese Officer Corps, 1949–1964*
*20. Toshio G. Tsukahira, *Feudal Control in Tokugawa Japan: The Sankin Kōtai System*
*21. Kwang-Ching Liu, ed., *American Missionaries in China: Papers from Harvard Seminars*
*22. George Moseley, *A Sino-Soviet Cultural Frontier: The Ili Kazakh Autonomous Chou*

Harvard East Asian Monographs

23. Carl F. Nathan, *Plague Prevention and Politics in Manchuria, 1910–1931*
*24. Adrian Arthur Bennett, *John Fryer: The Introduction of Western Science and Technology into Nineteenth-Century China*
*25. Donald J. Friedman, *The Road from Isolation: The Campaign of the American Committee for Non-Participation in Japanese Aggression, 1938–1941*
*26. Edward LeFevour, *Western Enterprise in Late Ching China: A Selective Survey of Jardine, Matheson and Company's Operations, 1842–1895*
27. Charles Neuhauser, *Third World Politics: China and the Afro-Asian People's Solidarity Organization, 1957–1967*
*28. Kungtu C. Sun, assisted by Ralph W. Huenemann, *The Economic Development of Manchuria in the First Half of the Twentieth Century*
*29. Shahid Javed Burki, *A Study of Chinese Communes, 1965*
30. John Carter Vincent, *The Extraterritorial System in China: Final Phase*
31. Madeleine Chi, *China Diplomacy, 1914–1918*
*32. Clifton Jackson Phillips, *Protestant America and the Pagan World: The First Half Century of the American Board of Commissioners for Foreign Missions, 1810–1860*
*33. James Pusey, *Wu Han: Attacking the Present Through the Past*
*34. Ying-wan Cheng, *Postal Communication in China and Its Modernization, 1860–1896*
35. Tuvia Blumenthal, *Saving in Postwar Japan*
36. Peter Frost, *The Bakumatsu Currency Crisis*
37. Stephen C. Lockwood, *Augustine Heard and Company, 1858–1862*
38. Robert R. Campbell, *James Duncan Campbell: A Memoir by His Son*
39. Jerome Alan Cohen, ed., *The Dynamics of China's Foreign Relations*
40. V. V. Vishnyakova-Akimova, *Two Years in Revolutionary China, 1925–1927,* trans. Steven L. Levine
41. Meron Medzini, *French Policy in Japan During the Closing Years of the Tokugawa Regime*
42. Ezra Vogel, Margie Sargent, Vivienne B. Shue, Thomas Jay Mathews, and Deborah S. Davis, *The Cultural Revolution in the Provinces*
43. Sidney A. Forsythe, *An American Missionary Community in China, 1895–1905*
*44. Benjamin I. Schwartz, ed., *Reflections on the May Fourth Movement.: A Symposium*
*45. Ching Young Choe, *The Rule of the Taewŏngun, 1864–1873: Restoration in Yi Korea*
46. W. P. J. Hall, *A Bibliographical Guide to Japanese Research on the Chinese Economy, 1958–1970*
47. Jack J. Gerson, *Horatio Nelson Lay and Sino-British Relations, 1854–1864*
48. Paul Richard Bohr, *Famine and the Missionary: Timothy Richard as Relief Administrator and Advocate of National Reform*
49. Endymion Wilkinson, *The History of Imperial China: A Research Guide*
50. Britten Dean, *China and Great Britain: The Diplomacy of Commercial Relations, 1860–1864*
51. Ellsworth C. Carlson, *The Foochow Missionaries, 1847–1880*
52. Yeh-chien Wang, *An Estimate of the Land-Tax Collection in China, 1753 and 1908*
53. Richard M. Pfeffer, *Understanding Business Contracts in China, 1949–1963*

*54. Han-sheng Chuan and Richard Kraus, *Mid-Ching Rice Markets and Trade: An Essay in Price History*
55. Ranbir Vohra, *Lao She and the Chinese Revolution*
56. Liang-lin Hsiao, *China's Foreign Trade Statistics, 1864–1949*
*57. Lee-hsia Hsu Ting, *Government Control of the Press in Modern China, 1900–1949*
*58. Edward W. Wagner, *The Literati Purges: Political Conflict in Early Yi Korea*
*59. Joungwon A. Kim, *Divided Korea: The Politics of Development, 1945–1972*
60. Noriko Kamachi, John K. Fairbank, and Chūzō Ichiko, *Japanese Studies of Modern China Since 1953: A Bibliographical Guide to Historical and Social-Science Research on the Nineteenth and Twentieth Centuries, Supplementary Volume for 1953–1969*
61. Donald A. Gibbs and Yun-chen Li, *A Bibliography of Studies and Translations of Modern Chinese Literature, 1918–1942*
62. Robert H. Silin, *Leadership and Values: The Organization of Large-Scale Taiwanese Enterprises*
63. David Pong, *A Critical Guide to the Kwangtung Provincial Archives Deposited at the Public Record Office of London*
*64. Fred W. Drake, *China Charts the World: Hsu Chi-yü and His Geography of 1848*
*65. William A. Brown and Urgrunge Onon, translators and annotators, *History of the Mongolian People's Republic*
66. Edward L. Farmer, *Early Ming Government: The Evolution of Dual Capitals*
*67. Ralph C. Croizier, *Koxinga and Chinese Nationalism: History, Myth, and the Hero*
*68. William J. Tyler, tr., *The Psychological World of Natsume Sōseki,* by Doi Takeo
69. Eric Widmer, *The Russian Ecclesiastical Mission in Peking During the Eighteenth Century*
*70. Charlton M. Lewis, *Prologue to the Chinese Revolution: The Transformation of Ideas and Institutions in Hunan Province, 1891–1907*
71. Preston Torbert, *The Ching Imperial Household Department: A Study of Its Organization and Principal Functions, 1662–1796*
72. Paul A. Cohen and John E. Schrecker, eds., *Reform in Nineteenth-Century China*
73. Jon Sigurdson, *Rural Industrialism in China*
74. Kang Chao, *The Development of Cotton Textile Production in China*
75. Valentin Rabe, *The Home Base of American China Missions, 1880–1920*
*76. Sarasin Viraphol, *Tribute and Profit: Sino-Siamese Trade, 1652–1853*
77. Ch'i-ch'ing Hsiao, *The Military Establishment of the Yuan Dynasty*
78. Meishi Tsai, *Contemporary Chinese Novels and Short Stories, 1949–1974: An Annotated Bibliography*
*79. Wellington K. K. Chan, *Merchants, Mandarins and Modern Enterprise in Late Ching China*
80. Endymion Wilkinson, *Landlord and Labor in Late Imperial China: Case Studies from Shandong by Jing Su and Luo Lun*
*81. Barry Keenan, *The Dewey Experiment in China: Educational Reform and Political Power in the Early Republic*
*82. George A. Hayden, *Crime and Punishment in Medieval Chinese Drama: Three Judge Pao Plays*

*83. Sang-Chul Suh, *Growth and Structural Changes in the Korean Economy, 1910–1940*
84. J. W. Dower, *Empire and Aftermath: Yoshida Shigeru and the Japanese Experience, 1878–1954*
85. Martin Collcutt, *Five Mountains: The Rinzai Zen Monastic Institution in Medieval Japan*
86. Kwang Suk Kim and Michael Roemer, *Growth and Structural Transformation*
87. Anne O. Krueger, *The Developmental Role of the Foreign Sector and Aid*
*88. Edwin S. Mills and Byung-Nak Song, *Urbanization and Urban Problems*
89. Sung Hwan Ban, Pal Yong Moon, and Dwight H. Perkins, *Rural Development*
*90. Noel F. McGinn, Donald R. Snodgrass, Yung Bong Kim, Shin-Bok Kim, and Quee-Young Kim, *Education and Development in Korea*
*91. Leroy P. Jones and Il SaKong, *Government, Business, and Entrepreneurship in Economic Development: The Korean Case*
92. Edward S. Mason, Dwight H. Perkins, Kwang Suk Kim, David C. Cole, Mahn Je Kim et al., *The Economic and Social Modernization of the Republic of Korea*
93. Robert Repetto, Tai Hwan Kwon, Son-Ung Kim, Dae Young Kim, John E. Sloboda, and Peter J. Donaldson, *Economic Development, Population Policy, and Demographic Transition in the Republic of Korea*
94. Parks M. Coble, Jr., *The Shanghai Capitalists and the Nationalist Government, 1927–1937*
95. Noriko Kamachi, *Reform in China: Huang Tsun-hsien and the Japanese Model*
96. Richard Wich, *Sino-Soviet Crisis Politics: A Study of Political Change and Communication*
97. Lillian M. Li, *China's Silk Trade: Traditional Industry in the Modern World, 1842–1937*
98. R. David Arkush, *Fei Xiaotong and Sociology in Revolutionary China*
*99. Kenneth Alan Grossberg, *Japan's Renaissance: The Politics of the Muromachi Bakufu*
100. James Reeve Pusey, *China and Charles Darwin*
101. Hoyt Cleveland Tillman, *Utilitarian Confucianism: Chen Liang's Challenge to Chu Hsi*
102. Thomas A. Stanley, *Ōsugi Sakae, Anarchist in Taishō Japan: The Creativity of the Ego*
103. Jonathan K. Ocko, *Bureaucratic Reform in Provincial China: Ting Jih-ch'ang in Restoration Kiangsu, 1867–1870*
104. James Reed, *The Missionary Mind and American East Asia Policy, 1911–1915*
105. Neil L. Waters, *Japan's Local Pragmatists: The Transition from Bakumatsu to Meiji in the Kawasaki Region*
106. David C. Cole and Yung Chul Park, *Financial Development in Korea, 1945–1978*
107. Roy Bahl, Chuk Kyo Kim, and Chong Kee Park, *Public Finances During the Korean Modernization Process*
108. William D. Wray, *Mitsubishi and the N.Y.K, 1870–1914: Business Strategy in the Japanese Shipping Industry*
109. Ralph William Huenemann, *The Dragon and the Iron Horse: The Economics of Railroads in China, 1876–1937*
*110. Benjamin A. Elman, *From Philosophy to Philology: Intellectual and Social Aspects of Change in Late Imperial China*
111. Jane Kate Leonard, *Wei Yüan and China's Rediscovery of the Maritime World*

112. Luke S. K. Kwong, *A Mosaic of the Hundred Days:. Personalities, Politics, and Ideas of 1898*
*113. John E. Wills, Jr., *Embassies and Illusions: Dutch and Portuguese Envoys to K'ang-hsi, 1666–1687*
114. Joshua A. Fogel, *Politics and Sinology: The Case of Naitō Konan (1866–1934)*
*115. Jeffrey C. Kinkley, ed., *After Mao: Chinese Literature and Society, 1978–1981*
116. C. Andrew Gerstle, *Circles of Fantasy: Convention in the Plays of Chikamatsu*
117. Andrew Gordon, *The Evolution of Labor Relations in Japan: Heavy Industry, 1853–1955*
*118. Daniel K. Gardner, *Chu Hsi and the "Ta Hsueh": Neo-Confucian Reflection on the Confucian Canon*
119. Christine Guth Kanda, *Shinzō: Hachiman Imagery and Its Development*
*120. Robert Borgen, *Sugawara no Michizane and the Early Heian Court*
121. Chang-tai Hung, *Going to the People: Chinese Intellectual and Folk Literature, 1918–1937*
*122. Michael A. Cusumano, *The Japanese Automobile Industry: Technology and Management at Nissan and Toyota*
123. Richard von Glahn, *The Country of Streams and Grottoes: Expansion, Settlement, and the Civilizing of the Sichuan Frontier in Song Times*
124. Steven D. Carter, *The Road to Komatsubara: A Classical Reading of the Renga Hyakuin*
125. Katherine F. Bruner, John K. Fairbank, and Richard T. Smith, *Entering China's Service: Robert Hart's Journals, 1854–1863*
126. Bob Tadashi Wakabayashi, *Anti-Foreignism and Western Learning in Early-Modern Japan: The "New Theses" of 1825*
127. Atsuko Hirai, *Individualism and Socialism: The Life and Thought of Kawai Eijirō (1891–1944)*
128. Ellen Widmer, *The Margins of Utopia: "Shui-hu hou-chuan" and the Literature of Ming Loyalism*
129. R. Kent Guy, *The Emperor's Four Treasuries: Scholars and the State in the Late Chien-lung Era*
130. Peter C. Perdue, *Exhausting the Earth: State and Peasant in Hunan, 1500–1850*
131. Susan Chan Egan, *A Latterday Confucian: Reminiscences of William Hung (1893–1980)*
132. James T. C. Liu, *China Turning Inward: Intellectual-Political Changes in the Early Twelfth Century*
*133. Paul A. Cohen, *Between Tradition and Modernity: Wang T'ao and Reform in Late Ching China*
134. Kate Wildman Nakai, *Shogunal Politics: Arai Hakuseki and the Premises of Tokugawa Rule*
*135. Parks M. Coble, *Facing Japan: Chinese Politics and Japanese Imperialism, 1931–1937*
136. Jon L. Saari, *Legacies of Childhood: Growing Up Chinese in a Time of Crisis, 1890–1920*
137. Susan Downing Videen, *Tales of Heichū*
138. Heinz Morioka and Miyoko Sasaki, *Rakugo: The Popular Narrative Art of Japan*
139. Joshua A. Fogel, *Nakae Ushikichi in China: The Mourning of Spirit*

140. Alexander Barton Woodside, *Vietnam and the Chinese Model: A Comparative Study of Vietnamese and Chinese Government in the First Half of the Nineteenth Century*
*141. George Elison, *Deus Destroyed: The Image of Christianity in Early Modern Japan*
142. William D. Wray, ed., *Managing Industrial Enterprise: Cases from Japan's Prewar Experience*
*143. T'ung-tsu Ch'ü, *Local Government in China Under the Ching*
144. Marie Anchordoguy, *Computers, Inc.: Japan's Challenge to IBM*
145. Barbara Molony, *Technology and Investment: The Prewar Japanese Chemical Industry*
146. Mary Elizabeth Berry, *Hideyoshi*
147. Laura E. Hein, *Fueling Growth: The Energy Revolution and Economic Policy in Postwar Japan*
148. Wen-hsin Yeh, *The Alienated Academy: Culture and Politics in Republican China, 1919–1937*
149. Dru C. Gladney, *Muslim Chinese: Ethnic Nationalism in the People's Republic*
150. Merle Goldman and Paul A. Cohen, eds., *Ideas Across Cultures: Essays on Chinese Thought in Honor of Benjamin L Schwartz*
151. James M. Polachek, *The Inner Opium War*
152. Gail Lee Bernstein, *Japanese Marxist: A Portrait of Kawakami Hajime, 1879–1946*
*153. Lloyd E. Eastman, *The Abortive Revolution: China Under Nationalist Rule, 1927–1937*
154. Mark Mason, *American Multinationals and Japan: The Political Economy of Japanese Capital Controls, 1899–1980*
155. Richard J. Smith, John K. Fairbank, and Katherine F. Bruner, *Robert Hart and China's Early Modernization: His Journals, 1863–1866*
156. George J. Tanabe, Jr., *Myōe the Dreamkeeper: Fantasy and Knowledge in Kamakura Buddhism*
157. William Wayne Farris, *Heavenly Warriors: The Evolution of Japan's Military, 500–1300*
158. Yu-ming Shaw, *An American Missionary in China: John Leighton Stuart and Chinese-American Relations*
159. James B. Palais, *Politics and Policy in Traditional Korea*
*160. Douglas Reynolds, *China, 1898–1912: The Xinzheng Revolution and Japan*
161. Roger R. Thompson, *China's Local Councils in the Age of Constitutional Reform, 1898–1911*
162. William Johnston, *The Modern Epidemic: History of Tuberculosis in Japan*
163. Constantine Nomikos Vaporis, *Breaking Barriers: Travel and the State in Early Modern Japan*
164. Irmela Hijiya-Kirschnereit, *Rituals of Self-Revelation: Shishōsetsu as Literary Genre and Socio-Cultural Phenomenon*
165. James C. Baxter, *The Meiji Unification Through the Lens of Ishikawa Prefecture*
166. Thomas R. H. Havens, *Architects of Affluence: The Tsutsumi Family and the Seibu-Saison Enterprises in Twentieth-Century Japan*
167. Anthony Hood Chambers, *The Secret Window: Ideal Worlds in Tanizaki's Fiction*
168. Steven J. Ericson, *The Sound of the Whistle: Railroads and the State in Meiji Japan*
169. Andrew Edmund Goble, *Kenmu: Go-Daigo's Revolution*

170. Denise Potrzeba Lett, *In Pursuit of Status: The Making of South Korea's "New" Urban Middle Class*
171. Mimi Hall Yiengpruksawan, *Hiraizumi: Buddhist Art and Regional Politics in Twelfth-Century Japan*
172. Charles Shirō Inouye, *The Similitude of Blossoms: A Critical Biography of Izumi Kyōka (1873–1939), Japanese Novelist and Playwright*
173. Aviad E. Raz, *Riding the Black Ship: Japan and Tokyo Disneyland*
174. Deborah J. Milly, *Poverty, Equality, and Growth: The Politics of Economic Need in Postwar Japan*
175. See Heng Teow, *Japan's Cultural Policy Toward China, 1918–1931: A Comparative Perspective*
176. Michael A. Fuller, *An Introduction to Literary Chinese*
177. Frederick R. Dickinson, *War and National Reinvention: Japan in the Great War, 1914–1919*
178. John Solt, *Shredding the Tapestry of Meaning: The Poetry and Poetics of Kitasono Katue (1902–1978)*
179. Edward Pratt, *Japan's Protoindustrial Elite: The Economic Foundations of the Gōnō*
180. Atsuko Sakaki, *Recontextualizing Texts: Narrative Performance in Modern Japanese Fiction*
181. Soon-Won Park, *Colonial Industrialization and Labor in Korea: The Onoda Cement Factory*
182. JaHyun Kim Haboush and Martina Deuchler, *Culture and the State in Late Chosŏn Korea*
183. John W. Chaffee, *Branches of Heaven: A History of the Imperial Clan of Sung China*
184. Gi-Wook Shin and Michael Robinson, eds., *Colonial Modernity in Korea*
185. Nam-lin Hur, *Prayer and Play in Late Tokugawa Japan: Asakusa Sensōji and Edo Society*
186. Kristin Stapleton, *Civilizing Chengdu: Chinese Urban Reform, 1895–1937*
187. Hyung Il Pai, *Constructing "Korean" Origins: A Critical Review of Archaeology, Historiography, and Racial Myth in Korean State-Formation Theories*
188. Brian D. Ruppert, *Jewel in the Ashes: Buddha Relics and Power in Early Medieval Japan*
189. Susan Daruvala, *Zhou Zuoren and an Alternative Chinese Response to Modernity*
*190. James Z. Lee, *The Political Economy of a Frontier: Southwest China, 1250–1850*
191. Kerry Smith, *A Time of Crisis: Japan, the Great Depression, and Rural Revitalization*
192. Michael Lewis, *Becoming Apart: National Power and Local Politics in Toyama, 1868–1945*
193. William C. Kirby, Man-houng Lin, James Chin Shih, and David A. Pietz, eds., *State and Economy in Republican China: A Handbook for Scholars*
194. Timothy S. George, *Minamata: Pollution and the Struggle for Democracy in Postwar Japan*
195. Billy K. L. So, *Prosperity, Region, and Institutions in Maritime China: The South Fukien Pattern, 946–1368*
196. Yoshihisa Tak Matsusaka, *The Making of Japanese Manchuria, 1904–1932*

197. Maram Epstein, *Competing Discourses: Orthodoxy, Authenticity, and Engendered Meanings in Late Imperial Chinese Fiction*
198. Curtis J. Milhaupt, J. Mark Ramseyer, and Michael K. Young, eds. and comps., *Japanese Law in Context: Readings in Society, the Economy, and Politics*
199. Haruo Iguchi, *Unfinished Business: Ayukawa Yoshisuke and U.S.-Japan Relations, 1937–1952*
200. Scott Pearce, Audrey Spiro, and Patricia Ebrey, *Culture and Power in the Reconstitution of the Chinese Realm, 200–600*
201. Terry Kawashima, *Writing Margins: The Textual Construction of Gender in Heian and Kamakura Japan*
202. Martin W. Huang, *Desire and Fictional Narrative in Late Imperial China*
203. Robert S. Ross and Jiang Changbin, eds., *Re-examining the Cold War: U.S.-China Diplomacy, 1954–1973*
204. Guanhua Wang, *In Search of Justice: The 1905–1906 Chinese Anti-American Boycott*
205. David Schaberg, *A Patterned Past: Form and Thought in Early Chinese Historiography*
206. Christine Yano, *Tears of Longing: Nostalgia and the Nation in Japanese Popular Song*
207. Milena Doleželová-Velingerová and Oldřich Král, with Graham Sanders, eds., *The Appropriation of Cultural Capital: China's May Fourth Project*
208. Robert N. Huey, *The Making of 'Shinkokinshū'*
209. Lee Butler, *Emperor and Aristocracy in Japan, 1467–1680: Resilience and Renewal*
210. Suzanne Ogden, *Inklings of Democracy in China*
211. Kenneth J. Ruoff, *The People's Emperor: Democracy and the Japanese Monarchy, 1945–1995*
212. Haun Saussy, *Great Walls of Discourse and Other Adventures in Cultural China*
213. Aviad E. Raz, *Emotions at Work: Normative Control, Organizations, and Culture in Japan and America*
214. Rebecca E. Karl and Peter Zarrow, eds., *Rethinking the 1898 Reform Period: Political and Cultural Change in Late Qing China*
215. Kevin O'Rourke, *The Book of Korean Shijo*
216. Ezra F. Vogel, ed., *The Golden Age of the U.S.-China-Japan Triangle, 1972–1989*
217. Thomas A. Wilson, ed., *On Sacred Grounds: Culture, Society, Politics, and the Formation of the Cult of Confucius*
218. Donald S. Sutton, *Steps of Perfection: Exorcistic Performers and Chinese Religion in Twentieth-Century Taiwan*
219. Daqing Yang, *Technology of Empire: Telecommunications and Japanese Expansionism, 1895–1945*
220. Qianshen Bai, *Fu Shan's World: The Transformation of Chinese Calligraphy in the Seventeenth Century*
221. Paul Jakov Smith and Richard von Glahn, eds., *The Song-Yuan-Ming Transition in Chinese History*
222. Rania Huntington, *Alien Kind: Foxes and Late Imperial Chinese Narrative*
223. Jordan Sand, *House and Home in Modern Japan: Architecture, Domestic Space, and Bourgeois Culture, 1880–1930*

224. Karl Gerth, *China Made: Consumer Culture and the Creation of the Nation*
225. Xiaoshan Yang, *Metamorphosis of the Private Sphere: Gardens and Objects in Tang-Song Poetry*
226. Barbara Mittler, *A Newspaper for China? Power, Identity, and Change in Shanghai's News Media, 1872–1912*
227. Joyce A. Madancy, *The Troublesome Legacy of Commissioner Lin: The Opium Trade and Opium Suppression in Fujian Province, 1820s to 1920s*
228. John Makeham, *Transmitters and Creators: Chinese Commentators and Commentaries on the Analects*
229. Elisabeth Köll, *From Cotton Mill to Business Empire: The Emergence of Regional Enterprises in Modern China*
230. Emma Teng, *Taiwan's Imagined Geography: Chinese Colonial Travel Writing and Pictures, 1683–1895*
231. Wilt Idema and Beata Grant, *The Red Brush: Writing Women of Imperial China*
232. Eric C. Rath, *The Ethos of Noh: Actors and Their Art*
233. Elizabeth Remick, *Building Local States: China During the Republican and Post-Mao Eras*
234. Lynn Struve, ed., *The Qing Formation in World-Historical Time*
235. D. Max Moerman, *Localizing Paradise: Kumano Pilgrimage and the Religious Landscape of Premodern Japan*
236. Antonia Finnane, *Speaking of Yangzhou: A Chinese City, 1550–1850*
237. Brian Platt, *Burning and Building: Schooling and State Formation in Japan, 1750–1890*
238. Gail Bernstein, Andrew Gordon, and Kate Wildman Nakai, eds., *Public Spheres, Private Lives in Modern Japan, 1600–1950: Essays in Honor of Albert Craig*
239. Wu Hung and Katherine R. Tsiang, *Body and Face in Chinese Visual Culture*
240. Stephen Dodd, *Writing Home: Representations of the Native Place in Modern Japanese Literature*
241. David Anthony Bello, *Opium and the Limits of Empire: Drug Prohibition in the Chinese Interior, 1729–1850*
242. Hosea Hirata, *Discourses of Seduction: History, Evil, Desire, and Modern Japanese Literature*
243. Kyung Moon Hwang, *Beyond Birth: Social Status in the Emergence of Modern Korea*
244. Brian R. Dott, *Identity Reflections: Pilgrimages to Mount Tai in Late Imperial China*
245. Mark McNally, *Proving the Way: Conflict and Practice in the History of Japanese Nativism*
246. Yongping Wu, *A Political Explanation of Economic Growth: State Survival, Bureaucratic Politics, and Private Enterprises in the Making of Taiwan's Economy, 1950–1985*
247. Kyu Hyun Kim, *The Age of Visions and Arguments: Parliamentarianism and the National Public Sphere in Early Meiji Japan*
248. Zvi Ben-Dor Benite, *The Dao of Muhammad: A Cultural History of Muslims in Late Imperial China*
249. David Der-wei Wang and Shang Wei, eds., *Dynastic Crisis and Cultural Innovation: From the Late Ming to the Late Qing and Beyond*

250. Wilt L. Idema, Wai-yee Li, and Ellen Widmer, eds., *Trauma and Transcendence in Early Qing Literature*
251. Barbara Molony and Kathleen Uno, eds., *Gendering Modern Japanese History*
252. Hiroshi Aoyagi, *Islands of Eight Million Smiles: Idol Performance and Symbolic Production in Contemporary Japan*
253. Wai-yee Li, *The Readability of the Past in Early Chinese Historiography*
254. William C. Kirby, Robert S. Ross, and Gong Li, eds., *Normalization of U.S.-China Relations: An International History*
255. Ellen Gardner Nakamura, *Practical Pursuits: Takano Chōei, Takahashi Keisaku, and Western Medicine in Nineteenth-Century Japan*
256. Jonathan W. Best, *A History of the Early Korean Kingdom of Paekche, together with an annotated translation of* The Paekche Annals *of the* Samguk sagi
257. Liang Pan, *The United Nations in Japan's Foreign and Security Policymaking, 1945–1992: National Security, Party Politics, and International Status*
258. Richard Belsky, *Localities at the Center: Native Place, Space, and Power in Late Imperial Beijing*
259. Zwia Lipkin, *"Useless to the State": "Social Problems" and Social Engineering in Nationalist Nanjing, 1927–1937*
260. William O. Gardner, *Advertising Tower: Japanese Modernism and Modernity in the 1920s*
261. Stephen Owen, *The Making of Early Chinese Classical Poetry*
262. Martin J. Powers, *Pattern and Person: Ornament, Society, and Self in Classical China*
263. Anna M. Shields, *Crafting a Collection: The Cultural Contexts and Poetic Practice of the* Huajian ji 花間集 *(Collection from Among the Flowers)*
264. Stephen Owen, *The Late Tang: Chinese Poetry of the Mid-Ninth Century (827–860)*
265. Sara L. Friedman, *Intimate Politics: Marriage, the Market, and State Power in Southeastern China*
266. Patricia Buckley Ebrey and Maggie Bickford, *Emperor Huizong and Late Northern Song China: The Politics of Culture and the Culture of Politics*
267. Sophie Volpp, *Worldly Stage: Theatricality in Seventeenth-Century China*
268. Ellen Widmer, *The Beauty and the Book: Women and Fiction in Nineteenth-Century China*
269. Steven B. Miles, *The Sea of Learning: Mobility and Identity in Nineteenth-Century Guangzhou*
270. Lin Man-houng, *China Upside Down: Currency, Society, and Ideologies, 1808–1856*
271. Ronald Egan, *The Problem of Beauty: Aesthetic Thought and Pursuits in Northern Song Dynasty China*
272. Mark Halperin, *Out of the Cloister: Literati Perspectives on Buddhism in Sung China, 960–1279*
273. Helen Dunstan, *State or Merchant? Political Economy and Political Process in 1740s China*
274. Sabina Knight, *The Heart of Time: Moral Agency in Twentieth-Century Chinese Fiction*
275. Timothy J. Van Compernolle, *The Uses of Memory: The Critique of Modernity in the Fiction of Higuchi Ichiyō*

276. Paul Rouzer, *A New Practical Primer of Literary Chinese*
277. Jonathan Zwicker, *Practices of the Sentimental Imagination: Melodrama, the Novel, and the Social Imaginary in Nineteenth-Century Japan*
278. Franziska Seraphim, *War Memory and Social Politics in Japan, 1945–2005*
279. Adam L. Kern, *Manga from the Floating World: Comicbook Culture and the* Kibyōshi *of Edo Japan*
280. Cynthia J. Brokaw, *Commerce in Culture: The Sibao Book Trade in the Qing and Republican Periods*
281. Eugene Y. Park, *Between Dreams and Reality: The Military Examination in Late Chosŏn Korea, 1600–1894*
282. Nam-lin Hur, *Death and Social Order in Tokugawa Japan: Buddhism, Anti-Christianity, and the* Danka *System*
283. Patricia M. Thornton, *Disciplining the State: Virtue, Violence, and State-Making in Modern China*
284. Vincent Goossaert, *The Taoists of Peking, 1800–1949: A Social History of Urban Clerics*
285. Peter Nickerson, *Taoism, Bureaucracy, and Popular Religion in Early Medieval China*
286. Charo B. D'Etcheverry, *Love After* The Tale of Genji*: Rewriting the World of the Shining Prince*
287. Michael G. Chang, *A Court on Horseback: Imperial Touring & the Construction of Qing Rule, 1680–1785*
288. Carol Richmond Tsang, *War and Faith:* Ikkō Ikki *in Late Muromachi Japan*
289. Hilde De Weerdt, *Competition over Content: Negotiating Standards for the Civil Service Examinations in Imperial China (1127–1279)*
290. Eve Zimmerman, *Out of the Alleyway: Nakagami Kenji and the Poetics of Outcaste Fiction*
291. Robert Culp, *Articulating Citizenship: Civic Education and Student Politics in Southeastern China, 1912–1940*
292. Richard J. Smethurst, *From Foot Soldier to Finance Minister: Takahashi Korekiyo, Japan's Keynes*
293. John E. Herman, *Amid the Clouds and Mist: China's Colonization of Guizhou, 1200–1700*
294. Tomoko Shiroyama, *China During the Great Depression: Market, State, and the World Economy, 1929–1937*
295. Kirk W. Larsen, *Tradition, Treaties and Trade: Qing Imperialism and Chosŏn Korea, 1850–1910*
296. Gregory Golley, *When Our Eyes No Longer See: Realism, Science, and Ecology in Japanese Literary Modernism*
297. Barbara Ambros, *Emplacing a Pilgrimage: The Ōyama Cult and Regional Religion in Early Modern Japan*
298. Rebecca Suter, *The Japanization of Modernity: Murakami Haruki between Japan and the United States*
299. Yuma Totani, *The Tokyo War Crimes Trial: The Pursuit of Justice in the Wake of World War II*

300. Linda Isako Angst, *In a Dark Time: Memory, Community, and Gendered Nationalism in Postwar Okinawa*
301. David M. Robinson, ed., *Culture, Courtiers, and Competition: The Ming Court (1368–1644)*
302. Calvin Chen, *Some Assembly Required: Work, Community, and Politics in China's Rural Enterprises*
303. Sem Vermeersch, *The Power of the Buddhas: The Politics of Buddhism During the Koryŏ Dynasty* (918–1392)
304. Tina Lu, *Accidental Incest, Filial Cannibalism, and Other Peculiar Encounters in Late Imperial Chinese Literature*
305. Chang Woei Ong, *Men of Letters Within the Passes: Guanzhong Literati in Chinese History, 907–1911*
306. Wendy Swartz, *Reading Tao Yuanming: Shifting Paradigms of Historical Reception (427–1900)*
307. Peter K. Bol, *Neo-Confucianism in History*
308. Carlos Rojas, *The Naked Gaze: Reflections on Chinese Modernity*
309. Kelly H. Chong, *Deliverance and Submission: Evangelical Women and the Negotiation of Patriarchy in South Korea*
310. Rachel DiNitto, *Uchida Hyakken: A Critique of Modernity and Militarism in Prewar Japan*
311. Jeffrey Snyder-Reinke, *Dry Spells: State Rainmaking and Local Governance in Late Imperial China*
312. Jay Dautcher, *Down a Narrow Road: Identity and Masculinity in a Uyghur Community in Xinjiang China*
313. Xun Liu, *Daoist Modern: Innovation, Lay Practice, and the Community of Inner Alchemy in Republican Shanghai*
314. Jacob Eyferth, *Eating Rice from Bamboo Shoots: The Social History of a Community of Artisans in Southwest China, 1920–2000*
315. David Johnson, *Spectacle and Sacrifice: The Ritual Foundation of Village Life in North China*
316. James Robson, *Power of Place: The Religious Landscape of the Southern Sacred Peak (Nanyue* 南嶽*) in Medieval China*
317. Lori Watt, *When Empire Comes Home: Repatriation and Reintegration in Postwar Japan*
318. James Dorsey, *Critical Aesthetics: Kobayashi Hideo, Modernity, and Wartime Japan*